D1035202

The
BOOKER T. WASHINGTON
Papers

The
BOOKER T. WASHINGTON
Papers

VOLUME 7
1903–4

Louis R. Harlan
and
Raymond W. Smock
EDITORS

University of Illinois Press
URBANA · CHICAGO · LONDON

© 1977 BY THE BOARD OF TRUSTEES OF THE UNIVERSITY OF ILLINOIS
MANUFACTURED IN THE UNITED STATES OF AMERICA

Library of Congress Cataloging in Publication Data (Revised)

Washington, Booker Taliaferro, 1856–1915.
 The Booker T. Washington papers.

 Includes bibliographies.
 CONTENTS: v. 1. The autobiographical writings.—
v. 2. 1860–89.—v. 3. 1889–95.—v. 4. 1895–98.—
v. 5. 1899–1900.—v. 6. 1901–2.—v. 7. 1903–4.
  1. Washington, Booker Taliaferro, 1856–1915.
2. Afro-Americans—History—1877–1964—Sources.
E185.97.W274   301.45′19′6073024   75–186345
ISBN 0–252–00666–6 (v. 7)

To the Memory of
William Henry Baldwin, Jr.

LIBRARY
ALMA COLLEGE
ALMA, MICHIGAN

CONTENTS

Contents

Contents

CONTENTS

Contents

Contents

CONTENTS

INTRODUCTION

THIS VOLUME FINDS Booker T. Washington at the height of his powers as an interracial diplomat and black spokesman. It also marks, on the other hand, the expression of outspoken criticism of him by leading black intellectuals that would continue until long after his death.

There had been criticisms earlier of Washington's compromise with southern white segregationists, but these went unheard in the general praise and sponsorship of the Tuskegean. At the meeting of the Afro-American Council in Louisville in the summer of 1903, the critics led by the Boston editor William Monroe Trotter failed to get a hearing from the pro-Washington majority. A month later when Washington spoke in a Boston church, in the camp of the opposition, Trotter led an effort to disrupt the meeting. While it did not succeed in stopping Washington from speaking, it was sufficiently disorderly to be headlined the next day as "the Boston Riot" and to earn Trotter a thirty-day jail sentence.

Washington believed the attacks on him were personal and motivated by jealousy, and Trotter's actions seemed to confirm his view. There was, however, growing dissent on intellectual grounds, a conviction that Washington's philosophy and leadership pointed in the wrong direction. In the spring of 1903, in a collection of essays entitled *The Souls of Black Folk*, W. E. B. Du Bois, the leading black intellectual of the period, criticized Washington's unsympathetic attitude toward higher education and the higher aspirations of the race, and the compromises dictated by Washington's need for support from southern white leaders and northern millionaires. Du Bois couched his criticisms in polite language, but after the Boston Riot the vindictiveness of Washington and his lieutenants toward Trotter drove Du Bois into outright opposition to the Tuskegean.

Faced with these black opponents who waved the banner of social justice and accused him of betrayal, Washington publicly ignored them but privately maneuvered against them. One of his methods was espionage. Melvin J. Chisum of New York, his paid spy, infiltrated the Trotter organization and gave Washington prior warning of the plans for disrupting another Washington meeting, possibly even acting as provocateur of the disturbance. A Boston lawyer, Clifford H. Plummer, also spied on Trotter and foiled his plans to embarrass the Tuskegean at the time of a banquet in Washington's honor in Cambridge. His friends in Boston, meanwhile, pushed the case against Trotter in the courts, and his lawyer, Wilford H. Smith, persuaded a black Yale student to sue Trotter and his co-editor for libel, and Washington secretly subsidized another Boston black newspaper to compete with Trotter's Boston *Guardian.* Washington also secretly subsidized other newspapers and journalists and through his secretary and ghost-writers made Tuskegee a center of pro-Washington propaganda. When a new magazine, *The Voice of the Negro,* was founded in 1903, Washington installed Emmett Scott as an associate editor.

In an effort in January 1904 to come to terms with his critics, Washington called a secret conference of leading Afro-Americans at Carnegie Hall in New York City. Washington could not resist the urge to stack the conference in his favor and also the Committee of Twelve for the Advancement of the Negro Race which grew out of it. Du Bois resigned from the Committee of Twelve, which confined its efforts to issuing pamphlets on the race problem instead of becoming the major force for black unity that it was intended to be.

Washington continued to advise President Theodore Roosevelt on political appointments in the South. He also worked to destroy the power of the lily-white Republicans over the party machinery in the southern states and was partially successful in this endeavor, although lily-whitism remained a force in Louisiana, Texas, and several other southern states after the presidential election of 1904. The appointment of William D. Crum as collector of customs at Charleston, S.C., dragged on for years and became a cause célèbre for Washington. Racial politics prevented senatorial approval of

Crum until 1905, but Washington convinced Roosevelt to keep Crum in office on interim appointments until confirmation could be achieved. Much of Washington's prestige as a political broker hinged on the success of the Crum appointment. Critics of the Tuskegean's role in politics were quick to point out that the long and frustrating battle over the Crum appointment revealed the limitations of Washington's power.

In answer to both black and white critics of his political activity Washington claimed that he never proposed candidates to the President but gave his best advice when the President called upon him. Despite his statements to the contrary, however, the correspondence reveals that Washington was an active and skillful political broker and machine boss.

Washington continued the secret civil-rights activity he had begun in the late nineties. When several states passed Pullman car segregation laws, he worked with W. E. B. Du Bois, J. C. Napier, and others in unsuccessful efforts to test the laws and to persuade Robert Todd Lincoln of the Pullman Palace Car Company to resist the change. Working through his lawyer, Wilford H. Smith, Washington financed and directed two tests of the Alabama disfranchisement laws, which reached the U.S. Supreme Court in 1903 and 1904. To keep his part in these suits secret, Washington resorted to code names in the letters between his secretary and his lawyer.

Much of the money to carry on these diverse activities came from the coffers of philanthropists friendly to Washington. H. H. Rogers of Standard Oil gave Washington hundreds of dollars in cash whenever he visited him, with instructions not to make public the source. The largest giver was Andrew Carnegie, who contributed $600,000 in U.S. Steel bonds in 1903, of which $150,000 was a personal gift to Washington and his family.

The editors are glad to acknowledge the assistance of the following staff members who have made valuable contributions to this volume: Sadie M. Harlan, Janet E. Hartman, Geraldine McTigue, Denise P. Moore, William M. Stowe, Jr., and Richard B. Wilkof. We acknowledge and appreciate the continued sponsorship and encouragement of the National Endowment for the Humanities, the National Historical Publications and Records Commission, and the University of Maryland.

ERRATA

VOLUME 5, p. 178, Reverdy Cassius Ransom died in 1959.

VOLUME 5, p. 195, James Harvey Anderson was a minister of the A.M.E. Zion Church, not the A.M.E. Church.

VOLUME 6, p. 242, add annotation: William Monroe Trotter (1872–1934) was BTW's most vehement and uncompromising black critic. A *magna cum laude* graduate of Harvard, he spoke for the elite black professional class through the Boston *Guardian*, a weekly newspaper he founded in 1901. His chief interests were civil rights and criticism of the conservative leadership of BTW. In July 1903 Trotter achieved the confrontation he had long sought with BTW in what became known as the Boston Riot. For his part in this disruption of Washington's speech he served a thirty-day jail sentence. Soon afterward, Trotter founded the New England Suffrage League, and in 1905 he aided W. E. B. Du Bois in founding the Niagara Movement. Distrusting the white founders of the NAACP, he withdrew from the organization at its formative stage. A supporter of Woodrow Wilson in 1912 in protest against the part of Roosevelt and Taft in the Brownsville affray, he soon quarreled with Wilson over the issue of federal segregation measures. Trotter's career was punctuated by irreparable breaks with his co-workers, and during his last decade he was increasingly isolated from the mainstream of black affairs. See Fox, *Guardian of Boston*.

SYMBOLS AND ABBREVIATIONS

STANDARD ABBREVIATIONS for dates, months, and states are used by the editors only in footnotes and endnotes; textual abbreviations are reproduced as found.

DOCUMENT SYMBOLS

1. A — autograph; written in author's hand
   H — handwritten by other than signator
   P — printed
   T — typed

2. C — postcard
   D — document
   E — endorsement
   L — letter
   M — manuscript
   W — wire (telegram)

3. c — carbon
   d — draft
   f — fragment
   p — letterpress
   t — transcript or copy made at much later date

4. I — initialed by author
   r — representation; signed or initialed in author's name
   S — signed by author

Among the more common endnote abbreviations are: ALS — autograph letter, signed by author; TLpI — typed letter, letterpress copy, initialed by author.

REPOSITORY SYMBOLS

Symbols used for repositories are the standard ones used in *Symbols of American Libraries Used in the National Union Catalog of the Library of Congress*, 10th ed. (Washington, D.C., 1969).

ATT	Tuskegee Institute, Tuskegee, Ala.
DHU	Howard University, Washington, D.C.
DLC	Library of Congress, Washington, D.C.
DNA	National Archives, Washington, D.C.
GEU	Emory University, Atlanta, Ga.
KyBB	Berea College Library, Berea, Ky.
MH	Harvard University, Cambridge, Mass.
MU	University of Massachusetts, Amherst
NN-Sc	Schomburg Collection, New York Public Library, NYC
ViHaI	Hampton Institute, Hampton, Va.

OTHER ABBREVIATIONS

BTW	Booker T. Washington
Con.	Container
NNBL	National Negro Business League
RG	Record Group
Ser.	Series

Documents, 1903–4

To Robert Todd Lincoln[1]

[Tuskegee, Ala.] January 2, 1903

My dear Sir: I very much hope that you can find time to read the enclosed statement in regard to the treatment, on one of your cars, of a young colored man, a graduate of a college in Iowa, and one of the most intelligent a[n]d refined men that I have met. It does seem to me that a rich and powerful corporation like yours could find some way to extend in some degree, protection to the weak. I believe it is possible to settle this matter in a business-like, high-toned way and not humiliate passengers in the way that the present policy or system permits. Yours truly,

[Booker T. Washington]

TLc Con. 548 BTW Papers DLC.

[1] Robert Todd Lincoln (1843–1926), son of Abraham Lincoln, was U.S. Secretary of War (1881–85), U.S. minister to Great Britain (1889–93), and president of the Pullman Co. (1897–1911).

From Cassius Carter[1]

San Diego, California Jany. 6. 1903

My dear Mr. Washington: I want to congratulate you upon the splendid impression you made in San Diego. Especially do I want to thank you for the realization brought to me personally that the education and moral uplifting of the Negro will reconcile the white man to his presence. Really, it is the inconsequential characteristics of the negro that mostly offend — loud-talking, assumption; more so than some serious shortcomings. I wish there were some strong energy working upon the Anglo-Saxon as you on yr. side, awakening his sense of justice, and stimulating his patience. Don't trouble to answer this note. I am very sincerely yr. friend,

Cassius Carter

ALS Con. 252 BTW Papers DLC.

[1] Cassius Carter, born in Virginia in 1857, practiced law in Virginia and Texas before moving to California in 1886. He was district attorney in San Diego from 1893 to 1903.

Thomas Junius Calloway to Emmett Jay Scott

Washington, D.C. Jan. 12, 1903

Dear Mr. Scott: You will be interested to know that we had an "anti-Booker Washington["] meeting at Bethel Literary society the other night.[1] "Upstart" Ferris, from everywhere in general and from nowhere in particular addressed the society on "The Boston Negro's Idea of Booker Washington." The burden of his complaint and, as he states, of the Boston Negroes, seems to be that Mr. W. ignores and actually harms the higher aspirations of the Negro, because of his public utterances of the Negro's need of industrial education. Of course this is the old, old story of Mr. W's being opposed to the higher education of the Negro, which has been refuted so often. Ferris attempted to belittle Mr. W's motives, and attempted to show that Mr. W. was losing hold of the New England people. He gave credit for the work done at Tuskegee, but deplored as a racial calamity the "gospel of work" which Mr. W. is preaching to the American people. If you have seen the Boston Guardian I suppose you know better than I can say the nature of Ferris' animadversions.

The interesting feature of the occasion, to me, was the evidence of a number of people here who, from their applause, indicated a feeling of hostility to Mr. W. In studying these malcontents I felt that I could account for each of them by reason of interest in rival institutions, Howard, Atlanta, &c. and the others under the not very elegant term of "sore heads" who have succeeded wonderfully in doing nothing themselves and hence have a grievance against any man who is doing something.

I must say, however, that except on the part of some over zealous "defenders" of Mr. W. the discussion was on a high plane, and interesting principally in the fact that with all the ingenuity of the "Boston Negroes" and their advocate (Ferris) so *little* could be trumped up in the way of grievances against Mr. W. whose sphere of influence has extended so immensely and whose utterances in detached statements are published so widely in the press.

As friends of Mr. W. Mrs. Calloway and I have agreed that the puerile result of this effort to find fault with Mr. W's motives and public service, has been one of his most eloquent tributes. Verily his life work is best praised by the enemies he has made.

Mrs. C. joins me in best regards to you, Mrs. S. and the little S (or s's). We hope you will honor us with a call in some of your "flights" through Washington. Sincerely,

Thos. J. Calloway

ALS Con. 252 BTW Papers DLC.

[1] An editorial, critical of Ferris's attack on BTW, appeared in the Washington *Colored American*, Jan. 17, 1903, 9.

From Theophilus B. Morton[1]

San Francisco, January 13, 1903

My dear Mr. Washington: After carefully considering the matter of the invitation so kindly given by you, to attend the annual banquet of the Unitarian Club this evening, at which you are to be the guest of honor, I have concluded that it will be more prudent and wise for me, and more beneficial to the cause to which you are so faithfully devoting your noble life, for me not to accept, for the following reasons:

First: it is a purely social function, held annually, for the pleasure of the members and such persons as are invited by the Club or its members to be their guests. I have therefore some delicacy of feeling about attending, unless the invitation should be tendered by the Club or some member thereof.

Second, I had, prior to your arrival, through the influence of a prominent member of the legal fraternity, made an effort to secure a ticket admitting me upon this occasion, in order that I might hear your address to this most cultured and critical assemblage, in the same spirit and sense that many of our white friends prefer to hear you address those of your own race. I did not know at that time, however, that the affair was of a strictly social character, and one that would naturally be confined to that particular social circle. When I did learn this, I informed my legal friend that I did not want an invitation, and would not go if he obtained a ticket for me.

Thirdly, I will not attend, because I fear indeed, [am] almost certain, that it will prove injurious to your cause and work in the future.

Fourth. While I am certain that I would be treated with the highest courtesy were I to attend, this would not relieve me of the humiliation which in the very nature of things would be felt by me, in the knowledge that I am not, in the true and proper sense, an invited guest of the real hosts of the occasion, and in the further fact that my presence was injuring the cause of my whole race.

Lastly: I rejoice to see you rise in every line, socially as well as otherwise, because as you go up, you carry the race, myself included, with you, and I will do nothing to impede your progress or injure the cause in the slightest degree. I shall be encouraged by your life and accomplishments to strive to elevate myself to that station where courtesies and high social recognition shall come to me because of my inherent worth and accomplishment in some line. This is my nature, ambition and determination. Go up I will: go down, I will not. I don't want to be a small crab to the great work you are doing me.

Trusting that you will accept my declination, viewing it in the broad, lofty and sincere spirit in which you tendered the invitation, I am, my dear sir, Very sincerely at your command at all times,

T. B. Morton

TLS Con. 267 BTW Papers DLC.

1 Theophilus B. Morton, born in Virginia in 1849, became a messenger and librarian in the U.S. circuit court of appeals in San Francisco. He was also a partner in Rivers and Morton, San Francisco bootblacks. BTW considered Morton a leader of the San Francisco black community. Morton was active in the Afro-American League.

To Hollis Burke Frissell

Tuskegee, Ala., Jan. 20, 1903

Dear Dr. Frissell: I have just returned from a trip to California where I put in thirteen days of pretty active work.

My purpose in writing is to urge you to consider the matter of going to California with the Hampton quartette. I believe that there is a field for Hampton and Tuskegee in California which we should take immediate advantage of. Having gone this year I shall not attempt to go before the end of two years at least, but if you could go a year from now that would keep alive the interest in Negro education. While traveling expenses would be considerable if you had to pay full fare, still in every case where I went in California I found the collections averaged nearly three times as large as collections in New England towns and cities. For example, in Oakland in the Congregational Church the collection was something over a thousand dollars. During the thirteen days that I was in the state, I got in cash from individuals and at meetings something over $8,000, and I believe that Hampton would do as well or better. There is a lot of wealth there which needs to be cultivated and educated. Mr. Harriman gave me transportation over the Southern and Union Pacific roads so that the trip and railroad expenses cost little. There is a large wealthy class of people who go to Southern California for the winter, aside from the wealth possessed by the native Californians. In case you go I would suggest your starting in time to begin work the first of February. My trip was a little too early to catch the greater part of the Eastern visitors. Aside from this, I should have planned to have remained in the state at least a month as there were many important places that I could not touch. I believe that looked at from another point of view, you would find the beautiful scenery and charming climate of California would be a great rest and tonic for you that would prove beneficial from many points of view. Yours truly,

Booker T. Washington

TLS   BTW Folder   ViHaI.

From Charles William Anderson

"Hoffman House"   Hampton, Va. Jan 23 1903

Confidential

My dear Doctor Washington: Yours of the 21st at hand. Just before leaving New York, I called on Gen. Clarkson and found Bishop Walters waiting in his office. The good bishop invited me to take part in his interview with the General and briefly outlined its tenor. It was a proposition in favor of the election of a committee of ten or a dozen Colored men to advise the President in relation to the colored appointments, and thereby to "relieve Brother Washington," as he put it. I took occasion to enter a gentle demurrer, on the ground that I felt that Mr. Washington was pre eminently the man to advise the President along these lines, and because I felt also that such a committee would get the President in more trouble than the war with Venezuela. I maintained that if the President was competent to name a good committee, he was competent enough to get along without one; and if it was to be named by parties other than the President, who could prevent its being packed, and standing always for the appointment of the friends of the boss of the packed committee, and against other worthy applicants. I also advanced the opinion that such a committee would probably endorse men who could not command the support of their state leaders and members of the U.S. Senate, and thereby bring the President into conflict with these high signatory powers, in case he acted on their recommendations. Clarkson concurred with me very fully, but I thought — I may have been mistaken — but rather got the impression that the bishop was a trifle disappointed. The bishop did not say anything against you or your leadership. He seemed to feel that you were being overworked. I am rather of opinion that his proposition emenated from his desire to be doing a little leading for the race, rather than from any scheme to displace you. At the same time, I thought you ought to know something about it — particularly as I have heard the scheme mentioned by several of the race "party-builders" during the past two or three weeks. It may be interesting to you to know that Genl Clarkson did not approve of the plan, but agreed with me entirely.

I pass this along in confidence. The General will doubtless tell you all about it, when you see him.

We leave here on next Wednesday or Thursday for New York. My wife directs me to send her regards to both Mrs Washington & yourself. Yours Faithfully,

Charles W. Anderson

ALS   Con. 249   BTW Papers   DLC.

From William Henry Baldwin, Jr.

Brooklyn, N.Y. Friday Jan 23. [1903]

Dear Mr Washington, I have watched your Western trip with great interest. Your letter today is full of encouragement, and inspiration. I have taken the liberty of sending copies (of your reference to your trip) to our close friends.

It is very important.

I have spent the evening on Genl. Edn. work. Getting ready for our annual meeting tomorrow.

On Thursday next we have our first meeting under our National incorporation at Washn. D.C. and also we meet the Peabody Board.

They have asked us to help them decide important questions, and to cooperate with them. My hopes are being realized. General Education, Slater & Peabody.

It scares Mr Murphy, but I am not afraid of the results of concentration.

There are lots of things to talk over. Our meeting of the Southern Board, the Ogden dinner, the Armstrong meeting (poor) the meeting in Phila. with the Academy of Political Science (good) My New York local Negro Conference,[1] (2nd meeting next Monday), My talk with DuBois,[2] etc.

Let me know soon when you expect to come North, so I can plan time for you. I am not going out much, as Mrs Baldwin[3] is not at all well.

I want to talk with you about Tillmanism, and the Prest. and Southern (mis)representation! My regards to all. Faithfully

W H Baldwin Jr.

ALS   Con. 792   BTW Papers   DLC.

¹ A private conference of about fifteen persons, including William L. Bulkley, Felix Adler, Wallace Buttrick, George Foster Peabody, Robert C. Ogden, W. E. B. Du Bois, Samuel R. Scottron, and Charles S. Morris. The conference was concerned with the welfare of blacks in New York City. It was one of several meetings out of which grew the Committee for Improving the Industrial Condition of Negroes in New York City.

² Du Bois, who attended the conference, later wrote that, following the conference, he was "whisked over to William H. Baldwin's beautiful Long Island home and there what seemed to be the real object of my coming was disclosed.... Both he and his wife insisted that Tuskegee was not yet a good school, and needed the kind of development that I had been trained to promote." (Du Bois, *Dusk of Dawn*, 78.) Two interviews with BTW followed, but Du Bois eventually decided to remain at Atlanta University.

³ Ruth Standish Bowles Baldwin (1865–1934) was the daughter of Samuel Bowles, editor of the Springfield (Mass.) *Republican*. A graduate of Smith College, she took an active part in educational, welfare, and peace movements. She maintained an interest in Tuskegee and friendship for BTW after her husband's death in 1905. She was one of the founders of the National League for the Protection of Colored Women, one of the organizations that merged to form the National Urban League, of which she was the first president and a lifelong supporter. She was also a founder and officer of the New York Probation and Protective Association and a trustee of Smith College for twenty-five years.

To Theodore Roosevelt

Tuskegee, Alabama. January 24, 1903

Personal and Confidential.

My dear Mr. President: I have just reached home from a three weeks trip to California, but I have kept closely in touch with matters in the South during my absence. I have received both of your letters on my return.

I cannot feel that it would be to the best interest of all concerned for me to see you just now, in person, and that I had better not do so provided the same end can be accomplished indirectly. If it cannot I will go to Washington at once. In any case I mean to see both Postmaster General Payne and Gen. Clarkson soon.

I am not afraid to do anything that I think is right, but I think it just as well to recognize the fact that the newspapers are making quite an effort just now to keep the South inflamed and if it can be avoided, without yielding in the matter of principle, I do not think it wise to do anything that will add to the flames, especially now that matters seem to be somewhat quieting down. I have studied matters closely from every point of view and I cannot see how you could have acted differently from what you have, and I am sure and believe that time will justify your actions.

I am keeping in close touch with the Advisory Committee in this state and matters are being handled cautiously and wisely. I had a talk with Mr. C. H. Scott this morning and he and the other members are most devoted and loyal.

I have written a separate letter today about Mississippi matters.

I am in close and constant touch with the Negro leaders and Negro papers in every part of the country, and with the exception of a few soreheads in Washington and Boston, no President has ever had the gratitude and loyal support of a race to the extent that you have it now. Of course, we must and shall watch closely, in the Southern States especially, every point that we may not be taken unawares by an enemy.

I am most anxious to see a really first class man go as Minister to Liberia, and if I can help you find such a man please let me know.

This note will reach you through my Secretary, and I have left the matter of the means of communicating it to you to his discretion. I hope that you will talk fully and freely with him regarding any matters that you want me to understand or anything you may want me to do. I have given Mr. Scott some memoranda to take up with you.

The marked copy of the Charleston News and Courier and your letter do not seem to have connection. I think you must have sent the wrong newspaper.

I am hoping that you thoroughly understand, Mr. President, that I mean at all times to stand firmly by you. Yours very truly,

Booker T. Washington

TLS Theodore Roosevelt Papers DLC.

11

From Edgar Stewart Wilson

Jackson [Miss.] Jan 24, 1903

My dear Mr. Washington: This morning I found a letter here from the Post Master General asking me for an immediate recommendation for a presidential office appointment. The incumbent appointed *not* by our friend, is short and its caused me — coupled with the uncertainties of the white cap situation with which I am called on to deal — to wire you that I could not go to Washington. There was no necessity for my going, I simply thought I might be of some service to the president, or the department, in the matter of suggestions concerning the Indianola matter, etc.

There is no news here of interest. I wrote you that Hill was back, and according to his own friends had a futile trip. The State committee is composed of 51. Some of them are good, some very good. About half of them — some 20 odd, hold federal offices and I am still building. Their signing the document to the president, was the result in some instances of lies, some of fear, and largely through the activity of those in the committee who have been turned out by the president or who have been office broking. Some of my best friends, and the presidents signed for the influence they would have with other members when the time for action arrives. With almost half the committee the president's friends and appointees and with the influence that can be exerted in the proper way at the proper time, I will have for the president at least 35, of the 51. I could now, if I wanted to — but this is not the time — have a majority of the committee sign a call for a meeting and depose Hill as chairman. He was so weak he could not get in the last State Convention from his own county (His friends) and got in by a proxy. He was made chairman by trading the few votes he had to a man favored by the Ohio influence, then potent here, for national committeeman. As soon as the fellows who are in politics for something find that Hill is utterly repudiated by the president, they will all drop him, they are doing so now. They will not beat a dead horse. He has been telling them that some body up there was his friend, and that he [will] win out yet. M M Montgomery, who is now Hills ally, and who went over the state getting signatures to the petition, is the man who remembered Hills selling offices, I have learned. I know he and Hill have been bitter enemies. Montgomery was appointed District atty before I was consulted. He is a dangerous man—not true to his friends. I warned the president against him a year ago, and it has turned out just as I feared about him. He is not big enough, or patriotic enough to rule and he will not serve. I told the president last October that he would have to be disciplined, and he said all right. Everything is fine so far as results go. Not a single appointment made has been criticised. On the contrary even the president's adversaries admit their fitness.

Please write me fully all you have in mind. Sincerely

Edgar S. Wilson

ALS   Con. 282   BTW Papers   DLC.

To Timothy Thomas Fortune

Tuskegee, Ala., Jan. 26, 1903

My dear Mr. Fortune: I am in receipt of your letter of January 10th and am very glad indeed to hear from you. I hope by this time you have received at least one of my letters. I am very glad to hear that your health is so good, and especially glad to know that you were not troubled by seasickness. You would have a pretty difficult time in making such a long journey if you were inclined to get seasick.

The South has become quite strenuous again. Their excitement is caused through the appointment of Dr. Crum and they are making quite an attempt to defeat his confirmation. The matter has not been settled as yet. And right on top of the Crum excitement it seems that three or four colored men in official life in Washington attended the Judicial Reception and took their wives and some lady friends with them. This was of course more than the South could stand nothwithstanding I am informed that colored people attend many such receptions.

I have had several conversations with important friends and I am more and more convinced that we ought to call together a meeting of 12 or 15 of our men who would represent the dominant forces in the race and I am rather convinced that we ought to come together periodically. Matters might reach such a point where it will be necessary to call such a committee before you return; in case we do, of course we shall leave a place on the board for yourself and I do not think we would do anything with which you would not agree.

It is rather lonesome when both you and Durham are out of the country.

I advise you to be very careful about what you say to newspaper men, especially in the Philippines, as they are rather treacherous. Yours very truly,

Booker T. Washington

TLS   Con. 249   BTW Papers   DLC.

From Wallace Buttrick

New York   Jan. 26, 1903

Dear Mr Washington: Yes, indeed, I saw that copy of the Richmond Times with its misleading and mischievous headline, and I had a sharp interview with the reporter regarding it. He apologized and explained to me that he did not put in the headline, and what was still better, he corrected the mistake, as you will see by the extract from the same paper later in the week, which I enclose. It should be said that this copy, which you have sent me, was printed before the conference assembled and was a bit of mischievous work on the part of an overzealous reporter. He interviewed a few superintendents and developed the idea that they were opposed to the higher education of the colored people. When we came to discuss the matter in the conference the conclusions reached were most satisfactory. By a unanimous vote, the commissioners decided that a minimum of eight grades should be given to all the colored people by the public schools, and before the vote was taken a number of county superintendents arose and said that they believed that there ought to be a high school for colored people in every county in the State, and Mr Glass,[1] Sup't of Schools at Lynchburg, and the head of the Virginia School of Methods, declared

14

publicly and with much feeling that the effort to repress the intellectual powers of the negro was inspired of the Devil. In fact, dear Mr Washington, I am sure that you would have been much gratified by the discussion of this whole matter at this conference. Dr Frissell was invited to lead the discussion and everybody concurred with what he said.

One of the sorrows of my life is that I cannot go to Montgomery this week. The members of our Board have simply vetoed it, feeling that it is absolutely necessary that I should be with them in Washington this week, where we are to meet the Trustees of the Peabody Board for an important conference. A further reason for sorrow is that this may make it necessary for me to postpone my visit to the Tuskegee Negro Conference until 1904. Let me ask your advice about this. Will it embarrass you in any way if, failing to go to the Montgomery conference, I should go to your conference? I do not want to do anything that will lead to unfavorable criticism. There is enough of that that I cannot anticipate and guard against, and I must be very careful in cases where my eyes are open to difficulties. Affectionately yours

Wallace Buttrick

TLS   Con. 249   BTW Papers   DLC.

[1] Edward Christian Glass was superintendent of the Lynchburg public schools for fifty-three years beginning in 1879, and also was an owner and editor of the *Virginia Journal of Education*.

From William Nicholas Sheats[1]

Tallahassee, Jan. 31, 1903

Dear Sir: Replying to your recent communication suggesting a conference between yourself and a dozen or more of the leading negro educators of this State, I will say that President N. B. Young[2] of the Normal and Industrial school of this place, at my suggestion, has sent invitations to about a dozen of the most influential colored teachers of the State.

They are asked to meet you on the 6th, of February, and have been told their railroad fare will be paid. The round trip fare for this number will not exceed the amount you named, $100.00, and if you will bring this with you it can be repaid to them at Gainsville.

I trust and believe that this meeting will be very profitable. Your truly,

Wm. N. Sheats

TLS   Con. 241   BTW Papers   DLC.

1 William Nicholas Sheats (1851–1922), a graduate of Emory College, was school superintendent of Alachua County, Fla., in 1892, when he wrote the educational provisions of the new state constitution. From 1893 to 1905 and from 1913 to 1922 he was state superintendent of education. Sheats invited BTW to speak in Gainesville, but the man who would be his rival for superintendent the following year sought to force a retraction of the invitation. Sheats stood by his position, and BTW offered to withdraw if it was believed best, but Sheats and others renewed the invitation and the speech was well received by a crowd of 2,000 about equally divided between black and white. The following year, however, Sheats lost his office to the leading opponent of the invitation to BTW, and he appealed unsuccessfully to Wallace Buttrick for money to sue his opponent for libel. (Sheats to Buttrick, May 25, 1904, Con. 18, BTW Papers, DLC.) A detailed account is White, "BTW's Florida Incident," 227–49.

2 Nathan Benjamin Young (1862–1933), born in Newbern, Ala., of a slave mother, was a graduate of Talladega and had an Oberlin B.A. and M.A. He was principal of two Alabama schools before going to Tuskegee, where he was head of the academic department from 1892 to 1897. He left to become professor of English at Georgia State College from 1897 to 1901, when he became president of Florida Agricultural and Mechanical State College for twenty-two years. Young sought to combine BTW's industrial education program with the liberal arts he had studied at Oberlin. He became president of Lincoln Institute from 1923 to 1927 and from 1929 to 1931.

From Edgar Gardner Murphy

Montgomery, Alabama. Jan. 31/03

Personal.

Dear Mr. Washington: The Conference[1] is over. Its technical value will not be as great as if Dr Buttrick had come, but its value as an awakening could hardly be greater.

I note your invitation to speak in Florida and I rejoice in it. I think it could have been managed here, but for the intense feeling which the President has aroused on the question of office holding. This feeling is largely morbid and unreasonable but it *exists* through all ranks and classes of our people. Every friend of the Negro is now put upon the defensive and it becomes impossible to do many things that would have been possible if the situation had been "let alone." There is more feeling against our Negroes than I have seen in many years. This is all very foolish, very cruel, very needless; but the feeling is *here* and it is useless — utterly useless — to challenge it. The people know your close friendship for the President. They absurdly believe that the President means to put Negroes into office practically everywhere through the South, and many believe, unjustly but sincerely, that this purpose is the reflection of your influence. You surely know how much this situation tries my heart; and I hope that at your convenience you will let me see you. Faithfully Your Friend

Edgar Gardner Murphy

ALS   Con. 249   BTW Papers   DLC.

[1] A meeting of Alabama county superintendents under the auspices of the General Education Board, one of a series of such meetings in southern states to promote public education.

From William Demosthenes Crum

Charleston, S.C., Jan. 31 1903

Personal

My dear Mr Washington: Appreciating all that you have done for me and relying implicitly upon your judgment I write to ask your advice at this critical time. My appointment has aroused a storm of opposition very embarrassing to me and I am sure equally so to the President and I am ready to accept any advice that you may be pleased to give, so far I have stood every test and am not ashamed of my record. I am profoundly grateful to the President and yourself for the stand taken in my behalf and yet I cannot understand the reported attitude of some of the republican senators on my case. It has been hinted to me that the President would be greatly relieved from an embarassing situation if I should withdraw from the fight.

Kindly let me know what you think of the situation.

Congratul[at]ing you on the great ovation given you on your Western trip. I am   Very truly,

Wm. D. Crum

HLS   Con. 249   BTW Papers   DLC.

An Account of Washington's California Tour
by Max Bennett Thrasher

Tuskegee, Alabama, January 31, 1903

During several years past Mr. Booker T. Washington has received many invitations to the Pacific Coast to speak in the interest of Tuskegee, but it has never been convenient for him to arrange to make so long a trip until this winter. He has just returned from two weeks spent in the State of California, during which time he made twenty-seven formal addresses, besides speaking informally a number of times at dinners, banquets, and receptions. I had the pleasure of making this trip with Mr. Washington, and it was so interesting in many ways, that I have thought the readers of The Student would be glad to know something of it.

Mr. Washington reached Los Angeles on New Year's morning, by way of the Southern Pacific Railroad, having stopped on his way from Tuskegee to speak for the Board of Trade of Houston, Texas, by invitation of that body. I had started to say that the morning he arrived in California, the first of 1903, was a beautiful morning, but I remembered in season that I learned while in California that I must not make comments on the weather. To say that a day was beautiful, was to intimate that there might be some days in California which are not beautiful, and that no Californian was ever willing to admit. As a matter of fact, every day we were in the state was cloudless, clear and sunny, and except for a few days in San Francisco, warm enough so that no overcoats were needed except at night. We were told, though, that this clear weather at this time of the year was not favorably looked upon by residents — that rain was needed now for the benefit of the next summer's crop.

Mr. Washington was met at the station by President A. E. Shumate of the California State Teachers' Association, and other officials of that body, for whom he was to make two addresses. He was also met by several reporters, a photographer, and two or three persons who wanted his autograph, but I hardly thought to mention these, as they were incidents of every city to which we went. As he had no speaking engagements for that day, he was able to devote the time to such callers, and to getting rested after the long journey across the continent. One of the best newspaper interviews had with him while in California, was obtained that day by Miss Bertha Crowell, for The Los Angeles Herald. Two other extremely good and appreciative interviews were written by Mr. Grant Wallace for The San Francisco Bulletin, from notes obtained during a ride with Mr. Washington on the train to Ontario, one day when he was to speak there, although people who saw the reproduction of the sketch of Mr. Washington, made at the same time, said it looked more like Bryan than it did like the Principal of Tuskegee.

Throughout the entire California trip, the press of the state was so uniformly kind that it was frequently commented upon. In all the places where we went columns of space were given to excellent reports of the meetings, and in many of the most influential papers, these reports were supplemented by encouraging editorials.

Mr. Washington's first public appearance in California was before the Friday Morning Club, at eleven o'clock, on Friday, January 2. This is a large and influential woman's club of the city, and, for that matter, of all Southern California. This is the building in which the Biennial Session of the Woman's Clubs of the United States met a few months ago. The audience room, which accommodates about a thousand persons, was jammed to suffocation, and when Mr. Washington entered the room, the audience accorded him the compliment of rising to greet him with the Chautauqua salute of waving handkerchiefs. One of the city papers, in fact, said that his welcome was more enthusiastic than even that given the late President McKinley, when he visited the city.

In the afternoon of the same day Mr. Washington made his first address before the State Teachers' Association, in Hazard's Pavilion, before an audience of three or four thousand persons, and in the evening spoke again in the same place to a still larger number. The next morning, January 3, we took an early train for Ontario, a beautiful village in the orange country, about thirty miles from Los Angeles. Mr. Washington spoke there in the Methodist Church, to an audience which more than filled the building. Some even put ladders to the windows and listened in that way. Although the time was 10:30 of Saturday forenoon, the banks and stores of the place accorded the rare compliment of closing during the hours of meeting, that every one might attend. We were indebted here for special courtesy to Rev. Mather, the pastor of the church.

After the meeting at Ontario, we had lunch with Rev. Ralph B. Larkin, the pastor of the Congregational Church, who had arranged for this meeting, and who was largely responsible for its great success, and then were driven by President George A. Gates,[1] of Pomona College, to Claremont, where Mr. Washington spoke to another large audience in the chapel of Pomona College. This drive of six miles through the orange country was one of the pleasantest features of the entire visit to California. The route led between groves of orange, lemon and olive trees, all in full fruit, and all irrigated by water brought down from the lofty mountains which tower behind this valley. We stopped several times on the way and were allowed to pick as much fruit as we wished, including oranges, lemons, persimmons — very different from the small Southern fruit of that name — olives, and grape fruit. Mr. Shaw, a fruit grower and packer of that place, who accompanied us, made the ride the more pleasant by his explanation of what we saw.

When we returned to Los Angeles that night, Mr. Washington was met at the station by a delegation of prominent colored men of the city. He was taken to Simpson's Pavilion, a very fine audience room accommodating three thousand persons, and spoke to an audience under the auspices of the colored people, which packed the house. While this was a meeting arranged by the colored people of the city, and more particularly that Mr. Washington might have a good opportunity to speak to the people of his own race, there were many white people in the audience. After this meeting the colored people gave him a banquet in an assembly room connected with the same building.

Sunday at 3 p.m., Mr. Washington spoke in the Methodist Church at Pasadena. This is one of the largest and finest church buildings in California, and though it will accommodate between two and three thousand persons, it was estimated that as many more were gathered in the grounds outside, who could not get in. After this meeting, by invitation of Mrs. Garfield, the widow of the late President Garfield, Mr. Washington was driven to her home for lunch, and later drove to call on Mrs. Ruth Brown Thompson, the daughter of John Brown. In the evening of the same day, he spoke in the First Congregational Church in Los Angeles, to another crowded house.

On Monday, January 5, we went to San Diego, in the extreme southwestern part of the state, and only eight miles from the Mexican line. The meeting here had been arranged for by Mr. George W. Marston, the largest and most successful merchant of the city. It was held in the Isis Theater, which was so full that the stage was covered with chairs to give additional seats. After this meeting Mr. Washington met the colored people again and spoke to them. One of the very pleasant features of the visit to San Diego, was a launch ride on the Bay, given by Mr. Marston and a number of men belonging to a club there, under whose auspices the meeting was held. San Diego Bay, set quite around with mountains, is said to be more beautiful even than the famous Bay of Naples, and as this day was the first time that either of us had seen the Pacific Ocean, we were glad to have this opportunity to ride upon it.

Tuesday we returned to Los Angeles, where Mr. Washington was the guest at dinner of Mr. and Mrs. Robert C. Owens,[2] colored, who had invited a number of the leading colored people of the city to meet him. Mr. Owens, although still a young man, is the owner of much valuable property in Los Angeles, including a business block on Spring street, the principal business street of the city, in which are three fine stores. When Mr. Washington came away, Mr. and Mrs. Owens gave him $120 for Tuskegee, a gift which the offer of the General Education Board to duplicate all sums given to the school this year by colored people, will make net the Institute $240.

Tuesday night was spent traveling to San Jose, and as our train was five hours late, we reached there too late for some minor engagements, including one to drive to Saratoga to visit some more relatives of John Brown. Two meetings were held at San Jose, one in a theater and the other in one of the churches. Both were crowded and enthusiastic, and the contributions made to Tuskegee amounted to an even $1000. These meetings in San Jose were arranged for by Miss Lucy Washburn, once a teacher of Mr. Washington at Hampton, and it was largely [due] to her warm interest and untiring energy that they were so successful.

On the morning of Thursday, January 8, we made an early start for Palo Alto, the site of Stanford University, where we were met by Vice-President J. C. Branner, President Jordan being in the East. We enjoyed an opportunity to go over the buildings being erected for the use of the University, especially the chapel which Mrs. Stanford[3] is erecting as a memorial to her late husband. These buildings, of brown stone, in the style of the old Mexican Missions, will be when completed, I think, the most beautiful and most complete specimens of a distinctive type of architecture in the United States. Although it was only the second day of the college term, the assembly room, seating 2000 persons, was packed. After the meeting we lunched with Mrs. Leland Stanford, and then drove to Belmont to visit Mr. Reid's[4] famous preparatory school. We reached San Francisco at 4 p.m. of the same day, and Mr. Washington spoke that evening in the Mechanics Pavilion to an audience, estimated in the papers the next morning, as from nine to eleven thousand. This meeting was under the auspices of the Collegiate Alumnae Association, and was arranged for by Mrs. Frederic Burke.

On Friday, at 3 p.m., Mr. Washington spoke before the students of Mrs. Mills'[5] College for Young Ladies, at Oakland, and in the evening spoke in Hearst Hall at the Pacific Theological Seminary. Previous to the meeting he was the guest at dinner of Prof. and Mrs. C. S. Nash, meeting among others there, President J. K. McLean, of the Seminary, for whose advice and help in the planning of the California trip Mr. Bedford, who made all the plans for this trip, has expressed himself as greatly indebted.

Saturday we went to Sacramento, where in the afternoon a reception was given Mr. Washington in the Crocker Art Gallery, under the auspices of the Tuesday Woman's Club, Mrs. Edinger,[6] president. In the evening we were guests at dinner of Mr. and Mrs. Harris Weinstock. [Mr. Weinstock,] who is the leading merchant of the city, visited Tuskegee about a year ago with his wife and daughter. Among the guests at dinner were Governor and Mrs. George W. Pardee, the recently elected governor of the state. Later in the evening Mr. Washington addressed an audience in the First Presbyterian Church. The meeting in Sacramento was arranged for by the Lecture Association of the city, Mr. Sparrow Smith, who is the President of the Capital Banking and Trust Company, being largely instrumental for its inception and success. Both at the reception and the meeting many of the colored residents of the city improved the opportunity to meet Mr. Washington.

Sunday morning Mr. Washington spoke at 11 a.m. in the First Congregational Church, in San Francisco, Rev. George C. Adams, pastor, and lunched at the home of Mr. and Mrs. John F. Merrill, who had been so kind as to invite a company of representative people of the city to meet him. At 3 p.m. he spoke at Starr King Zion A. M. E. Church, Rev. Thaddeus A. Brown, pastor. The Church was beautifully decorated with flags and flowers, and crowded with the best colored residents of San Francisco. At the close of the address Mr. Thomas B. Morton[7] offered a set of resolutions which were unanimously adopted. They pledged interest in, and loyalty to, the distinguished leader and full and free endorsement of his wise, manly and unselfish efforts in behalf of the race.

Sunday evening Mr. Washington spoke at the First Congregational Church of Oakland, and after this meeting spoke for a special meeting of the colored people of Oakland. At the meeting at the Zion Church the contributions for Tuskegee amounted to nearly $300, including $50 from the Fanny J. Coppin Club, $5 from the Aurora Club — five young ladies — $5 from the Booker T. Washington Relief Society for Homeless and Orphan Children, and several sums from individuals, including $5 from Captain Young, $10 from Mrs. Ida C. N. Porter, and $20 from Mr. Edward Berry. The contribution from the Oakland meeting, which was under the auspices of the Industrial Club, made through Mr. C. C. Riley, was nearly $100. As in the case of the other contributions mentioned from colored people, all these amounts will be duplicated to the school by the General Education Board.

Monday morning Mr. Washington spoke to the colored troops stationed at [the] Presidio, a few miles outside of San Francisco. His visit to the Presidio was by the invitation of Captain Charles

Young, of the Ninth U.S. Cavalry, seconded by invitations from several other officers. The meeting was largely attended by many people besides the colored troops. After the meeting Mr. Washington lunched with Captain Young at the latter's house in Officers' Row.

Monday evening Mr. Washington went to Stockton to speak, a large audience being gathered in the Methodist Church. This meeting was arranged for by Rev. R. H. Sink.

On Tuesday morning Mr. Washington spoke at the University of California, to an audience of five thousand persons. The contributions made at this meeting to Tuskegee were over $1,000, including a check for $500 from Mrs. Hearst,[8] with whom Mr. Washington had lunch after the meeting. On Tuesday evening he was the guest of the Unitarian Club of San Francisco at a reception and dinner given in his honor at the Palace Hotel, said to be the largest hotel in the world. About three hundred and fifty persons were present, all that the dining room of the hotel would accommodate, and Professor Louis Lisser, the president of the club, told me that a week before the dinner more than a hundred requests for tickets had been declined for want of room. The rooms of the hotel were beautifully decorated for the dinner, and the ladies present wore knots of cardinal, the color of Tuskegee. After the dinner Mr. Washington spoke for an hour or more upon the work of the school.

On Wednesday forenoon Mr. Washington spoke for the Ebell Woman's Club, of Oakland, in their club house. This is the oldest woman's club of Oakland, and one of the strongest woman's clubs on the Pacific coast. In the afternoon of the same day he was the guest at dinner of Captain Shorey,[9] a colored gentleman, at his home, West Oakland, to meet a company of about twenty representative colored men of the two cities.

In speaking informally at the dinner, Mr. Washington repeated what I had already heard him say, the surprise and pleasure which he had felt to find colored people of the Pacific coast, as a general thing, so prosperous, so intelligent, and so well informed not only as to matters pertaining to the race in the country as a whole, but particularly as regarding the history and work of Tuskegee.

On Wednesday evening we started by way of the Southern Pa-

cific and Union Pacific for Chicago and from there came directly
to Tuskegee.

Tuskegee Student, 15 (Jan. 31, 1903), 1, 3–4. A typescript version is in Con. 280,
BTW Papers, DLC.

¹ George Augustus Gates (1851–1912), a graduate of Dartmouth (1873) and An-
dover Theological Seminary (1880), was president of Pomona College from 1902 to
1909 and president of Fisk University from 1909 to 1912.

² Robert C. Owens, born in 1860, a wealthy black businessman who made his
fortune in real estate, was a frequent donor of scholarships to Tuskegee Institute.

³ Jane Lathrop (Mrs. Leland) Stanford (1825–1905).

⁴ William Thomas Reid (1842–1922) was president of the University of California
beginning in 1881. In 1885 he founded the Belmont School in Belmont, Calif.

⁵ Susan Lincoln Tolman (Mrs. Cyrus T.) Mills (1826–1912).

⁶ Mrs. Frank A. Edinger.

⁷ Theophilus B. Morton.

⁸ Phoebe Apperson (Mrs. George) Hearst (1842–1919).

⁹ William T. Shorey, born in Barbados of a white planter and a Creole mother,
became a well-known captain of whaling ships out of San Franciso beginning in 1887.

An Article in the *Southern Workman*

[January 1903]

ONE OF THE MAKERS OF TUSKEGEE

My brother, John H. Washington, joined me here at Tuskegee
in 1885, and has been closely identified with the work of the Tuskegee Normal and Industrial Institute ever since.

Back in the years when I, as a boy in West Virginia, was trying
in every way to plan how I could get to the Hampton Institute, it
was my brother and my dear mother who encouraged me and
helped me. It was my brother's savings, added to my own, that enabled me to start for Hampton, and when I was enrolled as a student there he cheerfully stayed at home and toiled in a coal mine
that his earnings might help to keep me at school. Later, he was
able to satisfy the ambition which he had suppressed for my sake,
and went to Hampton himself as a student. After he was graduated
he taught for a year, and then for five years held a position in the
United States Engineering Corps occupied in the improvement of

the Kanawha river, the great coal-bearing stream upon whose banks our boyhood home was built. I had tried for some time to have him join me in the work here before he decided to do so.

When my brother came to Tuskegee, in 1885, it was to act as business manager, and to take charge of the boarding department. A year and a half later he was put in charge of the industrial department, which, up to that time, I had looked after myself. The industries were then extremely primitive, compared with what they are now, but the lack of conveniences from which we suffered made the duties of the director all the more arduous. In addition to the farm and the brickyard, we had then a blacksmith shop with one anvil, a carpenter shop, and a printing office so small that I have heard my brother complain that when he went into it he had to back out, because the clear space in the shop was too small to turn around in. In addition to his other duties, my brother acted as commandant until the present officer, Major J. B. Ramsey, came here from Hampton to assume the duties of that position.

The first building which my brother erected, as director of industries, was Willow Cottage. Cassedy Hall, the laundry, and the boys' hospital followed, all built after his own plans. Several years ago, at the suggestion of Dr. J. L. M. Curry, he spent a part of a year in the North, studying the methods of the foremost industrial schools of the country, among them the New York School of Technology, the Pratt Institute of Brooklyn, the Worcester Polytechnic School, and the Drexel Institute of Philadelphia.

The interest which my brother has taken in the development of Tuskegee, and his determination to carry through a thing which he has begun, are illustrated in the establishment of our foundry. He believed it was possible for us to do foundry work here, and to teach it to the students. He showed so much enthusiasm on the subject that when the Alabama Polytechnic School at Auburn was preparing to put a new cupola into their foundry, they offered to give their old one to us. When some of us who were not so enthusiastic as my brother on the subject of foundry work, thought the experiment would not justify the expense of having so heavy an object freighted over from Auburn here, he took an ox-team and went after it and brought it himself. The cupola was set up, and the foundry work has been developed so successfully that it is now an important part of the industrial department. A dozen or more boys work at the trade each year, we have more than a hundred different patterns which we cast, and the work has increased to such an extent that we have recently bought and set up a larger cupola.

In the course of his work, the director of industries has sometimes found it necessary to make great exertions in order to push a building to completion against the time it was needed, especially when, at times, unavoidable delays have occurred. I remember this was the case when the new chapel was to be dedicated. He worked all night to direct the work, and I have heard him say that when the line was forming on the grounds to march to the chapel on the day of dedication, he and some of the men were just sweeping out the last of the litter of construction from the building, and that they went out the back door as the head of the procession entered at the front. Hard as it has sometimes been to do it, I believe he has never disappointed the school in having a building ready at the appointed time. I speak of this to show how completely and unselfishly he has thrown himself into the work at Tuskegee. For the last few years his position has been that of superintendent of mechanical industries. With the present year the scope of his work was broadened, and he was made general superintendent of industries.

Southern Workman, 32 (Jan. 1903), 30–32.

To Theodore Roosevelt

Tuskegee, Alabama. February 3d, 1903

Personal and Confidential
My dear Mr. President: I write according to promise bearing upon my interview with the editors of The Churchman and The Outlook. I had a long talk with Dr. McBee[1] of The Churchman! I found that Dr. McBee did not disagree with you in what you had done except perhaps in the case of the Indianola matter, but he did disagree as to the method and time of making the Crum appointment and the Lewis appointment especially. I tried to express as best I could how these matters came about, but the main thing that I tried

to impress upon him was the fact that notwithstanding the outcry about your placing Negroes in office the facts showed that you had nominated but one colored man to office in the South in a locality where no colored man was holding office before you came into the Presidency, and that was the case of Dr. Crum. On the other hand, the net result of your Negro Southern appointments shows that there are two less Negroes holding Presidential offices in the South than was true under President McKinley. You have increased the quality of Negro officials in the South and reduced the quantity. This fact I am getting into the ears of the people North and South wherever I have the opportunity. Dr. McBee said that he did not intend to have any more adverse editorials upon your position at present at least.

I had a long conference with Dr. Lyman Abbott and Mr. Lawrence F. Abbott. Both of them, especially Mr. Lawrence F. Abbott, feel that they have been supporting your policy as they have understood it and were somewhat chagrined to feel that you had the feeling that they had not stood by you. Mr. Lawrence Abbott has already sent you his most recent editorials. Dr. Abbott is going to have an editorial in an early number of The Outlook which I think will place matters in a more satisfactory condition so far as The Outlook is concerned. I furnished Dr. Abbott a statement, as I did the editor of The Churchman, as to what you have actually done in the South in the appointment of Negro officials, and Dr. Abbott is going to use these facts in his editorial.

I am now making an effort to get hold of some Southern editors with a view of trying to acquaint them with the facts in relation to your Southern appointments. Yours truly,

Booker T. Washington

TLS   Theodore Roosevelt Papers   DLC.

1 Silas McBee (1853–1924), a graduate of the University of the South (1876), was editor of *The Churchman*, a national weekly of the Episcopal Church, from 1896 to 1912.

To George Bruce Cortelyou

Tuskegee, Alabama. February 3, 1903

Personal.

My dear Sir: On the 12th of February, Lincoln's Birthday, the colored people are in the habit of holding large meetings especially in the Northern cities. Two on a large scale are planned for, New York and Boston, and in these meetings I am reasonably sure that strong resolutions endorsing the President's policy in the South will be passed. I cannot but feel in the present state of public feeling that such resolutions if pretty generally passed all over the country will rather serve to put the President in an awkward position rather than help. If you will be kind enough to let me know the feeling of the President on this subject I can take measures to control these meetings in a large degree if I am notified in time.[1] Yours truly,

Booker T. Washington

TLS Theodore Roosevelt Papers DLC.

[1] Cortelyou replied that Roosevelt agreed that any resolutions "should be put in the most mild and moderate manner." (Feb. 6, 1903, Con. 16, BTW Papers, DLC.)

To Timothy Thomas Fortune

Tuskegee, Ala., Feb. 3, 1903

My dear Mr. Fortune: I have your letter of January 17th written just on the eve of your leaving Honolulu and I am very glad to have it. I watch all of your movements with a great deal of interest.

I must confess that we are passing through a rather severe trial in the South just now. The closing of the Indianola post office and the appointing of Dr. Crum seems to have been made a peg upon which to hang a great deal of anti-Negro sentiment in the South. The feeling against the President at this time is rather intense. I hope, however, that present conditions are only temporary and that within a few months we shall settle down to a normal state of affairs. I should feel better if you were in this country. Notwithstanding the way the President is standing up and notwithstanding many things that I have tried to do to help the race, I notice that the enemies in Washingon and in Boston especially seem to be most active at the present time. Yours truly,

Booker T. Washington

TLS Con. 290 BTW Papers DLC.

From James H. Hayes[1]

N.Y. [City] Feb. 3, 1903

Dear Sir: Having been informed by Bishop Walters, that you are or have been under the impression that the work we are trying to do — pushing the Virginia Suffrage Cases — and arousing popular interest to the National Negro Suffrage Convention, Louisville, July 7th — is in some way intended to criticise you, I hasten to disclaim any such idea or intention. In me there is not the slightest desire for the usual "killing off" business in which the Negro has become an adept.

Your place in history has been made. Your name has been written where it will never be erased. Should God call you now, yours would be among the few immortal names which will never die.

I couldn't harm you if I would nor wouldn't if I could.

I do not write this so much to disclaim, as to let you understand that I am not so silly as [to] think that anything I can say will injure you. I enclose a clipping from the "Sun" of today. Res.,

Jas. H. Hayes

ALS Con. 249 BTW Papers DLC.

1 James H. Hayes (b. 1855), a graduate of Howard University Law School (1885), was a lawyer in Richmond. He was the first president of the National Negro Suffrage League in 1903, and opposed the adoption of the Virginia Constitution of 1902 because of its Jim Crow provisions and voting restrictions. Hayes was one of only a few black lawyers in the South who publicly opposed BTW.

A News Item in the Washington *Post*[1]

Washington, D.C., Feb. 3, 1903

ATTACKED BOOKER WASHINGTON
Local Negroes Indignant at Remarks of
W. H. Ferris, of Boston

The presence in the city, for the past three weeks of W. H. Ferris, from Boston, has stirred up considerable agitation among his race concerning the work that Dr. Booker T. Washington is doing along educational lines. Shortly after his arrival here, Ferris delivered an address before Bethel Literary and Historical Association, in which he took occasion to arraign Dr. Washington for catering to the prejudices of the white race in encouraging the Caucasian idea that the negro is an inferior being, asserting that Mr. Washington is opposed to the aspirations of the colored people, and higher education as a racial necessity; that he condones the "jim crow car" and the disfranchising clauses of the Southern States' constitutions, and finally, that he is departing from his life-work by engaging in politics. The speech aroused indignation among the better classes of the colored people of the city and the friends of Mr. Washington have been bringing evidence to the fore in refutation of what they feel is calculated to do him harm.

At a largely attended public meeting last Sunday, before the Second Baptist Lyceum, Mr. R. W. Thompson, assistant editor of the Colored American and a staunch advocate of industrial education as the basis of race progress, presented a carefully prepared paper, reviewing the true attitude of Mr. Washington upon the mental, moral, and material development of the negro, answering in detail the criticisms advanced by the detractors of the Tuskegeeian, quoting liberally from Mr. Washington's own speeches and letters to substantiate his argument.

To-night the agitation will be continued at the Metropolitan A. M. E. Church, M street, between Fifteenth and Sixteenth streets, under the auspices of the Bethel Literary and Historical Association, with Prof. Jesse Lawson as the principal speaker. He will speak in favor of the work of Mr. Washington, and the general discussion will be participated in by a number of well-known men.

Washington *Post*, Feb. 3, 1903, 10.

¹ Richard W. Thompson forwarded the news item to Emmett J. Scott with the comment: "Things are at a fever heat today. Big time promised for tonight. Am stirring the animals up. Chase says he is going to raise several kinds of sand. We are all loaded for bear. I send you a clipping from today's Post, which shows the situation. Mr. Washington's friends advise that he stand pat." (Feb. 3, 1903, Con. 278, BTW Papers, DLC.)

From Charles William Anderson

New York. February 4th, 1903

My dear Doctor: Supplementing my letter¹ and telegram of yesterday, I want to say that I have had six more telegrams sent today to the Senator. Among them was a good strong wire from the President and Secretary of the "Colored Republican Organization of the State of New York," and one from the President and Secretary of the "Colored Republican Organization of New York County."

I gave our friend Peterson the material for a good strong editorial on the situation for this week's issue of The Age, and advised him to emphasize the fact that without the Colored vote of New York State, no Republican Legislature would be possible, and therefore the Junior U.S. Senator from this State could not hope to be his own successor. I am sure Peterson will develop this feature very fully.

I forgot to say that I talked with Rev. Chas. S. Morris and Rev. Brooks² of St. Marks Church, before the Preachers meeting on Monday, and they both very kindly agreed to take charge of the resolution and have it passed. I also outlined the tenor of the telegram to be sent, and asked Dr. Morris to see to it that the telegram was properly worded and signed. Morris is, as you know, a man of some scholastic attainment and can be relied upon to dress up a matter of this kind in "apple-pie" shape. The Henry Hyland Garnet Republican Club of Kings County, of which Mr. Geo. E. Wibecan³ is President, will pass strong resolutions to-night, and a telegram will be signed and sent at once. The resolutions will be engrossed afterwards, and duly forwarded by mail. Thus, it seems to me that Greater New York has been properly covered, so I will take the afternoon train to-day for Albany and do what I can through the members of the Legislature. I am not confident of being able to have a resolution passed, although I should very much like to do so, but I hope to have the leading members of the Legislature communicate with the Senator as individuals. The objection to a resolution will come from two sources: the large democratic minority, which will of course oppose it; and those fastidious Republicans who will feel that they ought not to interfere in matters affecting another State. Of course this is merely a conjecture on my part. I shall, at the same time, do my best to have such a resolution passed, but will not have one introduced unless I can feel reasonably assured of its passage. To have one introduced and defeated would damage the cause greatly.

Keep me advised about the case, and believe me   Faithfully yours,

Charles W. Anderson

TLS   Con. 248   BTW Papers   DLC.

1 Anderson had written to BTW that in response to BTW's telegram he had had ten prominent black men in New York City send telegrams to Senator Chauncey M. Depew urging his support of the confirmation of William D. Crum. He persuaded several religious and political groups to pass resolutions, and he wired black leaders in seven other New York cities, urging them to have black preachers and heads of black organizations do likewise. (Feb. 3, 1903, Con. 248, BTW Papers, DLC.)

2 William Henry Brooks (1854–1923) was pastor of St. Mark's M. E. Church in New York City from 1897 until a few months before his death. Born in Maryland, he attended Morgan College and graduated from Howard University. After the New York race riot in 1900 he was chairman of the Citizens' Protective League. He encouraged blacks to work hard and live soberly so as to improve their bargaining position for equal rights, but he strongly criticized powerful whites when clear issues of unfair treatment were evident. Brooks was a director of the Afro-American Realty Co.

3 George Edwin Wibecan (1865–1946) was a postal employee in Brooklyn for forty-six years beginning in 1887. For many years he was the leading black Republican politician in King's County, although the Brooklyn Republican organization was rather weak during the years of his activity.

Richard W. Thompson to Emmett Jay Scott

Washington, D.C., Feb. 4, 1903

My Dear Scott— Last night's meeting at Bethel Literary was a "cracker-jack." It was "Washington Night" with a vengeance. The antis did a great deal of talking and earned some applause, but the force of the argument presented by the friends of the Wizard went to make up for lack in numbers and the hearty encores showed the spirit of the audience to be in sympathy with Dr. Washington. It was only the political phase that gave the opposition a chance to score. Lawson's paper was quiet in tone, but exhaustive in a scholarly analysis of the philosophy of the Tuskegeeian, and our friends saw to it that the salient points were greeted with acclaim. Our friends were out in force and the strength shown, even in reserve, disconcerted the most rabid of our enemies. Chase saw the situation and left early in the game. He was outclassed. Those who supported Dr. Washington by speech were Judge Terrell, Bishop Walters, Dr. W. Bruce Evans, J. H. Ewing and R. W. Thompson. We all got a "glad hand" and I can say without the suspicion of egotism that I never received a warmer reception in my life on my speech. The antagonists were W. H. Ferris, A. W. Scott,[1] L. M. Hershaw, T. M. Dent, S. J. Davidson[2] and Mrs. Ida D. Bailey. In number the orators were even, but I feel warranted in saying that I believe the expressions of approval that punctuated Lawson's speech, and which greeted the pro-Washington talkers, no matter what opposing partisans may say, gave us several shades the better of it. It may be added that our showing of reserve strength helped as much as did the oratory of our friends. I hope you will call the attention of the Wizard to this fact — and you can place upon it your own construction — that many heavy-weights were *present* at the invitation of Lawson and myself who maintained a *silence* rivalling that of the tomb. They were John C. Dancy, George H. White, Mrs. Daniel Murray,[3] R. S. Smith,[4] Kelly Miller, Prof. L. B. Moore,[5] and John P. Green. Why? Walters denied that any committee had been named on the patronage question, and asks me to assure Dr. Washington of his absolute loyalty to his leadership and that unity of action on the part of the educators, preachers, business men is his highest and only aim in pushing the Council. He wants the help of Dr. Washington at Louisville, and he tenders support to Dr. Washington for the Nashville meet. He wants harmony, and regards the appointment of myself as a happy event, since he feels sure of my devotion to the best interests of two men who by the gossip of the rabble are classed as rivals. He is fond of you, Scott, and desires that we all unite in promoting a union of the strongest forces that really mean business. I am, as you know, for the *right* — as God gives me to see the right.

I have been taking care of the Second Baptist Meeting in the several papers — Age, Freeman, Phil. Tribune, Baltimore Afro-American-Ledger, The Advocate, Charleston, W.Va., etc., as well as The Colored American. I have only seen Cooper once. He promised to attend the meeting of last night, but went to the theater to see a *coon show*. This is our friend and beneficiary.

Rev. B. J. Bolding talks next Tuesday evening at Bethel on "Should Educators and Ministers Take Active Part in Politics?" and promises to give a "hand" to B. T. W. and Walters.

I send the Post's account of the meeting, but do not regard it as wholly fair in its conclusions, for the meeting was a Washington triumph in enthusiasm, although the opposition made a fine showing. Ferris "fell down" badly, and it is an open secret that Trotter, who had contemplated sending him out on a lengthy itinerary, has recalled him as a failure. The net result of the series of meetings is that the friends of Mr. Washington have been aroused, and the enemies have not been increased nor encouraged. If the agitators of the antis have grown bolder, the supporters of Dr. Washington have grown correspondingly more aggressive.

When do you wish me to report? I can be there by 12th or 15th. I am raising some money to get off in good shape, but transportation is a bugbear just now. If necessary, can I, without embarrassment to you, draw in advance $20 to $25? — chargeable, of course, to my account. That's all for the present. Suggestions will be welcomed, Yours,

R. W. Thompson

TLS Con. 278 BTW Papers DLC.

1 Armond W. Scott was a Washington, D.C., black lawyer.

2 Shelby James Davidson, born in Lexington, Ky., in 1868, graduated from Howard University in 1893 and became a clerk in the Post Office and Treasury departments, meanwhile reading law in the office of William A. Cook until he passed the D.C. bar examination in 1900. The Treasury Department commissioned him to make a study of the manufacture and operation of adding machines. He prepared reform plans for auditing accounts in the Post Office and Treasury departments. He invented a device for tabulating and totaling accounts, an attachment that totaled money order reports at post offices, a special copy holder, and a coin machine counting device. He resigned from government service in 1912 to practice law.

3 Anna Evans Murray, born in Oberlin, Ohio, in 1858, married Daniel Murray in

1879. Anna Murray successfully lobbied for the introduction of kindergarten into the D.C. school system.

4 Reuben S. Smith.

5 Lewis Baxter Moore, born near Huntsville, Ala., in 1866, graduated from Fisk with a B.A. in 1889 and an A.M. in 1893. Three years later he took a Ph.D. at the University of Pennsylvania. Joining the faculty of Howard University, he became dean of the teachers' college in 1899. He was also an ordained Congregational minister, and was pastor of the People's Church in Washington from 1903 to 1910.

From Theodore Roosevelt

[White House, Washington, D.C.] February 6, 1903

Personal.

My dear Mr. Washington: That is excellent; and you have put epigrammatically just what I am doing — that is, though I have rather reduced the *quantity* I have done my best to raise the *quality* of the negro appointments. With high regard   Sincerely yours,

Theodore Roosevelt

P.S. By the way, don't worry about *me;* it will all come right in time, and if I have helped by ever so little "the ascent of man" I am more than satisfied.

TLpS   Theodore Roosevelt Papers   DLC.   Postscript in Roosevelt's hand.

From Albert Shaw

New York   February 6, 1903

My dear Mr. Washington: Thank you very much for your letter of February 3. I think you know without my telling you that I have long been in almost absolute agreement with what I have understood to be your point of view. I do not think that at present, in view of the conditions that exist and the feelings that prevail in the South, it is of the slightest advantage to single out here and there a worthy and successful Negro and appoint him to a federal office — that is to say, in the Southern States. On the other hand, since the Negro vote is actually and practically so important a factor in a great number of the Northern States, I deem it good politics to give the Negroes up here a fair and proportionate share of public offices, since here, I believe, if great care is exercised in the selection, such recognition is a helpful encouragement, while I think it does not react in any way to the prejudice or disadvantage of the race.

The Jews in this country are coming into a position of great influence and power, and the prejudice against them no longer operates to their disadvantage in politics or affairs. It keeps them out of certain New York fashionable clubs, but it does not prevent Mr. Louis Stern, a Jew, from being president of the Republican Club of New York at the present time; it did not prevent Mr. Isidor Straus, of New York, from going to Congress; it did not prevent his brother from serving as minister to Constantinople or from being appointed as one of the four American members of the permanent Hague Tribunal, and so forth and so forth. Now the Jews, historically speaking, in Europe — though of course not in this country — have been subject to shameful disabilities and discriminations. They have, however, made their way in spite of those things, and to some extent, I believe, they have benefited by their limitations. Being excluded from society and excluded from politics, the Jew devoted himself with the more assiduity to business success and to association with his fellow Jews for the care and protection of the poorer members of his race. He has thus grown in the domestic virtues and has developed a great business capacity. His character as a man, his success in business, his proficiency in our colleges and professions has at length delivered him from his few remaining disabilities.

We must then, I think, take the historical view rather than the purely logical or analytical view of all race questions. It is your ability to take this historical view that has long held my great admiration. Your mind is practical rather than theoretical. From the practical standpoint the Negro has no immediate chance, worth bothering with, to succeed in Southern politics. But speaking also from this practical standpoint, he has an excellent chance to succeed in Southern agriculture and industry, and through his own efforts and those of his friends he has an excellent fighting chance to secure about as good educational opportunities as his white neighbors enjoy. Inasmuch as he is allowed to till the soil, to work at trades, and to hold property under conditions at least tolerable and in the main favorable, and since there is a good chance to secure for him educational opportunities, I think you are perfectly right in putting all stress upon the desirability of his going ahead along these lines that are available to him. It requires great forbearance and a marvelous breadth of view to put up with certain discriminations in railroad service, hotels, at the polls, and so forth and so forth; nevertheless you have taught us to see that the best way to overcome some of these things is to ignore them as much as possible and to look at the bright side of the situation. I earnestly wish that Dr. Crum had declined the President's appointment. I think it would have been an excellent thing for all concerned. The better element of the South at the present time needs encouragement and help in its endeavor to prevent proposed divisions of the school fund and to do away with lynchings, mobs, and terrorism.

I wish you would take the time to write me again even more fully on the situation in two or three of the Southern States as it appears to you at the present moment. Believe me, Sincerely yours,

Albert Shaw

TLS Con. 275 BTW Papers DLC.

J. C. May [Wilford H. Smith]
to R. C. Black [Emmett Jay Scott]

N.Y.C. Feb. 6th, 1903

Dear Friend: Bishop Walters called and I have agreed to be in Boston at Fanuel [Faneuil] Hall meeting on the 12th inst. I would like to know if it is meant for me to include in the statement which I shall make of the amounts raised by the people in Alabama, the two M's.——— paid by "His Nibs," or shall I speak only of the fifteen hundred raised by the committee. If there is any special line he would suggest for me to pursue, I would be glad to have him indicate it; otherwise my address will be a plain statement of facts, and what we hope to accomplish through the cases.

I have taken out my subscription to the Guardian, and am examining the criminal statutes of Massachusetts. You shall hear from me again after the meeting in Boston. Very truly yours,

J. C. May

TLSr   Con. 25   BTW Papers   DLC.

From Alexander Walters

Jersey City N.J. Feb. 7, 19[03]

My dear friend: I did not receive your letter until I returned home to-day from Boston. I was delighted to hear from you. I will see Rev. Corrothers[1] and speak to him concerning the matter about which you wrote.

While in Boston I called to see the Editors of The Guardian, but could not get them to agree to any thing that is reasonable. I see by the New York Journal, of to-day, that the editorial quotes you as being against Negroes holding offices. If you could issue a statement denying this, and in some way assure the public that you stand for the Civil and Political rights of the Black man, it would greatly relieve the situation. If this is not done I am afraid that it will be utterly impossible to stem the tide of opposition to the policy that a large number of White papers both North and South are attributing to you. They know of your influence among the White people and they are taking advantage of it to advance their interest by misrepresenting you. A word from you in this crisis will spike their guns; without an expression from you it will be utterly impossible for me to control the Boston meeting, can't you send me a letter to be read there which can be given to the Press? The meeting promises to be a tremendous affair. Answer by special delivery. I remain, Yours truly.

A. Walters

TLS   Con. 272   BTW Papers   DLC.

[1] Sylvester L. Corrothers, born in York, S.C., in 1866, educated at Livingstone College, was a leading A.M.E. Zion minister for sixty-five years. Early in the twentieth century he was pastor of the Galbraith A.M.E. Zion Church in Washington, D.C. At the time of his death in 1948 he was pastor of a church in Westbury, N.Y.

From Charles William Dabney

Knoxville [Tenn.] February Seventh [1903]

Personal

My dear Dr. Washington, I wish to congratulate you upon your great *victory*, it was a real victory, over ignorance and prejudice, at Gainesville.

It was wisely, prudently, bravely and nobly done. The truly brave man is always prudent and wise. Your course has strengthened the Cause immensely. Very Cordially yours,

Chas. W. Dabney

ALS   Con. 255   BTW Papers   DLC.

An Article in *Outlook*

February 7, 1903

Two Generations under Freedom

I have often been asked to what extent the Negro race has the ability for self-direction and government, and the power to initiate and to make continuous progress unaided.

I want to try to answer this question, in part at least, not by abstract argument, but by telling the story of a self-governing community of colored people.

The group of negroes whose story I want to tell reside in Cass County, Michigan. Among the early settlers of that part of the State were several Quakers who had left their former homes in the South because they did not approve of slavery. In Michigan, as elsewhere, these Quakers soon let it be known that not only were they opposed to the institution of human slavery, and that runaway slaves would receive a friendly welcome among them, but that they would also receive physical protection if necessary. In addition to becoming an asylum for escaping slaves, this community of Quakers soon became a station on the "Underground Railroad."

The townships in Cass County in which the Quakers for the most part settled were named Calvin and Porter. It was about the year 1840 that a few colored people, mostly from Kentucky, began to find their way into these townships. Every year after that the number of escaped slaves grew larger, until in the year 1847 a determined effort was made on the part of some slaveholders to recapture their runaway negroes. Quite a number of slave-owners or their representatives appeared in Calvin township in that year, coming in one band, mounted and well armed, and made a bold and determined effort to regain possession of their property and return it to Kentucky. The effort at capture was successfully resisted by the Quakers, the colored people, and other residents of the community.

While a few of the colored people, as a result of this raid, became uneasy and fled to Canada, the ultimate result was to advertise Cass County, Michigan, as being a part of the country where negroes could enjoy a reasonable freedom from the constant fear of being snatched up and returned to their former masters. After the "raid" a still larger number of colored people began to go into the two townships named, and they covered a much wider territory than the first settlers. In addition to those who came directly to Michigan, not a few escaped slaves left Ohio, where they had first located themselves, in order to settle in Cass County, where the good Quakers had so effectually proved their courage and loyalty.

It was not, however, until the year 1849 that one of these townships, Calvin, began to assume the character which invests it with special interest at present. In 1847 a large slaveholder by the name of Saunders, who lived in Cabell County, Virginia — now a part of West Virginia — died. When his will was opened, it was found that provision had been made to the effect that all his slaves must be made free. The will further provided a generous amount of money which was to be used in removing all of the testator's slaves into a free State. In addition, the slaveowner made arrangements for the purchase of a tract of land in some free State to be divided among these people, and the building of a house for each of his former slave families, the will also providing the money to do all this.

The Saunders ex-slaves, forty-one in number, at last were started northward. One who was entitled to accompany them refused to go into a land of freedom, even with all the added advantages of this opportunity, because his wife was a slave and could not go with him. After a long journey, which was attended by many hard-

41

ships, the members of the party finally reached their Michigan home a few days before Christmas. A large tract of land which was a complete wilderness had been purchased by the executors. This tract was divided into parcels of eighteen acres for each individual — men, women, and even infants — the youngest baby getting as much as the oldest man. A small log house of such style as was common for the settlers in that country at that time was erected for each family.

The Saunders families — for each family took the name of the former master of the slaves — found their first winter in the wilds of Michigan in sharp contrast to the temperate climate they had left behind them in Virginia. They underwent a great deal of suffering. Not only were they unused to the climate, but they had to clear land for the spring planting in soil to which they were not accustomed. Their Quaker friends, as well as the colored people already residing in Calvin township, were most kind to them, but the rigorous climate, as well as the sudden change in methods of living, began to tell upon these people in rather a discouraging manner before many months in their new home had passed. It soon became evident that there were some things that the mere gift of freedom and the gift of lands and money could not do. Freedom, lands, and money could not give one experience in self-direction and self-dependence. In the words of another, "Freedom is a conquest, not a bequest."

For several years the Saunders families were in a majority in the township, and they prospered in a reasonable degree. But, as time passed, many of them began to let their wants increase faster than their ability to supply these increased wants. In their extravagant ideas and practices they began to demonstrate the truth of the old saying that a man values only what he has had experience in accumulating. Besides this, while these new settlers were in the possession of lands and houses, they were without education. Some of them began to give mortgages on their land, and while their good Quaker neighbors would protect them in their freedom, and help them to get an education, they were not averse at any time to driving a shrewd and safe business bargain. Not many years passed before a good part of the land once owned by the Saunders families began to fall into the hands of the Friends.

I will not recite in more detail the story of the Saunders community, except to say that most of the property owned by these people gradually passed out of their hands in one way and another, some part of it being secured by other shrewd colored men who had settled in Calvin township. I think I make a correct statement in saying that when I visited the township a few weeks ago I found only one of the original Saunders settlers who at the present time owns any of the land bought by the executors of the Saunders estate. The bare mention of "a Saunders family" would quite likely cause a quiet smile to creep over the face of one of the old inhabitants who did not belong to that group. These people not only had not held their own materially, but I found that, a few years after the newcomers began to get planted in their free homes, not a few of the young men began developing habits of idleness, not a few became criminals, while still others made themselves offensive to the whites and sensible blacks by becoming "uppish" and in other ways disagreeable. All these things resulted in giving the community something of a bad name for several years.

From the foregoing some may draw the conclusion at once that the whole effort was a failure. Not by any means. What I have stated simply emphasizes the fact that human nature is very much the same, no matter under what color of skin it is found. What I have related of the history of the Saunders community illustrates what I have often tried to say in relation to my race in general in this country — that the first one or two generations of freed people would naturally in many cases mistake freedom for license and would be overcome, in a large measure, by the first temptations of their new life; but that the second or third generations would begin to settle down to hard, sober business. If any one wants to get direct and specific proof of the truth of this statement, he should spend one or two days, as I have done, in making a first-hand investigation of the present condition of the negroes in Calvin township.

My visit of inspection, however, before I had been in the township two hours, taught me that the weak points exhibited by the people of the earlier generations had wrought a most beneficial work. It is often said that a thing that is bad has to get worse before it gets better. This I found to be true of Calvin township. At about the time when matters had gone down to their lowest ebb, industrially and morally, the more level-headed of the colored people began to realize the situation and to resolve that by strong and earnest effort they would bring about a reform. At about this time there began coming into the township a different class of people. These came mainly from Ohio, North Carolina, and Virginia. As a rule, they or their parents represented a class of people who had been set free — the class which in North Carolina were termed "free niggers," a designation which, strange to say, was used as a term of contempt by negro slaves as well as by their masters. The main point that I want to bring out here, though, is that these later settlers, either in Ohio or in some of the Southern States, had got over the first flush of freedom, and so were ready to settle down to business when they reached Calvin township. The money and the experience that these people brought with them to Calvin had been dearly earned by themselves. This new element joined itself with the better representatives of the earlier settlers, and very soon Calvin township began to acquire a new atmosphere. The real solid growth of the township began from this time.

My attention was first attracted to this settlement some years ago when I was in South Bend, Indiana, the site of the Studebaker wagon factories. I noticed that the colored people of South Bend seemed to be an unusually prosperous and solid lot of people, far above the average of those generally found in large cities, or anywhere in the North. I asked one of the Studebakers the reason for this difference, and he said that he thought it grew out of the fact that from the first the Studebaker firm had never permitted any color line to be drawn in any department of their works — that a negro was not made to feel that on account of his race he was assigned to a certain minor place in the factory, and could not hope to rise above that place, no matter how well he did his work. Mr. Studebaker said that they had held out to their negro workmen the same hope of reward in the way of promotion or increase of pay that the white workmen had held before them. There is a lesson in this treatment of the negro workmen by the Studebakers that has in it a solution for many of the problems connected with the negro. Take away from any race or individual the hope of reward, and you help destroy the race or individual.

From this discussion of the condition of the colored people in South Bend, Mr. Studebaker called my attention to the large community of colored people in Calvin township, Michigan, which is not very far from South Bend, since Cass County, in which Calvin is situated, is on the southern boundary of Michigan. When I asked Mr. Studebaker about these people he said in substance that for a number of years his firm had sold them wagons and other farm machinery, and had often sold on credit; and that in all their business relations of recent years they had proved themselves just as reliable and prompt as the white people in the same county, or anywhere in the State. This statement so interested me that I resolved to see this community for myself at the very first possible opportunity, because I had always been anxious to see just what progress in self-government any large number of people of my race could make when left absolutely to themselves and given the advantage of the climate and location that the average white man in America possesses.

In connection with what I am going to say it should be kept in mind that the unit of government in Michigan, as in Massachusetts, is the township — that is, each township has practically complete self-government. Besides this it is entitled to at least one representative on the Board of County Commissioners which controls the affairs of the county.

When I visited Calvin township recently I found that it contained a population of 759 negroes and 512 whites. In addition to these, a large negro population had overflowed into the adjoining township of Porter, and to some extent into all but two of the towns in the county. The county seat of Cass County is Cassopolis. The nearest boundary line of Calvin township is about six miles from Cassopolis.

As I drove, in company with the Hon. L. B. Des Voignes, the probate judge of the county, Mr. Max Bennett Thrasher, a newspaper writer, and Mr. Jesse W. Madrey, the latter one of the most prosperous colored farmers in the county, from Cassopolis in the direction of Calvin township, we soon began going through well-cultivated farms and past comfortable-looking farm-houses. The farms, for the most part, in their general appearance compared favorably with the average farms we saw in Michigan. Many of the houses were large, attractive, and well built. The yards were made beautiful with grass, shrubbery, and flowers. The barns, stock, poultry, and other farm attachments were in keeping with everything else that we saw. In our drive of nearly ten hours, in which we covered thirty miles of territory, through Calvin township and a part of Porter, the adjoining township, we saw little to indicate that we were in a negro town except the color of the faces of the people.

They were up to the average of their white neighbors. There are perhaps few townships in the South among the agricultural classes that would compare favorably with this one.

In a few cases it was interesting to see standing on the same premises the small cabin in which the people began life years ago, and then to see near it a modern frame cottage containing six or seven rooms. To me it was interesting and encouraging to note to what an extent these people "lived at home," that is, produced what they consumed. My visit took me through the community during the harvesting season, and at that time most of the farmers were engaged in threshing wheat and oats. On one farm we saw a large, modern steam thresher at work. Around it were employed some twenty men. This complicated piece of machinery was being operated wholly by negroes, and, what was more interesting, was owned by a negro by the name of Henry L. Archer. Mr. Archer not only threshed grain for the negro farmers in his township, but for the white farmers as well.

In speaking of the extent to which these people "keep themselves," I want to say that their home-raised and home-cured pork was, without any reservation, the best I ever tasted. I was particularly struck with this when visiting the home of Mr. Allen, of Porter township, the negro stock-raiser and stock-trader. "Bill" Allen has as high standing for probity and shrewdness among the people in the Chicago stockyards as the average white man. His many well-filled barns and the large number of valuable horses, cows, pigs, and sheep he owns were among the most interesting sights that I saw.

William Allen was born in Logan County, Ohio, but his parents were free colored people from North Carolina. To speak in more detail about Mr. Allen, I found that he owns seven hundred acres of land, and that the taxes which he paid last year in the two townships of Calvin and Porter amounted to $191. When I visited his farm, he had fifty head of cattle, ten horses, three hundred sheep, and twenty-five hogs. All of his property is paid for. Mr. Allen is one of the few men I have heard of as resigning a political office.

He was a Justice of the Peace for eighteen years, and resigned because it took too much of his time away from his farm.

It was rather remarkable to learn that Samuel Hawkes, a fine specimen of the race, pays the largest tax of any one, white or black, in the township of Calvin. His tax this year was $154.36. In addition to this, Mr. Hawkes paid over $50 taxes on property which is in his charge as an administrator. He owns about five hundred acres of land, free of encumbrance. He is highly spoken of by every one whom I saw, of both races, including the county officials and the cashier of the bank at Cassopolis, who said his credit was good at that institution. I was told on good authority that Mr. Hawkes is worth $50,000. He has perhaps learned the lesson that not a few white people have learned — not to give in all of their property for the purpose of taxation.

Samuel Hawkes was born in Nottaway County, Virginia, in 1828. In 1837 he moved to Jackson County, Ohio, and remained there until he came to Calvin in 1853. He is entirely a self-made man, beginning work for himself at the age of sixteen, cutting cordwood. He had saved up enough money so that when he came to Calvin in 1853 he was able to buy the eighty acres of land on which he still lives, paying for it $800 in, as he expresses it, "gold and silver." He then went back to Ohio and worked there six years longer before he came to Calvin to live permanently on his farm. For the last quarter of a century Mr. Hawkes has devoted himself to the general management of his property, loaning money, and dealing in real estate.

Cornelius Lawson, the Supervisor for Calvin, is a native of North Carolina, whose parents moved to Cass County after an intermediate residence of some years in Indiana. He has lived in Calvin since 1853. He was elected a Justice of the Peace in 1878, and retained the office until the present year. In 1899 he was elected Supervisor, and has been re-elected every year since. Mr. Lawson is a farmer, and lives about a mile from "The Corner" — the official center of Calvin. He is the first colored man to be elected to the County Board of Supervisors.

It would be difficult for me to give a better idea of the industry and prosperity of these people than can be obtained from reading the following extract from a letter which I received not long after my visit to Cass County. The letter is from one of the most reliable colored men in the county, and, I ought to add, was written with no thought that it was to be published:

Cassopolis, Michigan, November 3, 1902

Mr. Booker T. Washington:

Dear Friend—I will impose upon your precious time only long enough for you to read this, as no answer is necessary.

I wanted to tell you that I thrashed those stacks of grain that you saw when at our place. Mr. Archer did the thrashing in one day—944 bushels of oats and 884 bushels of wheat. I paid him $41.44. On the 29th I shipped a carload of hogs and sheep of my own raising to Chicago. I received $707.30 for the same. I have 167 sheep left and about 80 head of hogs; this includes all sizes. . . .

Your humble servant,

J. W. Madrey

I found that there was another colored man in the township, Mr. C. W. Bunn, who owns two sawmills and much other real estate. He is said to be worth $50,000.

In several cases I noticed that the carpets on the floors of the homes of the people were of the home-made kind, but they were handsome and substantial. A considerable number of the colored people in Calvin township own their homes, and many of those who are renting are doing so from negro landowners. In a few cases white people in the county are renting property owned by negroes.

There are, I believe, eight schools in Calvin, four of them taught by colored teachers. Not only are the teachers colored, but the schools are controlled by negro school officials for the most part. As we drove through the township I found a copy of the following notice posted:

ANNUAL SCHOOL MEETING
State of Michigan

NOTICE is hereby given to the qualified Voters of School District No. 8 of the Township of Calvin that the Annual Meeting of said District will be held at the Schoolhouse on Monday evening, the 1st day of September, A.D. 1902, at 8 o'clock, for the Election of School District Officers, and for the transaction of such other business as shall lawfully come before it.

Dated this 25th day of August, 1902.

C. F. NORTHROP, Director.

Mr. C. F. Northrop is a negro. So far as I could judge by the appearance of the teachers and the school buildings, they compared favorably with others in that part of the State. In addition to the negro teachers and ministers, there are two negro physicians in the township.

One question that is often debated is as to the ability of the negro for self-government from a political point of view, and I was extremely anxious to get information on this. In Calvin township in 1900 there were 759 negroes and 512 whites. I made diligent inquiry to ascertain if there was any friction between the two races, and could find no evidence that there was. Judge Des Voignes and other county officers informed me that there were no reports of cheating at the ballot-boxes, and that the affairs of the township were conducted as well politically as any in the county. For some years, the Judge said, it had been the boast of the negro tax collector of Calvin that he was one of the first collectors to secure and pay into the county treasury all of the township taxes. On one recent occasion it was said that when another town was trying to beat Calvin in this, and the Calvin tax-gatherer's report was delayed, largely through the tardiness of one negro taxpayer, whose tax was only three dollars, rather than have Calvin lose its reputation for promptness a number of the public-spirited negroes "chipped in" and paid the tax of the delinquent.

Each township in the county is entitled to one representative on the County Board of Commissioners which has the control of the affairs of the entire county. The representative of Calvin is a black man, and I was told by several white people of the county that the negro Commissioner voted intelligently and conservatively. So far as I could find evidence, there had never been in the township any "scandal" growing out of the misuse of money by public officials, notwithstanding, as I have said, that each township levies and collects its own taxes for schools and other public enterprises.

I was a little curious to see to what extent the colored people took interest in the large National questions. I asked a good many of them how they stood on the question of reducing the tariff on Cuban sugar. In spite of the fact that Michigan is producing much beet sugar, I found that most of the colored people in this township were in favor of helping Cuba, and they were not slow to give their reasons. Later I found out from the rural free delivery mail-carrier that forty daily papers were taken in the township.

Some years ago a certain Congressman who represented that district in Congress got into the habit of coming to Calvin whenever an election was pending, to speak to his colored constituents, but instead of discussing the broad National questions of the day he would "jolly" the colored people. They stood it for a while, and then they let him know, in no uncertain way, that if he wanted to speak to them he must discuss public questions in the same manner that he did in other portions of his district.

The seat of government for the township is the town hall, which is located near the center of the township. It is here that the town officials have their offices. The principal business of the town is transacted through the town meeting, very much after the manner in New England.

I was informed by several reliable white men of the county that there had never been any trouble worth mentioning growing out of political differences. When the war between the States broke out, as soon as colored soldiers were permitted to enlist, practically every negro man in the township who was eligible enlisted and went to the front. As a result, there is a Grand Army Post in Calvin named Matthew Artis Post, in honor of one of the old settlers and soldiers. The Grand Army Post meets in a hall on the second floor of the town house. The present commander of the Post is Bishop Curtis, who was a member of the Fifty-fourth Massachusetts Regiment. It is said that he was wounded by the same shell that killed Robert Gould Shaw. The post has been established twelve years, and is in a flourishing condition.

There are three churches in the township, two of which I saw — one an African Methodist and the other a Baptist. One of these was established in 1853 and the other in 1854. Both of these congregations have neat and attractive buildings. Although I had caused word to be sent ahead of me that I did not want to make any address to the people, but simply wanted to be permitted to visit them on their farms and in their homes, and thus see them when they were not on dress parade, I found that when our party reached the Methodist church rather late in the evening we were welcomed by a brass band composed of young men living in the community, and it seemed to me that the whole township had assembled. Nothing but a short address would satisfy them. The most general complaint that I heard at this meeting, and from several individual farmers with whom I talked, was to the effect that the young men were too much inclined to leave the township and go to the large cities.

In my inspection of their church houses there were two things that specially pleased me. One was the fine and neat appearing parsonage which stood near the Chain Lake Baptist Church; the other was the appearance of the graveyard near the same building. The church house, the parsonage, and the graveyard gave one a picture which made him feel that he was in a Massachusetts village. The graveyard was laid out in family plots, and most of the graves had marble slabs or headstones. There were evidences that the burial-place received systematic care.

I thought that it would prove of interest and value to get the opinions of some of the prominent white people of Cass County as to what they thought of the members of my race in Calvin. With this end in view several of the leading men in Cassopolis, the county seat — a beautiful, substantial town of several thousand inhabitants — were consulted, and the following questions were at some point in the conversation asked of each one of the five men interviewed:

How does the material condition of the colored people of Calvin compare with that of twenty years ago?

How does it compare with that of their white neighbors?

How do the moral conditions compare?

What is the nature of the relations between the two races?

Do many of the colored people move away, and if so, why, and where?

Have they contributed as much towards the prosperity of the county as the other residents?

Do you know of any other colored community so properous?

In criminal offenses in the township do the colored people assist the officers willingly? In other words, does civic pride outbalance race sympathy?

Judge L. B. Des Voignes, who has been Judge of Probate of Cass County for six and a half years, and previous to that was Prosecuting Attorney, said:

"The material condition of the people has greatly improved in the last twenty years. They have more wealth, better farms and homes — they live better. Their conditions have kept parallel with the whites. Considering their opportunities, they have advanced. Their moral condition has improved very much. There has been a great decrease in criminal conditions during the last twenty years. Calvin does not give us — the courts — as much trouble now as some of our white communities. There is increased membership in churches, and increased attendance at schools. There is more desire for education. There are six schools in Calvin in which white and black go together. The relations of the two races are mutually pleasant.

"I do not recall any instance where white residents of the township have objected to colored people buying land there. I do not think there is any depreciation in the price of land. To a stranger buying land the colored residents might be an objection; but I do not think it would be to those who know the colored people of Calvin. A slightly larger proportion of the young people go away to the cities of South Bend, Elkhart, Dowagiac, Niles, etc. They go because they can earn more money.

"The colored residents have helped to contribute to the prosperity of the county, considering the opportunities they have had and the length of time they have had to earn money. There is a prosperous colored community in Volunia which is frugal, etc. This is small, though, not more than one hundred persons, and might, perhaps, be called a part of this. There are colored residents in several of the townships in Cass County. The treasurer of Calvin was one of the first to report the payment of every tax in the town. The better element, the property-owning class, are quick to assist in the conviction of criminals."

Mr. Charles O. Harmon, clerk of the county, was born in Porter township, and grew up among these people. He taught his first term of school in the Mount Zion school-house. Mr. Harmon said:

"There is practically no difference in the material condition of the people of the two races in Calvin. They are more prosperous than twenty years ago, particularly in having better farms and better houses. The moral condition is equal or nearly equal to that of the whites. There is a low and illiterate class, but not large considering the opportunities of the people. They take advantage of their opportunities as much as the whites. They are quick to take advantage of improvements, such as the telephone and improved machinery. There has been great improvement morally in the last twenty years.

"Some of the best people of the county live in Calvin and mingle with these people in a business way with no distinction. I do not think that the fact of the colored settlers being there is considered any detriment to the community, although white people from communities which have no colored settlers might be adverse to buying land there. Certainly land does not sell for any less there. The land in Calvin is among the best in the county. The merchants of Cassopolis find these people extra good customers. That may be one criticism to make — that they buy too freely for their own good. As a general thing, though, they are good pay, and take a pride in meeting their obligations.

"They have, probably, helped the county as much as could be expected of any people with their opportunities. I should say that they have helped in this way only during the last ten years. The tendency in this respect is good. The present colored Supervisor is the first colored man to hold this office. He is an able man in official work. He is a member of the county Committee of Equalization, and of the Committee of Public Grounds and Buildings. He was a delegate from the last County Board to the State Board of Equalization of Taxes, at Lansing."

Mr. C. C. Nelson is an undertaker in Cassopolis, who does most of the work in his line in Calvin. He has lived in Cass County for sixty years, and has been postmaster, sheriff, and overseer of the poor. He said in substance:

"There is no township in Cass County that has made so much improvement in the last twenty or twenty-five years as Calvin has. The people were once haphazard and lawless. At one time Calvin furnished two-thirds the court business of the county. That is past now. They have improved more, proportionately, than the whites. As a rule, the whites feel friendly towards them; better than formerly. People who know them make no objection to them. People who live in Calvin would not sell their land there any cheaper because of the colored population. Probably more of the young people go away. They put civic pride before race pride."

The Hon. L. H. Glover is a prominent Democratic lawyer of Cassopolis, and has been a Justice of the Peace there since 1862. He said: "The first generation of settlers were fine men — none better. The second generation was bad. The third shows a very marked improvement. But through it all the best men have supported the law unfailingly. There is a steady improvement morally, and this compares favorably with that of the whites. There is no social mingling, but otherwise the relations of the races are entirely friendly. I do not know of more than a dozen marriages of whites and blacks in the entire county. So far as prejudice towards the colored residents of the county is concerned, the farther away people live, the greater the prejudice. As they approach, it grows less. These people have contributed as much to the prosperity of the county as ought to be expected of them."

Mr. Allison, the proprietor and editor of the Democratic paper in Cassopolis, practically confirmed all of Mr. Glover's opinions. Mr. Allison, like Mr. Glover, has lived in the county for many years, and knows the colored residents well.

As I mingled with the white people and tried to draw them out freely, I got the idea pretty strongly that while they saw the weak points as well as the strong ones in this interesting little African colony, yet, on the whole, the whites were very proud of Calvin township and watched its development with deep interest and not a little satisfaction. In the story of this development there is nothing startling or remarkable. It is simply the story of the growth of a people when given the American chance to grow naturally and gradually. With the negro, whether considered as individuals or in groups, I find that the bearing of responsibility is one of the chief essentials of growth.

Outlook, 73 (Feb. 7, 1903), 293–305. A copy is in Con. 967, BTW Papers, DLC.

From N. P. T. Finch

Birmingham, Ala., Feb. 8 1903

Personal

Dear Mr. Washington: I have your letter. I will tomorrow call attention to Secretary Root's speech,[1] and to the fact that President Roosevelt has appointed few of your race to office.

I have to be careful in such race matters, so that I will be in good position to attack any lynching that may occur, and I propose to back up Mr. London[2] when he attacks the distribution of school moneys in the Black Belt. These are the two things I keep in mind, and I have to be careful in other respects. I did not think it good policy to object to the unjust and ridiculous cartoons our fool

Blackman[3] has been drawing. You see my situation, I am sure. I was born in New York, and that makes a difference.

Do you know Mr. Putnam, chief of the Library of Congress? A great deal of "writing" is necessary in the Library and I would be glad to get a chance at it. Keep me in sight, please. Very Truly Yours,

N. P T Finch

ALS   Con. 290   BTW Papers   DLC.

[1] On Feb. 6, 1903, Root said before the Union League Club in New York that the Thirteenth, Fourteenth, and Fifteenth amendments to the U.S. Constitution were failures, since blacks had virtually been disfranchised. He also pointed out that Theodore Roosevelt had appointed fewer blacks to office than his predecessors and that public sentiment was more hostile to black appointments than it had been during the administrations of McKinley, Cleveland, and others. Root said that "it is probably but a matter of time—not so very long a time—when the overwhelming weight of opinion of the white men will succeed in excluding blacks from all offices in the southern States." (Address before the Union League Club, Feb. 6, 1903, Con. 221, Elihu Root Papers, DLC.)

[2] Alexander Troy London (1847–1908), a Birmingham lawyer and state legislator.

[3] Walter Blackman was an artist employed by the Birmingham *Age-Herald*.

From Francis Jackson Garrison

Boston, Febry. 8, 1903

Dear Mr. Washington: I am greatly obliged to you for sending me Gov. Jelks's message & have read with much pleasure his outspoken words on lynching.[1] It is good to have a gleam of light like this from the South just as Secy. Root is making himself the mouthpiece of the Administration & the Republican Party in declaring suffrage a failure, & that wholesale disfranchisement of the colored race a matter of no concern.

I am expecting to be in Atlanta a week from [to]night, & hope to run down to Tuskegee by the early morning train on Monday, the 16th, & spend a few hours in seeing your great institution. I feared I might miss you, but I learned yesterday that your annual conference comes off on the 18th (when I must be in Athens at my nephew's wedding), and so I am hopeful of seeing you, unless you are at the north & planning to make a close connection on your return. It will be my first trip south, & a "flying" one. Yours ever truly,

Francis J. Garrison

ALS   Con. 259   BTW Papers   DLC.

1 William D. Jelks, in his inaugural address, said that blacks were "entitled to full protection of the law." While he assumed that some blacks were disposed to assault white women, he argued that lynching was not the solution to the problem, and that innocent persons were often victims of the mob. "It is false, absolutely false," he said, "to assert that this evil spirit is merely anticipating the action of the Courts." Jelks promised to prosecute "to the uttermost" members of lynch mobs. (Montgomery *Advertiser*, Jan. 20, 1903, 1.)

An Article by J. Douglas Wetmore

Jacksonville, Fla., Feb. 8, 1903

The County Superintendents of Public Instruction of the state of Florida held a convention at Gainesville, Fla., from the 3rd to the 6th of this month, and W. N. Sheats, State Superintendent of Public Instruction was president of said convention. Mr. Sheats invited Booker T. Washington to visit Gainesville during the week of the convention and deliver an address on "Negro Education" the night of the 5th, and he also invited the leading Negro educators of the state to meet Mr. Washington and discuss plans for improving the methods of teaching, and for prolonging the term of Negro schools throughout the state.

The Gainesville newspapers announced that Mr. Washington had been invited to address the County Superintendents of Public Instruction in the auditorium of the white public school of that city, and immediately, Superintendent of Public Instruction Holloway[1] of Alachua county of which county Gainesville is the county site, published an article in which he declared that Mr. Washington should not speak in the auditorium of the white public school while he was county superintendent. This letter was published Friday, Jan. 30, and caused quite a stir throughout the state; and every big (?) white man in Alachua county and the state of Florida, who is a political opponent of Mr. Sheats, took this opportunity of denouncing him, and swearing vengeance against him for the insult that had been offered the "superior race" of which they were "leaders." This agitation cluminated in an indignation meeting Monday night, the 2nd inst., at which meeting resolutions were passed sustaining the actions of County Superintendent Holloway, and denouncing State Superintendent Sheats. While this meeting was in progress, and Mr. Sheats was being denounced in vigorous language, he arrived in the city, and went immediately to the place of meeting and surprised his critics in the midst of their deliberations; and I am reliably informed that he made the "fur fly" for a few minutes; and that some of the things that were said on that occasion would not look well in school reading books. Mr. Washington was expected to arrive on the 4th, but after hearing of all the excitement over his proposed visit, he did not leave Tuskegee on the 3rd as he had anticipated, but on the 4th he received a telegram signed by Mr. Sheats, County Superintendent Holloway and the mayor of Gainesville,[2] urging him to come and deliver his address and assuring him that he would be cordially received. Mr. Washington telegraphed me on the night of the 4th that he would arrive in Jacksonville, Thursday morning, the 5th and requested me to meet him, which I did.

He remained in Jacksonville until 2:10 p.m., and I accompanied him to Gainesville as his guest. A great many of Mr. Washington's friends wanted him to cancel his Gainesville engagement, as they feared he might have been the victim of violence on the part of some Negro-hater. And it was on account of this fear for his safety, that I decided to accompany him. Gainesville is an old-fashioned ante-bellum Southern city, and more than one outrage has been perpetrated upon Negroes in Alachua county; therefore I expected that Mr. Washington would at least be insulted and discourteously treated, if he was not injured physically. We went on a local train of the Seaboard Air Line railway and of course stopped at every cross road and saw mill and at every place we stopped, several men, both white and black, came into the car to see and shake hands with the famous Negro, Booker T. Washington. After we had stopped at several stations and all the white men who had spoken to him, had expressed their appreciation of him, and told him how glad they were that he was going to Gainesville to speak, all fears I had as to his safety, vanished. Two elderly white men got on at Waldo, Fla., and shook hands with Mr. Washington and told him that they were going to Gainesville just to hear him speak. A very amusing incident occurred at this place, Waldo; a typical "cracker" about sixty years old was on the rear platform of our [train] peering into the coach, and another white man who had just spoken to Mr. Washington, said to him: "There sits Booker Washington, go in and speak to him," and the fellow on the platform replied: "No, I don't want to speak to him; I used to think a lot of Booker, but since he took dinner with the President, I have no more use for him, and I don't want to speak to him;" but his friend insisted, and said: "I just shook hands with him, and I tell you he is a mighty fine fellow and want you to go in and shake hands with him, cause you may never get another opportunity; come right in and see him, come on now." And the old man said, "well I believe I will." I was standing on the platform smoking, and I followed them in to hear what the old fellow would say to Mr. Washington, and to my surprise he told Mr. Washington that he was very glad to meet him, and that he had been reading about him for years, and thought him the smartest Negro in the world, and always wanted to meet him and shake his hand; and told him how much good he thought he was to his race. In fact, he bored Mr. Washington by the profusion of his compliments and did not leave him until the train began moving.

When we arrived in Gainesville we were met by a reception committee and escorted to the beautiful home of Mr. and Mrs. J. N. Clinton, where we received the best of care and attention during our brief stay. I went down to the Brown House (a white hotel) about 6:30 p.m. ostensibly to see a friend of mine, who was stopping there, but in reality to see what the sentiment concerning Mr. Washington was, but I was agreeably surprised to find that there was no feeling whatever against him, but that all this noise about Mr. Washington's coming had been made by the political enemies of Mr. Sheats; and that even the majority of those who had protested loudest against his speaking in the auditorium of the white school, were as anxious to hear him as those who had endorsed his being invited. Mr. Sheats had electric lights put in the circuit court room, and had filled every available space with benches and chairs. Mr. Washington was to speak at 8 o'clock, so at ten minutes to 8 we drove up to the court house and the corridors and stairs leading to the court room were so crowded that the sheriff had to force a way for us to get through the crowd to the court room. There were nearly two thousand people in the room and crowds were on the stairs and in the hall ways, and the local newspapers said about six hundred people were turned away, because they could not get within hearing distance of the speaker. There were nearly as many ladies present as men, and more than half of those present were whites.

Mr. Sheats introduced Mr. Washington, and said if he were asked to name the greatest white man in America and the one who had done the most for humanity, he would be unable to do so; but that if he were called upon to name the greatest Negro America has produced, and the Negro who has done most for humanity, irrespective of color, he would name Booker T. Washington. The hearty applause from both black and white, with which this statement was received, and the uproarious welcome given Mr. Washington when he arose to speak, was all that his most ardent admirers could expect. I have heard Mr. Washington speak on several occasions, but as I listened to him on the 5th inst., and saw how he swayed his audience and how completely he had them under his control, I realized that I had never fully appreciated his greatness. While I have admired him for years, and we have been friends since Jan. 1, '98, I have criticised him severely at times; and I wish all of his critics could have been with me in Gainesville and heard his speech and seen with what a masterly hand he handled those Negro-hating "crackers," and heard them applauding him when he scored them for their misdeeds, and I am sure that none of them would ever again accuse him of being a "good nigger," which, in my opinion, is the meanest thing a Negro can be called; for there is no human being for whom I have more contempt than a "good nigger."

When he finished speaking he could truly have used Caesar's famous message: "Veni, vidi, vici," in acquainting his friends with the result of his trip to Gainesville. He spoke for an hour and thirty-five minutes, and when he finished the applause was deafening. I wish all the Negroes and whites in the South could have heard the manly defense he made for his race, and the touching appeal he made to the whites to be fair and patient with the black man. Enemies may criticise and newspapers may misquote him, but I am positive that Gainesville will be a better town for the Negroes to live in, and that the relations will be more cordial between the two races, as the result of Mr. Washington's speech; and it is my honest opinion that the result is the same wherever Mr. Washington speaks. On Friday morning several prominent white citizens of Gainesville urged Mr. Washington to speak again that night from the band stand in the court house square, so that more people could hear him. He thanked them very kindly but declined to remain, and we left for Jacksonville at 1:30 p.m. One of the most remarkable things about this affair is, that Mr. Sheats, who invited Mr. Washington to Gainesville to speak, has been all of his life one of the most unreconstructed rebels in the state and supposed to be a Negro hater of the deepest dye, but Mr. Washington seems to have converted him in the last year, and he is now a strong advocate of longer school terms for Negro schools, and higher wages for Negro teachers. I am not a blind devotee of Mr. Washington, nor do I think him perfect by any means, but I do believe the Negro race, as a whole, is better off for his having lived; and I pray God he may be spared many years to plead for peace between the two races.

Indianapolis *Freeman*, Feb. 21, 1903, 2.

1 William M. Holloway denounced Sheats for inviting BTW, and in 1904 he used the issue in defeating Sheats as Democratic nominee for state superintendent.
2 W. R. Thomas.

To James H. Hayes

[Tuskegee, Ala.] Feb. 9, 1903

Personal.
My dear Sir: I am glad to receive your letter of recent date and thank you very much for the information which it contains. The time has come when all of us should work together and in harmony. I have been very glad to note through the newspapers that your speech was misquoted and that you were misrepresented in your Washington address. The main thing, however, that I have in mind in writing just now is to suggest that I think it will be a mistake to have another national convention called. Could not the same work which you have in mind be done through the Afro-American Coun-

cil? We are likely to weaken ourselves if we multiply these conventions. I have rather kept apart from the Afro-American Council for the reason that I did not want to seem to interfere with the work which it has in hand. I realize fully that there are two lines of work — one is in the direction of radicalism and the other is in the line of education, and my work can best be done in the latter direction while others can do the work in the direction of arousing the interest of our people in the direction of public affairs. Yours truly,

[Booker T. Washington]

TLc Con. 249 BTW Papers DLC.

To Edgar Gardner Murphy

Tuskegee, Ala., February 9, 1903

Personal.

Dear Mr. Murphy, I have just sent a telegram to Mr. Cortelyou to see if it is possible to arrange for you to meet the President on Friday. I shall expect an answer some time within the next two or three days.

I hope you will read carefully the editorial in this week's Outlook, also, the one in the Churchman. I might say to you privately that I gave both editors the information on which these editorials are based. It makes me very nervous and unhappy to have the President misunderstood and misrepresented in the South as is true at present. I do not believe that any man has gone into the Presidency since the war who has been so sincere in his desire to be of real service to both races in the South, and it has been a severe trial during the past weeks for me to keep quiet when so much has been said in the wrong direction. But I have felt that it was the part of wisdom for me not to say anything that might make me lose what hold I have on the South and I think the President will appreciate my seeming silence. Some of my best friends in the North do not agree with me as to my views on the sincerity of the President's action. In case you see the President I hope you will feel free to suggest anything that you have in mind about Judge Jones. President Roosevelt of all things likes perfect frankness. Very truly yours,

[Booker T. Washington]

TLc   Con. 249   BTW Papers   DLC.

To Alexander Walters

Tuskegee, Ala., February 9, 1903

Personal and Confidential.
Dear Bishop Walters: I have just had a letter from the President. He is anxious that the resolutions passed in New York and in Boston on the 12th of February shall be very mild so far as they refer to him and his interest in the colored people. I hope you will see that his wishes are carefully followed. You can easily see that there is an opportunity for the President to be placed in an awkward position, and instead of such resolutions being a help, they may serve as a hindrance. Very truly yours,

[Booker T. Washington]

TLc   Con. 272   BTW Papers   DLC.

To William Henry Baldwin, Jr.

Tuskegee, Ala., February 9, 1903

My dear Mr. Baldwin: I have just returned from Gainesville and seize the first opportunity to write you. It was from every point of view a most satisfactory trip. The whole thing shows the advantage of a few individuals being strong enough to stand up and manifest a little courage. The mere fact that Superintendent Sheats, Dr. Buttrick, and a few of the business men stood up straight from the first served to bring the whole town, and in fact, that whole section of the country around, to a sensible view. The result was that I never spoke to a more satisfactory audience even in Boston than I did in Gainesville. It was composed of about equal numbers of both races, and among the white people a large proportion were women. They were very urgent in their invitation that I should remain over and give a second address in the evening, but this I could not do.

The more I see of Dr. Buttrick the more I am convinced of his marvelous wisdom, courage, and discretion. Very truly yours,

[Booker T. Washington]

TLc Con. 792 BTW Papers DLC.

From Lavinia Hartwell Egan[1]

Shreveport, Louisiana   Feb. 9–1903

My dear Mr. Washington: I am very sorry to tell you that I think a visit from you at this time would be ill advised and would not meet with the endorsement and encouragement you and your theories so heartily deserve. I need not tell you that the course of President Roosevelt has changed very materially the color of things throughout the South, and that you and your race are thus made to suffer the consequences of an act for which you were in no wise responsible. A few weeks ago, had you been able to come to us, you would have found our entire city, white and black, ready to welcome you. Just now we are forced into a false position toward you and your race which time alone can remove. I am quite assured that you yourself will understand the situation, and that you will keep Shreveport in your good books looking to a visit in the future. I have had a recent visit from McLane Berch,[2] and have on hand a bit of "stuff" which I have collected for him and his school. I hear only good reports of him.

I should like to know what Tuskegee and particularly Mrs. Washington are doing for the Louisiana Purchase Exposition. I am a member of the Board of Lady Managers, and so am directly interested in womans work. Will you or Mrs. Washington write to me in the matter?

With the kindest regards, and regrets that your coming seems just now inopportune, I am   Very truly

Lavinia H. Egan

ALS   Con. 257   BTW Papers   DLC.

[1] Lavinia Hartwell Egan, born in Texas in 1863, was a journalist, lecturer, and educator. In 1903 she was president of the Louisiana State Federation of Women's Clubs.
[2] McLane McClellan Birch.

To William Henry Baldwin, Jr.

[Tuskegee, Ala.] Feb. 10, 1903

Personal.

Dear Mr. Baldwin: I have read your letter to Mr. Shaw with interest.[1] You perhaps have noted that I am very slow to lose faith in a friend and I cannot but still cherish the feeling that Mr. Roosevelt has in his heart to do for the colored people just what you and I both are trying to do. If I felt thoroughly convinced that he or any other man was simply trying to use the race as a means of furthering his selfish and political ends I would drop him without a moment's hesitation. The more I study and observe conditions in the South the more I am convinced that ours is the only way out of the present difficulty, though I cannot shut my eyes to the fact that many of our people, especially in Boston and Washington, are growing very nervous and impatient, and they are visiting a great deal of condemnation upon me because I do not attempt to lead in a movement that will secure at one bound all the political and other rights that the Negro demands. I understand that the set of colored people who have always opposed me in Boston are to hold a meeting in Faneuil Hall on next Thursday night which will have for its object largely condemnation of me for not speaking out more strongly on political and public questions. Several of my friends have written me urging that I give out something to the press in order to ward off this threatened demonstration. I have said to all that I shall say nothing. I am perfectly content to trust to the future to vindicate the wisdom of what we are trying to do. It is the more

natural growth that is going to be our salvation and not the artificial
mushroom development. Yours truly,

[Booker T. Washington]

TLc   Con. 249   BTW Papers   DLC.

[1] Baldwin wrote Albert Shaw that it would have been better if Roosevelt had
not appointed William D. Crum in light of the sensationalism generated by BTW's
White House dinner. Baldwin said: "It only indicates that he does not know the
Southern question." Any action on behalf of blacks that the President took, Baldwin
surmised, would be viewed in the South as a move toward social equality, against
which the South was adamant. "I think you agree with me," Baldwin wrote, "that the
only progress that can be made with a backward race living alongside of a superior
race will be through just such methods as suggested by Booker Washington." (Feb. 5,
1903, Con. 249, BTW Papers, DLC.)

To Julius Daniel Dreher

[Tuskegee, Ala.] Feb. 10, 1903

Personal

Dear Dr. Dreher: I am very sorry indeed that we missed each other
a few days ago when I was en route South. I was on the train that
I told you I would be on and I cannot understand how you failed
to see me.

I told the President about your suggestion of writing an article
for the North American Review bearing upon his Southern policy
of appointing Negroes to office[1] and he seemed very much interested
in the matter, especially so that he told me to tell you to come up
and take lunch with him and talk the matter over. In this connection I want to suggest that if you will read the editorial in last
week's Outlook you will get hold of some valuable information. I
might say privately that I furnished this information to The Outlook and can give more in the same direction if you decide to write
the article. I hope you have had an answer from the North American Review by this time.

I am planning to be in New York for a short while on the 22d of
February and shall be there for a longer period sometime in March.
Yours truly,

[Booker T. Washington]

TLc   Con. 249   BTW Papers   DLC.

[1] Dreher wrote BTW on Feb. 1, 1903 (Con. 255, BTW Papers, DLC) that W. H. Page had encouraged him to write an article commending Roosevelt's appointment of blacks, but Frissell "said we must be careful about endorsing President Roosevelt's appointment of colored men to office" and "seems to think such appointments injure the Negroes." Dreher also echoed the fears of some of his advisers that such an article might weaken his own opportunity for a federal appointment in case he should resign or be removed from the presidency of Roanoke College.

To the Editor of the Cincinnati *Enquirer*

[Tuskegee, Ala.] February 10, 1903

Personal and Private.

Dear Sir: It may be of some value to have a statement from me to the effect that the enclosed statements are not true. I have never been refused a meal in a dining-car. I have never had the slightest difficulty or unpleasantness on a dining car anywhere in the country. The colored waiters and porters as well as the white dining car conductors have always served me in the most willing manner wherever I have come in contact with them. Very truly yours,

[Booker T. Washington]

TLc   Con. 249   BTW Papers   DLC.

From Charles Fleischer[1]

Cambridge [Mass.] Feb. 11th 1903

My dear Mr. Washington: Two days ago I had the privilege of addressing the Boston Literary & Historical Ass'n — a group of Negro men and women who represent, I should say, the best of that element in our community. I had occasion, in the course of my remarks on Zionism — one phase of the "Jewish Question" — to compare the different attitudes of Jews towards that problem to the attitudes of Bishop Turner and Booker Washington to the

Negro problem. I have the greatest regard for you and admiration for your consecrated labors. Naturally, then, I spoke of you in that spirit. To my astonishment I noted: that, at favorable mention of your name, a frost fell upon the audience, which had been warmly sympathetic and was again so when I finished with my use of you for illustration. I was not long left in doubt of the significance of this — to me — surprising incident, for, after the meeting, a number of excited men and women asked me — in the friendliest way, however — why I had at the same time suggested self-insistence to the Negro and the Jew, and a shaming out of existence of the prejudice against both by *proving* their intrinsic worth and dignity — while also mentioning Mr. Washington to enforce my point. They proceeded to "prove" to me how you were playing into the hands of their enemies, were a selfish time-server and what not. No amount of expostulation from me made the slightest impression upon them. I tried to tell them that they needed perspective, that you had vision and "faith in the longevity of your cause." But it was all of no avail. I was astounded at this discovery that you were without honor among your own people — though it serves negatively to prove you the prophet and the emancipator.

I have taken the liberty of writing to you thus frankly for a distinct reason: I feel that it is pathetic and unnecessary that you should be thus completely misunderstood and your motives misinterpreted by the very ones to whose welfare you are consecrated. I cannot believe that you would be indifferent to their good opinion, or that you are satisfied to trust to time to correct their judgments.

Therefore, I write to ask whether you would not think it worth while either to issue an address making quite clear, to this mistrustful element, the purpose and bearing of your recent remarks on the efforts towards the political and social restriction of the Negro's rights and privileges — or, if that would be distasteful to you, to publish an article on the subject in some magazine or paper.

For the progress of your cause it seems to me desirable that you should be backed by the united and enthusiastic support of the Negroes of the U.S. What I have observed is, I fear, only a sympton of a serious and growing disaffection which would long retard the success of those purposes which all Negroes and humanitarian

Whites hold in common. The deep desire for this success must excuse my writing thus to you. With great regard, I am   Sincerely Yours,

(Rabbi) Charles Fleischer

ALS   Con. 249   BTW Papers   DLC.

1 Charles Fleischer (1871–1942) was born in Breslau and immigrated to New York in 1880. He was educated at Hebrew Union College (1887) and the University of Cincinnati (B.L., 1893). From 1894 to 1911 he was rabbi of Temple Israel in Boston. A student of Emerson and the utopian philosophers, he eventually broke his religious ties and organized the secular Sunday Commons, a forum for the discussion of such issues as marriage, divorce, religion, and evolution. He also became a columnist for the Hearst syndicate. In 1922 he became an editor of the New York *American* and later was a radio commentator and editor of the magazine *Democracy*.

To William Goodell Frost

Tuskegee, Feb. 11, 1903

Personal

My dear President Frost: I call your attention to a matter in which you are quoted in the enclosed clipping taken from the N.Y. Tribune of Feb. 9. I dislike very much to see you quoted as stating that the white man should be educated before the Negro is educated. I regret also to note that other white men engaged in education in the South have been preaching the same doctrine recently. It seems to me wholly wrong. Several years ago in an address delivered in Carnegie Hall where Mr. Cleveland presided, I called attention to the fact that the time had come when the North should help to educate not only the Negro but the poor white man. I still stand by that statement, but I think it wholly unfair for anyone to make the statement that the white man should be educated first. There is but one interpretation to be put upon such a statement, and that is that the education of the Negro must be stopped while the education of the white man goes forward. A broader and more statesmanlike thing would be to say that both races should be educated.

I repeat what I said in the beginning of this note that I do not

know whether or not you have been correctly quoted. I know that
I often suffer from mis-quotation. Yours truly,

[Booker T. Washington]

TLc   Con. 258   BTW Papers   DLC.

To Edwin Chalmers Silsby[1]

[Tuskegee, Ala.] Feb. 11, 1903

My dear Prof. Silsby: Sometime I want to have a conference with
you or some member of your faculty in regard to the Rhodes Scholarships. Dr. Parkin,[2] who has charge of the matter, spent a day here
last week and we went over matters pretty fully. Enclosed I send
you an outline of the conditions decided upon bearing upon those
who are to go from the Southern States. I think Talladega College
is the only institution in Alabama from which we can hope to have
a colored student go and I believe that if the matter is taken in hand
in time enough and all of the conditions understood that there will
be a chance for a Talladega man to go to Oxford which of course
will be a great thing not only for the college but for the entire
race.[3] I hope you will be able to give immediate attention to the
matter. Let me know if I can serve you in any way. Yours truly,

[Booker T. Washington]

TLc   Con. 1   BTW Papers   DLC.

[1] Edwin Chalmers Silsby, born in Siam of missionary parents in 1851, entered
the service of the American Missionary Association and became principal of Burrell
Academy in Selma, Ala., from 1875 to 1885. He was secretary-treasurer of Talladega
College from 1885 to 1907, and dean, registrar, and professor at Talledega from
1907 to 1913. He later served as emeritus professor and secretary to the faculty. He
died in 1922.

[2] George Robert Parkin (1846–1922) was principal of Upper Canada College in
Toronto from 1895 to 1902. He moved to England in 1902 and became the first organizing secretary of the Rhodes Scholarship Trust, a position he held until 1920.

[3] The first Rhodes scholarship awarded to a black American went to Alain Leroy
Locke, a Harvard graduate, who studied at Oxford from 1907 to 1910.

To Samuel Somerville Hawkins Washington

[Tuskegee, Ala.] Feb. 12, 1903

My dear Dr. Washington: I am in receipt of your kind letter of recent date and hasten to reply. I have followed with care the matter of the Rhodes Scholarships from the time that Mr. Rhodes made the offer, and Dr. Parkin, the agent of the Fund, spent a day here last week going over matters in connection with this fund. I am sorry to say, however, that in spite of my efforts to see him first, he had already spent a day in Atlanta in conference with the presidents of Southern white universities, but he tells me that according to the plans agreed upon there is nothing to prevent a colored man from having an equal chance. I send you a copy of the conditions agreed upon by the Atlanta conference. According to these conditions it seems to me that Talladega College is the only institution in the state which could send a colored student. Only this morning I had written the president of Talladega[1] calling his attention to this opening. I repeat, Dr. Parkin insists that a colored man, under the provisions agreed upon, will have an equal chance; he says that he kept that point constantly before the conference in Atlanta. I have, however, some doubts upon our being able to secure a fair representation under these plans. Dr. Parkin assures me however, that if there is the least sign of injustice manifested that the committee already appointed will be dissolved and new ones created. I might add that everything that has been done is to still be approved by the central committee in England. Dr. Geo. R. Parkin whose address is Upper Canada College, Toronto, will be open for suggestions at any time. Yours truly,

BTW

TLcIr BTW Papers ATT.

1 George W. Andrews, acting president of Talladega College until Apr. 1, 1904.

To John C. Asbury

[Tuskegee, Ala.] Feb. 12, 1903

Personal.
My dear Mr. Asbury: I write to thank you for the editorial in the last issue of the Odd Fellow's Journal with regard to President Roosevelt and myself and our relations to the race and its interests. It seems to me you have gone to the very root of the matter in discussing the President's motives and all. He is a brave good man and is one of the best friends we have ever had in the White House. Yours truly,

[Booker T. Washington]

TLc   Con. 249   BTW Papers   DLC.

To William Edward Burghardt Du Bois

Tuskegee, Ala., February 12, 1903

Dear Dr. Du Bois: I am sorry that a tremendous pressure of work has delayed my sending out the letters[1] sooner, but I am sending to you copy of such a letter as I have sent out.[2] I shall keep you informed as to the answers. I find that I did not mention to you when you were here the name of Mr. Fortune as he is out of the country, but I find that it is probable he will return within a few weeks, and in that case, I should feel that it is proper to invite him to be present at this time. I understand that you and he do not agree on many matters. I have known Mr. Fortune for a number of years and while he has his weak points he also has his strong ones, and I think his counsel in such a meeting would be of great value. I am very anxious that the meeting be not confined to those who may agree with my own views regarding education and the position which the race shall assume in public affairs, but that it shall in every way represent all the interests of the race. Very truly yours,

Booker T. Washington

P.S. I rather think it would be better for you to write Mr. Morgan yourself. I do not know him very well and then besides I rather have the idea that he has some feeling against me and would not perhaps under the circumstances be inclined to consider favorably anything that I might say. Please let me know if you will write him.

B. T. W.

TLS W. E. B. Du Bois Papers MU. A carbon is in Con. 256, BTW Papers, DLC.

1 This was BTW's first attempt in conjunction with Du Bois to convene a private conference of black leaders of opposing factions. He soon abandoned the plan, but revived it in Jan. 1904 as the Carnegie Hall or New York Conference.

2 A carbon copy of BTW to Abram L. Grant, Feb. 12, 1903, is in the Du Bois Papers, MU.

From John Elmer Milholland

Philadelphia, February 12th, 1903

My dear Mr. Washington: Mr. Ogden is among the most conscientious of men, but he seems to see the entire solution of the Southern problem in education. I don't. I see in education only one of several important streams of reformatory effort, in the right direction. It is tremendously important, but it is not the whole story, not by any means. There is the legal effort, represented by Wise[1] and his friends; there is the political effort, represented by the relentless exponents of Lillie White scheming; there is the Constitutional effort, for which the President stands; there is the Press effort, the practical character of which I have intimated to you; and there is this effort to stamp indirectly, but effectively, the race prejudice by giving the man who delights to honor you an opportunity to do so in the eyes of the whole social and civilized world.

I stand for all of them; they are all needed. They should all be encouraged, and it is a great mistake for the exponents of one to do nothing to co-operate so far as possible with the exponents of the others.

Mr. Ogden, however, cannot see his way to do this. That in itself is bad enough, but he practically tells me that if you consent to be the guest of the evening you will injure not only yourself but the whole cause of education in the South.

We discussed the matter for a long time. He, apparently, is as strong as ever in his own belief, and I am utterly untouched by a single argument he put forth.

Yesterday I saw Mr. Baldwin. We talked for nearly two hours, and I think Mr. Baldwin understands me a little bit better than he ever did before, for the discussion was without gloves or evening dress. I think he is more in accord with me than he is with Mr. Ogden. We shall probably meet again Monday or Tuesday and decide the question one way or the other. I am sorry to keep you waiting, but I do not think the fault is at my door.

My dear Mr. Washington, the time is drawing very near when these rose water methods of dealing with a dangerous situation will not be discarded, but they will be relegated to their proper place, because the majority of the people of this country still believe the Constitution means something and its provisions are operative south of the Mason and Dixon line. Sincerely yours,

Jno. E. Milholland

TLS Con. 249 BTW Papers DLC.

1 John Sergeant Wise (1846–1913), the son of Governor John Alexander Wise and a Confederate veteran, became in 1880 a member of the Readjuster party in Virginia and subsequently a Republican leader. On several occasions he charged Democrats with corrupt and illegal denial of voting rights to blacks.

To Alexander Walters

[Tuskegee, Ala.] February 13, 1903

My dear Bishop: A number of influential and strong members of our race have requested me to put before you the matter of calling a conference to consist of twelve or fifteen of our best men, representing every phase, if possible, of Negro life and activity, to meet in, say, New York City, during the latter part of March or the 1st of April, for a two or three days quiet and private conference concerning the present condition and future of the race.[1] I write to ask if such a conference is held, if you can be present? It is probable that your traveling expenses to this conference would be paid, and if you agree with the suggestion, will you be kind enough to indicate what your probable expenses would be in case it would insure your attendance by having your expenses cared for. It is important that this matter be kept entirely private at present. Very truly yours,

[Booker T. Washington]

TLc Con. 281 BTW Papers DLC.

1 Similar letters were addressed to T. Thomas Fortune, Abram L. Grant, and others.

From Charles William Anderson

Albany, Feb. 13, 1903

My dear Doctor Washington: I came hither on Monday of this week, to use my good offices with the party-builders agreeably to your suggestion, and succeeded in inducing several individual members of the Legislature to send letters. I was fortunate enough, last week, to have twelve letters written — five by members of the House, and seven by members of the Senate. Hence you see, I have allowed no stone to go unturned, but I notice by the paper of this morning that all our work has gone to pot. It was really too bad, and I am afraid that it will be quite difficult to secure a federal appointment for any colored man, however excellent, unless he is to succeed another colored man or is an applicant for a foreign post. This is my rendition of the hand-writing on the wall. Is it not yours? I do not, however, apprehend much difficulty about the confirmation of a colored man appointed to a diplomatic post, or to succeed a colored office holder. I leave here to-morrow for New York, where I shall hope to hear from you. Yours very truly,

Charles W. Anderson

P.S. A mass meeting is advertised in New York for the 19th, approaching, and I am down to speak. Hayes is to be there, as also are Walters, Derrick,[1] Brooks, Morris and other preachers too numerous to mention. My first impulse was to decline, but on sober reflection I concluded that it might not be wise to sacrifice a good cause because of the indiscretion of one man, and that it might be best to attend and do all in my power to prevent any unwise or indiscreet utterance from being made. What do you advise? I will follow your advice in the matter.

C.W.A.

TLS   Con. 248   BTW Papers   DLC.   Postscript is in Anderson's hand.

1 William Benjamin Derrick (1843–1913), born in the West Indies, was an A.M.E. minister beginning in 1864. After fifteen years in Virginia he moved to New York in 1879 and was elevated to bishop about 1900. Derrick's duties took him to the West Indies, South America, and West and South Africa, in addition to several posts in the United States.

From Whitefield McKinlay

Washington, D.C., February 13, 1903

Dear Mr. Washington: Yours just at hand. Since I wrote you last Doctors Reybourn[1] and Purvis[2] talked with Sen. Perkins for nearly an hour and covered every phase of Crum and the Negro question, but they came away convinced that he is a sneaking hypocrite. I also called on Sen. Lodge who promised to appeal to Perkins and who believed when the final test came he would vote for him. His true feeling was disclosed in the Baltimore Sun to-day who quotes him as saying that the Negro question is analogous to the Chinese question.[3] By that I am led to infer that he might be the senator whom Sen. Hoar quoted as saying that he was sorry that slavery was abolished. I did not pay much attention to Jones as he defined his position several years ago in a speech in the Senate in which he referred to the Negro as being an inferior being. Gov. Pinchback, Terrell and myself will frame a letter on Sunday to be sent to each of the Republican Senators in order to force them up to a vote. I confess that I was very much disappointed that Sen. Nelson[4] who promised Lyons and myself that he would vote for him should dodge the vote and thereby cause an adverse report. You must by all means insist regardless of what may be done by the Senate he must be reappointed, for should we lose this case not even the letter carriers of the South will be safe from attack of the Press.

Root's speech has caused considerable adverse comment and is calculated to depress all colored office holders, and I had hoped that at one of the Lincoln birth-day meetings last night that another Cabinet officer might take occasion to explain Root's and the Administration's attitude.

I sent you the editorial in last Sunday's Tribune which was favorable. Bishop Ireland's speech[5] has the right ring to it and will help his church. Very truly,

W. McKinlay

DICTATED.

TLS   Con. 266   BTW Papers   DLC.

[1] Robert J. Reyburn (1833–1909), born in Glasgow, Scotland, an army surgeon during the Civil War, was dean and professor of hygiene and preventive medicine at Howard University Medical School.

[2] Charles Burleigh Purvis, born in 1842 in Philadelphia, was the son of the prominent black abolitionist Robert Purvis. In 1868, after serving as an army surgeon, he joined the faculty of Howard University Medical School, where he was professor of obstetrics and gynecology from 1873 to 1906. He was also chief surgeon of Freedmen's Hospital from 1881 to 1894.

[3] The newspaper reported that Perkins intended to oppose Crum's confirmation. "He says he realizes that the race question enters very strongly into the case, and he is in a position to sympathize with the Southern people by reason of his understanding of the Chinese question on the Pacific Coast, which, he declares, is analogous to the negro problem in the South." (Baltimore *Sun*, Feb. 13, 1903, 2.)

[4] Knute Nelson (1843–1923), Republican senator from Minnesota, 1895–1923. Born in Norway, he immigrated to the United States at the age of six.

[5] Archbishop John Ireland, guest of honor at a banquet of the Lincoln Club of Chicago, said that to deny the Negro access to the ballot box was "to war against American institutions" and "to set aside Lincoln principles." Though he rejoiced in "the territorial aggrandisement that has come to America," he said it would also be contrary to the principles of the Republic and the memory of Lincoln to hold overseas populations in perpetual tutelage. (Baltimore *Sun*, Feb. 13, 1903, 10.)

From Wilford H. Smith

New York City, Feb. 13th, 1903

Dear Friend: I have just returned from Boston, and write you this account of what occurred there. I also send several Boston papers giving an account of the meeting and showing the published resolutions.

After I wired you yesterday, I found Peter J. Smith, and made an effort with his assistance to find out what was in the resolutions. I am satisfied that the Guardian had framed the resolutions so as to give vent to their feelings against you, but several fortunate circumstances helped us to thwart them. They were these: Mr. Hayes had brought Bishops Derrick and Walters along to speak at the meeting, which very much enraged Trotter and Forbes, so much so that they insulted the Bishops and said if they undertook to speak it would precipitate a row in the hall. This treatment of the bishops made them bestir themselves among the preachers to get them to resent the insult. It turned out however, that the preachers could not do anything in the way of altering the program, but many of them were on the resolution committee, and when the committee met at 7 o'clock to pass upon the resolutions, they were in such a frame of mind towards the Guardian people as to not let them have their way, and I believe the resolutions were altogether changed from their original form. Both Bishops Derrick and Walters and Mr. Hayes, especially urged the members of the committee whom they knew to see to it that the Guardian did not assail you in the resolutions.

We tried in the early part of the evening to reach Mr. Pillsbury, but could not find him. Had we done so, we intended to try and dissuade him from attending Faneuil Hall meeting, and meant to hold another meeting at the Charles Street Church. The Bishops and Hayes and I went to the Charles Street Church and at first decided not to go to Faneuil Hall meeting at all, but when we found that we could not reach Mr. Pillsbury, Hayes and I went. After much persuasion they got Hayes to speak at the close of the meeting. I was not even invited to the platform. I think I am suspected. I heard all the speakers save Grimke, and none of them assailed you or your work, but I understand Grimke did in some way; you will find it alluded to in the report of the Globe.

I talked with Forbes, and his insolence and presumption is truly monumental; I left his office in disgust, and resolved more stoutly than ever that if a case could be found, to land him behind the bars.

It would be useless to bring any proceedings other than criminal, and I shall be careful to wait until I get everything dead certain before I make a move. I have my plans well laid, and will advise you as they progress.

I got your letter this morning before leaving Boston. Very truly yours,

Wilford H. Smith

TLS Con. 261 BTW Papers DLC.

From Whitefield McKinlay

Washington, D.C., February 14, 1903

Dear Mr. Washington: I had a very important interview with the President this morning and we went over the Crum situation thoroughly. He told me that Rev. Edgar Murphy had called on him and had urged him to withdraw Crum's name. Sen. Frye[1] had also done the same thing. I replied that there was no alternative but to fight it out. He stated that unless Crum and his friends were willing to withdraw his name he would not change his attitude. He was willing to provide for Crum elsewhere at a better salary, to which I gave no approval. On my return to my office I wrote him a copy of the enclosed letter which I think covers the situation. Unfortunately the President has a lot of weak friends who are piling on the agony. I have not entirely lost courage, but I confess the outlook is exceedingly dark.

Gov. Pinchback, Terrell and myself will meet tomorrow to frame a letter which will be sent to each of the Senators. The President realizes that the trust people have a hand in this dirty fight and he used some very strong language with reference to them.

I sent the telegram to Crum as directed. Leupp told me that he has an engagement with the President for tomorrow night and will talk very plainly to him.

I also told the President that both McLaurin and Capers were unworthy of confidence and were wholly responsible for this state of affairs, and that Capers last visit here was for the purpose of confusing the situation, in which he succeeded. Very truly,

W McKinlay

DICTATED.

TLS Con. 249 BTW Papers DLC.

1 William Pierce Frye (1830–1911), a Republican, was U.S. senator from Maine, 1881–1911.

From William Henry Baldwin, Jr.

Brooklyn, N.Y. Feb. 16, 1903

B.T.W. Your letter 10th about my letter to Shaw. My intuitions have played an important part in my judgment. The remark R. made about the Negroes in Oyster Bay Town sticks in my mind.

A friend of the President admitted the other day that he is a Sophomore a word meaning "foolishly wise." However, there is no reason for you to go back on a "friend," with the present Evidence, but there is every reason why you should beware of his weaknesses.

W H B Jr

ALS   Con. 792   BTW Papers   DLC.

From Alexander Walters

Jersey City, N.J. Feb 16 1903

Dear Friend: Your letters have been received and their contents greatly appreciated. After a careful reading of your letter concerning a statement from you, to be read at the Boston meeting — I came to the conclusion that you were right. Bishop Derrick, Mr Hayes, and myself went to Boston Wednesday night the 11th. On Thursday morning we met a part of the Committee at the home of Rev Stevens.[1] We were not long in discovering that the "Guardian" people had put up a "job" on us and were determined to make the meeting an Anti-Washington affair. We told them we would not have it. The fight was bitter; each side sent emissaries to have a full Committee to meet at 7:30 P.M. to consider resolutions &c. We secured a majority, but to win we had to remain away from the mass meeting. I will tell you all about it when we meet. I heartily approve the idea of a private conference as suggested in your last letter. Being near New York, I will not have any traveling expenses. I would consider it a pleasure to entertain the company at tea or dinner on the day of the meeting. Let me know as soon as possible the date agreed upon. Yours sincerely,

A. Walters

ALS BTW Papers ATT.

1 Probably George E. Stevens of the Calvary Baptist Church.

To Timothy Thomas Fortune

Tuskegee, Ala., Feb. 17, 1903

Personal.

My dear Mr. Fortune: I have not heard from you for some time. I am keeping immensely busy these days and hardly have time for a friendly letter to many people. Things are pretty squally just now and I miss you more and more. The nomination of Crum and the closing of the Indianola post office seem to agitate the South and keep the water boiling. Aside from this, the Boston crowd with Trotter, Ferris, Forbes, etc., at their lead, seem to have broken out afresh. The Senate committee reported adversely on Dr. Crum. I think the main man who was responsible for the adverse report was Perkins of California. You ought to tell Morton and the rest of the friends in California to sit down hard on Perkins. Crum has grown very nervous over the whole situation and I fear is ready to collapse. Just now is it hard to tell what is going to be done, whether Crum is going to withdraw or whether the President will re-nominate him in case he does not withdraw. The whole situation is very much mixed and there is a good deal of unrest among our people. Secy. Root's speech in New York a few weeks ago, which nobody seems to understand, has further complicated the matter. In the midst of it all, however, the President seems to be standing squarely and so far as I can get information directly or indirectly, he is with us. Various groups of our people are agitating the calling of all kinds of conventions, but as far as possible I am trying to stem the tide against the calling of conventions and direct-

ing the attention of the race to the importance of standing by the
Afro-American Council with a view of letting it be the medium
through which our battles are to be fought. I shall feel easier when
I know that you are in the country again. Yours truly,

Booker T. Washington

TLS Con. 249 BTW Papers DLC. Scott added a handwritten postscript:
"I'll write soon, too—busy as blazes—Scotty."

To Charles Fleischer

Tuskegee, Ala., Feb. 17, 1903

My Dear Mr. Fleischer: Your kind letter of February 11th finds me
very busy, arranging for our annual Negro Conference, but I cannot refrain from pausing to reply at once to the observations noted
by you.

I wish to say that I am not at all surprised at the statements made
in your letter. I have known for a number of years the feeling existing among a group of colored people in Boston, and have known
other occasions when their feelings have been manifested in the
manner described by yourself. Another group of similar caliber is
found in the city of Washington. Aside from a few individuals scattered about mainly in various New England cities, those to whom
I have referred constitute the only colored people in the country
of any considerable prominence or influence who do not approve
of my views and general attitude on the race question. I keep my
hand pretty closely upon the pulse of the race in several ways, particularly through a careful examination of the editorials contained
in the two hundred or more Negro newspapers published in various
parts of the country. I feel safe in saying that out of these 200, aside
from one published in Boston, another in Washington, and still
another in Chicago, practically all heartily support my views. As
an illustration of what I mean, I happen to be able to put my hand
upon several colored papers which have come into the office this
week, and I take the liberty of sending them to you for perusal.

I do not grow angry over the opposition of the group in Boston —
in fact, I must confess I pity them. It is not unlikely that if I had

81

been reared in the North, and schooled in the high schools and colleges of that section, with no opportunity of coming into contact with the real problem of the race, I might share their sentiments. As it is, they, having never come in contact with the rank and file, with no opportunity for doing effective work in their behalf, cannot in any appreciable degree touch or influence the real heart of the people.

There is nothing that I could say or do which I think would change the attitude of a number of these people. Notwithstanding the fact that I have explained my attitude on the questions of Jim Crow cars and the unjust election laws of the South in public addresses and in my books, they willfully misunderstand and misrepresent my words and actions whenever they feel disposed to do so. They even criticised the President of the United States for inviting me to dine with him. While a few, no doubt, oppose me on principle, I am convinced that among a large majority, the antagonism is based upon spite, to say the least. Though regrettable, the actions of these people are not without profit — I often conclude that, instead of doing harm to the cause for which I stand, they help both myself and the cause. I am sure that if I had back of me the entire Negro race, with no element in it watching for mistakes, and weaknesses, I should not be so careful of my words and actions, and should not work as hard as I do. The alertness of this group of critics may serve to make me more valuable to the race and nation. I rest content in the thought that there is not the slightest foundation for the objections raised, and in the belief, gained by experience, that in Boston and elsewhere, the colored people who constitute the bone and sinew of the race understand me and approve of my position. Mr. Wm. H. Lewis, whom the President recently appointed Assistant District Attorney, and who lives in Cambridge, I think can give you information as to the source and extent of the opposition in Boston.

I have just as strong an ambition as anyone could possibly have to see all the privileges come to our race, but I know, as you must know, that they cannot be gotten by merely making speeches, by cursing somebody, or seeking a scape-goat upon which to lay the blame for the failure to rid ourselves of all the ills complained of, without appeal to the natural law of time and industry. Some time when I am in the North, I shall be glad to talk these matters over further with you. Again, allow me to thank you for your letter, and let me add that I am not at all surprised that one who has not known these people and of the existence of this opposition, should be surprised as you were. By this mail I take the liberty of sending you two of my books, "Up From Slavery" and "The Future of the American Negro." In them you will find my views on the main questions fully and frankly stated. Yours very truly,

[Booker T. Washington]

TL Copy Con. 249 BTW Papers DLC. A carbon of another version is in Con. 290, BTW Papers, DLC.

From Charles William Anderson

New York. February 20, 1903

Personal

My dear Dr. Washington: The Cooper Union Mass Meeting has come and gone, without the explosion of the least bit of dynamite, as you will observe from the herewith enclosed clippings.[1] Agreeably to your suggestion, I sought out Bishop Walters on reaching the Hall, and had a talk with him. I then talked with each of the speakers of the evening, and admonished them to refrain from all expressions which might be used against the cause and the Race. In my own speech I used the following language:

"In approaching the subject which this meeting is called to consider, I want to assure you that I fully appreciate the advisability of caution, and I sincerely hope that the other gentlemen who are to address you will appreciate it also. In times like these, when we find so many men of conscience and scholarship who ought to be our natural allies, and so many journals of influence that ought to be our natural defenders and whose attention ought to be nailed to the high moral aspects of this controversy, growing cold and indifferent, we cannot be too careful. One rash word, and perhaps even one too ardent expression, may injure our cause and lose it friends." The other speakers were careful and discreet and nothing was said that would in any way damage the movement or expose the Race to criticism. Bishop Derrick, in one of his "sunburstery" flights, did use some rather unfortunate language, but the newspaper men some how or other did not print it. At the same time, he did not go very far out to sea. Bishop Walters was a trifle unfortunate, also I thought, in his reference to the late President McKinley, as you will see by the clipping from the New York Sun. I think the good Bishop will do well to abstain from reflections of this character in the future, as President McKinley is now one of the Nation's martyred Presidents, and criticisms of him will not help any cause, however just or righteous.[2] The resolutions endorsed Dr. Crum for confirmation in open Senate, as you will see. Hence, I think we are to be congratulated upon the successful issue of this meeting.

In my letter of yesterday I may have omitted to say that I will gladly serve on the Committee suggested by you, if our friends decide to hold the conference. If you have any other matters in which I can be of service to you, kindly command me. Yours faithfully,

Charles W. Anderson

TLS Con. 248 BTW Papers DLC.

[1] More than 2,000 blacks met in the Cooper Union on the night of Feb. 19, 1903, to protest against disfranchisement and to urge the U.S. Senate to confirm the appointment of William D. Crum to federal office. About $1,000 was raised to help fight disfranchisement in the state of Virginia. Bishop Alexander Walters blamed President McKinley for failure to stem the tide of disfranchisement in the South. The speakers, however, did not attack Roosevelt and generally endorsed his policies. John E. Milholland condemned the South for lynching blacks and denying them civil rights. (New York *Sun*, Feb. 20, 1903, 3; New York *Times*, Feb. 20, 1903, 6.)

[2] BTW wrote Anderson: "I am very sorry myself that our good friend the Bishop makes these unfortunate references to President McKinley; they certainly do us no good." He complimented Anderson on his handling of the meeting. (Feb. 28, 1903, Con. 248, BTW Papers, DLC.)

From Alexander Walters

Jersey City, N.J., Feb 21 1903

My Dear Friend: I write to ask your aid, in trying to defeat the Trotter "gang" in their Cleveland Convention which is called for no purpose, but to denounce you, President Roosevelt, and the Republican party. I have already written letters to a number of the leading editors calling attention to this fact, and I have urged them to fight the Convention to death. I have prepared an appeal which will be sent out in a few days. It is for the purpose of arousing interest in the Louisville Convention. At the Mass Meeting held in Cooper Union Thursday night we endorsed the Council and elected fifteen men to represent that body at Louisville. What can you do to help me? The following was received from Trotter last week; "Below you will find an editorial written last summer (a criticism of the Council for not denouncing President Roosevelt). I send it to show you why men feel that a body that favors Washington or that he controls is of no value to the race." I shall do all in my power to head off this inconoclast, a deceiver whose object is to build up himself at the expense of others. Let me hear from you as soon as possible.

The Cooper Union Meeting was a *great* success. Yours sincerely,

A. Walters

ALS   Con. 249   BTW Papers   DLC.

An Address before the Brooklyn Institute of Arts and Sciences

Brooklyn, New York, February 22, 1903

THE EDUCATIONAL AND INDUSTRIAL
EMANCIPATION OF THE NEGRO

Mr. Chairman, Ladies and Gentlemen:

I cannot bring myself to feel that I am worthy of speaking to the members of the Brooklyn Institute of Arts and Sciences on the occasion of the observation of the birthday of George Washington, the Father of our Country. Neither by education nor by experience am I fitted to perform such an important service. Occasions like the one which we celebrate tonight, that have to do with the great lives of the founders of the republic, are mainly valuable in giving us the opportunity to pause in the midst of our onward march, take our bearings, and learn lessons from the past that may perchance serve us greatly in the future.

Our republic is the outgrowth of the desire for liberty that is natural in every human breast — freedom of body, mind, and soul, and the most complete guarantee of the safety of life and property. It was the desire for liberty, ever burning in the hearts of the Pilgrim Fathers and the Quakers, that led them to cut loose from kindred and native land and risk the perils and hardships of an almost unsailed and unknown sea. It was the same aspiration that led these people in their new-found home in America to resolve to make an effort to rid themselves of all connection with the mother country, because of political and economic restrictions. A spirit of freedom was kindled that soon manifested itself in every valley and on every hill from Massachusetts to Georgia. The cry for liberty came in equally emphatic tones from the Cavaliers of Jamestown as from the Puritans of Plymouth Rock. I need not take your time to remind you how, under the leadership of George Washington, the result sought for was secured through the Declaration of Independence, through Lexington, Concord, and Yorktown.

Still later in our country's history we have another evidence of the growth of the sentiment of freedom in the promulgation of the Monroe Doctrine, which, in a word, said that the United States would not only contend against the world for its freedom, but for the freedom of all governments upon the two American continents. Half a century later we find the Southern section of our country entering into a political and physical war in a contention for freedom in the control of domestic and state policies, and still later we find ourselves demanding, at the point of the sword, the freedom of our neighbors, the Cubans.

During all the period that the majority and dominant races were contending for the most complete and perfect freedom and independence, there were living by their side two other races, different in color and different in history — the Indian and the Negro. The red man refused, in a large degree, to serve the white man as a slave, refused as a general thing to assimilate the white man's civilization, and refused, even when he had the opportunity, to enter into sympathetic coöperation with the government instituted by the conquering race. Strange to relate, during all the years in which the white American was making such heroic struggles for his own freedom, at nearly every point at which the lives of the red man and the white man touched each other there either was war between the two or injustice and oppression shown in the original American. The result is that because of oppression, or inability to stand the contact with a stronger and more numerous race, the Indian recedes and diminishes.

At any rate, you have so far practised absorption, colonization, or extermination, that the problem growing out of the presence and influence of the red man is small in comparison with the scope and depth of your other race problem. That is to say, in one way or another, you have got the Indian out of the range of your vision. And in this country it seems to be the fashion to consider a problem solved when we get it out of our sight to such an extent that its existence is unobtrusive and our consciences are eased.

Our most recent experiment in the way of race accessions — the Filipino — I shall not, on this occasion, discuss, for the reason that you seem as yet to be quite undecided as to how and where he shall be classed — that is, whether you will rate him as a black man or a white man. Just now the Filipino seems to be going through the interesting process of being carefully examined. If he can produce hair that is long enough and nose and feet that are small enough, I think the Filipino will be designated and treated as a white man; otherwise he will be assigned to my race. If I were to consider the question purely from a selfish standpoint, I should urge that our new subjects be classed as Negroes; but if I were to consider unselfishly the peace of mind of the Filipino himself, I should hope that he be so classified that, in addition to all his other trials, he will not struggle through all future generations considered and looked upon as a problem, instead of a man.

But this is a digression from the trend of our discussion. In the year 1620, just about the time when the sentiment in favor of national freedom was at its height, in some way a few members of my own race — twenty in number, it is said — were landed at Jamestown and were sold into physical bondage. The first representatives of your race preceded the first of mine by less than a score of years, if you reckon the landing of the English at Jamestown — the Pilgrims landed at Plymouth in the same year — 1620.

Cæsar, writing of the people out of which your race grew, describing them as he found them in England, says: "The inhabitants do not for the most part sow corn, but live on milk and flesh, and clothe themselves in skins. All the Britons stain themselves with a pigment which produces a blue color, and gives them a most formidable appearance in battle. They wear their hair long. Ten or twelve have wives in common." Another historian says of these people: "They appeared rambling about their islands with long beards like goats, clad in dark garments reaching to heels, and leaning upon staves. Their only navigation is in small boats of twisted osier covered with leather."

Two thousand years later — in round numbers — another explorer and historian, writing of the Africans — the stock out of which my race grew — has this to say of them (I quote from Dr. Livingstone): "I had been in closer contact with heathenism than I had ever been before; and although all, including the chief, were as kind and attentive to me as possible, and there was no want of food, oxen being slaughtered daily, more than sufficient for the wants of all of us, yet to endure the dancing, roaring, and singing, the jesting, anecdotes, grumbling, quarreling and murdering of these children of nature, seemed more like a severe penance than anything I had ever before met with in my course."

We come thus to the point where these two races, so unlike in physical appearance but so similar in their primitive life, meet. One becomes the owner, the other the slave. It is interesting, and perhaps instructive, to note that during the greater part of the period in which agitation and struggle were kept up for the most complete freedom for the white race, another and growing race was being held in servitude by the very people seeking liberty for themselves. Even George Washington, whose birthday we celebate, held slaves while he fought for freedom.

For nearly two hundred and fifty years the two races remained in close contact with each other in the capacity of master and servant. What was the result of this contact on the enslaved? I confine myself to a statement of cold, bare facts when I say that when the Negro went into slavery, he was a pagan; when he ended his period of bondage he had a reasonably clear conception of the Christian religion. When he went into slavery he was without anything which might properly be called a language; when he came out of slavery he was able to speak the English tongue with force and in-

telligence. Moreover, when he entered slavery he had little working knowledge of agriculture, mechanics, or household duties;
when he emerged from the condition of a chattel he was almost the
entire dependence in a large section of our country for agricultural,
mechanical, and domestic labor.

In spite of many wrongs and frequent cruelties, when the two
races faced each other in their new relations at the end of slavery,
there was a certain attachment and bond of sympathy existing between the individuals that composed them that few people outside
of the slave states could understand or appreciate.

Unlike the Indian, unlike the original Mexican or the Hawaiian,
the Negro, so far from dying out when in contact with a stronger
and different race, continued to increase in numbers to such an
extent that, whereas the race entered bondage twenty in number,
at the end of the slave period there were more than four million
representatives. In addition to that the race has continued to grow
in numbers in a state of freedom until there are now more than
nine millions. So I want to emphasize the truth that whether we
are of Northern or of Southern birth, whether we are black or
white, whether with or without sympathy for the colored man, we
must face frankly, gravely, sensibly, the hard, stubborn fact that in
bondage and in freedom, in ignorance and in intelligence, the
Negro, in spite of all predictions and scientific conclusions to the
contrary, has continued year by year to increase in numbers, until
he now forms about one eighth of the entire population, and that
there are no signs that are based upon proper evidence that the
same ratio of increase that has obtained in the past will not hold
good in the future. Further than this, in spite of setbacks here and
discouragements there, despite alternate loss and gain, despite all
the changing, uncertain conditions through which the race has
passed and is passing, you will find that every year since the black
man came into this country, whether in bondage or in freedom, he
has made a steady gain in acquiring property, skill, habits of industry, education, and Christian character.

But now we have the two races in contact with each other, not as
master and slave, but as freemen, with equal rights guaranteed by
the Constitution, and sheltered by the same flag.

If one had asked Cæsar when he first discovered your forefathers
in the condition that has been described, if in two thousand years

they could be transformed into the condition in which they are now found in America, the answer doubtless would have been an emphatic "No." If one had asked Livingstone, when he first saw my forefathers in Africa, if in the fifty years that have elapsed since then, or even in the two hundred and fifty years that have passed since the first African was brought to this country, a young Negro would be the class orator at Harvard University, the answer doubtless would have been a "No" — as emphatic as Cæsar's.

In mathematics and in the physical sciences we can lay down definite hard-and-fast rules, can be sure that a certain thing will be true tomorrow because it was true five hundred years ago, but in the evolution of races and nations it is hardly possible to be guided by or to reckon by mathematical rules. In fact, the higher one ascends, the further he gets away from the material, and the more nearly he approaches the intellectual and spiritual life, the more uncertainty surrounds him. The two races, facing each other in a state of freedom thirty-seven years ago, presented, we must acknowledge, a problem of life which could not be found anywhere in the history of the world. It was not left us, then, to be definitely guided by the mistakes or failures of others, but it became our duty to blaze, as it were, a path through a wilderness.

While, as I have stated, in dealing with races one cannot be guided by definite formulas, yet I do believe that study of the history of the races of the world, together with a close observation of the character and history of these two races during a period of two hundred and fifty years in America, ought to enable us to reach a few conclusions with some degree of correctness.

The Negro has lived for over two centuries in the midst of the people who from pulpit to rostrum, through the press and in school, in legislative halls and on many a battlefield, have been constantly upholding the doctrine that the most complete development of each human being can come only through his being permitted to exercise the most complete freedom compatible with the freedom of others. Under these conditions the Negro naturally has wrought into every fiber of his being a belief that if freedom is good for one race, it is equally helpful and necessary to the well-being of others. It is impossible that the impassioned plea of Patrick Henry, "Give me liberty or give me death," should have had no influence upon our black citizens. If the black man did not have in him that which spurred him toward the acquiring of those qualities which you consider most essential, neither the white man at the North nor the white man at the South would have any respect for him or confidence in his future.

This, then, after a long introduction to a short sermon, brings me to the pith of what I want to say:

What is liberty for a race, and how is it to be obtained?

In this respect we must bear in mind the words of another, that freedom in its highest and broadest sense can never be a bequest; it must be a conquest.

Black men must not deceive themselves or from others suffer deception. There are several kinds of freedom. There is a freedom that is apparent, and one that is real; a superficial freedom, and one that is substantial; a freedom that is temporary and deceptive, and one that is abiding and permanent; one that ministers to the lower appetites and passions, and another that encourages growth in the higher and sweeter things of life — a freedom that is forced, and one that is the result of struggle, forbearance, and self-sacrifice. But there is but one kind of freedom that is worth the name, and that is the one embodied in the words spoken centuries ago by the Great Master: "And ye shall know the truth, and the truth shall make you free." We can benefit a race only as we can an individual, and that is by dealing honestly, truthfully with it — by giving it that truth which shall make it free indeed.

It is my purpose this evening to take a historical, philosophical, and fundamental view of the Negro question. I do this because, in building a house, the main thing is to get the foundation laid correctly, to get it started upon the rock and not upon the sand, to be sure that the principal timbers are sound and true to measurement. Or, changing the metaphor, to say with Longfellow, of the ship:

> We know what Master laid thy keel,
> What workman wrought thy ribs of steel,
> Who made each mast, and sail, and rope,
> What anvils rang, what hammers beat,
> In what a forge and what a heat,
> Were shaped the anchors of thy hope!
> Fear not each sudden sound and shock,
> 'Tis of the wave and not the rock;
> 'Tis but the flapping of the sail,
> And not a rent made by the gale.

In the development of a race there are many temporary, local, and side issues to which one can devote himself if he so choose. On the other hand he can aim to keep true, in the main, to matters more fundamental and far-reaching, and trust in a large degree to time for a growth in the sense of justice — trust to time for the logical and natural readjustment of all human rights around any worthy and deserving race, which can never be permanently resisted.

> The dreamers who gaze while we battle the waves
> May see us in sunshine or shade;
> Yet true to our course, though our shadow grows dark,
> We'll trim our broad sails as before,
> And stand by the rudder that governs the bark,
> Nor ask how we look from the shore!

But to return to the main point. What is freedom, and how obtained?

The child who wants to spend time in play, rather than in study, mistakes play for freedom. The spendthrift who parts with his money as soon as it is received mistakes spending for freedom. The young man who craves the right to drink and gamble mistakes debauchery for freedom. The man who claims the right to idle away his days upon the street, rather than to spend them in set hours of labor, mistakes loafing for freedom. And so, all through human experience, we find that the highest and most complete freedom comes slowly, and is purchased only at a tremendous cost. Freedom comes through seeming restriction. Those are most truly free today who have passed through great discipline. Those persons in the United States who are most truly free in body, mind, morals, are those who have passed through the most severe training — are those who have exercised the most patience and, at the same time, the most dogged persistence and determination.

To deal more practically and directly with the affairs of my own race, I believe that both the teachings of history as well as the results of everyday observation should convince us that we shall make our most enduring progress by laying the foundation carefully, patiently in the ownership of the soil, the exercise of habits of economy, the saving of money, the securing of the most complete education of hand and head, and the cultivation of Christian virtues. There is nothing new or startling in this. It is the old, old road that all races that have got upon their feet and have remained there have had to travel.

Standing as I do today before this audience, when the very soul of my race is aching, is seeking for guidance as perhaps never before, I say deliberately that I know no other road. If I knew how to find more speedy and prompt relief, I should be a coward and a hypocrite if I did not point the way to it.

Efforts in other directions may assist and bring stimulation, but after all for permanent success and growth we must, in my opinion, go back to and depend upon the basic principles to which I have referred. In the case of a diseased person, when the blood is once purified and the body cleansed, it is surprising to note how soon nature will cure all the minor and temporary ills that grow out of an abnormal blood.

As a slave the Negro was worked. As a freeman he must learn to work. There is a vast difference between working and being worked. Being worked means degradation; working means civilization. There is still doubt in many quarters as to the ability of the Negro unguided, unsupported, to hew his own path and put into visible, tangible, indisputable form products and signs of civilization. This doubt cannot be much affected by mere abstract arguments, no matter how delicately and convincingly woven together. Patiently, quietly, doggedly, persistently, through summer and winter, sunshine and shadow, by self-sacrifice, by foresight, by honesty and industry, we must reinforce argument with results. One farm bought, one house built, one home sweetly and intelligently kept, one man who is the largest taxpayer or has the largest bank account, one school or church maintained, one factory running successfully, one truck garden profitably cultivated, one patient cured by a Negro doctor, one sermon well preached, one office well filled, one life cleanly lived — these will tell more in our favor than all the abstract eloquence that can be summoned to plead our cause. Our pathway must be up through the soil, up through swamps, up through forests, up through the streams, the rocks, up through commerce, education, and religion.

If you ask me to state in detail just what will happen, and how and when it will happen — just what attitude each race will assume toward the other, and how each will act in a given case, when the conditions of growth on which I have laid emphasis have been fulfilled — if you ask this of me, I must answer frankly that I do not know. One can no more tell that than he can tell the day and the hour when the corn will ripen. We only know that if conditions prescribed by nature are complied with, at some time in some manner the corn will ripen and be gathered into the garner. Duty is with us; results are with God.

I have referred to the task that my race must perform if it would effectually emancipate itself. But there is another side. The white race, North and South, also has a duty and a serious responsibility.

In connection with our presence in this country, it should always be borne in mind that, unlike other races, we not only were forced to come into this country against our will, but were brought here in the face of our most earnest protest. Both as slaves and as freemen we have striven to serve the interests of this country as best we could. We have cleared forests, builded railways, tunneled mountains, grown the cotton and the rice, and we have always stood ready to defend the flag. We have never disturbed the country by riots, strikes, or lock-outs. Ours has been a peaceful, faithful service and life.

In the face of all this I cannot believe, I will not believe, that a country that invites into its midst every type of European, from the highest to the very dregs of the earth, and gives these comers shelter, protection, and the highest encouragement will refuse to accord the same protection and encouragement to her black citizens. I repeat here what I have often said in the South. The Negro seeks no special privileges. All that he asks is opportunity — that the same law which is made by the white man and applied to the one race be applied with equal certainty and exactness to the other.

And when I say this, I repeat also that which I have said directly to the members of more than one state constitutional convention in the South — namely, that any revised state constitution that is capable of being twisted into one interpretation when an ignorant white man is concerned and another when an ignorant black man is concerned will not represent entire justice or the highest statesmanship. These new constitutions should place a premium upon good citizenship for both races, and wherever they fail to do this, they are weak and are not in accord with the best interests of the state.

When in any country there are laws which are not respected,

which are trampled under foot and made to mean one thing when applied to one race and another thing when applied to another race, there is not only injustice for which in the end the nation must pay the penalty, but there is hardening and blunting of the conscience, there is sapping of the growth of human beings in kindness, justice, and all the higher, purer, and sweeter things in life. No race can degrade another without degrading itself. No race can assist in lifting up another without itself being broadened and made more Christ-like.

Before I conclude, I want to make one request and suggestion, and I do so with all the earnestness of my soul—with a full knowledge and realization of the present condition and anxieties of my race. That request is that you white men of the North and the white men of the South approach the solution of the Negro question with coolness, with that calmness, that deliberation, and that sense of justice and foresight with which you approach any other problem in business or national affairs. On most other subjects white men use their reason, not their feelings; but in considering the subject of the colored man, in most cases, there are evidences of passion — a tendency to exaggerate and to make a sensation out of the most innocent and the most meaningless events. This is not the way to settle great national questions. While the North and the South argue in heated passion, the Negro suffers.

We must not grow disappointed or despondent because, forsooth, all that was hoped for thirty-five years ago has not taken place just exactly as we wish, or as had been planned. Man's way is not always God's way. The Ten Commandments and the Golden Rule were proclaimed centuries ago, and yet with all his growth and strivings, the Anglo-Saxon, citing him as an example, has not, I think you will agree with me, reached the point where he is living up to them in daily life. And yet, because of this failure, no one has yet been bold enough to propose that we should repeal the Ten Commandments and the Golden Rule. Every government, like every individual, must have a standard of perfection that is immovable, unchangeable, applicable to all races, rich and poor, black and white, towards which its people must continually strive.

I believe the time has come — and I believe it is a perfectly practical thing — when a group of representative Southern white men and Northern white men and Negroes should meet and consider with the greatest calmness and business sagacity the whole subject as viewed from every point. When there is division, when there is doubt on other great questions, this method is followed. Why not in this?

The age for settling great questions, either social or national, with the shotgun, the torch, and by lynchings, has passed. An appeal to such methods is unworthy of either race. I may be in doubt about some things connected with our future, but of one thing I feel perfectly sure, and that is that ignorance and race hatred are no solution for any problem on earth. No one can ever lift up a race by continually calling attention to its weak points. The Negro, like other races, should be judged in a large degree by its best element, rather than by its weakest.

It is hard to find those who can so far control themselves as to discuss this subject with complete absence of prejudice. In most cases there is an effort to prove the Negro a devil or an angel. He is neither, but just an ordinary human being. I deplore the spirit and the disposition of any person who can extract seeming comfort out of the habit of continually dwelling upon the mistakes and weak points of any individual or race, without trying to suggest a remedy for those mistakes and weaknesses. Anyone who is guilty of doing this lives among the briars, the thorns, the stubble and the stumps of life. He who is not content with cold, captious, negative criticism, but enters with body and soul into positive, progressive effort to strengthen and make more useful the most unfortunate of God's creatures, is the individual who is living in green groves and who is continually drinking in the sweet fragrance that comes from beautiful flowers.

When measured by the standard of eternal, or even present, justice, that race is greatest that has learned to exhibit the greatest patience, the greatest self-control, the greatest forbearance, the greatest interest in the poor, in the unfortunate—that has been able to live up in a high and pure atmosphere, and to dwell above hatred and acts of cruelty. He who would be the greatest among us must become the least.

Though often beset behind and before, and on the right hand and on the left, with difficulties that would seem well-nigh insurmountable, I have the most complete faith in the ultimate adjustment of all the perplexing questions that weigh heavily upon us.

More and more, as a race, we are learning to exclaim with one of old:

> The stormy billows are high; their fury is mighty,
> But the Lord is above them, and almighty and almighty.

Ernest Davidson Washington, ed., *Selected Speeches of Booker T. Washington* (Garden City, N.Y.: Doubleday, Doran and Co., 1932), 100–117. A typescript with some variations is in Con. 959, BTW Papers, DLC.

From Robert Curtis Ogden

New York   February 25, 1903

Dear Dr. Washington: I want to express my great pleasure at the wisdom and power of your speech at the Brooklyn Academy of Music on last Sunday night.

I also desire to raise the question as to whether it would not be desirable to print that speech for general circulation. A multitude of voices are proclaiming opinions founded upon partial information and are doing, in my judgment, immense harm; notably the sermon of Dr. Dewey[1] at the Church of the Pilgrim, Brooklyn, on Sunday last.[2]

I cannot but feel that the general cause of education in the South for both races has been seriously set back by the late unfortunate discussions. I greatly regret that it did not occur to me when we were together with Mr. Baldwin on Sunday afternoon that I did not raise the question whether it would not be very wise for Dr. Crum to withdraw from the contest for the Collector in Charleston. The President, of course, cannot withdraw his name.

I am very timid in expression of opinion on this matter but it occurs to me that such action on the part of Dr. Crum might in the present condition of affairs be a stroke of wise and triumphant policy.

I greatly regret that you are to be deprived of Mr. Carnegie's visit. Yours very sincerely,

Robert C Ogden

TLS   Con. 249   BTW Papers   DLC.

1 Harry Pinneo Dewey (1861–1937), a Congregational clergyman, was pastor of the Church of the Pilgrim from 1900 to 1907.

2 Dewey spoke in support of industrial education for blacks, but cautioned that it should not be completely divorced from higher education and liberal arts. Ogden was probably disturbed by Dewey's remark that he believed Abraham Lincoln was right when he said the two races could not live together. Dewey saw growing social segregation and heightened racial awareness in the future, but hoped that segregation would not lead to a denial of opportunities for advancement. (Brooklyn *Eagle*, Feb. 23, 1903, 12.)

To Alexander Walters

[Tuskegee, Ala.?] Feb. 26, 1903

My dear Bishop Walters: I have your letter of February 21st and am in thorough accord with you regarding the two conventions. I have thought out this matter pretty carefully and I feel convinced that you ought to do two things. First, get all the colored newspapers to ignore completely any discussion of the proposed Cleveland convention; to fight it openly will simply mean to advertise it all through the country. Second, bend all of your energies in the direction of advertising the Louisville meeting and get our papers to do the same thing, but by all means I insist that you do not get any of the Negro papers to refer to the Cleveland meeting. Silence will hurt Trotter and his crowd worse than anything else. If you can get the colored papers to completely ignore the Guardian and Trotter and his crowd the sooner they will die. You can depend upon me to do everything possible to promote the success of the Louisville meeting; it is in the hands of good conservative men and a body that really represents the race. I hope you will work in close conjunction with Cyrus Field Adams. He is a quiet man but thoroughly reliable and knows how to get results. Yours truly,

[Booker T. Washington]

TLc   Con. 272   BTW Papers   DLC.

From Timothy Thomas Fortune

Manila, P.I., Feb. 26, 1903

My dear Mr. Washington: I am very glad to have your letter, of the 21st of January, in the mail this morning. It has been a great trial to me to be cut off from communication with you, but I know that it was all unavoidable. I am glad that you had such an ovation in California. Mr. Morton sent me the papers so that I was able to read all about your reception before I left Honolulu. I am glad that you had good reports of me there. I have lived in the middle of the road ever since I left Red Bank, and am determined still to do so. I will give the enemy a mighty bad time of it on that score in the future. I am going to justify by my conduct and work the confidence of those who sent me on the mission I have. And what a terrible job and responsibility I have tumbled into. It is the hardest and toughest job I ever had. But I feel equal to it. Don't fail to have the President order my per diem from $6 to $10 per diem. The outlay for white and light clothes in this country alone has been $100, while a like outlay in the states and Hawaii was necessary. If I had known what was needed much could have been saved. The outfit in clothes and trunks and the like has been fully $300. But that is all right, and the department will not hesitate, I believe, to increase the per diem. You should keep Mr. Morton in mind. He is one of the best men we have in the West, and he is devoted to me and you, and we have to look out for our friends like him. What about Dancy? Is he to hang on the good thing?

The newspapers in the Philippines are all hostile to the race, those published by white Americans, and of course I am on my guard as far as they are concerned. I began the war on them and the Rebel sentiment here this morning in a long article defending the President, and there will be more to follow. But about my official business I have said nothing whatever to them.

I have written Mr. Scott my plans for March and April, and he will let you know them, which will keep me from repeating it here.

Yes; that Boston gang of strikers should be driven to the wall, and if there is an opening when I get back we should train our guns on them. If they insist on black-guarding better men than themselves they should be made to stand the consequences. Mr. Adams sends me clippings of what is being said and done, so that I am again in touch with the home situation. And it seems to me, as you say, that matters are in as good shape as possible under the circumstances, in the states. The President is pleasing me very much by the brave way that he is standing by his guns. The South is horrible brutal and vulgar in its conduct. Of course, the President has the Nation with him. Not a state will go against him at the ballot-box. The same condition on a small scale has grown up here on the vile McKinley policy towards us. No southern white man should be allowed to hold an administrative office in the Philippines. Their conduct towards off-color people will always cause more or less trouble. The Filipinos hate the whole tribe of southerners here, and so do I. You cannot temporize with southern white men.

My spirits are high and my health is gilt edged, and I hope to see you in June. Remember me kindly to dear Mrs. Washington and the children. Yours very truly,

T. Thos. Fortune

TLS   Con. 258   BTW Papers   DLC.

To Elizabeth Julia Emery[1]

[Tuskegee, Ala.] Feb. 27, 1903

My dear Madam: I hope you will forgive me for the seeming delay in answering your kind letter of January 31st. The fact is your letter came during the season of our annual Negro Conference which occupied my time completely, and as soon as that was over I had to go to New York to deliver an address on the occasion of the celebration of Washington's Birthday and have just returned to Tuskegee.

I want to thank you most earnestly and sincerely for your generous gift to our institution. It comes at a time to help and encourage us more than you can realize. We are going to use it towards the payment of the salaries of our teachers; this is our greatest need just now.

Your words are most encouraging, and I consider it a cause of constant gratitude that I have the opportunity to do something I hope not only for my race but for the lifting up of all the people in the South regardless of race or color.

Now I have thought much about what your brother[2] should do at Cincinnati and I cannot help but feel that no one who is desirous of benefiting humanity should object to the words going upon the slab your brother wants to be placed there. While this is my opinion regarding the slab, I do not think that the colored people would object to a separation on the inside of the hospital provided the accommodations for each race are equal; this course is often pursued in the South. Even in our Southern States there are hospitals that draw no color line, but on the inside the two races are completely separated. This it seems to me, ought to satisfy any reasonable person. I have written your brother to this effect.

I hope at some time you may be able to see our work at Tuskegee, and I shall hope that your brother may find it convenient to stop by here when in the South. Yours truly,

[Booker T. Washington]

TLc   Con. 249   BTW Papers   DLC.

[1] Elizabeth Julia Emery in 1903 was about seventy years old. She spent the first twenty years of her life in Cincinnati and thereafter lived abroad, for a few years in France and for more than forty years in England. Unmarried and with a memory from her childhood of injustices toward blacks, she sought at Tuskegee to put some of her considerable wealth to use. (T. J. Emery to BTW, Apr. 8, 1903, Con. 261, BTW Papers, DLC.) Out of her benefactions over several years the Emery dormitories, a series of small, unpretentious buildings, were built.

[2] Thomas J. Emery, Jr., brother of E. Julia Emery, was president of Thomas Emery's Sons, a real estate and investment banking firm in Cincinnati. He was also president of the Emery Candle Co.

To Theodore Roosevelt

Tuskegee, Alabama. March 1/1903

Personal and Confidential.
My dear Mr. President: I have not written you since I received Mr. Edgar Gardner Murphy's telegram for the simple reason that the

Crum case is so complicated that I have not been able to make up my mind as to what the best thing to do is, and I often find that when in doubt the safe thing is to go slow or do nothing. Of one thing, however, I am convinced and that is, if the Senate does not act and you decide to give him a recess appointment, the sooner it is done after Congress adjourns the better it will be as it will stop the discussion and the agitation.

As I see the situation it is about this: With very few exceptions the colored people North and South together with the regular white Republicans in the South, are back of Crum. While the majority of the people in the North favor him, there is an element including the trusts and those who have money invested in the South, that is making trouble. The rank and file of the Southern whites I believe have little interest in the Crum case, but the Southern Democratic press, and the "Lily Whites" are keeping the waters stirred.

There are some indications that the South is getting tired of the agitation and is beginning to see your actions in their true light, to see that in your policy you have really been most considerate of the South.

As I said in the beginning it is hard, very hard to decide as to the wisest and best thing to do, but of the above conclusions I am well convinced. Yours truly,

Booker T. Washington

TLS Theodore Roosevelt Papers DLC. An earlier draft dated Feb. 27, 1903, is in Con. 249, BTW Papers, DLC.

To Robert Curtis Ogden

[Tuskegee, Ala.] March 2, 1903

My dear Mr. Ogden: I have your kind letter of February 25th and I thank you very much for what you say regarding my Brooklyn address. I have been surprised to see how favorably it has been received throughout the country. I shall take advantage of your suggestion and see that the address is reprinted in pamphlet form at once and hope it may accomplish still more good. As you suggest, a number of unwise and discouraging things are being said but I cannot but feel that good will come out of the airing which the Negro question is receiving.

In regard to Dr. Crum. I would say that Mr. Murphy was here a few days ago and he and I and Mr. Baldwin talked the matter over at some length. The difficulty is just here; if Dr. Crum would of his own accord withdraw it would be all right, but the colored people throughout the country feel very strongly that he ought not to withdraw and that the President ought to stand by him. Under the circumstances if I were to influence Crum to withdraw the whole responsibility would be placed directly upon me. I am not a coward and would care little for the criticism if I felt absolutely sure that I was right, but I confess that the Crum case is so complicated in so many directions that I cannot feel that his withdrawal at the present time would be absolutely the wisest thing and I question whether much good would be accomplished. I have not made up my mind exactly as to this view of it, but there is something in it. On the other hand, the question is raised in my mind whether or not if Crum goes into the office and makes a good official, as several colored people have done in various parts of the South, the race would be more helped by his winning over the white people who are now against him to his side. The feeling of the colored people throughout the country is this, that if Crum is defeated that it means the end of colored people holding office in the South. Very few colored people are giving any attention to the matter of seeking office. If there was any wholesale effort on the part of colored people to push themselves into office in the South or if I discerned any evidence on the part of the President to pursue a wholesale policy of putting Negroes into office in the South I should not hesitate to speak out my opinion.

I know my letter is not a very satisfactory one.

It is my plan to be in New York sometime during the next ten or twelve days and I shall hope to have the privilege of talking all these matters over with you. Yours truly,

[Booker T. Washington]

TLc   Con. 249   BTW Papers   DLC.

From Timothy Thomas Fortune

Manila, P.I., March 3, 1903

Dear Mr. Washington: I am going to send you another line by the mail that leaves on the 5th instant, as I shall be away in the country the remainder of this month and may not have an opportunity to write you before I get back in April. I still plan to leave here for the states May 1, and shall labor hard to do so. By that time I shall have all the facts that I need about the Islands and the people to write a report that will cover the scope of my mission and investigations. It is a mighty tough, arduous and dangerous job, surrounded among other difficulties with endemic and epidemic diseases and robber bands, called ladrones, who are really suspected to be "Insurrecto" bands. But I like the work in itself and the dangers and difficulties of studying the topographical, ethnical and literary features of it appeal to me. And the perfect health that I enjoy is a source of constant gratification to me. But I shall be glad when I am able to turn my face homeward, as I am very anxious to spend all of the summer months at Maple Hall, and to see much of you during the summer, as in past years. One of the things that has bothered me most since I left the states is the constant isolation in which circumstances have compelled me to live. All of intercourse here and in Hawaii has been of a business character, with the least possible social feature in it. There are many causes for this, which can only be understood by one who has travelled in the Orient.

Additional California newspapers have reached me, and I am astonished and gratified beyond measure at the magnificent reception that you had in the state. You are a great tower of strength for the race.

With my kind regards for you and Mrs. Washington and the children, as well as Mr. Scott, Your friend,

T. Thomas Fortune

TLS   Con. 258   BTW Papers   DLC.

To William Edward Burghardt Du Bois

Tuskegee, Ala., March 4, 1903

Dear Dr. DuBois: I send you herewith list of persons who have been invited to the proposed conference. All of them have been written to with the exception of Mr. Clement G. Morgan. Very truly yours,

Booker T. Washington

TLS   W. E. B. Du Bois Papers   MU.

To James Edward Graybill[1]

[Tuskegee, Ala.] March 4, 1903

My dear Sir: In the New York Tribune for March 1st I notice a purported interview with you in which you make remarks to the effect that there was a vast difference in the address which I delivered in Atlanta and the one delivered in Brooklyn on February 22d.[2] Enclosed I send you a copy of the address which I delivered in Brooklyn and also copy of the one delivered in Atlanta at the opening of the Exposition. I cannot believe that after reading these two addresses and making comparison you will still contend that there is any difference in the spirit and object of these two speeches. Ever since I have been speaking in public I have without exception clung to two resolutions, first, that I would not make an address anywhere in the North that I could not make in the South; secondly, if I had anything in the way of adverse criticism of the Southern white people I would make this criticism directly to them in the South and not go out from the South to do so. The Southern people are like anyone else, one can speak very plainly and directly to them but they do not like to have an individual go away from home to tell strangers about their weakness. If I had been speaking directly to a Southern white audience on February 22d I should have put some things much more strongly than I did in Brooklyn, but I was speaking to a Northern audience and not to a Southern audience as I was in Atlanta.

Of course I am writing on the assumption that the words quoted in the Tribune are correct. I mention this because I suffer so much myself from misquotation of newspapers that I always make a good deal of allowance for anyone who is quoted in the papers. Yours truly,

[Booker T. Washington]

TLc Con. 249 BTW Papers DLC.

1 James Edward Graybill (1845–1916), a former Confederate captain, was a New York lawyer, active in Democratic politics in the state, and president of the Georgia Society of New York from 1902 to 1905.

2 Graybill, a New York commissioner at the Atlanta Exposition in 1895, said that he agreed heartily with BTW's Atlanta Exposition address but felt that BTW was not faithful to its philosophy in his recent addresses. Graybill criticized Theodore Roosevelt for consulting with BTW on political appointments and also for dining with him. "I do not object to receiving the negro on terms of social equality because of his color," Graybill said, "but because of his ignorance." (New York *Tribune*, Mar. 1, 1903, sec. I, 9.)

From Theodore Roosevelt

White House, Washington. March 4, 1903

Personal.

My dear Mr. Washington: The more I have thought it over the more convinced I have been that Crum must be appointed. I shall send in his name again to the Senate to-morrow. If it does not act I shall appoint him as soon as it adjourns. Sincerely yours,

Theodore Roosevelt

TLS Con. 16 BTW Papers DLC.

To William M. Stevens[1]

[Tuskegee, Ala.] March 9, 1903

Dear Sir: I am writing you at this time to say that very reluctantly we were compelled to send your son[2] from this institution Saturday night, March 7th. For several days he together with other students have been trying to incite rebellion on the part of the Senior Class of the institution, a thing which we could not permit even for a moment.[3] Unfortunately he and others seem to have got the idea that the institution is to be controlled and governed by its students rather than by its faculty. The best way to nip such an affair in the bud was to immediately send from the school the ring leaders; your son was one of these. His railroad fare we have paid and we shall send his clothing and other things to him today. We have had very great confidence in him and have been hoping that he would deport himself to the end of the term in a creditable manner so that he could receive a diploma from the school.

Regretting this unfortunate affair, I am, Yours truly,

[Booker T. Washington]

TLc   Con. 276   BTW Papers   DLC.

[1] Probably William Stevens, a black farmer born in Texas in 1856 who resided in Winchester, Tex.

[2] Junius Henry Stevens.

[3] The cause of the rebellion is unclear, but it may have been a forerunner of the student strike in the fall of the same year. See BTW to Baldwin, Oct. 20, 1903, below. For other evidence of student unrest, see Cicero Clarence Simmons and Washington Alexander Tate to the Tuskegee Institute Executive Council, May 26, 1903, Con. 275, BTW Papers, DLC.

From Louis Edelman[1]

Huntsville, Ala., 3/11/03

Dear Prof: Your letter of the 5th instant at hand. In reply would say that I am not lecturing for money. I am working for the cause of humanity, be it white, black, jew or gentile.

I have just returned from Washington where I went upon the invitation of the Southern Road to consult with them about colonizing the persecuted jews of Romania. My heart goes out for all weak and persecuted races and I know I would find sympathy in your heart for the persecuted jews and if there is any way you could help them, I know you would do so.

My lecture is on the Jew, its history, persecution and achievements, and it speaks of persecuted races, which is very appropriate in the present time.

I have been fighting [on] the side of the weak and poor all my life; it is they who need me, and to them my life and energy belong. Yours very truly,

Louis Edelman

TLS Con. 257 BTW Papers DLC.

¹ An eye, ear, nose, and throat specialist in Huntsville, Edelman was for many years a friend of Tuskegee and BTW.

To Theodore Roosevelt

New York. March 27, 03

My dear Mr. President: I have just had a conference with Bishop Walters and Mr. Hayes. They are holding meetings in various parts of the country, and I feel rather sure now that I have got them down to a sensible and helpful basis their work will be along right lines. Your suggestion in regard to having Wm. H. Lewis appear at some of the meetings is a good one and this will be done.

Just as far as possible I shall keep an eye on the whole situation during your absence in the West. I feel quite sure that your Western trip is going to result in placing you even deeper in the hearts of the people than you are today.

I am glad to note that the South is quieting down. Yours very truly,

Booker T. Washington

TLS Theodore Roosevelt Papers DLC.

To William Edward Burghardt Du Bois

New York City. March 27, 1903

Dear Dr. Du Bois: I am in receipt of your letter of March 20th. The definite date for the meeting has not been fixed. It is a very difficult matter to set a date where so large a number of busy people are concerned that will bring together the majority of the people we want, for that reason the matter has dragged. All the people invited, however, are willing to attend. I have been working at the matter ever since we had our meeting at Tuskegee. I am very much afraid however, that it will be impossible to have the meeting in any month except April unless we defer it until June. Yours truly,

Booker T. Washington

TLS   W. E. B. Du Bois Papers   MU.

To Glenn R. LeRoy[1]

New York. March 31, 1903

Dear Sir: I thank you very much for writing me regarding your employing a number of our people in your business. Although I am exceedingly busy and pressed with many important matters at the present time, I cannot refrain from taking a minute in which to write you.

In the first place, I want to thank you for giving this opportunity to our people to show what they can do in a new direction. There is perhaps no one question that is asked me more often by people in all parts of the country than the question as to whether or not it is possible for black people to succeed in any large extent in manufacturing enterprises where skill and regularity of hours are demanded, and I very much hope that you will say in my behalf to the colored people whom you employ that the effort in your factory is being watched and will be watched with the greatest interest by the people in many parts of the country. If they succeed it will open the way for our people to be employed in the same direction elsewhere; if they fail it will go a long ways toward making people hesitate about giving them a chance in the same direction anywhere else. For these reasons it is especially important that every individual try to take the greatest pride in his work and be just as prompt, careful and systematic in performing his duty as possible. One of the weak points in connection with our people being employed in such work is that too many of them yield to the temptation to go off on excursions, picnics, etc., when their work demands their time and attention. People who are not prompt in beginning their work at the hour specified and who stay away from their work one or two days in the week without notifying their employers that they are to be absent are not the kind of people to get ahead. When I was a youth I used to work in a coal mine and in a salt furnace, but I always made it a rule to try to get to my work some minutes before the hour to begin work in the morning and if necessary to remain longer in the evening than anybody else, in this way I soon got to the point where my employer was willing to raise my wages without my asking him to do it. It is the individual who can be depended upon from day to day to do his full duty that is always sought for and is the first one to be promoted when there is an opportunity for promotion.

It would be a matter of the deepest regret to me and to many members of the race if our people failed to take the fullest advantage of the opportunity which you are offering them in your factory. If the opportunity ever offers itself I shall hope to see for myself the people that you are employing and the work that they are doing; in the meantime it is my urgent wish that each one do his full duty and more than his duty. By following this course they will not only make your own business succeed but each one will be placed in a position where he can save money, buy a home and make himself happy, comfortable and useful. Yours truly,

[Booker T. Washington]

TLc   Con. 550   BTW Papers   DLC.

1 Glenn R. LeRoy, a white man born in South Carolina in 1859, was proprietor of the LeRoy Shirt Waist Co., in Berkeley, Va.

From Emmett Jay Scott

Tuskegee, Ala., March 31, 1903

Dear Mr. Washington: I write to say that Miss Anthony, accompanied by her sister, Miss Emily Howland, and five others, spent

Sunday and Monday at the school arriving here Saturday evening, however. It rained all of Saturday night and Sunday and so I had exercises at the Chapel at four o'clock instead of at night both for the benefit of the students and for the benefit of the visitors. The exercises were the same as are usually followed on Sunday evenings. Miss Howland and Miss Anthony and Miss Harriet May Mills,[1] New York Organizer of the National Woman's Suffrage Association, spoke. The others were introduced and all in all the occasion was one of interest and profit, I think to all here.

All of the girls were required to march across the platform single file and the opportunity provided for them to shake hands with Miss Anthony. I think that she and they both enjoyed it very much indeed.

Miss Howland has gone from Tuskegee to Miss White's school, to Calhoun, Kowaliga and Camp Hill. Her interest in the school has not abated one single bit. Yours truly,

Emmett J. Scott

TLS   Con. 249   BTW Papers   DLC.

[1] Harriet May Mills (b. 1857) was a lecturer on the poet Robert Browning and a leader of the New York State Woman Suffrage Association from 1892 to 1913.

To William A. Pledger

New York. April 6, 1903

Personal.

Dear Col. Pledger: Adams and I had a conference with Bishop Walters last night. It seems to be the Bishop's opinion that you are going to stand for the presidency of the Council against Fortune. As I remember our conversation when I passed through Atlanta you said that you were going to support Fortune. As you know, there is going to be sharp opposition to Fortune. You of course have a right to run if you desire, I simply however, want to know your views on the subject if you are willing to state them. It seems to me there are two reasons why Fortune should be re-elected; one is that it is the custom in all such bodies to give a man the second term; the second is he is absent and is not on the ground to look out for his own interests. I do not know where the Bishop got his information neither did I tell him what you said to me, but I thought I would take the matter up directly with you. Yours truly,

[Booker T. Washington]

TLc Con. 249 BTW Papers DLC.

To Emmett Jay Scott

Hotel Manhattan, New York. April 6, 1903

Dear Mr. Scott: I have your letter of April 2d regarding your interview with Bishop Clinton and thank you very much for the information which it contains. I can use it to good advantage.

Bishop Walters, Adams and myself had a long conference here yesterday. I think it is rather clear that Bishop Walters is going to try to be president of the Council again, though he promised Adams and myself to support Fortune, but he is laying a great deal of stress on the opposition which he seems to have found throughout the country against Fortune.

I am very glad to learn through your telegram that Dr. D. K. Pearsons[1] is at the school. I had no idea he was to be there and hope that he got a good impression and that no stone was left unturned to let him see the real work of the school. Yours truly,

Booker T. Washington

TLS Con. 275 BTW Papers DLC.

1 Daniel Kimball Pearsons (1820–1912), physician, businessman, and philanthropist, donated money on a matching-fund basis to more than forty small colleges and secondary schools.

From William A. Pledger

Atlanta, Ga., April 13th, 1903

My dear Washington: I have your letter of April 6th, and have to say in reply that I am a little astonished at your asking me the question you do, since your knowledge of me ought to convince you that I never desert a friend, and especially would I not when he was absent, though I wanted the Prize.

I told you plainly, when I saw you, that I was for Fortune's re-election; I so stand now. What you want to do, is to keep the Bee out of old man Walters' Bonnet.

With best wishes, I am, Yours truly,

W. A. Pledger

TLS   Con. 271   BTW Papers   DLC.   Addressed to BTW in New York.

Extracts from an Address in New York City[1]

Madison Square Garden Concert Hall, New York, April 14, [1903]

The Tuskegee Normal and Industrial Institute, at Tuskegee, Alabama, is the outgrowth of the efforts of General S. C. Armstrong of the Hampton Institute in Virginia. General Armstrong was one of the great seers and prophets who realized that the task of the nation was not fulfilled when the shackles of physical slavery were struck from the limbs of the millions of slaves of the South. He realized that nine millions of human beings steeped in ignorance, minus experience, could be but half free. He foresaw that the nation must have a new birth and a new freedom, and that this regeneration must include the industrial, intellectual, and moral and religious freedom of the ex-slaves. Further, in refusing to return to his comfortable Northern home after the surrender at Appomattox, and in deciding to remain south to help in fighting for freedom in the larger and higher sense, General Armstrong appreciated as few Americans have, that the North owed an un[ful]filled duty to the South.

General Armstrong said by word and action that it was unjust to leave the South with its industrial system disorganized and overturned in the midst of a poverty that forbade the proper education of the white youth — to say nothing of the millions of recently emancipated black children.

In this connection I am glad that we have another great American and Christian statesman in the person of Hon. Grover Cleveland, who is manifesting by his presence and words here this evening that he too is conscious of the fact that the lifting up of the Negro is not alone Tuskegee's problem, not alone the Negro's concern, not alone the South's duty, but is the problem of the nation, because the whole people were responsible for the introduction and perpetuation of American slavery. In behalf of our struggling race I want to thank you, Mr. Cleveland, for your deep interest, and to say to you that because of your interest and faith in us we shall see to it that the nation is not disappointed in our progress nor in our usefulness.

The most fundamental and far-reaching deed that has been accomplished during the last quarter of a century has been that by which the Negro has been helped to find himself and to learn the secret of civilization — to learn that there are a few simple, cardinal principles upon which a race must start its upward course unless it would fail, and its last estate be worse than its first. In teaching this lesson perhaps the Tuskegee Institute has had some small share. In the founding of this institution two special points were kept in view; first, to teach the Negro the difference between being worked and working; to teach him that being worked meant degradation, and that working meant civilization — to teach him that all forms of labor were honorable and all idleness disgraceful. Further, in the founding of the Tuskegee school it was kept in mind that all races that have got upon their feet and remained there have done so largely by laying an economic foundation and by beginning in the proper cultivation and ownership of the soil. With this in view from the first we have made agriculture in all its branches the basis of our training at Tuskegee. We began teaching agriculture with one hoe and a blind mule. The institution has gradually grown until it owns two thousand acres of land, over seven hundred of which are cultivated by the students. Not only are the students taught how to secure their living from the soil, but to love agricultural life to the extent that they will return to the country districts to reside and not yield to the temptation of going to a city and trying to live by their wits.

In addition to the 1418 students now enrolled at Tuskegee we have sent out into the world over six thousand men and women who have been more or less helped, and who are devoting their lives as industrial workers and teachers. The students at Tuskegee receive training in 22 industrial departments, each of which gives training at some work at which they can find immediate employment in the South. Largely by the labor of the students the institution has been built up to the point where it has property in lands and buildings to the amount of $430,000.

But the glory and the value of our work is not in land, buildings or industries. It is in the work of the men and women who have been trained at Tuskegee, who are willing to forget themselves — to lose themselves in earnest efforts to lift up their fellows. What is this work? In the case of a people long restrained in physical bondage it was but natural that at the beginning of their new life a large proportion of them should interpret freedom for license. But graduates from the Hampton, Tuskegee and other institutions in the South are teaching the race that there are several kinds of freedom, that there is a freedom that is apparent and one that is real, a superficial freedom, and one that is substantial; a freedom that is temporary and deceptive, and one that is abiding and permanent; one that ministers to the lower appetites and passions, and one that encourages growth in the higher and sweeter things of life; a freedom that is forced, and one that is the result of forbearance, struggle and self-sacrifice. After all, though, our men and women are teaching the people that there is but one kind of freedom that is worth the name, and that is the one embodied in the words of the great master centuries ago: "And ye shall know the truth and the truth shall make you free."

We can benefit a race only as we can an individual, and that is by dealing frankly, honestly with it — by giving it the truth which shall make it free in reality. Further, in the words of another, the Tuskegee workers are teaching that which is the bedrock of all progress, that freedom in its highest and broadest sense can never be a bequest — it must be a conquest. Freedom comes through seeming restriction. Those who are most truly free today are those who have passed through the greatest trials and discipline, and those who have exercised the most dogged persistence and determination.

In the development of a race there are many local, temporary and side issues to which one can devote himself if he so choose, or he can aim to keep true in the main to matters more fundamental, and trust in a large degree to time for a growth in a sense of justice — trust to time for a logical and natural re-adjustment of all human rights around any worthy and deserving race. The great human law which always recognizes and rewards merit is universal — is everlasting.

In the case of my race I believe that the teachings of history as well as the results of everyday observation, should convince us that we shall make our most enduring progress by laying the foundation carefully, patiently, in the ownership of the soil, the exercise of habits of industry and economy, the saving of money and in the securing of the most complete education of hand and head, and the exercise of the Christian virtues. There is nothing new or startling in this. It is the old, old road that all races have had to travel which have got upon their feet. Standing tonight before this audience, when the very soul of my race is aching and seeking guidance as never before, I say deliberately that I know no other road. If I knew how to find more speedy and prompt relief, and did not point the way at any cost, I should be a coward and a hypocrite. Other agencies can and should assist, but after all we must depend mainly upon the principles to which I have referred for success.

One farm bought, one house built, one home sweetly and intelligently kept, one man who is the largest tax payer or has the largest bank account, one school or church maintained, one factory running successfully, one truck garden profitably cultivated, one patient cured by a Negro doctor, one sermon well preached, one life cleanly lived, these will tell more in our favor than all the abstract eloquence that can be summoned to plead our cause. Our pathway must be up through the soil, up through swamps, up through forests, up through the streams, the rocks, up through commerce, education and religion.

I have referred to the task and the duty of my race. Your race also has a tremendous responsibility and a rare privilege in connection with the elevation of my people. Unlike other races we did not come among you unbidden; our presence here was forced.

When a weaker and inexperienced race is projected, as it were, suddenly, as was true of my race, into the midst of a stronger and more civilized people, there are two dangers to be guarded against; one is that the stronger race will have its conscience seared and high sense of justice hardened and blunted by yielding to the temptation to repress the growth of the weaker race — in a word that the stronger race will have its progress retarded by reason of the presence of the more unfortunate race. The other danger is that the new race will yield to the temptation to seek the more superficial appearances of growth and civilization, rather than the reality, that the weaker race, seeing all about it evidences of great progress in wealth, intellect, and government, will seek possession of these elements of civilization which it has taken other races centuries to obtain through hard, natural, logical struggle. We cannot get something for nothing. Every race that gets up has to pay the price of beginning at the bottom and struggling up, largely through its own efforts.

Your duty, then, as I see it, is to help your race to be patient and just in relation to my race. My duty is to help my race to be patient with itself and just to itself. This, I confess, for my race is not an easy programme. When patience is suggested it is not unreasonable that one should be reminded, as he often is, of the long years of servitude, of the unfortunate years of reconstruction, of the anxious present, and that many should cry out in the anguish of their souls: "How long? Oh Lord, how long?"

The real and vital problem before this country in reference to my race is not in the failure of the fundamental laws, but in our failure to prepare all the people to fulfill the duties of citizenship pre-supposed by the fundamental laws.

The solution of the great race problem question is not in the abuse of the South by the North, not in the abuse of the North by the South, not in condemning the Negro, nor the Negro cursing the white man, not in colonization, not in expatriation, not in amalgamation or extermination, but it is in honest, sympathetic cooperation between the races. In this connection may I add that there have been few greater opportunities in the history of the world for a great statesman and philanthropist to do something that should redeem nearly a third of our country, and lift up the ignorant of both races than is presented by conditions now existing at the South.

Let us lay aside narrowness and bitterness, and with calmness face the great problem now before us.

At the Tuskegee Institute, in Alabama, we are trying to do our duty not only to the Negro but to the whole South, by starting the

Negro off in his new life as an intelligent, skilled and conservative worker in the soil, in wood, metal, and in the home — as a producer and a tax payer — to the end that he may naturally, gradually grow into all the duties and privileges of citizenship.

In conclusion may I add that the Negro, unlike the Indian, the original Mexican, or the Hawaiian, so far from dying out when in contact with a different or stronger race has continued to increase in numbers and influence. We seem to be the only race that is able to look the white man in the face, to live by his side and not only exist but to increase. So, then, I want to emphasize the truth that whether we are of Northern or Southern birth, whether we are with or without sympathy for the Negro, whether we are black or white, we must face the hard, stubborn fact that whether in bondage or in freedom, whether in ignorance or intelligence, that in spite of all predictions and scientific conclusions to the contrary, the Negro has continued year by year to increase in number until from twenty slaves the race has grown into nine millions of freemen, and there are no signs based upon proper evidence that the same ratio of increase will not hold good in the future.

You of the North owe an unfulfilled duty to the Negro, and equal duty to your white brethren in the South in assisting them to help to remove the load of ignorance resting upon my race. Both as slaves and as freemen we have striven to serve the interests of this country as best we could. We have, in a large measure, cleared the forests, builded the railways, tunneled the mountains, mined the coal, grown the tobacco, cotton, rice and cane upon which a large part of the wealth of the country is founded. We have never disturbed the country by strikes, lockouts or riots. In the days of the civil war, when helpless women and children were entrusted to our keeping in the absence of the master, no one ever suffered harm or went without food. We always have stood ready to defend the flag, and have been true to the Stars and Stripes. This is our past. With such a record I believe that all will agree with me that there is in this country enough sympathy and generosity to make of our people a still stronger force in the power and civilization of our nation.

TM   Con. 956   BTW Papers   DLC.

[1] BTW spoke to an audience composed largely of his northern white backers and friends. Among those in attendance were Lyman Abbott, Nicholas Murray Butler, William H. Baldwin, Jr., George Foster Peabody, Mrs. Collis P. Huntington, St. Clair

McKelway, John D. Crimmins, Oswald Garrison Villard, Jacob Schiff, and William Jay Schieffelin. Mr. and Mrs. Andrew Carnegie shared their box with Mrs. Grover Cleveland while the former president presided at the meeting. Three days after this address Carnegie gave $600,000 worth of U.S. Steel bonds to Tuskegee for the school's endowment fund.

Grover Cleveland's remarks had a racist tone, but apparently this was largely unnoticed by the white audience. The former president referred to certain "racial and slavery-bred imperfections and deficiencies" that could not be changed by emancipation or civil rights. He stated that the nine million blacks represented "a grievous amount of ignorance, a sad amount of laziness and thriftlessness." Cleveland went on to say that the race problem would be solved if left in the hands of responsible white men in the South, and urged that northerners show more tolerance of southern prejudice. (New York *Times*, Apr. 15, 1903, 1–2.) Even Emmett Scott overlooked the effects of such remarks and wrote BTW that he was sure Cleveland's presence at the meeting would result in some large donations. (Apr. 15, 1903, Con. 249, BTW Papers, DLC.)

Other speakers also laced their praise of BTW and Tuskegee with racist remarks. Edgar Gardner Murphy of the Southern Education Board based his appeal for aid to blacks on the notion that if blacks represented a decaying race then "the rotting body of its dissolution is polluting the atmosphere we breathe." "The man who has so much time to waste," he said, "that he can afford to waste time in morbid apprehensions as to the lurid perils of racial amalgamation is the very last man who can afford to refuse approval to Tuskegee's work. For Tuskegee is peculiarly an institution which, amid all the bewildering and rasping nonsense of pro-negro sentimentality, has stood with incomparable dignity and sanity by the great evident landmarks of racial and personal self-respect." (Address of Edgar Gardner Murphy, Apr. 14, 1903, Con. 268, BTW Papers, DLC.)

Ellen Collins, one of those in attendance, wrote BTW: "I laughed when Mr. Abbott spoke of the superiority of the white race — for I remembered your having told me that it happened every time you had a white man to speak at a meeting. But it seemed to us a fine gathering, now for contributions." (Apr. 15, 1903, Con. 254, BTW Papers, DLC.)

From William Lewis Bulkley[1]

New York, N.Y., 4/16, 1903

Dear Mr. Washington; Great interest was aroused and great pleasure given, when I announced to teachers and pupils that you would probably be with us for a few moments to-morrow eve. I sincerely hope nothing will interfere with your coming. It would be a severe disappointment. The children and the young people look forward to a word of advice from their great leader.

I shall spread the news in the neighborhood, and hope to have as many as our small assembly-room will accom[m]odate. Very sincerely yours,

W. L. Bulkley

ALS Con. 251 BTW Papers DLC.

1 William Lewis Bulkley (1861–1933), after receiving a Ph.D. at Syracuse University in 1893, became a seventh-grade teacher in New York City. In 1899 he became principal of all-black P. S. 80, and in 1909 he became the first black principal of a predominantly white school, P. S. 125. Though ideologically a supporter of W. E. B. Du Bois, Bulkley considered industrial education useful, and was one of the founders of the National Urban League as well as the NAACP. (Osofsky, *Harlem*, 62–67.)

Andrew Carnegie to William Henry Baldwin, Jr.[1]

New York, April 17, 1903

My dear Mr. Baldwin: I have instructed Mr. Franks, Sec'y, to deliver to you as Trustee Tuskegee, $600,000. 5% U.S. Steel Co. Bonds, to complete the Endowment Fund as per circular.

One condition only — the revenue of one hundred and fifty thousand of these bonds is to be subject to Booker Washington's order to be used by him first for his wants and those of his family during his life or the life of his widow. If any surplus [is] left he can use it for Tuskegee. I wish that great and good man to be free from pecuniary cares that he may devote himself wholly to his great mission.

To me he seems one of the foremost of living men because his work is unique. The modern Moses, who leads his race and lifts it through Education to even better and higher things than a land overflowing with milk and honey. History is to know two Washingtons, one white, the other black, both Fathers of their People. I am satisfied that the serious race question of the South is to be solved wisely, only by following Booker Washington's policy which he seems to have [been] specially born — a slave among slaves — to establish, and even in his own day, greatly to advance.

So glad to be able to assist this good work in which you and others are engaged. Truly yours,

Andrew Carnegie

TLSr Copy Con. 18 BTW Papers DLC.

¹ This is a notarized copy of the original grant letter, which was revised later but given the same date. See below. Another copy of Carnegie's original letter is in Con. 961, BTW Papers, DLC, along with an autograph statement of thanks by BTW: "You have helped the school more than you realize, for in addition to the interest in your gift the institution will hereafter be relieved from paying any salary to either Mrs. Washington or myself. We could not think of accepting a salary in addition to your gift, and besides I feel quite sure that there will be a surplus for the school each year after the needs of myself and Mrs. Washington have been provided for."

Andrew Carnegie to William Henry Baldwin, Jr.¹

New York   April 17th 1903

My Dear Friend   I have instructed Mr Franks my Cashier to deliver to you as Trustee of Tuskegee Six hundred thousand dollars 5% U S Steel Co 1st Mortage Bonds for the Endowment Fund.

I give this without reservation except that I require that suitable provision be made from the gift for the wants of Booker Washington & his family during his own or his wifes life. I wish that great & good man to be entirely free from pecuniary cares that he may be free to devote himself to his great mission.

To me he seems one of the greatest of living men because his work is unique. The modern Moses, who leads his race and lifts it through Education, to even better and higher things than a land overflowing with milk & honey. History is to tell of two Washington's one white, the other Black both Fathers of their people.

I am satisfied that the serious race problem of the South is to be solved wisely only through Mr Washington's policy of Education — which he seems to have been specially born — a slave among slaves — to establish and in his own day greatly to advance.

Glad am I to be able to assist this good work in which you and others so zealously labor. Truly yours,

Andrew Carnegie

ALS BTW Papers ATT.

¹ This is the revised version of Carnegie's grant letter, omitting specific reference to the $150,000 that was to be set aside for BTW and his family. While it is dated Apr. 17, the date of Carnegie's original gift, it was probably written on Apr. 23 after BTW had a conference with Carnegie. BTW and several members of the Tuskegee

board of trustees were afraid that the mention of such a large sum given to BTW personally would generate controversy in the South. (See BTW to Baldwin, Apr. 21, Baldwin to BTW, Apr. 21, BTW to Baldwin, Apr. 22, BTW to Grover Cleveland, Apr. 23, BTW to Baldwin, Apr. 23, 1903, below.) Andrew Carnegie remembered the circumstances of the revision more romantically in his autobiography. "Mr. Washington called upon me a few days after my gift of six hundred thousand dollars was made to Tuskegee," Carnegie recalled, "and asked if he might be allowed to make one suggestion. I said, 'certainly.'

" 'You have kindly specified that a sum from that fund be set aside for the future support of myself and wife during our lives, and we are very grateful, but Mr. Carnegie, the sum is far beyond our needs and will seem to my race a fortune. Some might feel that I was no longer a poor man giving my services without thought of saving money. Would you have any objection to changing that clause, striking out the sum, and substituting "only suitable provision"? I'll trust the trustees. Mrs. Washington and myself need very little.'

"I did so, and the deed now stands, but when Mr. Baldwin asked for the original letter to exchange it for the substitute, he told me that the noble soul objected. That document addressed to him was to be preserved forever, and handed down; but he would put it aside and let the substitute go on file." (*Autobiography of Andrew Carnegie*, 265–66.)

To Grover Cleveland

New York City, April 19, 1903

My dear Mr. Cleveland: The enclosed copy of a letter which came yesterday will give you some idea of how the presence of yourself and Mrs. Cleveland helped us at our meeting on the fourteenth. We are not going to give this to the public just now. In addition to this great and unexpected gift we have received up to the present $17,000. and gifts are still coming in.

It is very encouraging to note how your address has been received throughout the country and to note especially the sensible manner in which my own people have received it.

You can never know just how grateful we are to both yourself and Mrs. Cleveland for your help and interest. Yours Sincerely,

Booker T. Washington

ALS   Grover Cleveland Papers   DLC.   Enclosed was the letter from Andrew Carnegie to William Henry Baldwin, Jr., Apr. 17, 1903, above.

From William Henry Baldwin, Jr.

Washington DC   Apl 21 [1903]

Page, Buttrick, Peabody and I approve provided paragraph of your statement is published complete by associated press. Ogden and Murphy dissent.

W H Baldwin Jr.

TWSr Con. 542 BTW Papers DLC.

To William Henry Baldwin, Jr.

[New York City] April 21, 1903

Telegram received, long talk with Jesup and he urges that Carnegie's letter be given public at once and a statement should accompany it to the effect that trustees will hold a formal meeting soon to take action in accepting gift and that at this meeting of trustees would be proper time for me to declare my intentions in regard to use of money given me personally. He further states that since the money is given to trustees it is not proper for me to state now what I will do regarding it but such statement should be made at trustee meeting and given to the public. He suggests not quote anything I have said to Carnegie now but later give action of trustees in accepting gift to public and also my letter to trustees in regard to use of money. This he thinks will give whole matter dignity and orderly appearance and do no harm. Shall not act until I hear from you. Answer.

W.

Might get opinion of C. W. Hare if there.

TWI Con. 542 BTW Papers DLC. Addressed to Baldwin at the Southern Education Conference in Richmond, Va.

To Roscoe Conkling Bruce

Hotel Manhattan, New York. April 21, 1903

Dear Mr. Bruce: Under all the circumstances I think it will be well to pay Dr. Du Bois' traveling expenses to Tuskegee and return for the sake of his lectures. If he chooses to be little we must teach him a lesson by bearing greater and broader than he is. Yours truly,

[Booker T. Washington]

TLc   Con. 251   BTW Papers   DLC.

To Oswald Garrison Villard

New York. April 21, 1903

Personal.
Dear Mr. Villard: In my address at Madison Square Garden the other evening you will perhaps recall that I brought out some rather plain facts regarding the poor school facilities furnished to the colored people. I had still other facts that told a more serious story but I did not use them for the reason that I did not want to give the impression that I was exaggerating. I think however, that you ought to see the enclosed copy of a contract made by a public school official with one of our students. In case you make any use of this in the Evening Post I think it well to leave out the names as it might get the individual teacher in trouble. The net result is that these people are giving $7.50 for five months with which to educate 200 children. Yours truly,

Booker T. Washington

TLS   Oswald Garrison Villard Papers   MH.   Copy of the contract is enclosed.

To William Henry Baldwin, Jr.

[New York City] April 22, 1903

Further thought makes Jesup fear effect of personal gift. McAneny[1] and Schurz[2] have same feeling. All suggest that I see Carnegie and get letter changed so as to make whole gift to trustees without naming sum for me and suggesting that trustees make larger provision for family and self or give some sum named by Carnegie. I agree to this. Call me on telephone at ten tonight.

W.

TWlr Copy Con. 542 BTW Papers DLC. A draft in BTW's hand is in Con. 281, BTW Papers, DLC.

[1] George McAneny (1869–1953), after several years as a New York newspaper reporter, became secretary of the Civil Service Reform League in 1894, when Carl Schurz was its president. As executive of the New York City Civil Service Commission in 1902 he helped write the city's civil service code. In 1909 he was elected president of the Borough of Manhattan on the Fusion ticket. He was a longtime member of the Armstrong Association of New York and a trustee of the Jeanes Fund for Rudimentary Negro Education.

[2] Carl Schurz (1829–1906), German-born publisher and reformer, came to the United States in 1852 after participation in the Revolution of 1848. Active in the antislavery movement and the Republican party, Schurz became a Union general, U.S. senator from Missouri (1869–75), organizer of the Liberal Republican party (1872), Secretary of the Interior (1877–81), and president of the National Civil Service Reform League (1892–1901). He continued throughout his life to demand civil and political equality for blacks.

From William Henry Baldwin, Jr.

Richmond Va   April 22 1903

Have message   will wire fully later today   dont believe Jesups Judgement good   endowment Committee have full powers to accept.

W H Baldwin Jr

HWSr Con. 542 BTW Papers DLC.

To Grover Cleveland

New York. April 23d, 1903

My dear Mr. Cleveland: After thinking the matter over very carefully and consulting with a few of my friends, I felt convinced that to have Mr. Carnegie's letter go out to the public in the form that it was originally written, of which I sent you a copy, would prove misleading and hurtful to my own influence. I could not feel that to have the public informed that I had had the interest on so large a sum as $150,000 placed at my disposal would be the wisest thing and so I had a full consultation with Mr. Carnegie on the subject and got him to re-write the letter, leaving, as you will see, the matter of provision for me and my family according to his request to the Trustees; in this way I am quite sure that the matter can be arranged in a satisfactory way in a manner to carry out Mr. Carnegie's original desire and at the same time not create a wrong impression.

I send you a copy of the new letter. Yours very truly,

Booker T. Washington

TLS   Grover Cleveland Papers   DLC.

To William Henry Baldwin, Jr.

[New York City] April 23, 1903

Long conference with Carnegie. Matter arranged in a way that I am sure will be most satisfactory to all concerned. Letter will appear in tomorrow morning's papers.

W.

TWIr   Con. 542   BTW Papers   DLC.

To Warren Logan

[New York City] April 23, 1903

You can announce to teachers and students that Mr. Andrew Carnegie has given six hundred thousand dollars towards endowment fund. Think it good idea for short telegram to be sent him representing feelings of students and teachers. He sails tomorrow night. Dont give this to papers as that will be done from this end.

Booker T. Washington

TWSr Copy   Con. 542   BTW Papers   DLC.

Warren Logan to Andrew Carnegie

[Tuskegee, Ala.] April 23, 1903

Principal Washington has just communicated to the school your generous gift of six hundred thousand dollars. Our students and teachers have hailed the news with every demonstration of joy because of the great relief it will afford Principal Washington no less than for the value of the gift in assuring the permanency of the work. Teachers and students alike ask me to transmit this expression of gratitude to you.

Warren Logan, Treasurer

TWSr Copy   Con. 542   BTW Papers   DLC.

To Margaret James Murray Washington

[New York City] April 24, 1903

Dont give out any interview to newspapers regarding that gift.

B. T. W.

TWIr   Con. 542   BTW Papers   DLC.   Addressed to Boston, Mass.

A News Item in the New York *Sun*

New York, April 24, 1903

MR. CARNEGIE GIVES $600,000
TO ENDOW BOOKER WASHINGTON'S TUSKEGEE INSTITUTE

IRONMASTER CALLS HIM THE MODERN MOSES
AND FATHER OF HIS RACE, AND REQUIRES
THAT PROVISION BE MADE FOR HIS FAMILY
THAT HE MAY WORK ON FREE FROM CARE

Andrew Carnegie, who attended the meeting to aid Tuskegee Institute, at which ex-President Cleveland presided, has now sent to the trustees of the institute a gift of $600,000 toward the endowment fund.

The gift is made through Trustee William H. Baldwin, Jr. One condition is attached to it, and with that the trustees will cheerfully comply. Mr. Carnegie requires that provision shall be made by the trustees for the wants of President Booker T. Washington and his family during his own or his wife's lifetime.

"To me," Mr. Carnegie writes, "he seems one of the greatest of living men, the modern Moses, who leads his race and lifts it through education to even better and higher things than a land overflowing with milk and honey."

The sum of $600,000 was what Booker Washington asked for at the Carnegie Hall meeting to add to the endowment fund. It was also announced that $56,000 was urgently needed for current expenses.

The trustees of the institute will meet next week to take formal action in accepting the gift and at the same time to take measures to increase the endowment still further. They will then provide for Mr. Washington and his family. Three members of the endowment fund committee, Mr. Baldwin, Robert C. Ogden and George Foster Peabody, are now attending a conference at Richmond, Va.

.   .   .   .[1]

To a SUN reporter who saw him last night at the Hotel Manhattan Booker T. Washington said that Mr. Carnegie's gift came as a great surprise to him.

"The expenses of the Tuskegee school," said he, "are $152,000 a year, the greater part of which I have had to raise. About $102,000 of that must be raised every year. The income from this $600,000 which Mr. Carnegie gives us will be used very largely toward decreasing the amount I have to raise annually by subscription. But it will not be sufficient to cover the whole amount.

"We have already about $410,000 in our endowment fund. Mr. Carnegie's gift will raise it to more than a million. But we really need $2,000,000 to relieve the school from all necessity. However, we are most grateful to Mr. Carnegie for this gift. Aside from that he has given us a library building at Tuskegee. He gave us $20,000 for the library about four years ago.

"I think that was the first time I ever saw him. I called upon him. He told me that he had read my book 'Up From Slavery,' had become interested and had a copy of the book in his library at Skibo Castle.

"I don't know of any special reason that induced him to make his gift at this time, but I think he had his mind made up to do something for the colored people.

"I think he had in mind the fact that I ought to have a chance to devote more of my time to remaining at the school, instead of being compelled to be away from it so much. The principal of the gift is not to be touched; only the income.

"As soon as I received the news I telegraphed it to the school.

"I may say that Mr. Carnegie has been giving us quietly, all along, $10,000 a year. That has not been known publicly. This morning I called to thank him for the new gift. We had a long and pleasant chat. Just what we talked about I cannot reveal. But I can say that the entire South, including the negro race, will thank Mr. Carnegie for his large gift. I think and I hope it will bring others.

"I wouldn't like it to go forth that this would relieve the school from all necessity, but, as I said before, we are very grateful. Mr. Carnegie had promised to go to the school in February, but he was under the weather and was compelled to forego the visit."

Mr. Washington said that there are now 1,408 students at the school. They pay their own board in labor or in cash, but mainly in labor. They buy their books, but the cost of tuition constitutes a large part of the school's expense account.

Asked if he thought Mr. Cleveland's speech at the Madison

Square Concert Hall meeting had in any way influenced Mr. Carnegie to make the $600,000 gift, Mr. Washington said he did not know. Mr. Cleveland, however, was Mr. Carnegie's guest while here to attend the meeting. As a result of that meeting $18,000 was raised, most of which will go toward paying the current expenses of the school.

Mr. Carnegie will sail for Europe to-morrow. He will go aboard the steamer to-night.

New York *Sun*, Apr. 24, 1903, 1.

1 The final version of Carnegie's letter of gift, Apr. 17, 1903, has been omitted here. See above.

From Francis Jackson Garrison

Boston, April 24, 1903

Dear Mr. Washington: I am rejoiced beyond measure by the announcement in this morning's paper of Carnegie's gift to Tuskegee. I remarked to your wife the other day, when she was calling here, that I felt that in your speech the other night you opened the door very pointedly for him to do this, and I have felt that he could not long refrain from making a large addition to your endowment fund. If I am not mistaken, this gift of his will carry it up to a million dollars, and as he has in some other cases added to or duplicated his first gift, I trust that he will not be content until he has added another million or two to your fund. I trust also his example will prove an example, and not deter others from doing likewise.

I read the report of the Cleveland meeting with deep interest, but not, I must confess, without much disturbance of mind, for I felt that Cleveland's speech would be received precisely in the way it was by the Southern press, and made the most of as an endorsement of their ever-emboldened demand for white domination. The speech was able and carefully worded, and its closing paragraph set no limit to the possibilities of the race, for it distinctly intimated that they were certain, with a proper foundation and equipment, to break through "any crust of prejudice," but the first effect of the speech is to weaken the already too weak moral resistance of the North to the unjust interpretation and application of the new constitutions, and to the dogged purpose of the Southern whites to shut the door of hope to all people of color, regardless of their intelligence and character. However, I hope the munificence of Carnegie, with his glowing letter of presentation, will do something to offset the ill effects of Cleveland's declaration, and that the good work will go steadily forward.

I am much disappointed at receiving a note from Mrs. Washington this morning saying that she cannot come and spend the night with us, as she had planned, but I hope we shall have you both later in the season. Yours very truly,

Francis J. Garrison

P.S. I am sending you the May *Atlantic* with an article on the Mulatto as a Factor in the Race Problem,[1] which I read for the first time last evening, & which I deeply regret that Mr. Perry has published, for it is vicious in spirit & purpose & alike contemptious & unchristian. I wish that it would be answered by a full-blooded negro, as Sam R. Ward[2] replied to Capt. Rynders in N.Y., in 1850. (See chapter on The Rynders Mob in Vol. 3, of my father's Life, when you have a chance.)[3]

TLS Con. 249 BTW Papers DLC. Postscript in Garrison's hand.

[1] Alfred Holt Stone, "The Mulatto Factor in the Race Problem," *Atlantic Monthly*, 91 (May 1903), 658–62. The article contended that blacks were "undeveloped" and innately inferior and that signs of their progress were traceable to the "white blood" in mulattoes and those of lighter skin.

[2] Samuel Ringgold Ward (1817–66) was a leading black abolitionist. Born on the Eastern Shore of Maryland, he became a teacher in black schools in New York City and an agent of the American Anti-Slavery Society and the New York Anti-Slavery Society; he was known as "the black Daniel Webster" because of his oratorical ability. Ordained as a Congregational minister in 1839, he was pastor of several churches in New York State.

[3] See *William Lloyd Garrison*, 3:272–312. Ward's demeanor and eloquence, during a confrontation between abolitionists and their northern critics, refuted the claim of a hostile speaker, Isaiah Rynders, that blacks were subhuman.

From Emmett Jay Scott

Tuskegee, Ala., April 24, 1903

Dear Mr. Washington: The following is the telegram sent to the different colored people as suggested by you: "Please wire Mr. Andrew Carnegie, 5 West 51st Street, New York, to-day sure thanks for gift of six hundred thousand dollars to this institution. Thank him for generous interest in race. Pay telegram and send memo, charge to me. (Signed) Emmett J. Scott."

It has been sent to the following: Mr. S. Laing Williams, Mr. George L. Knox, E. L. Blackshear, C. N. Love,[1] T. W. Jones, J. C. Napier, Dr. I. B. Scott, E. E. Cooper, R. H. Terrell, Dr. Courtney, and H. T. Kealing. Very truly yours,

E J Scott

TLS Con. 272 BTW Papers DLC.

[1] Charles N. Love (1862–ca. 1945) was editor and owner of the Houston *Texas Freeman* after E. J. Scott moved to Tuskegee in 1897. In the 1930s he was vice-president of the Informer Publishing Co.

Gordon Macdonald[1]
to the Editor of the Washington *Post*[2]

Montgomery, Alabama. [ca. Apr. 28] 1903

Editor Post: In the memorable words of David B. Hill, "I am a Democrat," but, unlike that illustrious statesman, I am a Democrat all the time. Hence, what I write in apology of a Republican President may well be taken as truth wrung from a most reluctant source.

The entire Democratic press has for months been assailing the President for his appointments to offices of negroes in the South in localities where such appointments are particularly offensive, the appointment of Crum at Charleston being a typical case. At the same time, and with singular accord, these same newspapers have been lauding Booker T. Washington for his educational and political wisdom. Even Mr. Carnegie has turned aside from his efforts to relieve the painful congestion of his finances by donating public libraries and "planked down" $600,000 for the benefit of this shrewd darkey and his alleged beneficial Tuskegee propaganda. Mr. Cleveland, eschewing for the time duck-hunting and fishing, has enlightened the world with what he thinks of Washington, and the utterances of this ponderous "occasional Democrat" have been praised by Republicans and Democrats alike. But they are all — even the quasi-Republicans — down on the President for doing exactly what this same Booker persuaded him to do! It is time that somebody was protesting against this injustice to the President. It is high time that these dark and disreputable political children were charged up to their real father and not to their mere wet-nurse. With all the commendable patience of Job's young friend, "Elihu, the son of Barachel the Buzzite, of the children of Ram," I have been waiting for some one to tell the truth, both of Theodore the Swift and of Booker the Crafty. But none has spoken. So, as did the indignant Elihu, &c., &c., &c., I will "lift up my voice," providing you give it utterance to the public.

It does not call for any excessive effort of intelligence or of memory to know that not one negro has been appointed to any office of importance in the South save at Washington's advice and persuasion of the President. Nor can any man be so absurdly foolish as not to know that Washington, born and raised in the South, knows as well as he knows anything (save, perhaps, "the feathering of his nest") the intense and immutable objections of all Southern white men to such appointments. Yet Washington is the man who secured all these appointments, especially that of Crum. It is possible that the President did not know any better. It is impossible that Washington could be ignorant; yet the deluded press and a few of the people continue to abuse the President and belaud Washington. This state of affairs is grossly unjust. Of course, some men would, on discovering their mistake, have retracted and done better. But the Lord did not construct Roosevelt on these lines. He must govern after the manner of the laws of the Medes and Persians, which alter not. He is of those who, having selected a road, will follow it even unto hell. That is the way he was made, and we must take him — or get rid of him — with this fixed fact in view.

So much in apology for the President. Of course, if this is ever called to his attention, he will vehemently repudiate the apology, perhaps speak swear words of his apologist. But what is that to the triumph of Eternal Truth?

Now having demonstrated who is really responsible for the negro appointments in the South, let me turn the searchlight of truth on the renowned Booker and his doings — his real doings. This wonderfully shrewd negro has convinced not only the naturally gullible Northern people that his propaganda is of infinite benefit to the negroes and whites of the South, that the aims and results of his Tuskegee performances are to give young negroes an "industrial education" and not to incite them to dreams of social equality with the whites; having obtained ponderous words of commendation from the Sage of Princeton, and much more valuable cash from Carnegie, Ogden, et al., really fools most of the Southern newspapers as well! Living in Montgomery, a county adjoining Macon, wherein Tuskegee is situated, I speak whereof I know, in saying that for one genuine hardworking husbandman or artisan sent into the world by Washington's school, it afflicts this State with twenty soft-handed negro dudes and loafers, who earn a precarious living by "craps" and petit larceny or live on the hard-earned wages of cooks and washwomen, whose affections they have been enabled to ensnare. The girls graduated at this school are taught to scorn hard work, while their poor mothers toil over the washtubs and the cook stoves that their daughters may be taught music and painting — God save the mark! — and to rustle in fine dresses in a miserable imitation of white ladies. What Washington teaches by precept is shown in its results on his scholars. What he teaches by example is clear to any man who is not an idiot by nature or blinded by preference. Example is ever the thoroughest teacher of the young, and the example of Washington is the most disastrous to the rising generation of negroes that can be imagined. It teaches to his deluded pupils that social equality is a possibility and that it is near. They hear of him hobnobbing on terms of perfect equality with the President of this country. They hear of his visiting rich Northerners as a favored and petted guest. They hear of his getting his child into a fashionable school for white girls in the North. Can any of his friends deny these things with truth?

I tell the people of this country that there is no one factor more disastrous to the negro in his life and ways than this same lauded Booker Washington. He is leading his people to dream a dream of death and disaster. His "industrial education" is a blind — an idle farce. His example is the only real thing.

We are a people who have walked the ways of trouble and misery and more trouble is before us. It must be met and we must meet it alone. We only understand. And our public men are afflicted with darkened counsel.

"And when these things come to pass — and lo! they will come — then shall we know that there has been a prophet among you."

Gordon Macdonald

Washington *Post*, Apr. 30, 1903, 6.

[1] Gordon Macdonald, born in 1848, was a Montgomery lawyer. In an interview with Max B. Thrasher, Macdonald attributed to William B. Paterson, BTW's long-time rival, much of the information and many of the charges against BTW and Tuskegee in this letter. Asked if he had ever been to Tuskegee, he answered: "No, I never had any curiosity to go there." (Interview, ca. June 1, 1903, Con. 277, BTW Papers, DLC.)

[2] The Washington *Post* contained an editorial on Macdonald's letter, stating that he was a reputable person who represented the views of "a large and very important class at the South." The *Post*, however, disagreed with Macdonald and said: "In some respects we know that his information is inaccurate." The editorial stated that it was well known that BTW "did not seek the now famous dinner," and added that BTW's role in appointments of blacks to office had been exaggerated. Furthermore, the *Post* defended BTW's work at Tuskegee and said: "Booker Washington's institute offers to the colored youth an opportunity to acquire useful preparation—some craft or training whereby they can maintain themselves afterward—and that is more than can be said of the average 'institution of learning.' " (Washington *Post*, Apr. 30, 1903, 6.)

From Charles Barzillai Spahr

New York   April 30th, 1903

Dear Mr. Washington: We are just in receipt of a note from Miss Katherine Coman, a professor in Wellesley College in which she states that you share her view (and mine) regarding the perils of negro disfranchisement. Her words are, "The most thoughtful man

I met in the South conceded that the suffrage had been necessary to guard his (the negro's) civil rights. That it is still necessary Booker Washington himself will tell you." If this correctly states your view and if you are willing to be quoted as holding it, it will help those of us at the North who believe that the now popular gospel of negro disfranchisement is not only one of sad tidings to the poor but one certain to result in the hardening of the white race and the degradation of the black. In my view no material or even educational gains can make up for the negro's loss of faith that he has the rights of a man if he shows himself a man. Yours very truly,

Charles B. Spahr

TLS   Con. 272   BTW Papers   DLC.

From Charles Waddell Chesnutt

Cleveland, O. May 2, 1903

My dear Dr. Washington: I meant to have written you sooner to congratulate you on your recent good fortune in the matter of the Carnegie bequest. Any personal advantage it may bring to you, you have certainly earned, and it will greatly enhance the usefulness of Tuskegee.

I wish I could see as good results, either now or in prospect, for the policy of conciliation of the South of which you have been the most distinguished advocate. Under it, whether because of it or not I do not know, the rights of the Negro have steadily dwindled, until, by the decision of the Supreme Court in the Alabama case,[1] the Negro in the South has no rights which the government, as constituted, can compel Southern white men to respect. I believe in manhood suffrage, and the speeches of the Northern men at Richmond, truckling away the fundamental rights of citizenship, have filled me, as they did some of the Southerners present, with a very wholesome disgust. Under that decision, aided by the acquiescence of the North, and the inability of the colored race to command, by

its votes, any attention from Congress, I confidently expect to see
still further assaults upon the liberties of colored people. A people
without representation are a people without liberty, as I think so
able a man as you must admit.

With kind regards to Mrs. Washington, believe me, Sincerely
yours,

Chas. W. Chesnutt

TLS BTW Papers ATT.

1 *Giles* v. *Harris*, 189 U.S. 475 (1903).

Emmett Jay Scott to E. Donaldson[1]

[Tuskegee, Ala.] May 4, 1903

Dear Sir: I boarded the sleeping car Boscebal at 12:50 o'clock Saturday, May 2d at Richmond, Va., and attempted to secure a berth on
that car from Richmond to Atlanta, Ga. The conductor, J. W.
Wood, peremptorily refused me accommodation with the statement that everything had been sold. This statement was absolutely
untrue as you can verify, I am sure, by reference to his record, etc.
It would have required forty-eight persons to have filled every seat,
as you readily understand, and there were only twenty persons, who
as a matter of fact, had seats even from Richmond to Danville.
With the cowardly spirit of his cowardly kind, he attempted to in-
timidate the porter who contradicted his statement in my presence
that all seats were sold. I was an interstate passenger and this man
had no right to refuse me service; and then, too, in the State of
Virginia, there is no law operating against the selling of sleeping
car berths to persons of color. The Pullman Company is in business
for the sake of business, and this man, serving his own prejudices,
deprived the Company of the sale of a berth from Richmond to
Atlanta.

I am not sure that you are the proper person with whom to enter
complaint in this matter, and so I am sending a copy of this letter

137

to Mr. Martin Superintendent of the Pullman service at Philadelphia.

Awaiting word from you in this matter, I am, Yours truly,

[Emmett Jay Scott]
Private Secretary
to Booker T. Washington

TL Copy   Con. 249   BTW Papers   DLC.

1 Superintendent of the Pullman Sleeping Car Service, Richmond, Va.

From Charles William Anderson

New York, May 13th, 1903

Personal

My dear Doctor Washington: This is merely to put you in possession of a little information about Mr. James H. Hayes. A meeting
was held at the house of Mr. George Wibecan, in Brooklyn, to arrange for a Suffrage Convention to be held in that City sometime
in the early part of June. Several of Mr. Wibecan's immediate followers were present, but the prominent Colored people of that
City were conspicuously absent. In reply to a question concerning
the movement, Mr. Hayes took occasion to say that the only person
of any importance who was at present opposing the movement was
myself, and volunteered the statement that he was in doubt about
meeting this opposition, but was rather inclined to take the bull
by the horns and assail me in a public speech. He accused me of
having either written or inspired the letter printed in the New
York Age some weeks ago, advising him and his friends to make
a statement of the amount of money already collected, and the
amount yet to be raised. When this information was detailed to
me, I sent word by my informant that I knew nothing about the
authorship of the letter in question, and had nothing to do with its
publication. I told my man to inform Mr. Hayes that I had addressed the Cooper Union Meeting in favor of the Suffrage move-

ment, and had given of my means to it; but at the same time, I felt that if he was at all displeased with my present attitude, he would do well to follow his first inclination and assail me in a public speech, as that was a game at which two could play. I further advised him that, while I had nothing to do with writing the letter complained of, I was in full sympathy with it. I told him that I felt an accounting ought to be made, in justice both to Mr. Hayes and to the Colored people here who are giving their money to help the good cause along, and reminded him that it ought not to hurt any movement to tell the truth about it, and to let the light in. With this, my informant went out under the everlasting stars.

Just how Mr. Hayes arrived at the conclusion that I am against his movement, I do not know, but I have a rather sneaking suspicion that Mr. Wibecan is responsible for it. Wibecan was present at your Madison Square Garden meeting, and was very much disturbed about Mr. Cleveland's speech. He returned to Brooklyn in company with Mrs. Anderson and myself, and after letting off quite a quantity of mountain air and lake scenery, he volunteered the statement that you were doing the Race a great deal of harm, and that the people were dividing rapidly into two camps, "the Hayes Camp and the Washington Camp," and added, "I want to be put in the Hayes Camp."

After this rather unexpected outburst, I took occasion to talk "brass tacks" to him, and told him he ought to be ashamed to mention you and Hayes in the same breath. I went on to talk about the advisability of giving a little publicity to the amounts being collected by Hayes and his friends, and called his attention to the fact that if once a suspicion was aroused, that the funds were not being properly applied, it would prevent Colored men from raising money in the future for any cause, however righteous. Wibecan evidently passed the matter along to Hayes. Hence his attitude toward me. Hayes has formed a very close alliance with Wibecan, John E. Bruce (Bruce Grit), Bishop Walters, James D. Carr[1] and D. M. Webster.[2] I am not so sure about Webster, but I am quite confident that the other men are in the combination. At the conference above mentioned, Hayes took occasion to ridicule the manner in which Wilford H. Smith conducted his case, and insinuated that Smith was not a lawyer. He informed his friends that many of the men who follow you, were of opinion that Smith's case was the strongest one pending before the Court, but added that he knew all along that it was the weakest. He said, in case an unfavorable decision was handed down by the Supreme Court, he would advise that prominent Colored speakers be sent into all of the doubtful States of the North and urge the Colored voters to go fishing on next Election Day. Thus you have his plans as outlined by him at the Wibecan conference. I thought you might like to know these things, and therefore send them along to you.

I am in receipt of a letter from Mr. Scott relative to the case of Arthur Flanagan, a young Colored man now under sentence of death for the murder of a jailkeeper in this City. Flanagan and another man attempted to break jail and struck the keeper with an iron bar, from the effects of which blow he died. Flanagan's accomplice was a Colored ex-convict, and was the leader in the attempt to break jail. He was killed by falling from the jail window, and Flanagan escaped. As it was impossible to punish the real culprit, the authorities here resurrected an old law which makes the killing of a keeper during a jail delivery a capital offence. And in this way, Flanagan was sentenced to die. Nearly everybody here has signed a petition asking the Governor to commute the sentence to imprisonment for Life. The fact that he was a mere boy at the time, and that they bound and gagged the keeper after striking him, proves conclusively that they did not intend to kill him, and that the murder was not therefore premeditated. It seems to me that the sentence under the circumstances was unduly severe. I am told by his Mother and Sister that both the District Attorney that prosecuted him, and the Judge that sentenced him, have joined in a recommendation to the Governor for commutation of the sentence to "Imprisonment for Life." I do not ordinarily take any interest in such cases, and would not have signed his petition, were I not fully convinced that the sentence was entirely too severe. I forgot to say that he was imprisoned in the first place for having assisted in disposing of some stolen goods. It is clear from the testimony that he did not know the goods were stolen when he disposed of them, and had he not joined the other man in the attempt to escape, would probably have been cleared of the charge. I shall not give you any advice about the case, further than the facts quoted above, and send them in response to Mr. Scott's letter of the 11th. Yours truly,

Charles W. Anderson

(Dctd, C. W. A.)

TLS   Con. 278   BTW Papers   DLC.

1 James D. Carr, born in Baltimore in 1868, was a graduate of Rutgers and Columbia University Law School. He was the first black assistant district attorney in New York City, beginning in 1898.

2 Deborcey Macon Webster, born in 1868, was a lawyer in New York City from the early 1890s. He was active in seeking legal redress from the police following the New York Riot of 1900.

To Joseph Oswalt Thompson

[Tuskegee, Ala.] May 15, 1903

Personal and Confidential.

My dear Sir: I want to congratulate you and the other Referees upon the outcome of the Montgomery conference and the meeting in Birmingham.[1] Under all the circumstances I cannot see how you could have conducted things more wisely and successfully than you have. You had a very hard, trying and delicate task. I regret that some of our own people should act indiscreetly, but that is to be expected; they have been very badly deceived and of course it will take some time to win back their confidence. You and Mr. Aldrich and Mr. Scott, I repeat, have shown your wisdom, courage and fidelity in this matter in a very remarkable manner. Yours truly,

[Booker T. Washington]

TLc   Con. 279   BTW Papers   DLC.

1 On May 6, 1903, William F. Aldrich, Joseph O. Thompson, and Charles H. Scott, three of the leading Republicans in Alabama, called a conference to overturn an earlier party ruling that no blacks could serve as delegates in state party functions. Thompson and his associates introduced a resolution to reorganize the Republican state executive committee, the same committee that had earlier excluded blacks. The resolution failed, but a compromise proposal passed which allowed blacks to participate as delegates. Lily-white Republicans were pleased that the state executive committee was not reorganized, and the black-and-tan faction was content that black delegates would be recognized.

On May 12, at the meeting of the state executive committee in Birmingham, the lily whites lost in their bid to influence the referees regarding the appointment of black delegates, and the party returned to "old time Republicanism," which included blacks. This was a substantial defeat of racial factionalism in the Alabama Republican party and signaled a victory for the pro-Roosevelt elements and the black and tans. (Montgomery *Advertiser*, May 6, 1903, 5; Birmingham *Age-Herald*, May 7, 1903, 1–2, and May 13, 1903, 5.

To William Ingersoll Bowditch[1]

[Tuskegee, Ala.] May 15, 1903

My dear Mr. Bowditch: I regret exceedingly the long delay in answering your letter of March 10; the fact is I have been away from the school for some weeks on a long campaign in the interest of the school and have just recently returned and got to the point where I could answer your letter. I am very glad that you wrote me as you did concerning my position on the franchise. I would say that I feel reasonably sure that practically all the colored people and most of the whites who are interested in the subject, understand my position on that subject except about a half dozen colored men in Boston who seem to get a good deal of satisfaction just now out of a continued effort to misrepresent my position on every occasion. I presume that what you have seen must have been an extract taken from some address without the proper context. In order that you may see clearly that I have always on every proper occasion made myself understood on the franchise, I send you first a marked copy of the address which I delivered a few weeks ago before the Brooklyn Institute of Arts and Sciences in Brooklyn, N.Y. I also send a copy of an Open Letter sent to the Louisiana State Constitutional Convention, and an Interview published in the Atlanta Constitution. I should also send you what I said to the members of the Alabama State Constitutional Convention when it was in session but for the fact that the address was signed by a committee and not by myself alone, hence it would hardly be proper for me to claim it as my own. After you have read thoroughly what I have said, I do not believe that you will feel that I have in any way shirked my duty. It is true that I do not speak on this subject every day or even every month; if I were continually harping on it when

I did speak my words would have little weight or attract little attention. There is no colored man in the South and few in the North, if any, who do not really know my position on these questions, and what is more important know what I have actually done in favor of securing the Negro's political rights.

The enclosed editorial from a white Democratic paper published in Alabama is evidence of the fact that even the white Democratic papers do not misunderstand me.

If I can serve you further please be kind enough to let me know. Yours truly,

[Booker T. Washington]

TLc   Con. 249   BTW Papers   DLC.

1 William Ingersoll Bowditch (1819–1909) was a Boston lawyer and former Garrisonian abolitionist, whose home was a stop on the Underground Railroad during the 1840s and 1850s.

To Erwin Craighead[1]

[Tuskegee, Ala.] May 15, 1903

My dear Sir: I thank you for your kind letter of May 13th and I am very glad to reply to it.

I think the document to which you refer must be a little book called "Tuskegee" which tells somewhat of the work being done by our graduates. By this mail I send you a copy of this book. I also send you a marked copy of my last report to the Board of Trustees which bears upon the subject of the occupation of our graduates.

Since your letter has been received, I have decided to get a trained and experienced newspaper correspondent, Mr. M. B. Thrasher, to go to Montgomery and make a hand to hand investigation into the facts as to the occupation of our graduates in that city and county, and without entering into any controversy with Mr. McDonald or anybody else Mr. Thrasher is going to send a statement to the Washington Post giving the results of his examination whether they are favorable or unfavorable, and I have thought that perhaps it might be of service if Mr. Thrasher were to send you a copy of the same letter with the understanding that it is to be sent only to the Register and the Washington Post. If you would like this please indicate it to me as soon as possible.

I would state in general that I feel very sure that there is not the least foundation for the statement made by the Montgomery lawyer. For example he states that our girls are given training in painting. I have been here since the foundation of the institution and do not know of a single case where a school girl has been given even one lesson in painting, so that if he is no nearer the truth in his other statements than he is in that one I feel very sure that the investigation will refute the statements made. But I do not like to deal in generalities but in facts, and for this reason I have sent Mr. Thrasher to make the investigation.

May I add that I am always grateful to you for your deep interest in our work. Yours truly,

[Booker T. Washington]

TLc   Con. 256   BTW Papers   DLC.

1 Erwin Craighead, born in 1852, was an editor of the Mobile *Register* beginning in the 1880s. In 1889 he became vice-president of the paper. He was a member of the Alabama State Board of Education beginning in 1904.

To Charles Fletcher Dole

[Tuskegee, Ala.] May 15, 1903

My dear Mr. Dole: Please forgive me for not answering your letter of April 8th earlier but the fact is I have been away from home on a long campaign in the interest of the school and scarcely had time to write a letter.

I thank you for speaking to me so frankly concerning my Brooklyn address. I think though, if you have time to re-read what I have said you will find that I did not commit myself to an endorsement of any of the wars engaged in by the United States but simply stated a historical fact in connection with these wars, at least that was my object. But on the main point raised in your letter I confess that when we first entered upon our connection with the Philippine

Islands that I could not see clearly what the outcome would be though I was warned by Mr. Garrison and other good Boston friends as to the result of our taking the Philippine Islands would have upon our race here in the South. Events I confess, have rather forced me to the conclusion that our course in the Philippines is going to make it more difficult to secure the rights of the Negro in the South. I believe that a large part of the country is sick of the Philippine Islands and would let them go if a proper opportunity offered itself. I shall not become discouraged, however, by any means, concerning our future here in the South but shall attempt to work all the harder because of the additional obstacles which seem to have been placed in our path. I shall hope to talk the whole matter over with you when I see you.

· · · ·

[Booker T. Washington]

TLfc   Con. 249   BTW Papers   DLC.

To Stella Houghton Scott Gilman[1]

[Tuskegee, Ala.] May 15, 1903

My dear Madam: I have received your letters and have read them with care.[2] I have had occasion to consider several times before the wisdom of establishing a domestic training school at Tuskegee, and there are several reasons why I do not think it wise to establish such a school here. I think it would be impractical from several points of view. At this institution we give training in every line of domestic work, hence any girl who finishes our course should be able to perform any of the usual duties connected with [a] servant's life, but one of the most important things to be accomplished for the colored people now is the getting of them to have correct ideas concerning labor, that is to get them to feel that all classes of labor, whether of the head or hand, are dignified. This lesson I think Tuskegee, in connection with Hampton, has been successful in teaching the race. The most economical thing that we can do in addition to teaching this lesson is to send out a set of people not only trained in hand but thoroughly equipped in mind and heart so that they themselves could go out and start smaller centres or training schools where servants if necessary might be given proper training. For instance, we would be doing a better service to the whole country if we can train at Tuskegee one girl who could go out and start a domestic training school in Atlanta, Baltimore, or elsewhere, than we would be doing by trying to put servants directly into individual houses which would be a never-ending task. I am quite sure the two kinds of work could not be brought together at Tuskegee.

Besides the reasons to which I have referred, I must confess that I cannot rid myself of the feeling that our people are better off in the South than they are in the North, and I have never been able to bring myself to the point of urging them or encouraging them to exchange their Southern residence for a Northern one.

I regret that my letter must be so unsatisfactory. Yours very truly,

[Booker T. Washington]

TLc Con. 546 BTW Papers DLC.

1 Stella Houghton Scott Gilman, born in Tuscaloosa, Ala., in 1844, was a founder, with her husband, Arthur Gilman (1837–1909), of the "Harvard Annex," later Radcliffe College. She was also active in women's clubs in Cambridge.

2 Stella Scott Gilman wrote BTW on May 6 and 7, 1903, urging him to establish a department for the training of domestic servants. "It is said that America pays the rent of Ireland through the sons & daughters who come here for work," she wrote. "Why should we not keep the money in the country & send it through our native born colored sons & daughters to their fathers & Mothers too feeble to work in the South." (May 6, 1903, Con. 546, BTW Papers, DLC.) The next day she wrote BTW that her idea had the backing of some of the best women in Cambridge, including the wife of a Harvard professor and a female professor at the Massachusetts Institute of Technology. (Con. 546, BTW Papers, DLC.)

To Robert Curtis Ogden

[Tuskegee, Ala.] May 15, 1903

My dear Mr. Ogden: I have received both of your letters of May 8th and 9th.[1] I shall not attempt to speak fully until I have an opportunity of seeing you. In the meantime I wish you to understand that whatever I have said regarding [the] Union League incident[2] has grown out of my intense love for you and loyalty to the work which you are leading in so helpfully. I confess that I may be over-solicitous that nothing should be done that would in any way cripple your present unique and wonderful influence for good among both races in the South. I thank you for calling my attention to the danger of getting into too close contact with your opponent;[3] Mr. Murphy has also spoken to me of the same matter. It was largely because of the weak character of such men as your opponent that I felt that it was wrong for you to cast your pearls before swine. In a personal conversation I had with him in New York however, I told him that neither myself nor the other colored people were agreed that reduction of representation in Congress of the Southern states was in the interest of the colored people. The Negroes ask the question in what position they would be left after the reduction has taken place. Nothwithstanding what I have said, wise conservative agitation looking towards the securing of the rights of the colored people on the part of the people of the North is not hurtful.

I shall hope to talk the matter out with you when I see you. Yours truly,

[Booker T. Washington]

TLc   Con. 269   BTW Papers   DLC.

1 Both in Con. 270, BTW Papers, DLC. See also Warner Miller to BTW, Apr. 10, 1903, Con. 249, BTW Papers, DLC.

2 Ogden, at the Union League Club of New York, took a stand against reduction of southern congressional representation on account of disfranchisement as "in the highest interests of my colored friends." He complained that "the private rejoinder to my position (which was assumed with dignity and perfect courtesy) is innuendo and personal criticism." He denied that he had cited BTW in opposition to the measure, but said that another club member had said that if BTW and H. B. Frissell had been present both would oppose the resolution. (Ogden to BTW, May 8, 1903, Con. 270, BTW Papers, DLC.)

3 Warner Miller (1838–1918), a paper manufacturer of Herkimer, N.Y., was a Republican congressman from 1879 to 1881 and U.S. senator from 1881 to 1887. In 1888 he narrowly lost election as governor. Miller supported reduction of southern representation in Congress as a measure to stem the tide of disfranchisement, and publicly debated this issue with Ogden at the Union League Club.

To Henry Clay Payne

[Tuskegee, Ala.] May 19, 1903

Personal

My dear Sir: I write to say that I think under all the circumstances Messrs. J. O. Thompson, W. F. Aldrich and C. H. Scott have managed affairs in this state in a very admirable and successful manner. As you know, this committee had a very trying and delicate task to perform and they have succeeded in a large degree in bringing the party back to its trusted moorings and have done so with less friction than I have dared to anticipate. Their work is not yet complete but they are continually making progress, as the recent meetings in Montgomery and in Birmingham will indicate. I do not think that we are to the point in this state where the interests of the President or the interests of the colored people can be taken out of the hands of this committee and I feel with the best light that is before me that they should be kept in power until the next National Convention. I shall hope to talk the whole matter over with you, however, when I am next in Washington. Yours truly,

[Booker T. Washington]

TLc   Con. 261   BTW Papers   DLC.

From Roscoe Conkling Bruce

Tuskegee Institute. May 20, 1903

Principal Washington: In glancing over my letter[1] to you on the conditions in which the Negroes of Montgomery live, I find that I failed to mention the most pathetic aspect, an aspect people don't like to talk about and yet one of grave importance to education and reform. There are fairly well educated young women, students from Fisk, Atlanta, Tuskegee, in the dives of Montgomery. I talked with several persons about this matter and one of the dives I myself visited. As far as I learned, these young people gravitate to these places much more from (1) accident for which they themselves were hardly responsible, (2) mere ignorance, (3) inability to earn a comfortable living, as from (4) vicious impulses.

As the close of this school year approaches, the need for some woman to talk plainly (calling a spade a spade) to our girls on these matters becomes urgent. Religious appeal I believe to be curiously ineffective; a common-sense statement of the facts is in my judgment the thing needful.

You will pardon me for making this suggestion. Faithfully yours,

R C Bruce

TLS   Con. 249   BTW Papers   DLC.

1 At BTW's request, Bruce had written him a letter on Apr. 18, 1903, giving an account of social and educational conditions in Montgomery, Ala. (Con. 250, BTW Papers, DLC.) On Apr. 30, 1903, in accordance with BTW's request, he suggested remedies for these conditions, including a social settlement. (Con. 261, BTW Papers, DLC.)

An Editorial in *Outlook*

May 23, 1903

Two Typical Leaders

Professor W. E. B. Du Bois; Booker T. Washington: they represent different types of character, different conceptions of the race problem, different methods for its solution, and they deal with it in a widely different spirit. These differences are strikingly illustrated in two volumes — one by Professor Du Bois, just published, "The Souls of the Black Folk," the other by Dr. Washington, published four years ago, "The Future of the American Negro."

To Professor Du Bois the negro and the American are ever separate, though in the same personality. The American negro is "two souls, two thoughts, two unreconciled strivings"; he is ever the subject of a "double consciousness"; dominated by a "sense of always looking at oneself through the eyes of others, of measuring one's soul by the tape of a world that looks on in amused contempt and pity." To Dr. Washington the negro race is a great race; during the Civil War the negro exhibited a remarkable "self-control," and was "to the last faithful to the trust that had been reposed upon him" by his master, yet was always "an uncompromising friend of the Union," and never, either in freedom or slavery, under a suspicion of being a traitor to his country; and since emancipation has he given abundant evidence that he can "make himself a useful, honorable, and desirable citizen." To Professor Du Bois the negro is a problem, and the question is ever present in his consciousness, and from it he confesses himself unable to escape, "How does it feel to be a problem?" To Dr. Washington America is the problem, and the white race is as much a part of it as the black: "The problem is how to make these millions of negroes self-supporting, intelligent, economical, and valuable citizens, as well as how to bring about proper relations between them and the white citizens among whom they live." Professor Du Bois is half ashamed of being a negro, and he gives expression to his own bitterness of soul in the cry which he puts into the mouth of his race, "Why did God make me an outcast and a stranger in mine own home?" Dr. Washington rejoices in the honorable record of his race; in his address at Hampton's last Commencement he cries out to his white auditors, "We are as proud of our race as you are of yours"; and his negro auditors applauded his declaration with great enthusiasm. The sense of amused contempt and pity for his own race, caught from the white people, is reflected in the title of Professor Du Bois's book, "The Souls of the Black Folk"; the spirit of race pride, of national patriotism, and of hope for the future of his race is reflected in the title of Dr. Washington's book, "The Future of the American Negro."

We shall speak hereafter more fully of Professor Du Bois's interesting and valuable book, as we have heretofore spoken of Dr. Washington's; here we take the contrast between the two as a text for some reflections on two parties or tendencies or influences in the negro race, which the two respectively represent. One of these parties is ashamed of the race, the other is proud of it; one makes the white man the standard, the other seeks the standard in its own race ideals; one demands social equality, or at least resents social inequality, the other is too self-respecting to do either; one seeks to push the negro into a higher place, the other to make him a larger man; one demands for him the right to ride in the white man's car, the other seeks to make the black man's car clean and respectable; one demands the ballot for ignorant black men because ignorant white men have the ballot, the other asks opportunity to make the black man competent for the duties of citizenship, and wishes no man to vote, white or colored, who is not competent; one would build the educational system for the race on the university, the other would build it on the common school and the industrial school; one wishes to teach the negro to read the Ten Commandments in Hebrew, the other wishes first to teach him to obey them in English; to one labor is barely more honorable than idleness and the education which makes "laborers and nothing more" is regarded with ill-concealed contempt, to the other industry is the basic virtue, and the education which makes industry intelligent is the foundation of civilization. The first view has frequently crude representation in negro journals and by negro orators — political and religious; but the ablest and most cultivated expression of it which we have ever seen is afforded by the volume of Professor Du Bois, albeit presented with qualifications which in this brief summary it is impossible to represent; of the second view the pre-eminent representative is Dr. Washington. The Outlook heartily accepts the second view. Something like this is what it would say to its Afro-American readers:

I. Have faith in yourselves. Cultivate the spirit of self-respect; only he who respects himself will be respected by his neighbors. Decline to look at yourselves through your white neighbor's eyes; look at yourselves through your own eyes. Do not take the white man as a standard; make your own standards. Be not imitators. There is no more reason why you should imitate the white man than why the white man should imitate you. No man can make himself into another man; no race can make itself into another race. The missionary makes a mistake who tries to convert the negro into an Anglo-Saxon; the negro makes a greater mistake who desires for himself any such conversion. The Anglo-Saxon was once a subject race; it did not win its present position by trying to be Norman. Do not try to be an Anglo-Saxon; be an Afro-American, and be proud that you are one.

II. Do not push yourself forward; do not allow would-be leaders to push you forward. Do not be ambitious for social equality, or industrial equality, or political equality, or any kind of equality.

Be ambitious to be men, and trust that in time the manhood will make for itself a place; it always does. The whole power of the Federal Government did not suffice to give you political power; it failed because you had not the necessary preparation for the exercise of political power. The United States Supreme Court has decided that it cannot give you political power by a judicial device. The slower way is the quicker way. Get political competence, and trust that political power will follow in due time. In most if not all the Southern States the possession of about three hundred dollars' worth of taxable property entitles you, under the amended constitutions, to a ballot. Set yourselves, by honest and intelligent industry, to get the property; then ask for the ballot. If registrars deny it to you, when you go before them with your tax receipt, appeal to the State courts to enforce the State law. If ignorant, shiftless white men vote, so much the worse for the State. It is neither for your interest nor for that of the State that you should be represented by an ignorant and shiftless negro vote. Nothing is for your interest that is not for the State's interest.

So also in the industrial and the social world. Acquire intelligence and virtue, and what usually accompanies them in this country, a moderate property, and the doors of industry and the respect of your fellow-men will follow. What Dr. Washington said at Atlanta, what Professor Du Bois calls the "Atlanta Compromise," is no compromise; it is a principle of universal application, just as true and just as applicable in the Northern factory as the Southern plantation: "In all things purely social we can be as separate as the five fingers, and yet one as the hand in all things essential to mutual progress." Never forget this principle; never demand social recognition; social recognition is never given on demand. Always work for mutual progress. What member of your race has risen to the position of social respect, won the opportunity of useful industry, and acquired the political influence of Dr. Washington? Follow in the path he has blazed for you, and you will arrive, sooner or later, at the same destination.

III. Therefore seek education — first, last, and all the time. But do not fall into the notion that education means ability to read and understand Homer and Dante. Do not let Professor Du Bois's picture of Socrates and Francis of Assisi deceive you. There are already enough "brothers of the poor" of your race in America; you do not need to add to their number. The first duty of every man is to earn his living; after that comes the duty of adding to the life of others. Seek for yourself, seek for your race, first the ability to earn a living. Is this materialism? Very well! materialism is the basis of life. What not only your race, what the great mass of the American people, need to-day is a broader education rather than a higher education. No education for any race, or for any individual of any race, is adequate which does not include manual training; and no education is worthy of the name which leaves its recipient helplessly dependent on his neighbors for his livelihood. Are you a teacher, or a preacher, or a doctor, or a lawyer, or a merchant? can you read Greek? can you enjoy Homer and Dante, Raphael and Titian, Beethoven and Brahms? Very well; but do not content yourself by the endeavor to pass your knowledge along to your race; use it to make them first of all self-respecting and self-supporting citizens; second, practical contributors to the welfare of the community in which they live. It is not true that Dr. Washington asks "that black people give up, at least for the present, three things — first, political power; second, insistence on civil rights; third, higher education of negro youth." It requires all our charity to think that Professor Du Bois really believes that Dr. Washington has ever asked anything of the sort. He asks his fellows to get political power by proving their capacity to exercise it; civil rights by obedience to law; and higher education by building it on a foundation of a broad industrial and ethical education. In this he is absolutely right. Political power without previously acquired capacity to use it is always dangerous to others and generally dangerous to the possessor; the civil rights of a freeman the lawless are not entitled to; and higher education without a foundation laid in elementary education is a castle in the air, which collapses at the first rude awakening of the ill-bred scholar to the exigencies of actual life.

IV. Do not think about yourself. Do not think about your woes or your wrongs. Meditate, not on "the souls of black folk," but on "the future of the American negro." Look out, not in; forward, not backward. Put your thought on your work, not on your soul; and take council of your hopes, not of your discouragements. Do not look too long on the one-roomed cabins, or on the mortgaged farms, or on the usurious rates of interest, or on the Jim Crow cars, or on the short-term schools. Remember that forty years ago few negroes in Virginia owned themselves, and that now they own seventeen and a half million dollars' worth of taxable property; that forty years ago it was a penal offense to teach a negro to read, and that now there are public schools for him, supported at public cost, in every Southern State; that forty years ago no negro could vote, and now that negroes are registering and voting and having their votes counted in every State and in nearly every county in the South.

The negro still suffers injustice; he is still subject to a sometimes cruel prejudice. The Outlook does not condone the first nor apologize for the second. But what is the remedy? Not Federal Force Bills; not Supreme Court decisions enforcing political equality; not a veneer of culture on a nature ill developed in the essentials of practical life; not self-assertiveness and clamorous demand for political rights or social equality. Character. Character — developed by broad systems of education in the negro and not less in the white race. Character — wrought in the individual and extending by a gradual process throughout the community. Character — the foundations of which are truth, honesty, chastity, temperance, industry, intelligence; the superstructure of which is material property, mutual respect, personal culture, political freedom, and social peace.

Outlook, 74 (May 23, 1903), 214–16.

William Henry Baldwin, Jr.,
to the Trustees of Tuskegee Institute

N.Y. City. May 23, 1903

At a meeting of the Committee on Investment of Endowment Fund held in New York City on Thursday, May 7th, at 4:30 P.M.
There were present Messrs Robert C. Ogden,
George Foster Peabody,
J. G. Phelps Stokes, and
W. H. Baldwin, Jr., Chairman.

A letter from Mr. Andrew Carnegie, (certified copy of which is attached) dated April 17th, was submitted, and after discussion it was unanimously agreed to accept the Trust under the terms and conditions of the gift.

The following Resolution was thereupon adopted:

WHEREAS, Andrew Carnegie has made to this Committee of Endowment of the Board of Trustees of the Tuskegee Normal & Industrial Institute a gift in trust of Six hundred thousand dollars ($600,000.) in five per-cent. United States Steel Company first mortgage bonds from which he has required that One hundred and fifty thousand dollars ($150,000.) in par value thereof shall be set aside for the purposes hereinafter specified; and

WHEREAS, This Committee, in behalf of such Board of Trustees, has, with a deep appreciation of the splendid generosity of Mr. Carnegie's gift, accepted the same; and

WHEREAS, It is the duty of this Committee to set aside such One hundred and fifty thousand dollars ($150,000.) in the par value of such bonds for the special purpose designated by Mr. Carnegie — Now, therefore, it is

RESOLVED, That one hundred and fifty thousand dollars, ($150,000.) in par value of the five per-cent. United States Steel Company bonds received from Andrew Carnegie shall be set apart and held by this Committee for the said Board upon special trust with power from time to time to change or alter the investment or investments thereof and out of the net income thereof to pay annually to Booker T. Washington during the term of his natural life the income thereof in quarter yearly installments, the same to be used by him for the support of himself and his family; and after his death, if he shall leave widow him surviving, then to pay the said income to her in like quarter yearly installments, the same to be used by her for the support of herself and family during the term of her natural life; subject, however, to the right to the said Booker T. Washington during his life and after his death to his widow (if he leave one him surviving) during her life to apply any portion of said income not required for such support as aforesaid to any of the purposes of the Tuskegee Normal & Industrial Institute; and upon the further trust after the death of the said Booker T. Washington and of his widow, if any shall survive him, to apply said One hundred and fifty thousand dollars ($150,000.) in the said bonds or the securities or property which shall represent the same, to the purposes of the said Institute.

I may state also that the terms and conditions of this gift were explained to me personally by Mr. Andrew Carnegie after receipt of his letter, and the whole matter was submitted by resolution of the Committee on Investment of Endowment Fund to Mr. Edward M. Shepard,[1] as Counsel, who, after considering the letter transmitting the bonds, prepared the resolution above recited.

I am instructed by the Committee to forward this communication to the Board of Trustees, and ask for their formal approval with appropriate resolution, and to transmit such resolution, through the Secretary, to me, so that I may forward the same to Mr. Andrew Carnegie.

W. H. Baldwin Jr
Chairman
Committee on Investment
of Endowment Fund

TLS Con. 18 BTW Papers DLC.

[1] Edward Morse Shepard (1850–1911), a leading New York lawyer, public servant, and Democratic politician, was a close personal and political friend of George Foster Peabody, a neighbor at his summer home on Lake George. He often gave his legal services to the philanthropic organizations to which Baldwin, Ogden, and Peabody belonged, and was legal counsel of Tuskegee Institute.

To Matthew T. Driver

Tuskegee, Ala., May 25, 1903

Mr. M. T. Driver: After careful consideration and consultation with several of our Trustees, I am now convinced that the school ought to receive your resignation as Business Agent June 1st. You are aware of the fact that I have said to you on several occasions that your work as Purchasing Agent was not wholly satisfactory but you had improved to some extent since you took hold of the work. In addition to the rather unsatisfactory work you now have added the correspondence between yourself and the Cincinnati woolen firm to which I have already called your attention. The meaning of such correspondence is that you put yourself in a position to be obligated to this firm in a way that would make you of no value as a disinterested agent purchasing thousands of dollars worth of goods for the institution each year. For the reasons above stated I am quite sure that you will see with me the wisdom of the course that I suggest.

In view of your long faithful connection with the school, for which we are grateful and most thoroughly appreciate I wish to add that if we can find other work for you on the school grounds or be of assistance in securing a position elsewhere we should be very glad to do what we can in either direction in case you desire it. Yours truly,

Booker T. Washington

TLpS Con. 282A BTW Papers DLC. A draft is in Con. 255, BTW Papers, DLC.

From William Henry Baldwin, Jr.

N.Y. [City] May 25th., 1903

My dear Sir: I enclose herewith a communication addressed to the Board of Trustees of the Tuskegee Institute, on behalf of the Committee on Investment of Endowment Fund, which should be presented and approved at the meeting of the Board of Trustees on Wednesday, the twenty-seventh.

The final form in which it has been put has been delayed so that I have only received it a few minutes ago from Mr. Edward M. Shepard.

The Committee gave serious consideration to this matter, and was not willing to do anything except to carry out the terms of Mr. Carnegie's gift, and therefore they put upon you any responsibility that you may have in connection with the funds which are to be turned over to you for your use. I do not know that the Board understands that such a large amount of money has been put at your disposal; and at the same time that the matter is presented, I think it would be well for you to give them some impression that you will pay back to the Institute the salary which you receive, keeping it in that form so that you are regularly employed by the Institute, and that you will also be able out of the funds placed at your disposal to make some contributions in various lines that will be of benefit to the Institute. I would not commit myself as to the amount which you will give to Tuskegee, but I would have it clearly understood by the Trustees that you will not expect to use all of the money set aside for you. This is a very delicate question, and the South will be very sensitive about it unless you handle it in a tactful manner.

I think you should explain to the Board of Trustees that we have nothing to do except to accept the gift just as it is given, and they should be very guarded out of loyalty to you and the Institution in whatever they may have to say about this personal gift.

If at any time in the future any one should call you to account in an audience or anywhere for receiving so much money, you will have to be prepared to answer it.

I should make no definite promises until after you have had sufficient time to consider just what you will need for yourself, but I would not permit the impression to exist that you will use it all. Yours very truly,

W H Baldwin Jr.

TLS Con. 18 BTW Papers DLC.

From Matthew T. Driver

Tuskegee, Ala., May 26, 1903

Dear Sir, I received your letter of the 25th inst. suggesting that I tender my resignation as Business Agent of this school.

I must confess Mr. Washington that this was a great blow to me. As you know I have been here fifteen years, during which time I have made every effort to work for the best interest of the school. I feel that I have grown up with it and am a part of it.

You cannot imagine how hard it is for me to sever my connection after so many years of faithful work.

I do hope that you can possibly see your way clear to reconsider this action and let me continue my work.

For the last twelve months, I have thought that there was marked improvement in my work. I know I have worked hard to this end, and so far as I know there have been few just causes for complaint.

Regarding the correspondence with the Bruner Co., will say that I am very sorry that I wrote this letter, as it seems to mean so much. I certainly had no idea of doing anything that would in the least obligate myself or the school to anyone and as I said to you a few days ago, that this is the only letter of the kind that I have ever written but it does seem strange that this only one should fall into your hands as it did, written as it was.

Now Mr. Washington I hope you will grant my request and let me continue my work. I will assure you that you will never have occasion to call my attention to the like again.

You say you are willing to give me other work on the grounds or be of assistance in securing a position elsewhere. Will you kindly let me know what the work will be if you have it in mind, also if you have in mind a good position to which you could recommend me.

I thank you for what you have done for me and will appreciate anything you may do for me in the future. Very kindly yours

M. T. Driver

ALS   Con. 255   BTW Papers   DLC.

John Andrew Kenney[1]
to the Tuskegee Institute Executive Council

Tuskegee, Ala., May 26, '03

Esteemed Body: I wish to invite your attention to the general sanitary condition of the institution. I would say that for the health & welfare of this large community of persons, 'tis in a rather bad state. On the highways, where every one walks & sees, conditions are more favorable, but in many instances, down in the secluded places, where germs hatch & multiply, and diseases propagate the spectacle is all but favorable.

To speak in detail, there is more trash, paper, and other rubbish around the grounds and especially in vicinity of certain buildings at times, than there should be. I have spoken to the boys assembled, to Maj. Ramsey, to Mr. J. H. Washington, & to Mr. Smith[2] individually about the vicinity of Rockefeller Hall. Those in charge of the work appear to be making efforts to keep it clean, but behind the building are certain old rags & paper which have been there quite a while. (Mr. Smith promised today to have them moved). I want to speak of the grounds in the woods behind that building. They are filthy and polluted & the nuisance is continuing daily. The whole place is one general toilet & the odors which arise at times are fierce. One has only to step through the fence near the new bathhouse to have his esthetic senses shocked. Follow this road down the hill a little way & we come to the dumping ground for coarse rubbish. For those two evils I'd suggest the stationing of regular guards at certain hours during day & until after taps at night for the former. This is no new suggestion, but I urge its enforcement. For the second I suggest that this dumping ground be abandoned. 'Tis too near. I further suggest the burning of all useless & worthless rubbish as a sanitary precaution, rather than a general dumping ground.

Next I'd speak of the general, almost systematic custom of throwing trash, & slops from windows. In Rockefeller Hall one does not leave bedding or anything hanging in window to air & sun a little while, for fear of being bespattered with slop water from windows above. This has been experienced more than once in my own case. Behind Cassidy this morning were several wet spots & windows where water had been thrown out, and, passing the annex, I saw a girl throw slop water from window. Behind Senior practice Cottage, to-day & more than once previously I've seen slop water poured on ground at back door. The same is true of basement of Senior Cottage, & to-day water is standing to small extent in that basement — may be pipe-leakage. At boys barracks water is generally all along poured out from back doors. This morning was scrub morning — many had swept the water from places across porch to ground. The grounds around these buildings & just over the fence are very unsatisfactory.

As a further topic of consideration I'd mention the toilets. I don't speak on this subject without due consideration & sympathy for the management of the institution in its struggles to keep it on

a high level. A proper sewage system for this large place would require another princely donation from Carnegie or some other philanthropist, but we must recognize the evil as it confronts us and
do our utmost to combat it.

As a twin-sister to the toilets, I must speak of the drainage. They
are most unsatisfactory. They are menaces to the public health.
Earth closets never have been & never will be successfully used by
1500 people in small area. For drainage or sewage we have no convenient outlet. Some of the toilets are frightful. I'd mention two
especially. The large general toilet below Cassidy is fearful. The
stench meets one several yards away. Water from the bath room
runs through underneath the house & stands in a very unsightly
pool below, & then seeps away down into that mosquito breeding
swamp, where it stands and pollutes the air with its malodorous
stench.

I know it is much easier to criticise these ills than to offer the
remedy. Still I'd suggest thorough drainage by ditching that entire
swamp, collect all this water in pipes & lead it some distance down
the stream. *That* I am sure would help *some*. Next I'd suggest more
care about the toilet. Every particle of excrement should be collected in the pails & more lime or simple dry earth mixed & then
hauled away. One of the best & simplest deodorants is dry earth. A
barrel of it should be in each closet and a man should be appointed
whose duty it is to keep them in proper condition & see that this
earth or lime, or both are freely used quite frequently during day.
This I am sure would help matters without any great outlay.

The toilet behind the barracks ought to be attended or condemned. The boys have made that whole field, nearly, the fence
sides, & the field beyond, a veritable toilet, and I can't blame them.
For what human being can voluntarily consent to use that place
that stands for the toilet there? The toilet is nearly filled, a large
heap of excrement is behind it, & the urine seeps or trickles down
in the sand from the urinal with no provision for its removal. The
sight & stench are revolting. Behind this house runs a little slow
sluggish, lazy stream with dark, dirty water from upon the hill behind the trade building where the oxen stand. This water runs
through the refuse from the above named toilet & spreads out in a
marshy dirty place below.

We wish much that the girls toilet could be moved. I heartily approve of the work Mr. Williston[3] is now doing drawing that waste water away from behind the kitchen. The two things to-gether have made it very unpleasant. If the old gutter were kept fully free from obstructions, so the water would not stand, 'twould be much better. What can be done with that toilet? The girls should not have to go further away, and we can't very well put it in the building for want of a sewer system. I invite you to seriously consider the matter. I wish something might be done whereby the lady-teachers & girl-students might not be exposed to the unpleasant and unhealthy odors from that source next year as they have been during the past. I was surprised to see that the night soil from the toilet at Dorothy Hall was pulled out and banked instead of every particle being hauled away. The drainage from the laundry also needs attention.

Some time ago I saw a communication to Dr. Kenniebrew from you, in response to his suggestions concerning that stream which runs down the valley past the hospital. 'Tis a very crooked, sluggish, ragged affair. It contains much filth, & is contaminated from its source; first from Dorothy Hall, then the drainage from up about the kitchen, (small amount), the slop water from the sink near bath house, sewage from Alabama Hall & then from Huntington. If you were to cross that valley to hospital just after a rain and at many other times, you'd be convinced that it needs attention. The odor is sometimes fierce. The contents of this stream at flood seasons are washed upon the banks & lodge amidst the debris present & there remains a source of repugnance, often after the flood has ceased. It soaks into the soil & remains during a dry season to exhale its bad fumes. I wish that you might take under consideration the best thing to be done about it. Eliminating some of the curves, in places deepening the channel, and clearing away some of the rubbish, would I think, help matters some.

The sinks or places made for dumping slop water in many instances are not very satisfactory. Two in particular, I mention. The one back of Rockefeller Hall. The pipe leads it just 20 or 30 ft away and turns it loose to spread out on top the ground almost under the very windows of that magnificent building. I have no need to speak further on that. The other is down behind Huntington Hall and empties into the road.

There is one other nuisance of which I am forced to speak. It is the slaughter house. Yesterday & to-day the odor from that place was sufficient to nauseate a delicate stomach, & those odors were detected[?] in the regular thoroughfare, & when the wind is in favorable direction, the hospital, which of all places should be secure from such things, is invaded. One of head nurses mentioned it yesterday or to-day. On investigation I find a rather bad state of things down in that locality. The only thing I saw right at the house to speak of unfavorably was the drainage. All liquids run out at the back of the pen & much of the fluid spreads & soaks into the ground as the sight & odor will convince one. It then finds its way in a slow, shallow, lazy stream down the ravine, percolating the soil all the way. Some 200 or 300 yds down, I think I saw the cause of the bad odor. I was out quite early & watched the buzzards gathering, apparently, for their morning meal. I went to the spot and there seemed about fifty. The object of their attention was a pen into which is thrown all the offal & refuse from the slaughter house & here the buzzards feed. The odor present at the time led me to conclude that this caused the odor of which I spoke & of which some of the barn boys, on asking them, told me they get at times.

On the hill above this, but a little further over is the dumping ground, & from the fact that two poor belabored curs were getting their breakfast from this heap, we may conclude that offensive matter was present.

The night soil cart stood near. A more repulsive object you need not wish to see. I'll not disgust you by a description. I no longer wondered why it smells so badly in passing at night, nor did I blame the horse I was riding for being frightened. Suffice to say, a new one is much needed, one that is closely made & lined with zinc or sheet iron and will not leak. (I again urge here that more lime but especially an abundance of dry earth be used in these earth closets). Further down the hill seems to be or to have been at some time a dumping ground for this night soil cart. I don't wish to invade the farmer's territory, but to my mind, this is a waste as well as unhealthy. Let this stuff be put on some of the poor land & thoroughly mixed with earth. There it will be inoffensive & will enrich the soil. The hospital should not be menaced by these odors. They are dangerous to the strong & healthy. Certainly the sick, weak and enfeebled should not be exposed. Again, there seems to be *some* possibility that the resident physician's cottage at some distant day will be located nearer this nuisance than the hospital is now.

I urge that the slaughter house be moved, that the general rubbish, or garbage be burned, that this dumping place be moved, & that night soil be thoroughly mixed with dry earth on poor land some distance away from any kind of building. Most persistently do I urge that some step be taken at once to prevent that odor molesting people at the hospital, road & barn.

Lastly, I'd mention the grounds around the hospital. They are not as well kept as they should be. I sent Mr. Williston a note today, asking him to have some immediate attention given.

I have especially dwelt upon the dark side of this subject. I did so purposely. Every-body, every day sees the bright side, the pretty, flowers, trimmed grass, clean walks & well-kept lawns, but it is in the back places that the trouble lies, and with these I am dealing.

I have dwelt upon this at length that you may see if possible with the eyes with which I saw. If not I invite you to go and see. I am placing no criticism upon anyone. I am only stating the conditions. I don't ask who is responsible. We all *are* to an extent. The burden is ours, and as your health representative, which I have the great honor to be, I beg you to give my report a fair consideration. If you don't agree with me, as you won't in all things, at least consider some of them, and give us some help along these lines. I do strongly urge that at once a force of men, equal to the task, be put to work to at least give the whole place a thorough cleaning, and then the other matters be taken up as soon as convenient.

I don't try to be an alarmist, & know that I am not a pessimist, but should some communicable or zymotic disease gain a foothold among us, the conditions are ripe for a wide-spread epidemic, and I know that on investigation by experts we should be condemned & severely criticised. Since we can not begin earlier to straighten matters, let us not stop to ask whose fault or who is responsible, but let us all take hold of it and place our grounds, at once, in a more sanitary condition.

With great respect I beg to subscribe myself humbly,

Jno. A. Kenney

ALS Con. 551 BTW Papers DLC.

1 John Andrew Kenney (1874–1950), trained at Hampton Institute and at Freedmen's Hospital in Washington, D.C., was resident physician at Tuskegee from 1902 to 1924. He and BTW worked to establish National Negro Health Week. In 1913 he

became head of the John A. Andrew Memorial Hospital at Tuskegee. Moving to Newark, N.J., he operated the Kenney Memorial Hospital from 1927 to 1935. A president and for many years an active member of the National Medical Association, he founded its journal in 1908 and was its editor for many years. He returned to live in Tuskegee from 1939 to 1944.

2 William C. Smith, assistant landscape gardener in 1902–3.

3 David A. Williston, chief landscape gardener in 1902–3. In 1910 he returned to Tuskegee as superintendent of buildings and grounds.

From Edward Augustine Benner

Wellesley, Mass. May 30, 1903

My dear Mr. Washington: My present communication will cause you great grief, and it pains me very much to make it. For a month or six weeks past I have noticed Booker's willingness to play with the truth and several times he has been guilty of plain falsehood. Since that time I have talked with him seriously and at such times the consideration of his conduct in connection with his attachment to you has seemed to move him. But the spell passed. I have designedly kept positive restraint in the back ground, because I wanted to see how resolute he might be to resist temptations. I have cogent reasons to believe that contrary to the rules he has done considerable smoking in his room. He has neglected his hours and one night he came into his room by the window after hours.

Some time ago he planned, saying nothing to me about it, to meet his sister in Boston to spend his birthday with her. On May 19th she wrote him saying she "was so glad he could come." Meanwhile he continued his plans and finally on the 28th he came to me asking that he be excused on Friday morning to go to Boston. I said it was not my custom to excuse any one during school sessions, and that his work in Algebra was so far behind that I could not see my way clear to excuse him; yet I wished to please him and his sister, and I would speak with him again. That night I excused him from study-hour that he might drum and drill with the Boys' Brigade for Decoration Day. His uniform instruction is to return at once after drill. He should have appeared at about nine, but went down town with some boys of the brigade and appeared at ten and hid behind the cottage, apparently intending to enter by his east window. There I found him and asked him to explain. In the morning I said I would let him off on the 2.24 p.m. train but up to that time he must attend to his work. When the bell rang for school at one, instead of obeying it he went to the 1.07 train for Boston and returned at nine. This morning I asked him to explain his conduct. He said it was a case of distinct disobedience, but he had thought it all over and made up his mind to do it; he thought that was best.

I conclude, in view of his conduct and his attitude of defiance that I can do but one thing and that is to ask you to remove him from the school, and I await a prompt telegram from you instructing me where to send him. With much sympathy and the highest regard, I am   Sincerely Yours

Edw. A. Benner

ALS   Con. 249   BTW Papers   DLC.

J. C. May [Wilford H. Smith]
to R. C. Black [Emmett Jay Scott]

New York City, N.Y. June 3rd, 1903

Dear Friend: I think we have the article we want in the Guardian of the 30th ult., reflecting upon William Pickens,[1] the Yale man. I have just written him, suggesting that his friends here who had read the article were willing to furnish the expenses, if he would consent to make the complaint and furnish the testimony for the prosecution.

The Guardian folks were at the Hayes meeting in Brooklyn yesterday, which was a convention of New England, New Jersey, and New York people, to elect delegates to attend the Suffrage Convention to be held in Louisville, on the first of July, and they tried to get through a resolution reflecting on "His Nibs," but it did not go. The thing got so warm at one time, that Forbes and Hayes had to be separated. Forbes called Hayes a coward and a hypocrite because he did not stand by Trotter's attack on "His Nibs." The convention was simply a huge pow-wow and nothing more.

I am impatient to hear something from you in reply to my several letters, as time is running on my writs of error. Very truly yours,

J. C. May

TLSr Con. 25 BTW Papers DLC.

1 William Pickens (1881–1954), born in South Carolina, graduated from Talladega College in 1902 and from Yale in 1904. In the spring of 1903 Pickens won an oratory prize at Yale for a speech on Haiti, but in his speech he ridiculed that nation's political history and even suggested that it might have been better governed by whites. The *Guardian* attacked Pickens for "throwing down his own race." The *Guardian* was outraged when Pickens repeated the speech in Cambridge and described Pickens as "the little black freak student at Yale . . . with his enormous lips, huge mouth, and a monkey grin co-extensive with his ears." (Boston *Guardian*, May 9, 23, 1903, quoted in Fox, *Guardian of Boston*, 68–69.) Pickens was willing to prosecute the *Guardian* editors for libel, with aid from Washington and Smith, until they published an apology.

Pickens turned down an offer from Tuskegee Institute and went to Talladega from 1904 to 1914 as a teacher of Greek, Latin, and German. A member of the Niagara Movement, he became outspokenly critical of BTW after the founding of the NAACP, and this may have hastened his departure from Talladega. After teaching at Wiley College in 1914–15, he was dean of Morgan College from 1915 to 1920. He was field secretary of the NAACP from 1920 to 1942.

From Charles William Anderson

New York. June 4, 1903

Personal

My dear Doctor: Enclosed please find clippings "anent" Brooklyn Convention.[1] It was a failure. About two hundred present — principally spectators who were friendly to you. I was named on the Committee on resolutions, but withdrew last Friday, & had Chairman Gilbert[2] of the Arrangements Committee, name a substitute who was "one of us." I called on most of the local delegates & advised them to watch for resolutions & expressions reflecting upon you. Nearly all of those seen, were as sound as a gold dollar. I did not attend, & my club did not send delegates. Hayes disavowed any intention of exploding dynamite, and assured Gilbert that no assault would be made on any individual. Trotter of Boston, presented his resolution to committee & it was voted down, but through the weakness of the permanent Chairman, or by some underhand arrangement, he was allowed to speak on the floor. His speech created something a little short of a riot. He was greeted with cat-calls, and cries of "put him out." The women wanted to mob him. The entire "push" was strongly reminded that New York was not the place to assail you. They all fell to defending you, and turned on the very man they had encouraged to come there to assail you. My impression is, that "the lawyer" and "the bishop" arranged the assault with the intention of defending you, and thus demonstrating the importance of the work they are doing in your interest. Else why did they confine the call to New York, New Jersey and New England, and give the Trotter people the management of the New England wing? Sabe?

The New York papers ignored it almost completely. The "Sun" was the only paper to notice the row. All told, it was a farce and a fizzle. Look out for letters from "high clerics" telling you how strenuously they defended you. Hastily yours,

Anderson

ALS   Con. 278   BTW Papers   DLC.

1 A convention of the Henry Highland Garnet Republican Club of Brooklyn.

2 Francis H. Gilbert of Brooklyn, N.Y., was born in 1852 and attended Wilberforce College in 1868–69. He was owner of the Saratoga Cab Co. from 1900 to 1906, and was active in Republican politics in Kings County. He was a member of the NNBL, and later served as treasurer and board member of the Brooklyn branch of the National Urban League.

To Mrs. A. F. D. Grey[1]

[Tuskegee, Ala., ca. June 5, 1903]

Dear Madam: A story of persecution, of outrage and massacre of any people should never fail to stir the deepest sympathy of all right-thinking men and women of every nation, regardless of race, creed or form of government.

The report that has come of the horrors of Kishineff is shocking to the last degree, and civilization justly revolts against the cruelties that have been visited upon the heads of a people so law-abiding and peace-loving as the Jews.

Not only as a citizen of the American Republic, but as a member of a race which has, itself, been the victim of much wrong and oppression, my heart goes out to our Hebrew fellow-sufferers across the sea, in this hour of their dire extremity. I rejoice, however, that the latent conscience of the earth is liberally responding to your righteous appeal for aid, for in the awakening of refined feeling throughout the world, there rests an assurance that the safeguards of liberty, religious and civil, will be increased and more vigorously maintained. That a repetition of the frightful scenes of Kishineff may be rendered impossible, is a duty to which I pray this advanced century may seriously and at once address itself.

[Booker T. Washington]

TL   Con. 263   BTW Papers   DLC.

1 Secretary of the Ladies' Auxiliary of the Kishineff Relief League, Chicago. A massacre of Jews in this Russian city occurred in Apr. 1903 at the instigation of Russian officials.

From Charles William Anderson

New York, June 5th, 1903

Personal

My dear Dr. Washington: Supplementing my report of the Suffrage convention, which was mailed to you on yesterday, I beg to say that I have been informed that the secret plans of the convention were disclosed from the floor, by Mr. Trotter of Boston. He openly charged Mr. Hayes with having entered into an agreement with him to permit the passage of the resolution censuring you, and insinuated that the "good Bishop" and the "young statesman of Brooklyn" were in the plot. Mr. Trotter has been going about the City since the adjournment of the Convention, declaring that the managers had given him charge of the New England end of the movement, and had arranged to have his resolution pass without showing their hands in it, but were frightened off, because the house was so unmistakably in your favor. He is said to be very bitter against Hayes, the good Bishop, and Wibecan, and is charging them with all sorts of high crimes and misdemeanors. Thus it seems to be plain, that the plan originally was to have this un-friendly resolution aired in convention, and then have it tabled, under the plea of conservatism of action. By this scheme it was hoped, in my judgment, to be able to please your enemies without exposing the managers to the charge of having a hand in the plot. But the whole thing miscarried. Every man, woman and child present, was a stalwart supporter of yours, excepting the New England contingent. This frightened the managers and forced them to run away from their own clothes. This hasty retreat succeeded in bringing Trotter out with his charges of bad faith. So after all, the atmosphere is considerably clearer than it was before. The good Bishop did not attend, and was charged, by one of the delegates from New England, with having encouraged the "New England idea" and then remained away from the Convention that he might disclaim responsibility for it. I pass this along as the aftermath of the pow wow. Am glad you will be in the City shortly when we can go over the matter fully.

Hoping you are very well, I remain   Yours truly,

Charles W. Anderson

TLS   Con. 278   BTW Papers   DLC.

From Archibald Henry Grimké

Boston   June 6, 1903

Dear Sir: I was glad to get your second note, and the assurance which it contained that at some convenient time you would take occasion to explain further your position on the suffrage question in the South. I think it wise to do so. For I am told that, while it is true that you have several times endeavored to prevent the dis-franchisement of your race by certain Southern states, you have, after adverse action of those states, counseled, in effect, if not openly, acquiescence on the part of your people in such adverse action. It seems to be, therefore, under the circumstances highly expedient that you take or make an early occasion to set yourself right on this point. You could not possibly mean that the revised constitutions of those Southern states do, in fact, put a premium on property, intelligence, thrift, and character, for you and I know that they do not, either in spirit or in operation. It seems to me vastly important, then, that you make the public and the press clearly understand just what you did mean.

I appreciate the difficulty and danger of your relations with the South, and of those of Tuskegee also. But since you have been so often cited by that section and at the North, too, as commending those revised constitutions which have disfranchised the great bulk of the colored voters in certain Southern states, without at the same time depriving a single white man, however ignorant or worthless, of the right to vote, it is due to your race and to the principle of equality on which this republic was founded, that you define clearly, positively, and publicly the meaning of your much quoted and, I must believe, misunderstood remark that every revised constitution of the South puts a premium on property, intelligence, character and thrift.

I have known in the course of my life many noble men and women some of whom I have been intimately associated with, and I greatly admire the ability you have shown in redeeming yourself from the condition of slavery and I hate to think you are unfaithful to your own nobleness or the rights of your race to the exercise of the ballot on the same terms as white men enjoy the right. Respectfully yours,

[Archibald H. Grimké]

TL Copy   Archibald H. Grimké Papers   DHU.

A Statement in the Philadelphia *North American*

Philadelphia, June 7, 1903

NEGRO AND THE WHITE

I believe it is the duty of the negro — as the greater part of the race is already doing — to deport himself modestly in regard to political claims, depending on the slow but sure influences that proceed from the possession of property, intelligence and high character for the full recognition of his political rights.

I think that the according of the full exercise of political rights is going to be a matter of natural, slow growth, not an over-night, gourd-vine affair. I do not believe that the negro should cease voting, for a man cannot learn the exercise of self-government by ceasing to vote, any more than a boy can learn to swim by keeping out of the water; but I do believe that in his voting he should more and more be influenced by those of intelligence and character who are his next-door neighbors.

I know colored men who, through the encouragement, help and advice of Southern white people, have accumulated thousands of dollars worth of property, but who, at the same time, would never think of going to those same persons for advice concerning the casting of their ballots. This, it seems to me, is unwise and unreasonable, and should cease. In saying this, I do not mean that the negro should truckle, or not vote from principle, for the instant he ceases to vote from principle he loses the confidence and respect of the Southern white man even.

SUFFRAGE LAWS UNJUST

I do not believe that any State should make a law that permits an ignorant and poverty-stricken white man to vote and prevents a black man in the same condition from voting.

Such a law is not only unjust, but it will react, as all unjust laws do, in time; for the effect of such a law is to encourage the negro to secure education and property, and at the same time it encourages the white man to remain in ignorance and poverty. I believe that in time, through the operation of intelligence and friendly race relations, all cheating at the ballot-box in the South will cease.

It will become apparent that the white man who begins by cheating a negro out of his ballot soon learns to cheat a white man out of his, and that man who does this ends his career of dishonesty by the theft of property or by some equally serious crime.

In my opinion, the time will come when the South will encourage all of its citizens to vote. It will see that it pays better, from every standpoint, to have healthy, vigorous life than to have that political stagnation which always results when one-half the population has no share and no interest in the government.

As a rule, I believe in universal, free suffrage, but I believe that in the South we are confronted with peculiar conditions that justify the protection of the ballot in many of the States, for a while at least, either by an educational test, a property test, or by both combined; but whatever tests are required they should be made to apply with equal and exact justice to both races.

Philadelphia *North American*, June 7, 1903, 7.

A Statement by Louise Hadley in the Philadelphia *North American*[1]

Philadelphia, June 7, 1903

WHY I WOULDN'T DO IT

I refused to make up the bed of Professor Washington on general principles.

For a white girl to clean up the rooms occupied by a negro, I don't care who he is or how great he is, is a disgrace. I realized that if I cleaned up Booker Washington's rooms I would be looked down upon, and the slurs and insults of others would be thrown into my face at every turn.

I have always felt that the negro was not far above the brute. He is as calm as a lamb when talking to you, but ready to kill you when your back is turned. Of course, I don't say they are all that way; that is, man for man.

I admire Booker T. Washington in his place, but unfortunately he is out of it most of the time. He is the leader of his race, and no doubt has done more to elevate his people than any other man.

He is brilliant, and a man of great education no one can deny, but at the same time reveals all the characteristics of the negro.

Booker T. Washington has a national reputation, and he never hesitates to take advantage of the fact. He seeks the most aristocratic and seclusive company of the white people, and what arouses my indignation is the fact that some of the members of my own race seem glad of the opportunity to welcome him into their homes.

A RACIAL CHARACTERISTIC

Why doesn't Booker Washington seek the company of the men of the race of which he is the leader? In every city he enters there are a number of prominent colored families who would be proud to entertain their leader as a guest, and no doubt these same people wonder why their race's representative slights them and turns them aside for the company of men who are far his superiors.

But this is the negro for you. Give one an inch and he'll take a mile — that's a racial characteristic.

I can stand the negro when he is in his place, but I have no use for him when he is out of it. Booker T. Washington is an educated negro, and when he is in the South be behaves himself, but when he comes North he seeks to put himself on a level with white men. I have no use for him. Booker Washington's education has made him a leader of his race, but no amount of education can take the negro out of him.

I am not Southern born, but I am a Southern woman in spirit. My people were slaveowners in the South, and my grandfather was Joshua Morris, a United States Judge in Alabama. My father and mother were born in the South, but years ago they moved to Anna, Ill., where I was born, and where my home is to-day.

My father was a Union soldier, a member of the Eighteenth Illinois. He fought to save his country, but not to free the negroes. My parents lived in the slave district, and I have been taught to look upon the negro as the inferior of the white man, and created for his service.

I dislike very much the notoriety that my refusal to make Booker T. Washington's bed has brought upon me.

I come from the South where a white man is treated like a gentleman and white women are respected. But in Indianapolis it is entirely different. White people are treated as ruffians, and elbowed off the sidewalk.

Negroes are black and you cannot expect them to receive the respect from people, especially Southern people, that a white man receives. Even now since this matter has come up the negroes in my neighborhood are beginning to hoot at me on the street, and as they pass the house make remarks.

I am a Southern woman and am proud of it. No woman in the South would clean a negro's room, and I take the same stand that they do, although I do not live in the South.

Colored men, both great and small, are all the same to me.

President Roosevelt making Booker Washington a guest at the White House is the most unheard of thing that could have happened. The President has lowered himself and his country by welcoming the negro to the chief home of the nation. That is carrying matters entirely too far, and I think, as President, Roosevelt should be impeached for it.

I am an out-and-out Republican, agreeing with the party of my choice in everything, with the exception of the negro wing. That's where I object strenuously, as, in fact, I do with everything in which the negro attempts to force the effect or influence of his presence. That's the whole secret of why I refused to make Booker T. Washington's bed.

I simply stood by my principles, and did what I thought was right. To my many unknown friends in the South and a few in the North, who have so nobly and substantially expressed their appreciation of my act, I feel the deepest gratitude. The course of events has decided me. I have determined to go South to take one of the numerous positions awaiting my acceptance. There the negro knows his place, and he keeps it. There white men and women are treated by them with due respect, and are not insulted as they are in the North by being asked to become the servants of the negro.

Philadelphia *North American*, June 7, 1903, 7.

¹ This statement was coupled on the same page with BTW's statement above, though they had no connection. The *North American* mentioned that after Louise (Lulu) Hadley, an Indianapolis chambermaid, lost her job because of her refusal to make BTW's hotel bed, southern sympathizers sent her several thousand dollars and numerous job offers. Fate took an ironic turn, however, when the bulk of the money was stolen. Persons in Indianapolis said that her convictions were not as deep as she claimed, and the housekeeper of the Hotel English said that Louise Hadley had previously made BTW's bed, once or twice, without expressing any aversion.

Emmett Jay Scott
to Maybelle W. McAdoo [Wilford H. Smith]

[Tuskegee, Ala.] June 9, 1903

Hope you will push Pickens matter with all speed. Telegraph me our expense how it stands. Will write about other matters.

E. J. S.

TWIr   Con. 266   BTW Papers   DLC.

Maybelle W. McAdoo [Wilford H. Smith]
to Emmett Jay Scott

New York   6/9 1903

Pickens hesitates about matters   have written again urging him.

McAdoo

HWSr   Con. 266   BTW Papers   DLC.

To Walter Hines Page

[Tuskegee, Ala.] June 11, 1903

My dear Mr. Page: I thank you for the suggestion you have made regarding my World's Work article and for your reference to the recent address of Senator Simmons[1] in North Carolina. I wish to say that I have watched the discussion with some care on the part of Southern whites and others regarding the industrial education of the Negro, and in its bearing upon economic competition between the two races, so far as my observation and experience are concerned, I am convinced there is nothing in it. It is all barking and no biting. Every Negro in the South that learns to do something which the South wants done finds ready employment, and in my opinion it will be a hundred years before that condition is changed, if ever. Only yesterday we received urgent telephone and telegraphic messages from a large firm in Birmingham urging us to send some of our graduates there to replace white skilled workmen who had proven unsatisfactory. The demand for our graduates is simply overwhelming. Senator Simmons simply does not know what he is talking about. Yours truly,

[Booker T. Washington]

TLc Con. 550 BTW Papers DLC.

[1] Furnifold McLendel Simmons (1854–1940), U.S. congressman (1887–89), U.S. senator (1901–31).

To John Davison Rockefeller, Jr.

[Tuskegee, Ala.] June 11, 1903

My dear Mr. Rockefeller: I am sorry that the amount left over after the completion of Rockefeller Hall is not as large as I thought it would be, still I take great pleasure in returning to you in the enclosed check Two Hundred and Forty-nine ($249.00) Dollars.

You do not know how very grateful we are to your father for this generous help. It has made a very large number of our boys much happier and placed them in a position to do better work than they have ever done before.

I hope at some time your father can see the school that he has done so much to put upon its feet. The students and teachers would give him a great welcome if he could ever see his way clear to come. Yours very truly,

[Booker T. Washington]

TLc Con. 709 BTW Papers DLC.

To James Earl Russell

[Tuskegee, Ala.] June 11, 1903

Dear Dean Russell: Since writing you a few days ago to the effect that $300 are not enough to cover all the expenses of the students who have been sent to the Teachers College from Tuskegee, I have been glad to see the letter written by you to Mrs. Trumbull[1] in Colorado in which you also state that it will require $400 or $450 to pay the expenses of the students.

In regard to the matter of Tuskegee students going to the Teachers College I would say that after carefully investigating the matter I am glad to say that all those who have been sent there have been greatly benefited and have not at all been spoiled by living in New York City. I am quite sure that the same will be true of those we intend to send next year.

I think I know two of the donors, Mr. Brown[2] and Mr. Macy. These have both stated to me at various times that they would be willing to pay the expenses of a student from Tuskegee as long as we found it helpful. The other donor I believe is Mr. Rockefeller although I am not sure of this. As soon as I hear from the individuals who bear these expenses I shall be glad to write them. Yours very truly,

[Booker T. Washington]

TLc Con. 273 BTW Papers DLC.

1 Mary A. Sisson (Mrs. Frank) Trumbull.

2 John Crosby Brown (b. 1838), a banker and director of several railroads, or his son, William Adams Brown (b. 1865), a professor at Union Theological Seminary and a guest of Robert C. Ogden on his southern tours.

To Oswald Garrison Villard

[Tuskegee, Ala.] June 16, 1903

My dear Mr. Villard: The death of Mr. Thrasher was a great shock to all of us. Enclosed I send you a marked copy of our little paper, The Student, which [contains] some detailed account of his sickness and death.[1] Mr. Thrasher came as near being a perfect man as any, it seems to me, with whom I came into contact.

It may interest you to know, if you are not already in possession of the facts, that we owe to Judge Thomas G. Jones, who was appointed by President Roosevelt recently, a great debt of gratitude for what is being done in regard to exposing the peonage system in Alabama. I notice by this morning's paper that he has just declared the labor contract laws of the state unconstitutional.

The state's attorney, who lives in Tuskegee, was in my office a few days ago and he was detailing to me the efforts that he had made to bring those guilty of enslaving the colored people to justice but was baffled at [that] point until the Federal authorities took hold.

I have the Atlantic with your article on the Negro Soldiers [and] have not had time to read it but I shall do so soon.

I am planning to be in New York before many days and shall plan to see you. Yours truly,

[Booker T. Washington]

TLc Con. 249 BTW Papers DLC.

[1] Max Bennett Thrasher died of peritonitis in the Tuskegee Institute hospital on May 29, 1903, after an operation for acute appendicitis. (*Tuskegee Student*, 15 [June 6, 1903], 1.)

From Emmett Jay Scott

New Orleans June 21/03

My Dear Mr Washington: I came here this morning and found Montgomery[1] & Roscoe[2] waiting for some[one] — they knew not whom. I got right down to business with Montgomery & went over the whole, entire case in all of its details. The man is terribly broken up & disconcerted. He has refused in stated words to admit his guilt — except to say that the Special Agent was no doubt justified in the kind of report that he made — that he could have made an easier one if he had desired & that he could have also made a more damaging one & treated him with less consideration than he did show. He very *immodestly* on leaving showed the telegram asking him to come here to all of his office force & citizens of the town (as he has confessed to me under pressure) & so is all the more disconcerted for that reason. He seemed to feel that a special representative of Secretary Hitchcock was to come from Washington on here to give him instructions to do certain work. It is evidently a bolt from a clear sky as the agent had told him that all would be well & that he could rest easy as everything was finally accounted for, etc.

I wish to acquaint you with this fact however — *Brant*[?], the Special Agent in question, has given it out in this town that he has recommended Montgomery's dismissal, since two (2) persons have mentioned that fact to me — persons who know absolutely nothing of my mission here & who have so spoken only because they know that M. is here, & that fact caused them to make the suggestion to me. I knew nothing of the matter (to them).

Well, Montgomery, as I have wired you is hesitant & halting because he knows the people of Jackson will see a connection between his visit here & his resignation & desires to have it go in later to take effect September 30, the ending of the next quarter instead of June 30, the end of the present quarter. I have not parleyed with him. I have told him that he cannot now seek "to save his face," that he ought to feel mighty glad "to save his neck." He is thoroughly appreciative of the President's great consideration, as well as Secretary Hitchcock's & of your interest & only exhibits quite naturally it seems to me just the same kind of action that most men w'd exhibit. I shall stick here till he freely agrees to send in his resignation — as he can hope for nothing by sticking. I have asked you to wire me that there is no hope for a modification to Sept. 30 — so as to help me with the pressure I am putting on him. I have waited 5 hours & have not yet received answer of any character, but hope to shortly. I shall wire you as to outcome & you will have it before you get this letter. It is a pity that you have been betrayed by one whom you had trusted, but, but — it is the fates *again!!*

I beg to suggest that Col. Lewis has been holding over since January 19. There can be no doubt as to the President['s] intention to appoint him, & I wish you might suggest it to the President. It w'd do great good & would please the Colonel very much, as well as the masses of our people throughout the country. Walter Cohen[3] is also holding over, has Hanna's support & sh'd be reappointed. I have incidentally got both of them to agree to go to Louisville. They go to fight for the Administration (if necessary) & will be for anything you want.

If you should decide to send this report to the President w'd suggest that it be copied on typewriter, as I have no ink. The first part (as you note) refers alone to Montgomery. The latter leaves the whole thing to your final decision & your expected wire ought to settle it. Will wire when I go home.[4] Respectfully

Emmett J. Scott

ALS   Con. 274   BTW Papers   DLC.

[1] Isaiah T. Montgomery.

[2] Roscoe Conkling Simmons.

[3] Walter L. Cohen, a black former saloonkeeper and a Catholic, was for many years receiver of the federal land office in New Orleans and leader of the black-and-tan faction of Republicans in Louisiana. He and James Lewis were BTW's chief political lieutenants in that state. He also frequently aided BTW by arranging in New Orleans for Pullman accommodations on trains passing near Tuskegee.

[4] The next day Scott wrote BTW that he had secured Montgomery's resignation as receiver of public moneys in Jackson, Miss., because of "the pressure of personal interests." (June 22, 1903, Con. 274, BTW Papers, DLC.)

An Interview in the Boston *Transcript*

[South Weymouth, Mass., June 21, 1903]

His Place at Tuskegee

Booker T. Washington realizes that his place is at Tuskegee, and has no intention of accepting the offer of Lord Grey to go to British South Africa to undertake a similar work.[1] At his Weymouth summer home he said, yesterday: "One very practical reason why I cannot accept the offer is that Tuskegee needs about $100,000 a year which I have to raise. Lord Grey wanted me to examine the condition of the black people, and to make a report as to what methods would increase their industrial and moral value. I considered the offer carefully, but found the task fraught with such responsibility that I decided to reject it at this time. Some day, perhaps, I shall go, but it will be when my labors here are not so great as they now are.

The blacks there represent every grade of intelligence and education from savagery to the college graduate, but the majority of the work of advancement is being done along industrial lines."

Boston *Transcript*, June 22, 1903, 5.

1 BTW was approached indirectly in Mar. 1903 to undertake a tour of British South Africa for the purpose of finding ways to improve black life there. The British journalist William Thomas Stead, founder of the English *Review of Reviews*, contacted his American counterpart, Albert Shaw, on behalf of Albert Henry George, Earl Grey, former administrator of Rhodesia. (Shaw to BTW, Mar. 7, 1903, Con. 277, BTW Papers, DLC. See also Stead to Shaw, Feb. 11, and Stead to BTW, June 3, 1903, Con. 277, BTW Papers, DLC.)

To Theodore Roosevelt

South Weymouth, Mass. 22 June, 1903

Personal.

My dear Mr. President: While speaking to you Thursday concerning the attitude of the colored people in Indiana, Ohio, and Illinois, I meant to have said that I find most unrest existing in the state of New York, especially in New York city. This unrest is not the result of opposition to yourself, to your policy, or to the Republican party as such; but is due to the fact that a great number of colored people have formed the habit of voting with Tammany Hall on local issues; which habit is due to the activity of Tammany Hall in furnishing a large number of our people with employment. Very truly yours,

Booker T. Washington

TLS   Theodore Roosevelt Papers   DLC.

From Charles Barzillai Spahr

New York   June 23, 1903

Dear Mr. Washington: The clippings you sent Dr. Abbott — regarding the peonage cases before Judge Jones — were of great service. They practically gave us our second editorial on this subject. We want soon to prepare another paragraph upon the disposition the court makes of the cases now before it and particularly upon Judge Jones's attitude toward the Alabama Contract Law under which so many negroes seem to be held in involuntary servitude. We do not wish to ask your personal attention to this matter but if you would ask one of your assistants to send us the necessary clippings from the Montgomery papers, we should be still further indebted to you. Yours very truly,

Charles B. Spahr

P.S. — Any reply should be addressed to the Managing Editor, as I am just starting off for a short vacation.

TLS   Con. 270   BTW Papers   DLC.

From John Davison Rockefeller, Jr.

New York. June 24th, 1903

Dear Mr. Washington: Your favor of June 11th to my father enclosing check for $249 being the balance of his pledge authorizing the expenditure up to $34,000. for a boys dormitory, which balance you state was not required in the completion of the building, is received. My father is gratified to know that the building has been constructed so well within the estimated cost, the more so since it so frequently happens that the opposite is the case. He takes pleasure in returning the check for $249., desiring that the same be applied as you may see fit. Very truly,

John D Rockefeller Jr

TLS   Con. 249   BTW Papers   DLC.

Theodore Roosevelt to Edgar Stewart Wilson

White House, Washington. June 24, 1903

Personal.

Dear Mr. Wilson: For reasons which will be explained to you Montgomery has resigned. Give me at once a first-class colored man to put in his place.

The question of the political importance of the colored man is really of no consequence. I do not care to consider it, and you must not consider it. Give me the very best colored man that you know of for the place, upon whose integrity and capacity we can surely rely. Sincerely yours,

Theodore Roosevelt

TLSr Copy   Con. 282   BTW Papers   DLC.

R. C. Black [Emmett Jay Scott] to J. C. May [Wilford H. Smith]

[Tuskegee, Ala.] June 25, 1903

Dear Friend: Giles[1] is here to-day and has just had a talk with me. He is seeking a contribution from Mr. Washington. I have told him how thoroughly impossible it is for us to contribute toward the cause for reasons which I gave him, and which I thought he would understand. I have said to him, however, that I would wire you to see the Wizard in New York, and perhaps he would at least be able to put you in touch with some strong, influential persons. I wish you would write Giles to the effect simply that following a suggestion you saw the Wizard and that the interview was satisfactory. Do not leave him to think at all that the interest was substantial. Yours truly,

R. C. Black

TLSr   Con. 25   BTW Papers   DLC.

[1] Jackson Giles (b. 1859), a Montgomery black man, was the plaintiff in the Alabama suffrage cases. He worked as a janitor in the Montgomery Post Office. It is clear from this letter that Giles did not know that BTW was a major contributor toward the legal expenses of these cases.

From Francis Ellington Leupp

Washington, D.C., June 27, 1903

My dear Mr. Washington: Enclosed is the letter to Wilson,[1] which, as I wrote you, the President dictated while I waited. Before it could reach its destination, however, Wilson, who had been in New York, slipped into Washington. I contrived to get him into and out of the White House without anyone's discovering his presence; and it was arranged between him and the President that the acceptance of M——'s resignation should be made "on the appointment and qualification of his successor"; that Wilson should hunt up the right man, and get his appointment and qualification papers into shape; and that then the announcement should go forth casually and among a lot of others, that "so-and-so has been appointed, vice M—— resigned." There will thus be no interval.

Wilson was very badly cut up over this case. "He is a traitor to his race!" he exclaimed. "Where shall I look for another, when I have endorsed him as the best, and the ideal man?" Sincerely,

Francis E. Leupp

TLS Con. 249 BTW Papers DLC.

[1] June 24, 1903. See above.

From William H. Moss[1]

Boston Mass   June 28/03

Dear Doctor — Wm. M Trotter Forbes & Scott will leave Monday or Tuesday for Louisville Ky. I think it would be advisable for you to send Clifford H Plumer or someone, as the object of their going is to make a personal attack upon yourself. Kindly advise what day next week you can give me a[n] audiance. Yours very truly

Wm H Moss

ALS Con. 268 BTW Papers DLC.

[1] William H. Moss, a member of the Boston branch of the NNBL, published the pro-BTW newspaper the Boston *Advocate* in 1902. When it did not succeed, he

joined with Peter J. Smith, Jr., to publish the Boston *Enterprise* briefly in 1903. (Fox, *Guardian of Boston*, 70–71.)

To Timothy Thomas Fortune

[South Weymouth, Mass.] 29 June, 1903

Greatest importance your opening address be of calm conservative nature.

B. T. W.

TWIr Con. 542 BTW Papers DLC.

To the Editor of the *Independent*[1]

[South Weymouth, Mass.] 29 June, 1903

Prefer expressing in my address before National Afro-American Council at Louisville this week what I have to say concerning lynching.

Booker T. Washington

TWSr Con. 540 BTW Papers DLC.

[1] William Hayes Ward.

From James Sullivan Clarkson

New York, N.Y., June 30th, 1903

My dear Doctor Washington: I received your letter of 28th. Mr. Peter J. Smith came the same day, and we fitted him out with transportation from here to Louisville and return. I was glad to do this, and especially after receiving your letter, as it is important that he should attend the convention. Chas. W. Anderson concluded not to go, as he had very important business here. Dr. Morris[1] has gone, leaving today. Anderson says that the Hayes people have come in and proposed to support the regular order. Sincerely yours,

James S. Clarkson

TLS   Con. 252   BTW Papers   DLC.

[1] Charles Satchell Morris.

An Address before the
National Afro-American Council[1]

Louisville, Kentucky, July 2, 1903

RIGHTS AND DUTIES OF THE NEGRO

In the midst of the present deep interest growing out of matters connected with our race, it can be stated that recent events, as regretable as they are, have tended to simplify the problem in one direction at least. The events to which I refer show that the questions pertaining to our race are each day more and more becoming national ones, rather than local and sectional ones. When we carry the question up into the atmosphere where men of all races, North and South, will discuss it with calmness, with absence of passion and sectional feelings, I believe we shall have made a distinct advance.

While my remarks tonight will relate to the race in its national aspect, I speak also as one who was born in the South, who loves it, and expects to abide there permanently. I am glad this great meeting is held south of the Mason and Dixon line. It is in the South that the great masses of our people dwell, and will abide in the future as now. It is fitting that this body should have its hearing and perform its work in the section of our country where the Negro race lives; it is equally important that this organization speak its words and perfect its plans in the midst of the white people who are most directly concerned about the future of the race.

Whatever progress is made in the years that are to come will result largely from open, frank discussion and a sympathetic cooperation between the highest types of whites and the same class of blacks. One thing of which I feel absolutely sure is that without mutual confidence and cooperation there is little hope for the progress which we all desire. In the present season of anxiety, and almost of despair, which possesses an element of the race, there are two things which I will say as strongly as I may.

First, let no man of the race become discouraged or hopeless. Though their voices may not be often or loudly lifted, there are in this country, North and South, men who mean to help see that justice is meted out to the race in all avenues of life. Such a man is Judge Thomas G. Jones, of Alabama, to whom more credit should be given for blotting out the infamous system of peonage than to any other. Judge Jones represents the very highest type of Southern manhood, and there are hosts of others like him. There is a class of brave, earnest men in the South, as well as in the North, who are more determined than ever before to see that the race is given an opportunity to elevate itself; and we owe it to these friends as well as to ourselves to see that no act of ours causes them embarrassment.

Second, let us keep before us the fact that, almost without exception, every race or nation that has ever got upon its feet has done so through struggle and trial and persecution; and that out of this very resistance to wrong, out of the struggle against odds, it has gained strength, self-confidence, and experience which it could not have gained in any other way.

And not the least of the blessings of such struggle is that it keeps one humble and nearer to the heart of the Giver of all gifts. Show me the individual who is permitted to go through life without anxious thought, without ever having experienced a sense of poverty and wrong, want and struggle, and I will show you a man who is likely to fail in life. "Whom the Lord loveth, He chasteneth."

No one should seek to close his eyes to the truth that the race is passing through a very serious and trying period of its development, a period that calls for the use of our ripest thought, our most sober judgment, and frequent appeals to Him who has promised strength to the weak.

During the season through which we are now passing, I wish to ask, with all the emphasis I am able to command, that each individual of the race keep a calm mind and exercise the greatest self-control; and that we all keep a brave heart. Let nothing lead us into extremes of utterance or action. By this method of procedure we shall be able to justify the faith of our friends and confound our enemies. In the affairs of a race, as with great business enterprises, it is the individual of few words and conservative action who commands respect and confidence. Vastly more courage is often shown in one's ability to suffer in silence, or to keep the body under control when sorely tempted, than acting through the medium of a mob. In the long run it is the race or individual that exercises the most patience, forbearance, and self-control in the midst of trying conditions that wins its course and the respect of the world. Such a course will, in the end, draw to our side all men, North and South, whose good will and support are worth having. Let nothing induce us to descend to the level of the mob, but rather direct our course in a dignified atmosphere.

In advocating this policy I am not asking that the Negro act the coward; we are not cowards. The part which we have played in defending the flag of our country in every war in which we have been engaged is sufficient evidence of our courage when the proper time comes to manifest it.

The recent outbreaks of government by the mob emphasize two lessons, one for our race and one for the other citizens of our country, South and North; for it is to be noted, I repeat, that the work of the lyncher is not confined to one section of the country.

The lesson for us is that we should see to it that so far as the influence of parent, of school, of pulpit, and of press is concerned, no effort be spared to impress upon our people, especially the youth, that idleness and crime should cease, and that no excuse be given the world to label any large proportion of the race as idlers and criminals; and that we show ourselves as anxious as any other class of citizens to bring to punishment those who commit crime, when proper legal procedure is sure. We should let the world know on all proper occasions that we consider no legal punishment too severe for the wretch of any race who attempts to outrage a woman.

The lesson for the other portion of the nation to learn is that, both in the making and the execution, the same laws should be made to apply to the Negro as to the white man. There should be meted out equal justice to the black man and the white man whether it relates to citizenship, the protection of property, the right to labor, or the protection of human life. Whenever the nation forgets, or is tempted to forget, this basic principle, the whole fabric of government for both the white and the black man is weakened and threatened with destruction. This is true whether it relates to conditions in Texas, Indiana, or Delaware.

To show how far we have already been led astray by those who disregard the majesty of the law and would insult governors and judges, by those who would uphold the law in one case and trample it under foot in another, we have but to call attention to the lamentable fact that the most careful and systematic investigation into the subject of lynching that has ever been made in this country shows that only thirty-five per cent of those lynched have ever been charged with violence to women. To attempt to say that all these thirty-five per cent were guilty would be to argue that the judgment of the mob is more unerring than that of the court. We cannot, and should not, escape the punishment for our sins of commission or of omission.

It is with a nation as with an individual: whatsoever we sow, that shall we also reap; if we sow crime, we shall reap lawlessness. If we break the law when a helpless Negro is concerned, it will not be very long before the same law is disregarded when a white man is concerned. Out of the present conditions there is one sign more encouraging than all others; and that is that in the South as well as in the North the voice of the press is speaking out as never before in favor of upholding the majesty of the law.

The Negro in this country constitutes the most compact, reliable, and peaceful element of labor; one which is almost the sole dependence for production in certain directions; and I believe that, if for no higher reason than the economic one, the people will see that it is worth while to keep so large an element of labor happy, contented, and prosperous, by surrounding and guarding it with every protection and encouragement of the laws. In the long run, nothing is more costly and unsatisfactory than discontented, unhappy, and restless labor. Few people are wise enough to learn the economic value of justice.

In our efforts to go forward, we should keep in mind the difference between the problem presented previous to the Civil War and the one now confronting us. Before our freedom a giant tree was growing in the garden, which all considered injurious to the progress of the whole nation. The work to be done was direct and simple — destroy the hurtful tree. The work before us now is not the destruction of a tree, but the growing of one. Slavery presented a problem of destruction; freedom presents one of construction. This requires time, patience, preparation of the soil, watering, pruning, and the most careful nursing.

In this connection we should bear in mind that our ability and our progress will be measured largely by evidences of tangible, visible worth. We have a right in a conservative and sensible manner to enter our complaints, but we shall make a fatal error if we yield to the temptation of believing that mere opposition to our wrongs, and the simple utterance of complaint, will take the place of progressive, constructive action, which must constitute the bed-rock of all true civilization. The weakest race or individual can condemn a policy; it is the work of a statesman to construct one. A race is not measured by its ability to condemn, but to create. Let us hold up our heads and with firm and steady tread go manfully forward. No one likes to feel that he is continually following a funeral procession.

Let us not forget to lay the greatest stress upon the opportunities open to us, especially here in the South, for constructive growth in labor, in business and education. Back of all complaint, all denunciation, must be evidences of character and economic foundation. An inch of progress is worth more than a yard of complaint.

The whites and the blacks are to reside together in this country permanently, and we should lose no opportunity to cultivate in every straightforward, manly way the greatest harmony between the races. Whoever, North or South, black or white, by word or deed needlessly stirs up strife is an enemy to both races and to his country. While making our appeals for help and sympathy, we should not forget that in the last analysis the most effective appeal will consist in laying our case before the community and state in which we reside; nor that usefulness in our own homes will constitute our most lasting and most potent protection.

I appreciate from the bottom of my heart the tremendous and trying strain that is now upon us, and how difficult it is for us to make progress under such circumstances; but I believe the momentous period through which we are now passing will draw to our assistance in larger numbers the good will, the sympathy, and helpful cooperation of white men in the South, as well as in the North, if we only exercise due patience, self-control, and courage.

Ernest Davidson Washington, *Selected Speeches of Booker T. Washington* (Garden City, N.Y.: Doubleday, Doran and Co., 1932), 92–100. Incorrectly dated June 2, 1903.

1 Though W. M. Trotter and others of his faction sought a confrontation with BTW and bitterly criticized him on the convention floor, the Tuskegean's forces outnumbered and outmaneuvered the dissidents. BTW's address received a long ovation, and Fortune was re-elected president.

From Alfred Holt Stone[1]

Washington, D.C. July 2, 1903

Personal

Dear Sir: It is, and has always been, my opinion that a man should hold his peace, rather than, in attempting to discuss any phase of our "race question," give utterance to any expression in the least calculated to mar kindly relations, or beget feelings of harsh[n]ess or distrust between men who have the good of both races at heart.

I have faithfully tried to live up to this idea, and it is because in one instance I am placed in the attitude of departing from it that I write you this letter. I allude to an "interview" appearing in the Post this morning,[2] by Mr. Raymond Patterson.[3]

I shall not attempt to go into particulars, nor enumerate the instances wherein I have been misquoted, or my meaning utterly misinterpreted: I shall only say that I have never heard, nor claimed to hear, any mulatto "boast of his white ancestry," nor give any indication of feeling "degraded" by any "negro blood" he might possess. That I have never for a moment questioned the honesty of any views entertained by you, Dr. Du Bois, or any other man, in regard to the comparative capacities of the negro and mulatto, or any other subject, nor held to any such notion as that you were "dissembling" as to this, or any other question.

Mr. Patterson called on me a few nights since, and we had a lengthy conversation on the general subject of the so-called race question. It is in attempting to translate my ideas into his own words, and in confusing many of them in the process, that Mr. Patterson has done me the entirely unintentional injustice of misquoting me.

Mr. Patterson made no notes of our conversation, and I did not see the "interview" until its publication. The two paragraphs under the caption "Mulatto & Black Contrasted" are correctly quoted, being taken from a letter written after the appearance of your interview, though with no view to its publication.

I am writing this to place myself in the proper attitude as regards this interview, in so far as this may be possible through letters to two or three people, as against the circulation of a newspaper. In doing this I do not wish to be understood as charging Mr. Patterson with having intentionally misquoted me, though the wrong done my ideas, in numerous instances, is none the less great. Very truly yours,

Alfred H. Stone

ALS   Con. 277   BTW Papers   DLC.

[1] Alfred Holt Stone (1870–1955), a graduate of the University of Mississippi, was a gentleman scholar who divided his time between management of the family plantation Dunleith, the practice of law, and the study of sociology and economics. In 1900 he edited the Greenville *Times* for about a year, and spent most of the period from 1903 to 1910 studying in Washington, D.C. In 1908 he published *Studies in the American Race Problem*, which argued that the South should be left alone to handle the racial problem. Stone maintained that ignorant blacks were their own worst enemies, and he attributed the intelligence of some race leaders to their white blood.

[2] Stone allegedly said that the mulatto was not a degenerate but on the contrary superior to pure blacks. He reportedly said that men like BTW and W. E. B. Du Bois who denied that being of mixed ancestry made any difference secretly harbored the belief "that the white strain does tell, and that practically all of the men of so-called negro blood who have done anything in the world are of the mulatto type." (Washington *Post*, July 2, 1903, 3.)

[3] Raymond Albert Patterson (1856–1909), a Yale graduate (1878), was a regular columnist for the Chicago *Tribune* and other papers, writing from Washington, D.C.

To Theodore Roosevelt

Tuskegee, Ala., 6 July, 1903

My dear Mr. President: Perhaps you remember that you suggested that Mr. Wm. H. Lewis, of Boston, be invited to speak before the Afro-American Council at Louisville this week. He delivered two speeches, and I think I am safe in saying that he captured the entire meeting in the most effective manner. A great opportunity was offered him in the occasion, and he took advantage of it. The rank and file now know him, and he is acquainted with real conditions. I think he will as a consequence be a much more helpful and stronger man.

I beg to enclose a copy of the resolutions unanimously adopted by the National Afro-American Council at its Louisville meeting last week.[1] Very truly yours,

Booker T. Washington

TLS   Theodore Roosevelt Papers   DLC.

[1] The resolutions condemned disfranchisement and called upon the President to recommend to Congress that laws be passed guaranteeing constitutional rights for blacks. The Afro-American Council also endorsed Roosevelt and expressed "our unshaken confidence in his principles and policy of an open door to all American citizens." (Louisville *Courier-Journal*, July 4, 1903, 3.)

To William Edward Burghardt Du Bois

Tuskegee, July 6, 1903

Mr. Booker T. Washington will be pleased to have you take dinner with him at his home, "The Oaks,["] at 6:30 o'clock this evening.

HL   W. E. B. Du Bois Papers   MU.

To Julius B. Ramsey

[Tuskegee, Ala.] July 6, 1903

Major Ramsey: I find that in the barracks, Washington cottage, brick cottage and several other places where the boys sleep, they are troubled by bed bugs. I wish you would begin at once and take extra measures to see that all bed bugs are killed, and are kept entirely out of the boys' rooms. In order to carry out this order, I advise that you hire three or four women from the outside and let them devote themselves during the next two or three weeks, or for a month, if necessary, to getting all the bugs out of the rooms. This matter ought to receive constant and systematic attention all through the year.

[Booker T. Washington]

TLp   Con. 282A   BTW Papers   DLC.

From Charles William Anderson

New York, July 6th, 1903

Personal

My dear Dr. Washington: Immediately on the receipt of your first telegram I 'phoned General Clarkson about the passes, and was informed by him that he had secured two to Cincinnati and return, and one for me, clear through to Louisville and return. I told him that I could not use it, and asked him to give it to Mr. Smith of Boston, as he was one of our friends, and the other two men, Revs. Hunt[1] and Morris, ought to be instructed to support Fortune before supplying them with transportation. He agreed to act on this suggestion, and on the following day advised me that Hunt and Morris had agreed to support Fortune and to act generally with our friends at Louisville. On receipt of your second telegram, I called him up and gave him the information about Bruce. He was very much disturbed about it, and promised to read the riot act to him. Bruce did not secure his transportation from Clarkson. I rather think he got it from Hayes, as he is not in the habit of paying for things himself. It is exceedingly gratifying to know that our friends were victorious all along the line. Doubtless you have noticed that the New York newspapers have been giving splendid editorial approval of your Louisville speech. The "Times," "World" and "Evening Post" have all printed editorials along this line.

I forgot to mention that Clarkson told me that Mr. Smith of Boston was in town, and that he, Clarkson, was in doubt whether to give him the pass clear through to Louisville or to give him one of those from here to Cincinnati and return. I told him in reply that there was certainly no doubt about Mr. Smith, and therefore he ought to be given the through pass, while the other two men should be properly instructed. Did Morris and Hunt act with our friends? I think it is high time that we should line up these fellows, and find out just where each man stands.

You may be interested to know that Mr. Belmont[2] has purchased the Buffalo Race Track upon the report made by me as a result of my examination on last Thanksgiving Day. His own expert accountant reported against the investment, and I reported in its favor. I feel a little bit pleased that my judgment was accepted in a transaction, amounting to about $250,000.

Hoping you are very well, and that I will see you soon, I remain Yours truly,

Charles W. Anderson

TLS Con. 278 BTW Papers DLC.

[1] Reverend Granville Hunt, an associate of Bishop Alexander Walters.

[2] August Belmont (1853–1924), investment banker and promoter of New York's first subway system, the Interborough Rapid Transit Co.

To Charles Waddell Chesnutt

[Tuskegee, Ala.] July 7, 1903

Private and Confidential

My dear Mr. Chesnutt: I am in receipt of yours of June 27th[1] and thank you very much for your letter. I appreciate especially your reference to my friend, Mr. Thrasher; he was a very rare and helpful man, and his place will be difficult to fill.

I thank you for the freedom and frankness with which you write me regarding public matters pertaining to our race. Much that you say concerning the condition of our people in the South is true. I think there is little disagreement between us as to the actual state of affairs. In the last analysis I believe you will agree with me in this, that the Negro is like any other weak people. No one can give him strength which he does not intrinsically possess, and I fear, in one form or another, the Negro will have to continue to take his medicine until he gains material, mental, moral and political strength enough to enable him to change his present condition. If he wishes to, the strong man can always find a way to defeat the aspirations of the weaker one. That the Negro will always remain the weaker one I do not believe. With the same training I believe that the Negro will show as good results as other races, but until we do get that strength which can only come by education and experience, we shall be in an unenviable position. If a white man has upon his plantation in the South 500 Negro voters the majority of whom depend upon him for houses, for land, for food and clothing, this white man is going to control the franchise of the majority of those people. No law passed by congress or any state can prevent it, especially when there is ignorance mixed in with their poverty. Africa with her teeming millions is as old as Europe with its millions. Why the Africans did not go and take possession of the continent of Europe as the Europeans have of the continent of Africa I do not know, but I do know in some way that the European has gotten on top in Africa just as he has in America and I fear it grows out of the fact to which I referred in the beginning, that at present at least the Negro is the weaker race. This, however, is no excuse why justice should not be meted out to the weak in the South the same as is true in the North and in the West, and if we go on agitating and educating I believe that such justice will come. You will assist in bringing it about in your way and those of us who are laboring in the South will do the same to bring it about in our way. Our race has disadvandages in every part of the country. In the North you have Jim Crow work, in the South we have Jim Crow cars. In most sections of the North as much of a sensation would be created by a Negro going into a shoe factory or a printing office as if he went into a railroad car set aside for white people in the South. You say you have no faith in the Southern people's sense of justice so far as the Negro's rights are concerned. I have yet the most faith in the sense of justice of a large proportion of them, but just now in proportion to those who would do us wrong the number is small, but we should not condemn the good with the bad. Judge Thomas G. Jones of this state, a white Southern Democrat, is as pure, brave and honest a man and as good a friend to the Negro as any white man in this country.

You seem to imply in your letter that I have only expressed myself and am only interested in the subject of education and property.

Enclosed I send you two recent utterances of mine, one bearing upon the franchise and the other upon the subject of lynching. I say "recent utterances," but this does not indicate that I have not said the same thing over and over again in different words. If you would have me say any more or any less than I have said in these two utterances bearing upon lynching and the franchise I should be very glad to have you say so. I am not speaking on these subjects all the time either in the press or upon the public platform; if I were saying the [same] thing all the time the world would pay no attention to my words when the proper time came, but whenever I feel that the proper time has come for an utterance upon any subject concerning my race I have never hesitated to give that utterance. Some have claimed that I have been afraid to do anything that would not please the Southern white man in the way of asserting the Negro's rights as a citizen. When I accepted the invitation to dine with the President of the United States and his family it was with my eyes open. The invitation was in my hands for a day and during that period I had ample time to discuss the whole matter in all of its bearings with friends and to count the cost. Notwithstanding that I felt that in accepting this invitation I was not doing so as a personal matter but it was a recognition of the race and no matter what personal condemnation it brought upon my shoulders I had no right to refuse or even hesitate. I did my duty in the face of the opposition of the entire Southern press and at the risk of losing my own life.

I repeat I cannot understand what you or others want me to do that I have left undone. I should be very glad to hear from you at any time on this or any other subject whenever you feel in a mood to write. Yours very truly,

[Booker T. Washington]

TLc   Con. 551   BTW Papers   DLC.

1 See Chesnutt, *Charles W. Chesnutt*, 193–94.

To James Carroll Napier

Tuskegee, Ala. July 7, 1903

My dear Mr. Napier: I write you concerning two matters. First, I want to ask all of the officers of the National Negro Business League to be my guests at a dinner to be given in Nashville the evening previous to the meeting if you will be kind enough to arrange with some first class caterer to provide this dinner, of course at my whole expense.

Second, it has never been my purpose to attempt to remain at the head of the Business League. I felt when the organization was started that there was a field in which it could accomplish a great amount of good for our people, and at the time it was started I was in a position to inaugurate the movement in a way that perhaps no one else could have done, but the organization is now upon its feet and there is no special reason why I should remain as its president, especially in view of the fact that there are any number of people in it who are devoting themselves wholly to business while I am devoting the greater proportion of my time to education. While it is not generally known, I presume my individual business trans-actions outside of educational matters are in bulk equal to those of most of the members connected with the League, but this is a side matter. As I view the situation now, my present inclination is to ask you to [consent to serve as president of the Business][1] League. I would not alienate myself from it and would be willing to aid it in every way possible, in fact in the same way that I am now doing if desirable, only your name would be used instead of mine. In this connection I ought to say to you that in organizing and advertising the League it has been necessary to spend a considerable amount of money which the public does not know about, and you would find that in order to keep the League thoroughly before the people from year to year it will still be necessary to spend considerable money. I should be willing to relieve you of all expenses if desired and see that the work of advertising is kept up in the same way that it has been in the past. As I look at the matter now I can be of just as much service to the League and to the race out of the presidency as in it and perhaps more. I should not however, think for a moment of giving up my present office unless I was sure that some man of your temperament and standing would take the place. Yours very truly,

[Booker T. Washington]

TLc Con. 269 BTW Papers DLC.

1 At least one line is missing from the bottom of the page.

From Timothy Thomas Fortune

Washington, D.C., July 7, 1903

Dear Mr Washington: Your telegram of even date was received. It is indeed of the greatest importance that the work of the National organizer be difinitely mapped out. I have no faith whatever in Hayes. He and Wa[l]ters and McGhee will seek from now on to capture the organization. Upon discovering any crooked business I shall call the Executive committee together and have him fired.

Bishop Walters took snap judgment on me in my absence by calling the executive committee together and getting himself elected Chairman. *He was not a member of the committee* and had no right to call the new committee to order and could not be legally elected chairman when he was not a member of the executive committee. What should be my attitude in the matter?

I shall be head over heels in work from the time I reach Red Bank tomorrow night or Thursday noon until August 1.

I want to see Gen. Clarkson Thursday morning. I expect to see the Secretary of Treasury and Commissioner of Immigration tomorrow morning. They have my appointment and accounts badly snarled. I am an unfortunate and unlucky member.

Send matters to Red Bank after Thursday noon. Yours truly

T. Thos. Fortune

ALS Con. 258 BTW Papers DLC.

To Clark Howell

[Tuskegee, Ala.] July 8, 1903

Dear Sir: Your kind favor of July 6th has been received and I thank you very much for writing to me and also for withholding the publication of the communication referred to until after you had heard from me.

I think you will agree with me that it is practically impossible to meet all the criticisms that are likely to be made upon an institution of the character of ours. One day an individual, as in the case of Judge Griggs in his address before the Atlanta Institute of Technology, will object to industrial education for the Negro on the ground that the Negro by reason of being taught trades is taking work from the white man.[1] The next day some one else will claim that the Negro does not work at the industries taught at the various industrial schools.

Just now I have not the time to prepare a special article showing what our graduates and ex-students do, but I take the liberty of sending to you a copy of an article[2] which I have just completed for the World's Work in New York. This article is to be published August first, and under the circumstances of course it would not be proper for it to be used by any other publication, but I do not believe that the World's Work would object to your basing any editorial on it that you might care to make, using a few specific cases as illustrations of what our graduates are doing. You will see that I have given names and post office addresses all through this article, and I could multiply such instances almost without end. Frankly, I want to say that the only embarrassment that this institution experiences in regard to the employment of its graduates is in the matter of not being able to turn out students as fast as the demand comes for them. These demands come from both white and colored people.

You have been so very kind and generous to us through your editorial columns and in other ways that I hope at some time you can find time to come here and see for yourself something of our methods and can thus get a better idea of what our students are prepared for and what they really do after leaving us than in any other manner.

If I have not answered your questions fully please let me know.

I ought to add that the portions of the article which I have run around in red ink are not in the World's Work article and you are free to use them in full in any way that you may see fit.

I call your attention especially to the record of our graduates in Montgomery, Alabama, as shown by this report. The information in Montgomery was gotten a short time ago through a personal investigation. Yours truly,

[Booker T. Washington]

TLc Con. 249 BTW Papers DLC.

1 James Mathews Griggs (1861–1910), a Georgia judge who served in the U.S. House of Representatives from 1897 to 1910, spoke on June 18, 1903, at the commencement exercises of the Georgia School of Technology. He uttered the platitude that the South was best equipped to solve the race problem. He stated that "the negro race is not the equal of the white race and never can become so, no matter what its environment or accomplishment." Griggs maintained that those who emphasized industrial and technical training for blacks as a solution to the race problem were admitting that blacks were inferior. He argued that industrial training would not solve any problems but would only thrust black labor into competition with white labor and increase racial tensions. (Atlanta *Constitution*, June 19, 1903, 1, 4.)

2 BTW, "The Successful Training of the Negro," *World's Work*, 6 (Aug. 1903), 3731–51.

To Theodore Roosevelt

Tuskegee, Alabama. July 9, 1903

My dear Mr. President: The enclosed[1] is a true story. Yours very truly,

[Booker T. Washington]

TLS Theodore Roosevelt Papers DLC.

1 The enclosed clipping from the Baltimore *Herald* of July 3, 1903, read: "An old Florida colonel recently met Booker T. Washington and in a bibulous burst of confidence said to the negro educator:

" 'Suh, I am glad to meet you. Always wanted to shake your hand, suh. I think, suh, you're the greatest man in America.'

" 'Oh, no,' said Mr. Washington.

" 'You are, suh,' said the colonel, and then, pugnaciously: 'Who's greater?'

" 'Well,' said the founder of Tuskegee, 'there's President Roosevelt.'

" 'No, suh,' roared the colonel. 'Not by [a] jugful; I used to think so, but since he invited you to dinner I think he's a blank scoundrel.' "

For an eyewitness account of the incident, see An Article by J. Douglas Wetmore, Feb. 8, 1903, above.

According to Ray Stannard Baker, who was interviewing the President when BTW's letter arrived, Roosevelt read it aloud with "the greatest gusto" and "laughed uproariously." (Baker, *American Chronicle*, 171.)

To Timothy Thomas Fortune

[Tuskegee, Ala.] July 9, 1903

You will be doing me personal favor if you will write short letter to Brooklyn Eagle taking ground that there was no serious opposition to my policy at Louisville and showing up something of light character of the three Boston men.[1] Same editorial refers to you in praiseworthy terms. See Eagle July fifth.[2]

Booker T. Washington

TWSr   Con. 542   BTW Papers   DLC.

[1] W. Monroe Trotter, William H. Ferris, and George W. Forbes.

[2] The Brooklyn *Eagle*, July 5, 1903, 4, ran a story entitled "Booker T. Washington and the Negroes," which praised BTW for his "sanity and statesmanship." The article sympathized with BTW's frustration when black leaders refused to follow his ideas and instead agitated for political rights. BTW was under attack from a small number of delegates at the Afro-American Council meeting, the *Eagle* stated, for his conservative stand on agitation for rights and his opposition to higher education.

Fortune followed BTW's suggestion and wrote to the editor of the *Eagle* that 101 of the 117 delegates and the crowd in the galleries supported BTW, and that it was only a handful of detractors, mostly from Boston, who feebly tried to discredit him. (Brooklyn *Eagle*, July 12, 1903, 7.)

To Clark Howell

[Tuskegee, Ala.] July 9, 1903

Personal

Dear Sir: In further answer to your very kind letter of a few days ago making inquiry as to the work of our graduates and ex-students,

I would say that one of our officers[1] is employed almost continuously in visiting and inspecting the work being done by the men and women that we turn out, and he makes periodical reports to me of what he finds, and I take the liberty of enclosing to you a copy of the last report which he sent in. An analysis of this report will show that 57 cases are covered. Four are engaged wholly in teaching, 27 work wholly at their trades, 26 teach in connection with working at their trades. Yours truly,

[Booker T. Washington]

TLc Con. 249 BTW Papers DLC.

[1] Robert C. Bedford.

To Oswald Garrison Villard

[Tuskegee, Ala.] July 9, 1903

My dear Mr. Villard: I note that you have a special correspondent in Montgomery reporting special conditions bearing upon peonage. Either now or sometime in the future would it not be a wise plan for you to send some such man through the South reporting the actual condition of the Negro schools. I have just been notified through a certain source that in Lafayette Parish, Louisiana, where there are between 9,000 and 11,000 colored people there is only one school in the entire parish for these people. Yours truly,

[Booker T. Washington]

TLc Con. 261 BTW Papers DLC.

To the Editor of the Brooklyn *Eagle*

[Tuskegee, Ala.] July 9, 1903

Personal
Dear Sir: Enclosed I send you a copy of the address which I delivered in Louisville before the Afro-American Council a few days

ago. In this connection I note an editorial which appeared in your paper a few days ago and also which I attach herewith as a memorandum. I think by careful inquiry you will find that the picture incident has been very much exaggerated and means very little as showing any opposition to the policy on my part by the solid colored people of the country. The opposition was made by three colored men from Boston, the same ones who raised opposition in a recent meeting held in Brooklyn. In reality these men make such asses of themselves, and every one knowing that their object is to gratify a mere personal spite, the colored people in conventions do not take them seriously and for that reason pay little attention to them in the way of opposing or giving notice to what they say. Aside from gratifying a personal spite, their main object is to get their names into the newspapers which they know they can easily do by opposing some man whose name is well known to the public. Yours truly,

[Booker T. Washington]

TLc Con. 249 BTW Papers DLC. BTW sent the same letter to the editor of the Philadelphia *Ledger* on the same date, Con. 265, BTW Papers, DLC.

From Francis Jackson Garrison

Boston, July 13, 1903

My dear friend: I have just read for the first time the full report of your Louisville speech as printed in this morning's Herald & I must not lose an hour in telling you how complete & perfect it seems to me. In this crucial hour you have spoken with a calmness & wisdom that could be surpassed by no living man, and you have proclaimed the full doctrine of absolute equality before the law, and demanded that justice be dealt to white & black alike. This, with your reminder that a white offender against a woman's virtue is as guilty as a black, will cause a fresh outcry against you at the South,

& will bring you abuse from many who have hitherto pretended to approve you & your work, & have eagerly misquoted & perverted your utterances as to dabbling in politics or as to the higher education, &c., but it will be welcomed by the new generation of Southern men, like Chancellor Hill,[1] Profs Mims,[2] Trent,[3] Page, &c., who realize that the reactionary talk of men like Lyman Abbott & Secy. Root is the worst possible obstacle to them in their effort to rebuild the South on the only foundation — equality of rights & privileges — that will endure; and it will serve powerfully to stiffen the North & waken it to its duty & opportunity. I hear that Roosevelt & Hay are deeply moved by the present situation, & that Hay is bracing up the President on the subject, but he (Roosevelt) is a creature of impulse, & everything that he does is first weighed & measured by its possible or probable effect on his political fortunes. He will occupy a far lower position in history than you, who have so wisely realized the greater permanent influence & power of the man who, waging a moral warfare, keeps out of political life, with its inevitable bargains & compromises.

I should not say this to you if you were giving the remotest thought to what your place in history will be, or whether you will have any place in it. Your absolute self-consecration & self-abnegation in your work; the simplicty & modesty which have been unspoiled & unaffected by all the praise you have received & are constantly receiving; your unfailing sanity & balance, which would be impossible without the blessed & saving sense of humor; and the wonderful way in which you have held your rudder true through stormy & smooth seas alike, all these are proofs to me that you were appointed & chosen for your work, and that you have been & will be upheld not only by millions of hearts & hands of your countrymen, but by an unseen host of those who fought the battles of freedom two & more generations ago, and whose labors for the race have not yet ceased. I have said repeatedly during the past year that I regard yours as the most valuable life in America to-day, and I am far from being alone in this opinion. And as "this treasure is given to us in earthen vessels," pray do not ignore or neglect the necessity of taking proper rest & relaxation now & then.

We are hoping to see you & Mrs. Washington at our home in Lexington before long, and await your convenience & possibilities in the matter. Mr. Staples is also eager for your coming, as he has doubtless written you.

With best regards to Mrs. Washington, I am   Faithfully yours,

Francis J. Garrison

ALS Con. 267 BTW Papers DLC.

[1] Walter Barnard Hill (1851–1905), chancellor of the University of Georgia from 1899 until his death, was a member of the Southern Education Board and was host to the Conference for Education in the South at Athens in 1903. He struck his northern colleagues as more liberal than almost any other southerner on racial and sectional issues.

[2] Edwin Mims (1872–1959) was professor of English at Trinity College in Durham, N.C., from 1894 to 1909. He was the founder in 1902 and co-editor of the *South Atlantic Quarterly*, a journal that reflected his moderate reformism and faith in the "advancing South." He was a close friend of his stormier colleague John Spencer Bassett. He was head of the English department at the University of North Carolina from 1909 to 1912, and head of the English department at Vanderbilt from 1912 to 1942.

[3] William Peterfield Trent (1862–1939) was professor of English at the University of the South from 1888 to 1900, and professor of English literature at Columbia University from 1900 to 1929.

J. C. May [Wilford H. Smith]
to R. C. Black [Emmett Jay Scott]

[New York City] July 15th, 1903

Dear Friend, R. C. Black; The Dan Rogers case was affirmed on the 10th. Have applied to the Supreme Court of Alabama for a writ of error, which was refused on the 13th.

Have wired Clerk at Montgomery to make out and send certified copy of record, and as soon as it arrives, will apply to Mr. Justice White[1] for the writ as in the other cases.

Owing to the fact that the Supreme Court of the U.S. is out on recess, I shall have to arrange to secure the clerk's costs in this case until I can get a chance to file a motion to be allowed to proceed in forma pauperis.

The requirements of the other cases and this will more than consume what I now have on hand, and I would ask that you arrange to let me have another D as soon as possible. It may be time enough when I come to M to serve papers on the Governor and Attorney General in this case, if the writ be allowed by Mr. Justice White. Very truly yours,

J. C. May

TLSr   Con. 25   BTW Papers   DLC.

1 Edward Douglass White (1845–1921) of Louisiana was Associate Justice of the U.S. Supreme Court from 1894 to 1910, and Chief Justice from 1910 to 1921.

From Richard W. Thompson

[Washington, D.C.] July 15, 1903

Dear Mr. Washington: Mr. W. Allison Sweeney,[1] an old acquaintance of mine, as you know, has written to me, asking me to exert whatever influence I might possess with you in his behalf. He points out that he is your most aggressive partisan in Chicago, and has done yeoman service in Tuskegee's interest. He states that the $50 sent him some time ago was spent largely in expense of paper, and that he derived no direct benefit from it. He has severed his connection with the Monitor, and says he is in bad shape financially, intimating that he is really too proud to bring his actual condition before you. I had some weeks ago, while Mr. Sweeney was on the Monitor, suggested to Mr. Scott that Sweeney be given a surety of about $10 per week, and that he address himself to the attacks of the Conservator and the Boston Guardian, in such a manner as to escape the suspicion of being subsidized. I had not mentioned this to Sweeney. His getting off the paper nullifies that plan, for the time, at least, even if you should think well of it. I have written him a letter, a copy of which you will find enclosed. I lay the whole matter before you, with the suggestion that if you can arrange to put him to work, in a way that will guarantee the "delivery of the goods," he will prove a strong factor for good. Both as a writer and speaker he is powerful — but needs only a "balance-wheel" adjustment from time to time. The letter I have written in answer to his, is given here. It commits you to nothing, and you can answer him in accordance with your best interests.

R. W. Thompson

TLS Con. 261 BTW Papers DLC. Written on Tuskegee Institute stationery.

1 W. Allison Sweeney, a black man born in Michigan and educated in the public schools of Ann Arbor, was an active Republican and newspaperman in Detroit and West Virginia before moving to Indianapolis around 1890. In his youth he was an "uncompromising champion of civil rights." (Thornbrough, *Negro in Indiana*, 385–88.) He worked for the Indianapolis *Freeman* for a number of years before 1895, when he joined with Alexander E. Manning, a Democrat, in editing the Indianapolis *World*. About 1900 he moved to Chicago, where he was editor of the *Monitor*, the *Conservator*, and the *Leader*, black weekly newspapers.

From Henry Hugh Proctor

[Atlanta, Ga.] July 16, 1903

My dear Mr. Washington: I take pleasure in enclosing you check for $50.00 in appreciation for your services. We wish it were twice so much. The short time we had to work it up and the threatening weather in the forenoon prevented our doing as well financially as we had hoped.

But it was a great meeting and the effect has been very good. You will be happy to know that on the day following your address the constitutional amendment to divide the school fund was taken up and defeated.[1]

I think a number of the members of the legislature was present. I enclose you a clipping from the Constitution, an article by one of the members present.

Some of the white men who were there desire to make up a fund to have you return some time and speak to the colored people with free admission. Would you like to do so some time next year, say?

With high appreciation for your services, I remain, Yours very truly,

H. H. Proctor

ALS Con. 271 BTW Papers DLC.

1 BTW's speech to an audience that included some legislators was a warning that if school opportunities were denied, black farm workers would move to the cities. Other factors, particularly the conflicts between white and black counties, were more powerful than BTW's speech in defeating the amendment. (Harlan, *Separate and Unequal*, 228–30.)

From Timothy Thomas Fortune

Red Bank, N.J. July 16, 1903

Dear Mr. Washington: I had a long and pleasant and satisfactory talk with Mr. Ogden[1] at 1 O'clock yesterday, and he says he will be glad to give good consideration to any matter for publication that I may send him. I was also introduced to Mr. Villard, who seems to be a very genial and superior man.

I also had a long talk with Gen. Clarkson. He wanted to know if you had written to the President anything concerning me and I told him I did not know.

I wish you would think over the matter of taking on the Chicago Conservator. I will send you a copy of it and a sample of the make up it should have, in a short time. I have asked Laing Williams in a letter to-day to ascertain who owns it, what it is worth in circulation, if [it] can be bought and at what price, and his estimate of its actual cash value in plant and good will, all in strict confidence.

Jessie[2] is not a bit well to-day, and I shall not go to South Weymouth this week, on that account and because I am still behind with accumulated work, and donot feel like stirring out of Red Bank after driving the typewriter all day.

The New York Sun has an editorial on you and Du Bois to-day, which I enclose.

With kind regards for the family, Yours truly,

T. Thos. Fortune

What think you of my Eagle article?

TLS Con. 258 BTW Papers DLC.

1 Rollo Ogden (1856–1937) joined the staff of the New York *Evening Post* in 1891 and became editor-in-chief in 1903. He remained with the *Evening Post* until 1920, when he became an editor of the New York *Times.*

2 Fortune's daughter, born in 1883, later Mrs. Aubrey Bowser.

From Peter Jefferson Smith, Jr.

Boston, July 17th, 03

My dear Doctor: I write to inform you that the Enterprise did not appear last week owing to a lack of funds, and there is a strong probability that it will not issue this week owing to the same cause.

Mr. Moss is very anxious to have a talk with you regarding the matter of carrying on the paper with the hope of securing aid from you either directly or indirectly as the case may be, notwithstanding the fact that you have assured him through me that it was not your policy to own any interest in the newspapers of the country. I have tried to impress this fact upon Mr. Moss, but he insists that in view of the fact that he has carried on the paper alone for the period that he has and solely because of his admiration for you and the great work for the Race that you represent that you ought to give him evidence of more substantial interest and sympathy in the matter.

I beg to say in this connection that I engaged in the work with Mr. Moss because I admired his pluck and appreciated what seemed to me on his part real enthusiasm and loyalty. I feel however now as I think you do in the matter, (ie) that the influence of any colored paper spending its force against you and Tuskegee is of no avail, and hence need cause your friends no anxiety, and so with the Enterprise owing me for faithful services $45.00 I sever my connection with it. With kindest wishes I beg to remain faithfully yours,

P. J. Smith

TLS   Con. 277   BTW Papers   DLC.

From Mary Church Terrell

Washington, D.C. July 17 1903

My dear Dr. Washington: Many, many thanks for the fine letter you sent me. Enclosed is the article which has at last appeared in the Post.[1] It was so long appearing that I went to see Mr. Bone[2] to ascertain when it would be printed. He told me it had been in type for three weeks, but there had been so much in the Post on the Problem, he was saving it. Mr. Raymond Patterson of the Chicago Tribune has been touring the South and has written articles for some papers up this way on the various phases of the Problem. These have been appearing in the Post.

Please tell me what you think of my article. Criticise it, if you dont like it. I shall be glad to know just what you object to. It will help me in the future. I hope to see you the next time you are in this city which is so very dear to your heart. We are not all alike here. You must not bundle us all into one class.

With best wishes and a great deal of gratitude for the letter to the Lecture Bureau, I am sincerely yours,

Mary C. Terrell

ALS   Con. 278   BTW Papers   DLC.

[1] Terrell's account of the Tuskegee Institute commencement. "One might have closed his eyes," she wrote, "and have easily imagined himself at a commencement of the best of our Eastern colleges, with the slips of memory which sometimes occur there left out." She wrote that "whether one agrees with all of Dr. Washington's utterances or not, he can not help admiring the indefatigable industry, the rare executive ability, and the commanding powers which have made Tuskegee possible." (Washington *Post,* July 16, 1903, 5.)

[2] Scott C. Bone (1860–1936), managing editor of the Washington *Post,* founded the Washington *Herald* in 1906, and later was editor-in-chief of the Seattle *Post-Intelligencer* and governor of Alaska from 1921 to 1925.

W. Allison Sweeney to Emmett Jay Scott

Chicago, July 17, 1903

My Dear Mr Scott: It has just come to me by grape vine rumor, that a movement is taking head engaged in by a number of "nigger" editors notably Trotter, Wilkins[1] and a bunch of Southern men egged on by a number of "nigger" schoolmen in different sections of the country to secure and tabulate for the purposes of publication all requests for publication of Tuskegee "Copy," the amount in straight "reading matter" so printed by Negro journals within the last few years and the sum of money paid all sources by Tuskegee for same.

The object seems vague but at the same time distinctly "niggery" if subsequent information which I shall hope to secure authenticates the truth of the same.

Did not know but that the information might have a certain interest for you hence this action. Fraternally Yours

Sweeney

ALS Con. 274 BTW Papers DLC. Docketed by Scott: "Ref'd to in my typewritten letter this mail. It may be well to talk with Fortune about it. 7/20."

[1] D. Robert Wilkins, manager of the Chicago *Conservator* Publishing and Printing Co.

From Harry Thacker Burleigh

[New York City] July 18th 1903

Dear Mr. Washington: I have just finished reading "The Outlook's" review of Du Bois' book;[1] and it is so strong and true an article that I can[not] refrain from writing you, because it states your position so clearly that a blind man can see that Du Bois' work is purely personal whereas your work is general; you are for the masses while he pleads for the classes. It is obvious who has the greater and higher field. The article is a truthful justification of your methods and is timely, for many others of the (highly educated and cultivated class)? may be influenced by what Du Bois says.

I trust you have read it. It is The Outlook of July 11th 1903.

I trust I may hear from you soon as to definite arrangements as to places for our summer meetings. With kind regards I remain very truly yours

H. T. Burleigh

ALS Con. 249 BTW Papers DLC.

[1] The review of *The Souls of Black Folk* devoted several paragraphs to a defense of BTW's racial policies, and criticized Du Bois for offering no remedies of his own. (*Outlook*, 74 [July 11, 1903], 669–71.)

From Emmett Jay Scott

Tuskegee, Alabama. July 20, 1903

Dear Mr. Washington: I send you herewith list of thirty newspapers as per your telegraphic request today. I also call your attention to a letter just received from W. Allison Sweeney. I believe that there is something in this matter because of the stuff which the Conservator printed sometime ago with such gusto. I think it would be well to let me write each of these 30 newspapers to the effect that your publishers have been authorized to send advertising matter to them; this will counteract, no doubt, the effort being made.

I shall be able to send out very soon a full list of advertising matter respecting the Phelps Hall Bible Training School and this together should be effective. Yours truly,

Emmett J. Scott

TLS   Con. 274   BTW Papers   DLC.

From Edwin Mims

Cambridge, Mass., July 20, 1903

My dear Sir, I am a teacher in Trinity College, Durham, N.C., and am spending the summer here in Cambridge. Let me tell you how greatly stirred I have been by your speeches at Louisville and Atlanta. If more significant messages have been delivered to the American people during the past decade I am not aware of them. In fairness, maturity of judgment and constructive wisdom they are preeminent. As a Southern white man I rejoice in you, and the work you are doing. In the future even more than in the past I shall do what I can to produce a spirit among people of my race that will respond to your message.

We at Trinity have always been glad that we had you to lecture to our students. I was not there at the time but I have heard others speak of you. I hope you saw Dr. Bassett's[1] article in *South Atlantic*

Quarterly for July.[2] I ordered one sent to you. I believe we have the right point of view at Trinity. We shall always be glad to help you; *we believe in you* and bid you God-speed. Yours very sincerely,

Edwin Mims

ALS Con. 267 BTW Papers DLC. Docketed in Scott's hand: "A very fine letter. Told him letter ref'd to you—7/25."

[1] John Spencer Bassett (1867–1928), a graduate of Trinity College and of Johns Hopkins, taught at Trinity College from 1893 to 1906, and was co-editor with Mims of the *South Atlantic Quarterly* from 1902 to 1905. He was professor of history at Smith College from 1906 to 1928, where he wrote and edited many works in U.S. history, including a six-volume edition of the correspondence of Andrew Jackson.

[2] "Stirring Up the Fires of Race Antipathy," *South Atlantic Quarterly*, 2 (Oct. 1903), 297–305.

To Emmett Jay Scott

South Weymouth, Mass., 21 July, 1903

My dear Mr. Scott: I enclose a batch of letters from Montgomery regarding his matter, which I shall not answer unless you think there is something in them worthy of attention. When you acknowledge them, tell him that I have no power to change the decision of the Administration: I merely acted as a go-between, and as a shield to him; and that anything he has to say which he thinks would affect the President's decision, would be better sent directly to the President himself, or to the Secretary. Be careful how you word your letter, as Montgomery is likely to show it to some one.[1] Very truly yours,

Booker T. Washington

TLS Con. 249 BTW Papers DLC.

[1] Scott sent to Montgomery a cautious letter nearly duplicating BTW's language. (July 24, 1903, Records of the Office of Secretary of the Interior, RG 48, DNA.)

From James Carroll Napier

Nashville, Tennessee, July 21st. 1903

Dear sir: Replying to your letter of the 7th. instant I have to say first that I shall at the proper time look after the matter of the dinner and write you the details. Please let me know the number of persons you may wish to entertain. Second: I regret very much to learn that you are thinking of severing your connection with the League as its president. It will in my opinion fail to accomplish the great amount of good which present prospects seem to indicate unless you continue your connection with it as its official head. The name of no other living man can do for it what yours will. I therefore hope that you will at once reconsider your determination to relinquish the presidency of the League and make up your mind to continue as its head and guiding spirit. When I say this I am confident that I voice the sentiment of all friends of the League both within and without its ranks. The responsibility of the president I know is great; the executive ability, the time, money and travel necessary to keep the League and its affairs in proper shape are greater. From any of these view points you, above all men, are best fittted to serve the interests of the League. However, if after due consideration, you still wish to retire from the presidency I would be willing to confer with you as to who is best fitted to become your successor. While I feel that this honor could fall upon shoulders far more deserving and far better qualified than my own I would feel inclined to be largely governed in the matter by your good judgement. But I must of course not lose sight of the fact that almost my entire time is already consumed in looking after my own affairs and in the effort to preserve my health. For these reasons I would want to understand fully all that would be required of me before I could agree to assume such grave responsibilities. But about all these things I shall be glad and pleased to confer with you when next I see you if that would not be putting the matter off to too late a period.

By some mistake one of our papers published, about ten days ago, that the League would meet in July. We undertook to correct this mistake as best we could. But it seems that the correction did not reach some of our friends, for there have been a number of inquiries this morning as to whether you were in the City and a carload of persons came down from Lebanon to see and hear you.

I went to Springfield on Sunday last and found the people there greatly enthused over our coming meeting of the League. Our committees here are all working harmoniously and earnestly for a successful entertainment. These, I take it, are slight indications of what we may expect next month.

I have just called upon the Governor, Hon. James B. Frazier,[1] and he promises to use his utmost endeavors to be present and to say a few words of welcome to the League. He, as I have just written Mr. Scott, has authorized the use of his name in this connection. I am sure I shall secure the Mayor also, but he will not return to the City until August 1st. I have told Mr. Scott to also place his name on the program.

Hoping to hear from you, I remain, Very truly yours etc.,

J. C. Napier

TLS BTW Papers ATT.

[1] James Beriah Frazier (1856–1937) was governor of Tennessee from 1902 to 1905, when he resigned to take a seat in the U.S. Senate, where he served from 1905 to 1911.

From Emmett Jay Scott

Tuskegee, Alabama. July 22, 1903

Dear Mr. Washington: You will note, if you have seen the Guardian for last week, that they make much of the article which appeared in the New Jersey newspaper, claiming that request was made for the publication of certain matter, etc., the same stuff that appeared in the Conservator. I have gone over again with Mr. Thompson this entire matter, and he tells me that he tried to explain it to you as to how it happened. Remembering your statement to him in a note that I should pass on all matter of this character, I reminded him of it. He advises me that that note stands except that he is himself to send out certain matter under certain conditions. I do not know what those conditions are and would like to be advised as to how far I am to be responsible in this matter. We certainly should guard against any subsequent troubles of this kind. Yours truly,

Emmett J. Scott

TLS Con. 272 BTW Papers DLC.

W. Allison Sweeney to Emmett Jay Scott

Chicago, Ill. July 22, 1903

Personal

My Dear Mr. Scott: I had Wilkins in tow 'till past the "witching time of night"; fed him, drinked him, pumped him; drove to his lodgings not 20 minutes ago.

Grapevine rumor I forwarded you (did it reach you) authenticated.

The purpose of the scheme is to reveal to the country through the thoughtless Cooperation of the Associated Press, quoting the exact language of W. — "*disclosures that will astound the whites who have been buncoed into standing by this Irish-Negro Mountebank and cause the niggers to repudiate him as one man.*"

He was chary of names, and I hesitated to press him *too close* at *this* time.

Take it, when the scheme is ready for use, some A.P. Agent, either at Boston, N.Y. or Chicago will, if not forestalled, be whedeled into assisting their dirty work.

In time of peace prepare for war.

The course of Tuskegee *is plain.*

As between this horde of scoundrels, and the good name and future usefullness of the great school and its wonderful chief, the Associated Press *belongs* to you, ie. Tuskegee, See?

I will, as events may develop to my view, and I shall help them to, apprise you from time to time. Fraternally

Sweeney

ALS Con. 274 BTW Papers DLC.

R. C. Black [Emmett Jay Scott]
to J. C. May [Wilford H. Smith]

[Tuskegee, Ala.] July 23 [1903]

Friend J. C. May: I enclose herewith an editorial for Chisum's[1] paper.[2] I think this ought to draw out Trotter if anything does.

You say not to fear Bruce. *I do fear Bruce.** I do not think he can be trusted at all, and while for the present we have him absolutely under our control because of place he holds under Gen. Clarkson, at the same time he could quietly use the information against us and would be only too glad to do it. The point I have in mind is that, I do not believe that Bruce should be permitted to know anything of the probable lawsuit nor of our connection with that in any way. Let me know how far he has been advised in the matter.[3] I think, however, it is going to be a royal scrap to see Bruce, as he will be represented as doing, fighting the Trotter gang when they have been trotting together so much. Yours truly,

R. C. Black

* Reference is to Bruce Grit! Who edits Chisum's paper.

TLSr Copy   Con. 281   BTW Papers   DLC.

1 Melvin Jack Chisum, born in 1873, attended high school in Chicago, a technological school in Boston, and a business college in New York. E. J. Scott knew him in Texas in the early 1890s, but he first appeared in the BTW Papers as the proprietor of a "Training School for Colored Servants." (Circular letter to "Dear Madam," Mar. 19, 1901, Con. 213, BTW Papers, DLC.) From 1903 to 1906 Chisum was Washington's paid spy—and perhaps sometimes provocateur—in the ranks of BTW's black critics. In Boston he infiltrated the New England Suffrage League of W. M. Trotter. Later he moved to New York, where he became a member of the Brooklyn branch of the Niagara Movement. He met BTW on park benches and other clandestine places to pass on his information. In 1906 he secured a position on the anti-Bookerite Washington *Bee*, and persuaded its editor to accept a bribe to change his editorial position. (Harlan, "Secret Life," 405–6, 410–12.)

Chisum engaged in a number of enterprises in real estate, banking, and journalism. During World War I he was a labor agent for northern employers. In the 1920s he was ostensibly a syndicated journalist for black newspapers but also engaged in espionage for Tuskegee Institute. A Tuskegean interviewed by Pete Daniel in 1968 described Chisum as "like an armadillo" because of his bullet-proof vest, adding: "He was short, stubby, and ugly. He had a big belly...." He was alleged to have carried a pistol all the time. (Interview of G. W. A. Scott, Nov. 7, 1968.) In the 1930s he worked for the employers against the Pullman car porters' union. (Harris, *Keeping the Faith*, 53–55.)

2 *The Impending Conflict*, edited in New York by Melvin J. Chisum and John E. Bruce.

3 Smith replied: "I did not mean in speaking of Bruce that he would be trusted with any of our affairs whatever. He knows absolutely nothing and will not be told anything. All my dealings are with Chisum in a very private and confidential way." (J. C. May [Smith] to R. C. Black [Scott], July 30, 1903, Con. 25, BTW Papers, DLC.)

From Charles William Anderson

New York   July 23rd, 1903

Confidential

My dear Dr. Washington, Permit me to acknowledge the receipt of your esteemed favor of the 17th inst., and to thank you for its kindly tenor.

As you may know, or as you may not know, I have organized the "Colored Republican Club of the City of New York," which bids fair to be a splendidly successful movement. We have now nearly 800 resident members, and expect to have 2000 by the first of January next. The last meeting was held on the 15th inst., at which 167 new members were elected; all of whom duly qualified by paying their fees. As President, I have offered a prize of $25.00 in gold to the member who shall turn in the largest number of applications for membership, with the fees accompanying them. I fully expect to receive five or six hundred proposals in this contest, which concludes on October 1st. I enclose herewith a sample of the proposal card with which all the members are now supplied. We have two classes of members, resident and non-resident, and the Constitution provides that every Colored Republican Club of the state which shall file a list, giving the names and addresses of its members, shall become Associate members of our Club, and shall be entitled to all the privileges of our Club House whenever they may visit this city, and the Presidents of all clubs so qualifying shall become members of the "Advisory and Allied Clubs Committee" of this club. Thus you will see we hope to be able to be in touch with every Colored Republican Club in the state, and be in possession of the names and addresses of its members. In this way we shall be able to reach every mother's son of them at any hour of the day and night, and shall also be able to put them in possession of proper literature. Already we have established outposts in twenty-six cities and towns throughout the state, and have placed them under the leadership of men who will stand "Without hitching." Later on I mean to make a personal tour of the state, and make talks to each of these organizations. It is my purpose to include something more than politics in these talks, and [I] shall take occasion to urge the members all along the line to stand solidly behind you. Some days ago I mailed you a poster of an Emancipation Celebration to be held in Corning, New York, on August 4th. You will notice that the men in charge of that celebration have got the right motto as a heading for their bill. Of course, I regret the notice of the "cake walk contest," which you will find in the lower right hand corner of the bill, and shall do my best to shame them out of the desire to waste time in such silly amusements. I hope to be able to bring the membership of this organization up to ten thousand in time, and mean to do so if untiring industry and dogged determination will accomplish it. I am devoting all the time and money that I can possibly spare to this work, and when it is finished I think you will agree with me that it will be the most complete organization of Colored men in the United States. I am working quietly and without preliminary puffs, as I do not want it to seem to be a movement inspired by the President. As far as possible, I am preventing the formation of "Roosevelt clubs," as I do not think it advisable that the President's name should be associated with distinctively Colored Republican Clubs. Now, if at any time, you should have a few minutes conversation with the President, I would like to have you call his attention to this work. I have not said much about it to his friends hereabouts, as I was anxious that the information should reach him only after the movement had become an assured fact.

In my Corning speech I shall admonish our folks against improper deportment in public places, and against all those who commit, and those who condone the commission of crime. I shall, of course, take a fling at lynching, but at the same time, will talk "Brass tacks" against the cause of lynching. Do you approve of this idea? We leave for Saratoga on Saturday, where I can be addressed at the Thompson Cottage, Hamilton Street, Saratoga Springs. Yours respectfully,

Charles W. Anderson

P.S. (Confidential) Griffin, the body-servant of General Clarkson, has lately organized a "J. S. Clarkson Colored Rep. Club." It is a fake club, organized for the purpose of making him solid with the General. The newspapers have been criticising the General about it editorially. They regard it as another case of "Clarkson and his niggers." Why do sensible white men encourage these black fakirs?

TLS   Con. 278   BTW Papers   DLC.   Postscript in Anderson's hand.

Melvin Jack Chisum to Emmett Jay Scott

New York City   July 23, 1903

My Dear Mr. Scott: I believe that our mutual friend, Hon. Wilford H. Smith, wrote you concerning a letter to appear in this month's issue of the little book. I am holding it back from press on account of this letter. Please push it. Put all the fish hooks in it that a Texas genius can string on a fishing line.

I have been intending to write you for quite more than a month. I haven't done so for the very good reason that any member of the press gang would understand; you being one of the gang, I refrain from detail, suffice to say, this is the first issue.

You will notice on the title page, that this is neither a corporation nor a partnership. Before having employed the editor, I had an express agreement which is in writing, one clause of which reads, "I do hereby consent, pledge myself, and agree, that so long as I am retained as Editor of 'The Impending Conflict,' that I will not write, publish, nor cause to be published, any letters or articles whatsoever, that can be, even remotely construed as being antagonistic to Dr. Booker T. Washington or his policy." This agreement was signed before the able man, left for the Louisville Convention. He had written that "blasted stuff" that appeared in the Denver Statesmen and mailed it, which I very much regretted.

I have good reason to know, and believe you have, that "Bruce Grit" has never been regularly employed on the staff of any publication through all of his experience, where he received a stipulated salary and could count on getting it. This fact, I believe, will cause him to keep his contract with me and you may depend upon it that I am going to insist upon this document being observed to the letter. You'll see no more of this "tommy rot" from his pen.

You understand that I haven't a million, you understand also that I am a Texas Negro and keep my promises, and when salaries are due they will be paid, million or no million; and "The Impending Conflict," I hope, through observing our Texas principles to give a life of lasting usefulness.

I promised Bruce that I would not expose our agreement. You understand why he exacted this promise. I could not, however, refrain from having you understand that I do not endorse the Anti–Booker T. Washington camp, or any of the performances of its campers; but for my desire to have myself rightly understood, I should not have deviated from my promises. I ask you to regard this letter as strictly confidential between yourself, Dr. Washington, and myself. I am, Yours faithfully,

Melvin J. Chisum

TLS Con. 252 BTW Papers DLC.

From Charles Woodroph Hare

Tuskegee, Ala. July 23rd, 03

Dear Sir: Since I wired you about the organization of the East End Gin and Mill Co., Mr. T. Y. Conner came to the stock holders and proposed to sell his entire mill, and ginnery outfit, land, good will &c, obligating himself not to [in] any manner engage in the oil or gin business in Tuskegee, for the sum of $30,000.00, payable $10,000.00 cash the balance in ten years, allowing the privilege of the entire sum being paid up at any time directors wish. Judge Hurt and Mr. Thompson had Dr. Tennile, of Montgomery who is already in the oil business to come to Tuskegee and inspect the machinery and advise as to the price, profits &c. On his recommendations the East End concern was allowed to go by the board, and said parties with others organized as The Tuskegee Cotton Oil Company, capital stock $30,000.00. Prof. Logan and I both believing that this was by far the better investment took stock, and acting on your telegram I subscribed for six shares for you. One third of this only will now be called for. I believe it a very fine scheme.

Trusting that this will be entirely satisfactory to you, and that you will authorize some one in Tuskegee to pay your first installment when it is called for, I remain, Very truly yours,

Chas. W. Hare

TLS   Con. 264   BTW Papers   DLC.

From Emmett Jay Scott

Tuskegee, Alabama. July 24, 1903

Dear Mr. Washington: There is one peculiar phrase in Mr. Garrison's letter[1] which did not appear to him I am sure. For instance, he says that President Roosevelt "is a creature of impulse" and that everything he does is first weighed and measured by its possible and probable effects on his political fortunes. As a matter of fact, a man who is a creature of impulse would not weigh and measure what he does, and further, both you and I know that the President is not actuated at all by anything that has to bear upon his political fortunes. He is the strongest & sturdiest force in American life today as concerns the absolute equality of all men before the law. Yours truly,

Emmett J. Scott

TLS   Con. 272   BTW Papers   DLC.

1 See above, July 13, 1903.

To Emmett Jay Scott

South Weymouth, Mass., 25 July, 1903

Dear Mr. Scott: It is very important that our friend May be instructed to have no dealings of a confidential nature with J. E.

Bruce, who is very unreliable. I greatly fear that Chisholm[1] is not much better, although you may know him. Very truly yours,

Booker T. Washington

TLS   Con. 275   BTW Papers   DLC.

1 Melvin Jack Chisum.

To Emmett Jay Scott

South Weymouth, Mass., 27 July, 1903

Dear Mr. Scott: In case the Boston crowd persist in advocating the holding of another Afro-American Council, I should like you, so far as you can exercise influence to exert it in the direction of causing the colored Press pay absolutely no attention to this understaking. Very truly yours,

B. T. W.

TLI   Con. 275   BTW Papers   DLC.

William Henry Baldwin, Jr.,
to Francis Jackson Garrison

[New York City] July 27th, 1903

My dear Mr. Garrison: I thank you for your letter of 24th. I have just finished reading three or four letters from Mr. Washington, and the last word I dictated to him, before receiving your letter, was that I wanted to see him at once on several matters, and one of the principal ones was to urge him to go away for a few weeks and get a rest before the fall campaign. I shall certainly urge him to take a trip across the water and back, although I would not advise him hardly to go on shore on the other side because he would be bound to get into social duties and that would not rest him.

Mr. Washington sent me copy of the letter which you sent him after he made the speech in Louisville, and I told him that I thought it was one of the most valuable that he had received for a long time. I have felt sure for ten years past that his course is just right, for him and for the negro race. It has taken courage for him to take his position. The ill-tempered and noisy position taken by some of his negro opponents does not take courage. The people who should take up the other side of the question — that is the political question — are you and the rest of us white people.

I have been very much pleased to see the enormous amount of friction that has been stirred up during the past few months. It is the beginning of the new education for the whole people. The mass of our people will certainly see justice done, although it will come over a very rough road. I think the only safe position for the negro to take is one of patient and peaceful methods, and that the rest of us must do whatever fighting there is to be done.

I wish I might see you and talk over this whole question with you. I would like so much to meet you with Booker Washington and talk it all out.

With very sincere regards, I am   Yours very truly,

[William H. Baldwin, Jr.]

TL Copy   Con. 292   BTW Papers   DLC.   Copy marked: "For Mr. Booker T. Washington, So. Weymouth, Mass."

An Interview of Edward H. Morris[1]
in the Chicago *Inter Ocean*

[Chicago] July 28, 1903

"Booker T. Washington is largely responsible for the lynching in this country," said Edward H. Morris, past grand master of the United Order of Odd Fellows, a member of the State Legislature, and one of the leading colored attorneys of Chicago.

Mr. Morris made his attack upon the head of the Tuskegee school when commenting yesterday upon the recent Danville lynching.[2] He continued:

"The learned doctor teaches the colored people that they are

only fit to fill menial positions. The spirit of his teaching is illustrated by a rag-time song. 'Mr. Coon, You're All Right in Your
Place.' When the colored pupils are taught that they are fit only
to follow the plow, wield the ax, or push a plane, and are not qualified to fill the higher positions occupied by the white people they
act in a manner subservient to the whites.

"By the same pernicious doctrine the whites come to regard the
colored people as inferiors. In fact, I believe there are a great many
white people who are ready to come out flatfooted and say that the
negro is not a human being — that he has not the finer sensibilities
of the whites.

"The result is that the whites think the negroes are not entitled
to the same consideration as themselves, but should be looked upon
in about the same manner as a master looks upon a dog. When a
negro commits a crime they think there ought to be some system to
try him different from that by which white criminals are tried. If
he is lynched they think, 'Oh, he's only a negro. It doesn't count
much.'

"As far as the good of the colored race is concerned I prefer a
radical like Senator Tillman of South Carolina to Booker T. Washington. Tillman comes out openly and attacks the negroes and
condones lynching. The colored people think it doesn't matter so
much what he says, since he says he is an enemy of the colored
race. But the colored people believe that Washington is their friend
and look upon him as a prophet. Many of the colored people believe
and do what he tells them. Then they don't insist upon being
treated as the equals of the whites. The only reason Washington is
tolerated in the South is because he teaches that the negroes are fit
only for menial positions."

Chicago *Inter Ocean*, July 28, 1903, 2.

1 Edward H. Morris, born in Flemingsburg, Ky., in 1860, was educated in Chicago.
He began a law practice in Chicago in 1879 and became well known as a criminal
lawyer, often defending gamblers. Active in Republican politics, he was an assistant
attorney in Cook County and was elected to the state legislature in 1890 and 1902.

2 John Metcalf, a black man, was lynched by a mob in Danville, Ill., on July 25,
1903.

From Edgar Gardner Murphy

Concord [Mass.] July 28/03

Dear Mr W. This is confidential. Mr. Villard admits that he is paving the way for the agitation for the enforcement of the Amendments.

He has wrought untold harm already. When he discusses wrongs in the West he criticises the *wrongs:* when he discusses wrongs at the South he criticises the *South.* He has caused more race hatred in Alabama than I have seen in years.

The agitation for the enforcement of the terms of the 14th Amendment will *certainly* stampede the South against the Negro, and will cause untold wretchedness.

This letter from Mr. Glass[1] is confidential. Please return it to me. Truly Your Friend

Edgar Gardner Murphy

ALS   Con. 268   BTW Papers   DLC.

[1] Franklin Potts Glass (1858–1934) bought a half-interest in the Montgomery *Advertiser* in 1886 and was general manager until 1915. He was also editor-in-chief of the Birmingham *News* from 1910 until 1920.

From Emmett Jay Scott

Tuskegee, Alabama. July 28, 1903

Dear Mr. Washington: I do not think Chisum is a very brainy man, but I do know he is resourceful and I think at the same time honorable. I enclose herewith a letter from him which I have guardedly answered without in any way mentioning Bruce's name. What he says respecting his agreement with Bruce would seem to assure the man's (Chisum's) friendship and support. Our New York friend[1] can use Chisum in any way that we desire. Chisum formerly lived in Texas and I know him very well. Yours truly,

Emmett J. Scott

TLS   Con. 272   BTW Papers   DLC.

[1] Wilford H. Smith.

To Emmett Jay Scott

South Weymouth, Mass. July, 29. '03

Dear Mr. Scott, Of course it is well we keep in mind all that Mr. Sween[e]y is saying, but I cannot rid myself of the feeling that he is shrewd enough to use what he hears, or says he hears, as a means of ingratiating himself into our favor. Very truly yours,

B. T. W.

HLI Con. 275 BTW Papers DLC.

An Account of the Boston Riot[1] in the Boston *Globe*

Boston, July 31, 1903

NEGROES MAKE RIOTOUS SCENE

Booker T. Washington Was Speaking to Them

His Opponents Sought to Have Him Answer Certain Questions

Large Force of Policemen Called to Zion A. M. E. Church—One Man Stabbed and Had to be Sent to the Hospital—Three Persons Arrested, One of Them William M. Trotter

Surrounded by a struggling mass of angry people of his own race, in the confusion of fainting women and fighting men, unable to address his audience or to persuade them into a state of sanity, Booker T. Washington met his first really hostile demonstration in Boston last evening at the Zion A. M. E. church, corner of Columbus ave. and Northampton st.

What at first promised to be an episode in a program which often breeds disquiet among a people quick in anger, developed into a condition of riot. At one time it seemed as if nothing could prevent the wholesale shedding of blood, and in consequence of this every available police officer in division 5 and many of division 16 were hurried to the church, prepared for harsh measures.

The Zion church was packed to its doors with colored people. They fairly swarmed inside, and there was not an inch of standing room to spare. A program had been prepared which embraced all the speakers who have locally made themselves heard among the negro race. They seemed peaceful enough at first, yet there was an ominous hush in the big auditorium when William H. Lewis, the presiding officer, arose to introduce the speakers. A wave of anti-Washington sentiment was unmistakably abroad.

WASHINGTON'S NAME HISSED

Mr. Lewis is assistant U.S. district attorney, of football fame at Harvard, calm and generally respected by his people. Ordinarily there would have been an immense outburst of enthusiasm to greet him as presiding officer at the welcome to Booker T. Washington. When he arose to speak, there was only a faint clapping of hands from men and women who were frightened at the sound of their own welcome.

Mr. Lewis started to speak. As a matter of course, his very first words had relation to the man who was supposed to be the honored guest, and when he mentioned the name of the great leader, when he pronounced the name "Washington," there were hisses from every part of the hall. Mr. Lewis called for silence, and some one volunteered that the hissers should be ejected. A movement to do this met with such decided failure that the attempt died, and the disturbers remained within the walls.

The little swirl caused by those first hisses died out, and the audience settled back in their seats again. It had been distinctly said by George Washington Forbes at the beginning that there should be no hissing in the house of God. Rev. James H. McMullen[2] echoed the sentiment, and added that there should be no stamping of feet, catcalling or other demonstrations. Yet here was the audience doing all.

Granville Martin,[3] 44 years old, of 103 Falmouth st., was the first man to begin the trouble. He arose when Mr. Lewis mentioned the name of Washington and refused to be put down. Scott Robinson, one of the trustees of the church, again arose to state that there should be no hissing, and immediately followed a fusillade of hisses that forced him back into his chair.

The meeting rested a few moments until things became quiet enough for intelligent action. Mr. Lewis again attempted to address his people, and succeeded in introducing T. Thomas Fortune of the New York Age, an appointee by President Roosevelt to investigate the labor problems of the Philippines. He opened his address with a loyal and eloquent support of Booker Washington, in which he arraigned his people for some of their faults in a manner that plainly did not take well with the audience. He had not proceeded far with his speech when he began to cough violently. He reached for the accustomed water bottle, only to find that some one had emptied it in the heat of the first conflict.

His coughing became so marked, and sneezing among the other speakers who occupied the platform so prevalent, that it was evident that something was decidedly wrong. It proved that the "opposition" had sprinkled the platform carefully with cayenne pepper. This necessitated another pause until Mr. Fortune could catch his breath. He finally got through with his address, and was paying a final tribute to the honored guest, when Martin, who had come back into the hall at the very first opportunity, again made himself heard. He hissed and stamped his feet. The chairman told two patrolmen, who had come into the church, to preserve peace and quiet, to put the man out. This they did.

William M. Trotter of Boston, editor of the Guardian, jumped to his feet, and cried vociferously, "Put me out; arrest me!" He was forced into his seat, and told by the patrolmen to keep quiet or his defiance would be challenged by the whole police force. Trotter sat down.

RIOTOUS SCENE

Harry Burleigh, a New York singer of some repute, arose and opportunely sang "King of Kings." The song had a quieting effect. Encouraged by the lull in the proceedings, Edward Everett Brown,[4] a Boston lawyer, was called upon by chairman Lewis to say something to insure further peace among the people. Mr. Brown scored them heavily for making a disturbance in the house of God. He warned them that the police would be called in to quell the next disturbance that took place. Then Lewis himself arose and said:

"This is a disgrace to every individual in Boston. Those who wish to be free should know how to govern themselves. Their first duty is to preserve order in the church of God."

Mr. Fortune arose and said: "You don't indorse such vulgarity in a public meeting. (Applause.) Your duties as citizens should make you rebuke all riot and disorder." At the words "riot and disorder" the trouble commenced anew. Disregarding all the good words of the speakers, the people began to move suspiciously toward the doors to be ready at any time to take to flight. Those nearest the platform got as far back as possible and jammed against the wall in a solid mass. Some had already begun to depart.

To depart, and to attempt to depart were two very different things, under the condition of affairs existing. The stairways and lower hall were jammed full of people who could not move in any direction, and refused to leave the building.

At the point where Mr. Trotter had to be ejected, which was immediately following the arraignment of Fortune and Lewis, officer Underhill attempted to push through the crowd and get upstairs. He got up a little way and was forced back. Then reinforced by two patrolmen of the squad that was pouring from all parts of the district to the scene, he got up to the first landing of the stairway.

There someone ripped Underhill's coat up the back. "Pat" Malley, another patrolman, who had hurried down to make peace among men, was jabbed in the side with a hatpin by some woman who sympathized with Trotter in his great humiliation. Then, without warning, the whole crowd swayed a moment, and literally fell downstairs. Women fainted in the crush, and had to be taken out in the air and later sent home in carriages, and it was here that Bernard Charles,[5] 20 years old, of 111 Bow st., Everett, was stabbed with some sharp instrument, and taken away to the station house and booked, and later carried to the City hospital.

MARTIN AND TROTTER ARRESTED

Martin and Trotter were also locked up at the East Dedham st. station for disturbing the peace. Maude Trotter, a sister of the editor, was later taken to the station, but no charge was made against her and she was set free. Mrs. Trotter, mother of the editor, went bail for Martin and Trotter, and both went back in the church and tried to gain admittance, but were halted at the door.

Booker Washington, throughout the struggle that was going on about him, remained calm, and succeeded in going through his address, with the aid of a few periods when the noise was too terrific. He said in part:

"What I shall say this evening will relate in the main to the condition of our race in these large northern cities. It is a matter of constant regret to me that my duties call me in different directions of the country, and render it almost impossible for me to meet the members of my own race and speak to them face to face as often as my heart would lead me to do.

"The number of colored people who, for one reason or another, settle in the northern cities, is constantly increasing. The city of Philadelphia, for example, stands fourth among the cities of the whole country in the number of colored people living in it. We must see to it that our race not only makes progress in the south, but that those who have the privilege of living in the north do not fall short of the greater things expected and demanded of them.

"You here in Boston are favored with many advantages, compared with the people of the south; and I am frank to say that you are hampered by some disadvantages. One of the problems that more and more confronts our people in the northern cities is that of finding employment of such a nature as will give opportunity for progress and constant promotion. In the south, very largely, the field of labor is open to us with few restrictions. The young colored man in the north is surrounded on every hand by temptations, which will drag him down, unless he fortifies himself with the best education, and with a strong moral and religious sense of responsibility, and with the earnest cultivation of habits of industry and thrift.

CONDITIONS IN BOSTON

"You will find it easier to enter a college in Boston than to enter a shoe factory or a counting room. In other words, it is easier to secure an education in the north than to find opportunity to use it after it is secured. This leads me to emphasize a point which we, as a race, I fear, especially those men and women of us who are educated, have overlooked in too large a measure. We have attained to the place where we should no longer depend upon the good nature of other people to give us employment, but where we should so educate our heads and hands that we can create positions for ourselves.

"We must encourage that pioneer spirit, that dogged determination, that spirit of self-sacrifice, which was exhibited years ago by the Huntingtons, and Stanfords, and a host of others, who went out into the wilderness, and created towns, industries, and railroads, where none had existed before. Those men were not content with merely seeking positions; they created positions for themselves and for their relatives and friends.

"Hundreds of young men leave Harvard, the Institute of Technology and Amherst and begin in life at the bottom by working with the hands, and in this way actually create within a few years large industrial enterprises, which make them independent and powerful.

"A wealthy and progressive colored man whom I met a few months ago in California was the son of a negro farmer, who went to the state 50 years ago, bought a farm and cultivated it successfully and intelligently. Now, by reason of this economic foundation laid by his father the son is a college graduate, and receives a large income from the rental of his storehouses and dwellings, located in a city which has grown up on the former farm.

"All about you here in Boston are numerous examples of what Italians, Germans and other foreigners who have come here are doing. The Italian boy, in many cases, finishes the public schools and starts in life as an humble bootblack, and most probably only one chair. But he is not contented with this, and in a few months has a half dozen chairs, and later, a half dozen stands. Soon he has money in the bank, is wealthy, and is dependent upon no one for a job.

"I should like to see our young colored men graduate from the high school or college, and then go out and start, for example, a dairy farm, that will grow and improve until it is one of the best farms in Massachusetts. No white man will refuse to buy milk and butter because their producer is a negro college graduate. I would not in any sense limit the education of the negro, north or south, but would encourage him most emphatically to lay the foundations of future prosperity in these primary, original, and wealth-producing occupations.

"Right here let me say that the seeming difference in opinion as to whether the negro shall receive a college or industrial education is a mere quibble. All those who are engaged in the work of education at the south realize that he needs both parts of education just as any other people do. But for the masses emphasis should be placed upon industrial education.

"We need not go far to find examples of colored men who have themselves practiced what I am emphasizing. Right here in Boston, in the persons of Mr. J. H. Lewis, and of scores of others, we find colored men and women who have begun at the bottom in some industry, trade or commercial enterprise, and who have worked themselves up to a place where they are independent, and have the respect of all classes of their fellow citizens.

"We complain a great deal, and rightly, about the treatment accorded us on the railroads of public carriers in some parts of our country. We should remember, however, that the securities that largely govern these public carriers are on the market, and are as easily bought by black men as by white, and that the men who own the securities in the long run control the policy of the public carriers.

"In the last analysis the world cares very little what you or I know, but it does care a great deal about what you and I do. An educated man on the streets, with his hands in his pockets, is not worth one whit more than an ignorant man with his hands in his pockets. It is the application of our knowledge in such a way as to help the world onward materially, mentally and spiritually, that is in the long run recognized and applauded by mankind.

EDUCATION AND WORK

"Every colored parent in Boston should see to it that his child secures the very best, and completest, education; and with that education, a sense of the dignity and beauty of labor, a conviction of the disgrace of idleness, together with the mastery of some special trade or calling, by which at all times, if necessary, a living may be earned. Mere literary education whether of a black, or of a white man, increases one's wants; and one's ability to supply these wants should at the same time be increased, along lines in which he can find employment.

"We should not overlook the gospel of thrift. As a race we are not, I fear, willing enough to sacrifice today for tomorrow, and to do without this year, in order that we may possess in years to come. We are inclined to spend too much of what we earn, and to part ourselves from our money as fast as we earn it. It is in the savings banks, as well as in the school and the church; in the home and in the farm, that New England today finds her greatness and power.

"If the colored people of Boston owned as many shoe factories as they own churches, I suspect that the race in this city would be advanced immensely. We do not need fewer churches, but more farms and factories.

"As an encouraging instance, however, I should like in this connection to state that the negro race has contributed more this year to the support of the Tuskegee Institute than it has ever before done in the history of the Institution.

"I wish that every colored youth who hears my voice this evening would make a new resolve to put forth more earnest effort. He should not feel discouraged because he is poor and black, and should not feel that there is no future for him. If we exert ourselves with ability and determination in the difficult present, we make a future for ourselves and for those who come after us.

"In the increasing disposition of colored men and women, who have received their education here, to go into the south itself, and throw themselves into the work of uplifting their fellows, I see one of the most encouraging signs I have noted within the last few years. At the Tuskegee Institute, in Alabama, we are able to employ a larger number of colored college graduates than does any other one negro institution, and this is due largely to the fact that the institute was founded years ago upon the economic principles to which I have referred.

"In proportion as the institute has grown in the direction of agriculture, mechanics and other industries, in the same proportion has it been able to create positions for the educated members of our race, and the students trained at Tuskegee have gone out to teach the same lessons in every section of the south.

"However, while we are emphasizing the industries, and material wealth and prosperity, we should not overlook the fact that all this is useless and impotent unless backed and supported by strong moral and religious character.

"Let us not be discouraged as to our future, for the great human law, that merit shall be rewarded, will in the end be recognized, nor be nullified in any part of our country."

QUESTIONS FOR WASHINGTON

Here follows the letter that was prepared for use when Booker Washington arose to speak at the meeting in the Zion A. M. E. church. It was constructed in parts, each one to be separately launched at Washington by some one in the opposition. The list of questions includes all those that the trouble of last evening hinged on:

"1. In your letter to the Montgomery Advertiser, Nov. 27, you said, 'Every revised constitution throughout the southern states has put a premium upon intelligence, ownership of property, thrift and character.' Did you not thereby indorse the disfranchising of our race?

"2. In your speech before the Century club here, in March, you said, 'Those are most truly free who have passed the most discipline.' Are you not actually upholding oppressing our race as a good thing for us, advocating peonage?

"3. Again you say, 'Black men must distinguish between the freedom that is forced and the freedom that is the result of struggle and self-sacrifice.' Do you mean that the negro should expect less from his freedom than the white man from his?

"4. When you said, 'It is not so important whether the negro was in the inferior cars, as whether there was in that car a superior man, not a beast,' did you not minimize the outrage of the insulting jim-crow car discrimination and justify it by the bestiality of the negro?

"5. In an interview with the Washington Post, June 25, as to whether the negro should insist on his ballot, you are quoted as saying, 'As is well known I hold that no people in the same economic and educational condition, as the masses of the black people of the South, should make politics a matter of the first importance in connection with their development.' Do you not know that the ballot is the only self-protection for any class of people in this country?

"6. In view of the fact that you are understood to be [un]willing to insist upon the negro's having his every right (both civic and political), would it not be a calamity at this juncture to make you our leader?

"7. Don't you know you would help the race more by exposing the new form of slavery just outside the gates of Tuskegee than by preaching submission?

"8. Can a man make a successful educator and politician at the same time?

"9. Is the rope and the torch all the race is to get under your leadership?"

TROTTER'S EXPLANATION

William M. Trotter gave the side of the anti-Washington men as follows:

"The cause of the riot at the colored Methodist church was due to the absurd ruling of the chairman, W. H. Lewis, when he said that any one who hissed or manifested objection to the speaker of the evening, or who demanded the right to ask him to explain some of his previous statements favoring disfranchisement, and discriminating in Jim Crow cars, would be subject to arrest.

"The dissatisfaction was at once manifested by those who opposed Mr. Washington, and, to add to it all, Mr. T. T. Fortune, who had been brought over from New York to make a political speech, made an attack on the New England representatives to the recent Afro-American council which was called to protest against disfranchisement, but was turned into a republican rally.

"This naturally brought objection to Mr. Fortune's remarks. This hissing was increased when Mr. Washington attempted to speak and when he refused to entertain any questions."

Rev. J. Henry Duckery[6] of Cambridge said:

"Some of us preachers learned at 1:30 today that there was a deeply laid plot in operation to prevent Dr. Washington from speaking in Boston tonight. I have frequently warned Mr. Trotter relative to his tirade upon Mr. Washington and other persons. We understood this afternoon that Messrs. Forbes and Trotter had arranged and had placed men in different places of the church to hiss and to spread cayenne pepper around.

"What makes us look with greater horror upon the proceedings of that mob is that the leaders are men who have graduated from Harvard and Amherst colleges, and others who are in some way connected with the local and national government as employees. As for the Guardian it represents nothing more or less than yellow journalism, and will soon put the race in a very bad light in the east. I was pleased with the way the great majority of the people in spite of the persistent efforts of the disturbers conducted themselves, and I think that Dr. Washington tonight is stronger with the colored people in Boston than ever before. When he had finished his address he was given a grand ovation. Boston colored people like fair play."

Mr. Lewis said: "Two or three men made an abortive attempt to break up a meeting by a hostile demonstration against Mr. Washington. The disturbers were promptly ejected by the police and the meeting went on as scheduled. The address of Mr. Washington was the most eloquent I ever listened to, and he was heartily applauded throughout by the great audience."

In regard to the trouble, Napoleon B. Marshall,[7] a lawyer and deputy collector at city hall, who was present, said:

"The movement against Mr. Washington, was started by the colored people in Boston, who have been much displeased of late at the method that he has taken of trying to uplift the race. He has advocated the jim-crow car, and shows up unnecessarily the failings of the people. Thus the people took this opportunity of showing to the country their disapproval of Mr. Washington and his methods."

Boston *Globe*, July 31, 1903, 1, 3.

1 The episode was not a true riot, though popularly called so. Trotter had for years been frustrated by the refusal of the white press to recognize that there existed alternative philosophies and programs to those of BTW. In Boston he succeeded at what he had failed to accomplish in Louisville a month earlier. He temporarily disrupted a meeting in which BTW was the chief speaker, though there was no violence and the meeting was not completely shut down.

Washington and his Boston friends through strenuous efforts succeeded in putting Trotter and a cohort in jail for a month. The incident marked a rise in the level of intensity with which Washington harassed his critics, as though he felt panic at the prospect of losing his power and influence. Trotter's action did not, however, result in his becoming leader of the opponents of BTW, as W. E. B. Du Bois soon assumed that role.

2 James H. McMullen, A. M. E. Zion pastor of the Columbus Ave. Church, where the Boston Riot took place, testified against Trotter at both of his trials, and was later part of a citizens' committee that called upon Boston's mayor to fire George W. Forbes for his part in the incident.

3 Granville Martin, after policemen forcibly removed him from the church for interrupting Fortune's speech, returned to the hall to interrupt W. H. Lewis. The police rearrested him at Lewis's request. He was tried and convicted with Trotter and served a jail term. He later moved to New York. (Fox, *Guardian of Boston*, 51–52, 54, 57, 156.)

4 Edward Everett Brown, born in New Hampshire in 1858, was a black lawyer. In 1907 he was deputy health commissioner of Boston, and later held the position of deputy tax collector of Boston.

5 Bernard Charles was prosecuted by BTW's supporters along with Trotter and Martin, but the judge decided he acted without premeditation and fined him $25.

6 James Henry Duckrey (or Duckery), a black clergyman born in Delaware in 1861, was a member of the board of public licenses in Cambridge.

7 Napoleon Bonaparte Marshall, a black Bostonian and supporter of Trotter, was deputy tax collector in Boston from 1902 to 1906, when he moved to Washington, D.C., to practice law.

A Statement in the Boston *Globe*

Boston, Mass. July 31, 1903

COMPARED WITH FLIES
MR. WASHINGTON COMMENTS ON THE
ACTION OF A "FEW ILL-MANNERED
YOUNG COLORED MEN"

After the close of the meeting Mr. Washington said:

"Just as a few flies are able to impair the purity of a jar of cream, so three or four ill-mannered young colored men were able to disturb an otherwise successful meeting of the colored citizens of Boston tonight.

"I have rarely seen a greater triumph of the masses in favor of decency and order than I saw tonight after the police removed the three or four disturbers. I have rarely received a more hearty and welcome reception on the part of the masses than I received tonight, as was shown by their hearty applause and approval of my remarks and position.

"The colored citizens of Boston as a whole should not be held responsible for the unwise acts of a few rioters. Nine-tenths of the colored people in Boston have stood by and supported me in my work, and they were never more hearty in their approval than they are today. The men who disturbed the meeting have found this an easy way to get their names into the daily newspapers and to secure a little notoriety, which they otherwise could not obtain."

Boston *Globe*, July 31, 1903, 3.

An Account of the Boston Riot[1]

Boston, Mass., July 31. [1903]

RIOT AND CONFUSION IN BOSTON

Last night, at the A. M. E. Zion Church, on Columbus Avenue, at a public meeting of the Boston branch of the National Negro Business League, one of the most disgraceful and riotous scenes in the history of Boston was precipitated by five men, under the leadership of William Monroe Trotter, editor of the Boston Guardian, who has become insane in his opposition to Dr. Booker T. Washington, and his methods of leadership. The plan to break up the meeting was deliberately premeditated, and was of the coarsest, most vulgar sort, such as is employed everywhere by the hoodlum, rowdy elements to create riot and confusion. Trotter was backed up in his rowdyism by a half-dozen women of the street, whose vulgar services were obviously purchased. Martin, the man who began the interuption, and was most persistent in rowdyism, insisting that Mr. Washington is opposed to social equality, is a butler in a white family, and appeared at the meeting in his waiter's jacket.

But behind Trotter are the following men, who have more brains, if no more character, then he: Archibald H. Grimké, brother to Rev. Francis J. Grimké, of Washington, and recently appointed consul to San Domingo, as a democrat, by President Cleveland, Clement G. Morgan, George W. Forbes, W. H. Ferris, all college-bred men, and Jno. W. A. Shaw, a democratic soldier of fortune, who has always been down at the heels. By their action these men have lost character with the white and colored people of Boston, not because they are democrats at heart, but because they have shown a rowdy and vulgar disposition in their opposition to Mr. Washington, which places them among the hoodlums of the population.

There were seen two thousand people in and about the church, drawn there by a laudable desire to see and hear Dr. Washington speak. They were honest and intelligent people, among them being many of the distinguished and respected colored people of Boston, people proud of their city, and zealous for its high reputation for intelligence, sobriety, and for law and order. Scattered among these two thousand people, were Trotter and his henchmen, who had contrived to throw red pepper about the altar before the meeting was called to order, for the purpose of confusing the speakers. As soon as the chairman, Hon. W. H. Lewis, called the meeting to order, the disturbance was begun by one Martin, with hissing by his associates. When T. Thos. Fortune, of New York, was announced as the first speaker, the man Martin became so boisterous in his talk and action that the audience was thrown into confusion, and the police had to be called in to eject him. Just before Mr. Fortune concluded his remarks, the man was allowed to return to his seat on promise of good behavior; but the interruptions continued through the address of Mr. Edward Everett Brown.

When Mr. Washington was introduced, the five men created so much disorder and confusion that the audience became panicky and riotous in temper. The managers of the meeting then decided to have Trotter and all of his fellow conspirators ejected from the church. A squad of policemen, commanded by a sergeant, was called in, and in the confusion that ensued both inside and outside of the church, arrested Trotter and his sister, and two of his henchmen, and, with handcuffs on their wrists, marched them off to the station house. One was badly cut with a razor, and two policemen were injured, one of them stabbed with a hat pin in the hands, it is alleged, of Miss Maude Trotter. When the rioters were removed, after two hours of confusion, the meeting proceeded in an orderly and decorous manner. At the close of the meeting, Mr. Washington was given an ovation, and was overwhelmed by the crush of people who desired to shake his hand, and assure him personally of their hearty good will and sympathy.

It will be recalled that this man Trotter and two companions from Boston, came near precipitating a riot on three occasions at the Louisville convention of the Afro-American Council, early in July last, and succeeded by their lawless acts and words in coloring the reports about the convention in such a way as to confuse the thoughtful people of the country. It is safe to say that by their conduct at Louisville, and at the Boston meeting of the National Negro Business League, Trotter and his crew have done more to injure the cause of the race in the estimation of the people of the country, than can be overcome by years of hard honest effort. It is high time that the race frown down such crazy, desperate characters as Trotter, and place the seal of their disapproval upon them in such an unmistakable way that he who runs may read.

It is worth while to emphasize the fact that Dr. Washington has during the past six months spoken a dozen or more times in white churches in Boston, but Trotter and his gang made no disturbance in any of them; they waited until Dr. Washington was to speak at a church of his own race, crowded by the flower of the race's womanhood and manhood of Boston, to carry out their program of riot and confusion. Why did they not carry it out at some one of the white churches in Boston, where Dr. Washington has spoken during the last six months?

"Professor" Wm. H. Ferris, the prime mover in the riotous conduct at Louisville, was not present to assist his fellow-rioters in Boston Thursday night, for the reason that he is completely on his uppers in Louisville. It seems that Trotter and Forbes, after using Forbes [Ferris] for their own selfish ends, abandoned him, and left him stranded in Louisville. Ferris is a type of the tramp who goes South to attend meetings, and to instruct the colored people as to the solution of their problems. It is very pitiful to read the urgent letters he is writing to Boston, entreating his friends to send him even the smallest amounts to assist him to get home.

TM   Con. 978   BTW Papers   DLC.

[1] Probably written by E. J. Scott.

From Emmett Jay Scott

[Tuskegee, Ala., July 31, 1903]

My Dear Mr. Washington: I sympathise greatly with you because of the nasty mess last night — that Forbes, Trotter & the rest of that gang sh'd have made the "muss" they did. It all only shows their impotent fury that 2M(2000), people sh'd come out to hear you — in the face of all their dirty attacks. It must have exasperated them. I shall be greatly surprised if they do not receive the condemnation of all decent people — & if the end of their dirt is not in sight. Hudson had resolutions as per his draft herewith passed by the Convention.[1] He gave his consent for any changes I desired & I have sent to Advertiser, Constitution & Associated Press the report copy of which I also attach. I hope the report will go out & that you will have seen it even before this letter reaches you. It will break the force of their attack & will do good — great good! Yours Sincerely Ever,

Emmett J. Scott

ALS   Con. 249   BTW Papers   DLC.

[1] A convention of leading Alabama black Baptists, meeting in a Tuskegee church under the chairmanship of R. B. Hudson, passed resolutions condemning the effort of "a few irresponsible men at Boston last night to insult and humiliate Dr. Booker T. Washington of the Tuskegee Institute." They pronounced BTW "a conservative, worthy and safe leader." (Press release, July 31, 1903, Con. 250, BTW Papers, DLC.)

From Burwell Town Harvey

Peru, Ind. July 31–1903

Dear Prof. Washington: I just read in the evening paper an associated press dispatch from Boston, Mass., where you were interrupted by some of your opposers in attempting to ask questions during the delivery of your speech at the Zion church there. It is reported as almost precipitating a riot. One policeman was stabbed with a hat pin and one of your opposers was badly cut with a razor. I pray God that nothing will happen to you in such meetings. Such self-constituted leaders are disgracing the race. To-day, while the Negro race is passing through the crucial test of its worthiness to be engrafted into the civilized life of the American people; and when God has favored the race with such a modern "Moses" as you are; having manfully worked your way up the ladder of fame and now has the ear of the American nation and the civilized world, for that matter; and is at present exerting an incalculable influence in behalf of the poor ignorant and dependent race to which you belong; the Negro who would intentionally oppose or try to reflect or detract one iota of honor from you is an enemy to the race! Any one that will envy or oppose another because he persists in magnifying *his work* is a crank, pure and simple. The prayers of thousands of loyal supporters, black and white, go out to you in this your trying hour of opposition from the ranks of your own race. Shame! Shame!! With best wishes I remain your humble friend and student.

B. T. Harvey

ALS   Con. 260   BTW Papers   DLC.

From James H. McMullen

Boston, Mass. [July 31, 1903]

Dear Dr. Washington: I am not yet over the excitement of last evening. But our victory is complete. You will never be troubled in Boston again. The Guardian is "done for" and its thick headed Editor will be prosecuted to the fullest extent of the law. White and black are with you now as never before. A leading white citizen whose name I cant just recall but will name later said to me yesterday in the Court House, "Mr. Washington can get any kind of money he needs to carry on his work from me." I regret more than I have words to express the riotous proceedings of those individuals Thursday evening, but the end had to come and let us hope this is the end. The trial will come off next Tuesday and every effort on the part of my church will be made to punish the offenders of *decency*, *law* and *order*. You have won a *signal* victory and the colored people to a man appreciate your wise leadership and great statesmanship as displayed in all of your public utterances. I sincerely regret the disgrace which may, by unthinking ones, be charged to my church, but I am glad that I had a part in the ending of these *hood-lum* leaders and *scandel-mongers* who constantly speak disrespectfully of you. God bless you and your family. I am sorry that I did not get the opportunity to be presented to Mrs. Washington and your daughter and to have them meet Mrs. McMullen. Hope the opportunity will come again.

Count us in the future among your admirers and friends. You shall have my earnest support the remainder of my days. I am yours etc,

J. H. McMullen

N.B. I send you a card from my friend Rev. Marshall, W. H. of Saratoga N.Y. which will explain itself. If you desire you can answer it. He is alright.

J. H. M.

ALS   Con. 266   BTW Papers   DLC.

From Peter Jefferson Smith, Jr.

Boston Mass   July 31 1903

Case continued to Aug 4 Lewis counsel for church. Church determined to push case to the end.

P J Smith

HWSr   Con. 542   BTW Papers   DLC.

From Wilford H. Smith

New York City, July 31st 1903

Dear Dr. Washington: I have read with much shame for the people of Boston, the account of the disgraceful affair at your meeting there last night. It will be used to reflect on the race, to prove its want of appreciation, and criminal instincts, by our enemies.

By all means Trotter and Forbes must be muzzled, and at once. Just as early as possible I shall go to New Haven and exert my best endeavors to bring it about through the matter there. Very truly yours,

Wilford H. Smith

ALS   Con. 277   BTW Papers   DLC.

From James Carroll Napier

Nashville, Tenn., August 1st 1903

My Dear Mr. Washington: I see that the crowd of malcontents with whom we had to deal at Louisville have again been trying to give trouble — this time in Boston. They are indeed a hard and trouble-some set. They are themselves continually in hot water and it is their purpose and aim to draw every one else into it with them. At Louisville they thoroughly convinced me that they are utterly un-fit to govern or control themselves and therefore entirely unfit to champion the rights of others. They deserve to be severely sat down upon. I trust that the courts will mete out to each one of them his just deserts.

I wish very much I could have been present at this meeting to tell them what I think of them. No self respecting colored man in the South desires to have his cause championed by any such horde of loud-mouthed, blatant blatherskites. Their course brings no good to themselves or others. Their course is severely condemned on every hand. You will not meet men of this class or make up when you come to Nashville.

Every thing looks well for the League. Be sure to leave no stone unturned to secure a large attendance. I am sure that every delegate will receive the same general courteous treatment in Nashville that he would get in Boston.

Mrs. Napier has been quite sick and for three days has been con-

stantly confined to her bed. I am thankful to say that she is somewhat improved today. Very truly yours,

J. C. Napier

ALS   Con. 269   BTW Papers   DLC.

An Article in the San Francisco *Bulletin*

Aug. 2, 1903

TRAINING DUSKY GRISELDAS
MRS. BOOKER T. WASHINGTON'S MISSIONARY
WORK AMONG NEGRO HOUSE-WIVES

One has only to look out of the window of a passing train almost
anywhere from Virginia to Louisiana to see the dilapidated one
room cabins which shelter a large proportion of the eight million
descendants of slavery in this country today. It was during a recent
trip through the rural districts of the Black Belt, where shiftless
crowded negro homes abound and one discredits for the moment
the possibility of any member of the race being sufficiently alert to
stir up controversy through the obtainment of Federal office or anything else implying the exercise of the slightest energy, that the
writer was given an opportunity to see some successful results of
the work of an enlightened colored woman who had devoted years
of her life to the task of bettering the miserable conditions in the
homes of her people. The name of this woman is Margaret Murray
Washington. She is the third wife of the well known president of
Tuskegee Institute, Booker T. Washington.

Any one who has seen the outside, still more the inside of an
Alabama cabin can appreciate the magnitude of the undertaking
which confronts the reformer. From a roomless, often windowless,
hut, where light and air are admitted solely through cracks in the
dilapidated four walls and five or six persons are crowded under a
roof which hardly sheds water; where a bed with sheets and pillow
cases is as unusual as a glass window, and the family crawl in between some old covers without even taking the trouble to remove

their scant clothing — from such an abode to a clean, decent, well-ventilated house is a long step, but this is only a part of what Mrs. Washington is trying to accomplish, and in some cases has already achieved.

In childhood, Booker Washington's wife says, she ran away from a home little better than the worst of those she is now trying to reform. To some strict but kindly Quakers who took her to live with them and subsequently sent her to a university she owes her own careful training. Perhaps the best idea one can get of Mrs. Washington's methods was summed up in the words of a friend who said of her: "Mrs. Washington works on the principle that cleanliness is not only next to godliness, but before it."

In speaking of the way she started her "missionary work," as she calls it, Mrs. Washington said that six or seven years ago she became impressed with the conditions on a plantation about eight miles from Tuskegee, where a settlement of twenty negro families live in some old slave "quarters." When she first went to them five to ten persons were living in one room houses, and the children were allowed to go round with little or no clothing on them.

"It was just like Africa," she said, speaking of that time. "I felt something must be done, so one day I went down there with a good stiff broom, determined to see what I could do. I went to the most promising house of the lot and proposed to hold a meeting, first suggesting that we sweep up the place in honor of the occasion. The sweeping I gave that room made the woman who lived in it so ashamed of her own slack work that I have never since found her home in the same condition." After her first visit Mrs. Washington went periodically to the different cabins on the estate, showing the women how to remove [improve] even the most unpromising surroundings and urging them to take an interest in the decency of their homes for their own sakes and the sakes of their husbands and children.

In the course of time the planter for whom most of these people work gave the use of an abandoned cabin for a "settlement house," where a young woman graduate of Tuskegee was sent to carry on the work that had already been started. Since that time Mrs. Washington has raised sufficient funds to provide in its place a serviceable frame dwelling house on ten acres of adjoining land. This house is designed not only for a place for Mrs. Washington's meetings and classes, but is kept by Miss Davis,[1] who lives there, as an object lesson in housekeeping for the neighborhood.

Last February I was one of the party who visited this "settlement." The house with its fresh, white paint and shining glass windows, stands out in striking contrast to the dingy surroundings. The front door opens directly upon a bedroom absolutely shining with cleanliness. The bed, with its white spread and snowy pillows, was as smooth as a piece of glass. Every day it is made up by one of the neighbors' children, who is thus taught a useful lesson to carry into her own home. The floor, which could have been eaten from, had been scrubbed by another little black girl. The kitchen was equally well kept. There was a polished stove, with bright pots and kettles. In the middle of the room there was a well set table, where the visitors are invited to "model" meals, says the New York Herald.

Among the families of the "settlement" there was everywhere a marked superiority to what former observations of negro cabin life had led us to expect. Beds and floors were well kept. Cracked roofs and walls were filled in with clay. In many cases two or more rooms had been added. In fact, there was altogether an unusual air of neatness and order in all of the houses. Of course this plantation is only one of many places where Mrs. Washington is carrying on her work. In a building near the market place of the town of Tuskegee, where the negro farmers come every Saturday morning to trade, bringing their wives with them, Mrs. Washington holds what she calls "mothers' meetings." She has a weekly attendance of sixty to 100 women. There are two rooms in the building, one of which is fitted up with a cook stove and bed for practice lessons, and the other is used as a meeting hall.

On a Saturday morning the writer attended one of the meetings. The women who gathered there were neatly dressed, and although there was a wide dissimilarity in their costumes, ranging from shawls and picturesque sunbonnets to straw hats and imitation sealskin coats, and although some of them had even undertaken to lace their shoes with calico strips, there was evident in every case a regard for appearances seldom found in a gathering composed of negro farmers' wives. The topic of Mrs. Booker T. Washington's talk that day was "Self-Respect." "If we don't respect ourselves," she said, "how can we expect the white folks to respect us?"

It was not long after this that Mrs. Washington took me to the home of one of these "mothers." It is situated a short distance out of the town. This woman has been attending the meetings and classes for years. The house in which she now lives was originally similar to the cabins surrounding it, but it has been enlarged until it has now the appearance of a good sized house. Several windows have been cut in it and her husband has built a fence around a pretty front yard. At the time I saw her she had barely finished the noonday meal, but the table was already cleared and the children, in their clean gingham aprons, looked as unlike the half-clothed "pickaninnies" one finds in most Alabama cabins as could possibly be imagined.

When we first saw her the woman was sweeping the porch and as the sunlight fell on her well smoothed hair and fresh calico dress she seemed the very personification of that "self-respect" of which Booker Washington's wife had spoken in the meeting. Just across the way from this woman's house there is a broken down twelve foot cabin. Through the open door of it we saw a woman cooking dinner on a skillet hung over the chimney place. Outside a barefoot girl was washing some tattered clothing in a little water she had heated in a black pot placed over a rude fire of scraps and brushwood. We went inside of the house. It was almost dark, the only ray of light coming through a hole just big enough to put one's fist through and which had evidently been cut out with a penknife.

It is a contrast like that between these two homes which shows better than anything else possibly could what the wife of Booker Washington has done and may yet do for the negro homes in the black belt. Of course, Mrs. Washington's own home and the residences of the families of the other teachers at Tuskegee are models of home making and home keeping and serve more than anything else possibly could to shame the negro farmers and their wives, who are obliged to pass them continually on the road to and from the market.

San Francisco *Bulletin*, Aug. 2, 1903, Clipping   Con. 866   BTW Papers   DLC.

1 Probably Anna (Annie) Rosetta Davis, a Tuskegee graduate of 1895, who taught in Macon County after graduation.

To Whitefield McKinlay

South Weymouth, Mass., 3d August, 1903

Dear Mr. McKinlay: Enclosed I send you two letters from Gov. Pinchback. Please let me know what in your opinion is the wisest plan to secure without fail this position for his son, and whether there are any hindrances in the Civil Service Rules, which would prevent or make difficult his appointment.

You will be glad to know that Trotter, Forbes, Grimke, and two or three others, have by their actions completely killed themselves among all classes both white and colored, in Boston. Trotter was taken out of the church in handcuffs, yelling like a baby. They are to be tried in Court tomorrow, and every effort is being exerted by the citizens of Boston to secure their conviction. Very truly yours,

Booker T. Washington

TLS   Con. 4   Carter G. Woodson Collection   DLC.

To Francis Jackson Garrison

South Weymouth, Mass. Aug. 3. '03

My dear Mr. Garrison, I thank you very much for your letter of August first. While the experience in Boston, Thursday evening, was painful and disagreeable, it was one of the things that had to come to a head. It was like a severe surgical operation. During the past few months I have been asked to deliver an address before the colored people of Boston. I refused to accept, chiefly because I feared that trouble might occur. When I refrained from speaking, Trotter and others began to circulate the report that I would not speak before a colored audience.

Throughout the episode and the present agitation, the thing that gives me the greatest satisfaction is to note the sane sensible view that the rank and file of our people take with reference to conditions and to note how loyally and faithfully they support any policy that has in view the actual improvement of our people.

I do not become angry with Mr. Trotter and his clientelle, but I do pity them. If he had deliberately planned to kill himself and his influence with the colored people of Boston, he could not have done it in a more successful manner. Very truly yours,

Booker T. Washington

P.S. I thought you might care to see the enclosed copy of a letter from Mr. Mims.

B. T. W.

HLS   Francis J. Garrison Papers   NN-Sc.

From Emmett Jay Scott

Tuskegee, Alabama. August 3, 1903

Dear Mr. Washington: No doubt you have noticed that four of my editorials appeared in the Colored American last week. I was especially desirous of placing Kelly Miller in direct opposition to Du Bois which I think I succeeded in doing. Cooper got out a splendid issue of the paper last week from all points of view, although he may have emphasised too much Tuskegee and its interests. This is a thing I have especially asked him to guard against.

I hope that my telegram has had attention and that the Herald and Transcript were sent out promptly to various Negro newspapers. A report from them will weigh greatly I think with the Negro press and they should have first hand information upon which to base any comments they may make. I wonder if it is not possible now to reach Forbes in this matter for his part in this disgraceful riot and also the man put down as Assistant City Prosecutor, Marshall I believe his name is. Yours truly,

Emmett J. Scott

TLS   Con. 272   BTW Papers   DLC.

To Emmett Jay Scott

South Weymouth, Mass, Aug. 4 '03

My dear Mr. Scott, I thank you very much for your letter regarding the Boston episode and for the resolutions. They have appeared in all of the Boston papers and in the Associated press.

The whole affair was painful and regret[t]able from every point [of] view and it has resulted in killing Trotter and his element in the minds of both races. Even the colored people who before sympathized with him, have withdrawn. They are to be prosecuted in the courts tomorrow and they are putting up most humble pleas begging not to be punished. I have never seen the colored people of Boston so stirred up as they now are. We have certainly won a signal and far-reaching victory! Very sincerely yours

Booker T. Washington

HLS Con. 281 BTW Papers DLC.

From W. Allison Sweeney

Chicago   Aug. 4, 1903

My Dear Sir: Please accept my acknowledgement of your's under date of 28. ult. enclosing $10 as your contribution to the fund I am gathering for the purposes I had indicated to you.

In a line to your secretary thereto,[1] not knowing your address I said "to say that I was surprised is putting it mildly" etc.

There are good and recent reasons, not to mention antedating claims upon your sense of appreciation and an impulse to do the just thing, that caused surprise at your parsimonious offering.

That you yourself must have anticipated and shrunk from the disappointment you felt would result from your offering, is re[a]dily discerned in the veiled apology contained in the first sentence of your communication, to wit, "*I enclose a very small amount, only ten dollars.*"

At the risk of being impertinent permit me to suggest that upon your return to Tuskegee you review with *Your Own Eyes* the recent correspondence between your secretary and myself. It may serve to rarafy and broaden your vision, failing, you *are not* the man you should be.

I shall certainly send you a copy of the first issue of *The Blackman*, which event will transpire *only* when the funds in hand will *guarentee* a year's publication.

He who helps well helps quickly. Had you put into action *Now*, your promise at some future time to "assist" me "more generously," my first issue might at this moment lie before you. Fraternally your's

W. Allison Sweeney

ALS   Con. 274   BTW Papers   DLC.

1 Sweeney wrote sarcastically to Scott: "The $10 bill sent me by Mr. Washington is a silent but potent reminder of your wonderful sway over the man not to mention the exalted value placed upon any services he has so kindly permitted me to render him." He said he would file all of the correspondence, "and if its many features may not serve to point a moral, who knows, it may adorn a tale." (Aug. 4, 1903, Con. 274, BTW Papers, DLC.)

From Monroe Burroughs

Robertson, Va.   Aug. 6–1903

Dear Nephew: I write to let you hear from me.

I am well, hope this will find you and family well.

I am glad to say, I am keeping up very well, age considered.

Tho I am not able to walk about, much. We have contracted to buy a farm of 75 a[cres] which costs $375. If you can, I want you to please help me out a little on it; if it is only a little, it will be gratefully received. I think, if we have luck we can pay it in less time, than stipulated in contract. We have three yrs.

I have two sons in O. who are going to help pay and two daughters — one in O. and one in Bedford City, Va — who are going to help pay for this property. Tell John Washington I say, please help me a little if he can. I wrote to John last year and received no answer. I don't understand it.

All of the Burroughs family is dead, except Newt. Five of his girls are living they are all widows.

Lucinda, Martha, Ann, Eliza and Laura are living. Ellen has been dead a good while. They live in Franklin Co. Newt lives in Bedford Co. Tom Burroughs died last year.

None of my family is at home with me except my wife and a grandson.

I have a nice little crop of corn. Wheat crop is poor in Va. My daughter, Mary says send her your families' picture and names.

Tell John to please send me his families' pictures and names.

My wife is named Sallie, she is about 50 yrs. old.

I am 77 yrs. old. I feel that my time is growing short, in this world. If I never see you all again meet me beyond the smiling and the weeping, for I shall be there.

Your Uncle till death

Monroe Burroughs

ALS   Con. 249   BTW Papers   DLC.

J. C. May [Wilford H. Smith]
to R. C. Black [Emmett Jay Scott]

New York City, New York. August 6th, 1903

Dear Friend, R. C. Black: Justice White has allowed the writ of error in my case,[1] but requires a bond for cost, and as soon as it comes back from Alabama I will be ready to come down and serve papers. I shall be compelled to remain there long enough to get my man back from the penitentiary where he now is. I calculate to be there next week sometime.

If you find that you have to leave home before I come I wish you would leave the — D. — heretofore arranged for, with our good friend Adams.

Pickens was in to-day and he consents to what we wish. I have just wired "His Nibs." As soon as I return from Alabama we will go to Boston. Very truly yours,

J. C. May

TLSr   Con. 25   BTW Papers   DLC.

1 *Rogers* v. *Alabama*, 192 U.S. 266 (1903). The court ruled that Rogers's indictment for murder was unconstitutional, since blacks had been excluded from the grand jury that indicted him.

To Emmett Jay Scott

Petersburg Ill's   Aug 7th [1903]

Trotter and Two others sentenced thirty days in Jail.

B T W

TWIr   Con. 542   BTW Papers   DLC.

To Emmett Jay Scott

Shelbyville, Ill., 8 August, 1903

Dear Mr. Scott: Please let the enclosed[1] appear in two or three colored newspapers which you can thoroughly trust, as coming from a correspondent at Boston. The facts of course, can be used from time to time as editorial squibs, as you may think best. You may be interested to know that the whole crowd are thoroughly scared, and are on their knees, begging for mercy. Very truly yours,

B. T. W.

TLI   Con. 275   BTW Papers   DLC.

1 See A Press Release, ca. Aug. 8, 1903, below.

A Press Release[1]

Boston, Mass. [ca. Aug. 8, 1903]

The colored people of Boston feel that they have won a great and far-reaching victory in the direction of decency, law, and order, in securing the conviction and punishment of three of the leaders, including Wm. Monroe Trotter, in the disorder at a recent meeting where Booker Washington spoke here. Trotter has been sentenced to spend thirty days in the work house. The ignorant waiter, who was filled with whiskey, and was carefully groomed to do the bidding of Trotter and others, received a like sentence; and the man Charles was fined. It is very likely that Trotter's stay in the public jail will give him an opportunity to review his foolish life. From Harvard College to the gaol — the distance is great; but Trotter has travelled it in short order.

It is well known, however, by the colored people of Boston that the men who were sentenced were not the most guilty. Behind them, and urging them on, it is currently reported, are George Forbes, A. H. Grimke, and C. G. Morgan, who were not so brave as those who were arrested, but in the most cowardly manner stood in the dark, urging them on, without showing their own hands.

The most interesting and encouraging thing in connection with the whole matter is to note that almost unanimously the colored people of Boston condemn the riotous acts, and are determined to see the guilty ones punished. An example made in this case will have a good effect for a long time.

Examination into the plot reveals the further information, practically reliable, that several women from the streets were hired, and drugged with whiskey, to go into the church, and do the hissing. The colored people are especially incensed over the acts of these rowdies, because it is well known that while Mr. Washington has spoken many times recently in the white churches of Boston, he has not been interrupted by Trotter, Forbes, or any of their followers. They waited until they could get the opportunity to insult a colored audience, in a colored church, filled with colored ladies & gentlemen.

Amos Joy

TMdSr Con. 262 BTW Papers DLC. Scott dated the release July 15, probably meaning to write Aug. 15.

From William Henry Baldwin, Jr.

N.Y. [City] August 10, 1903

Dear Mr. Washington: I have just returned from Lake George. I could not find a moments time to write you from there.

We have just completed a three days session of the Southern Education Board, which was filled with interesting discussion. Fortunately on Friday morning, just as the meeting began, I was asked a question by Mr. Ogden which made it possible for me to speak on all the questions which are closest to your heart. We spent fully three hours at that first meeting, and after it was over Mr. Ogden, Mr. Buttrick and some others told me that it was the most important meeting which we ever had, and expressed their appreciation of the way in which I analyzed the general situation as it is today. My talk was based on my meeting with you Tuesday, and I began by saying that I had seen you and your family and that I noted the anxiety and sense of responsibility which you have in view of the increasingly strained relationship between the two races in certain parts of the country. I went right to the bottom of it. I talked right out plainly about all the things that one seldom talks [about] with Southern men. I laid everything bare. You know what I said without my attempting to repeat it, because I covered the whole subject as I know it, and I talked in just the way that I talked with you and did not mince matters.

We had meetings either two or three times each day, and yesterday had three meetings. The reports from various States were very encouraging to me as far as relates to the general question of education, but my constant question was, What has been done for the negro? In short, I showed my true color from beginning to end in this Conference and made myself the representative of negro justice.

At the session yesterday afternoon we had a very spirited meeting. I pictured the dangers, as I see them today, and then I dealt entirely upon the need of having some close connection between the negro representatives and these educational boards. It stirred up a mighty discussion and it brought out the characters of several men. I even went so far as to say that, as I knew that the negro race doubted us and doubted me because of lack of representation, if this doubt could not be dispelled in some other way I should feel that it was my duty more to leave the duties as a Director of the Boards and satisfy my own particular opportunity in siding with the negro race. Of course, that was a strong statement to make, yet I modified it by saying that I believed absolutely in the wisdom and good faith of all the members of that Board, and that I believed they would think honestly for the best interests of both the negroes and the white people in the South. My position, you will note, was that my own service could be greater to your people by keeping their confidence than by running any serious risk in staying with the Board if the doubt continued. I confess that my arguments, which were elaborate, were somewhat answered by the fact that Hampton, the Peabody Board, the Slater Board had no negroes as members, and that the A. M. A. has no negro representation. And I also learned more clearly than ever before the great embarrassment under which these Southern men live amongst their insane people. They admitted that their people were insane in these questions.

Dr. Alderman is simply great. Do you know that there are men in New Orleans who will not permit their sons to go to Tulane University because you were introduced by him on the stage in New Orleans. My only fear is that a man of such fine sense of honor will be driven, like so many others, from the southern country, and come to the land where he can be free.

Dr. Murphy is a man of true courage, and he *loves* your race.

I called Dr. Dabney down, and so did the other members of the Board, because he had not referred to negro education sufficiently in the Monthly Bulletin (the Bulletin will be stopped).

In short, I turned loose on the whole situation, and although Mr. Peabody and Mr. Ogden did not agree with me, I have certainly set them all to thinking. I do not know whether my actions were entirely wise or not. Dr. Frissell says he thinks it was all right, but I did one thing at least. I left the southern members, as well as the northern members, understanding that I, personally, would not be influenced by anything except a policy which would accord justice to the negro. It was a very intense time; the key note was struck high and it stayed there all the time.

A Committee consisting of Dr. Murphy, Dr. Buttrick, Dr. Shaw and Mr. Ogden has been appointed to submit a plan for re-organization of the Board, and to find ways and means, and the report to be submitted at a special meeting to be held in October or early in November. The idea is to secure the co-operation of the ministers of the South, both white and black, and to secure the co-operation of all Women's Clubs possible; to have local auxiliary boards in each State; or general auxiliary boards of white men and auxiliary boards of negroes. I am inclined to think that they will find some way to meet my suggestions.

Dr. Alderman has promised to stay with me when he comes to New York in the next week or two, and I shall talk it all out with him. He is magnificent and his heart is in the work for the negro, as well as the white man.

It was not decided where the next conference would be held.

Use discretion in referring to this letter, because I am telling confidential things. Yours very truly,

W H Baldwin Jr

TLS Con. 792 BTW Papers DLC.

From William Henry Baldwin, Jr.

N.Y. [City] Aug. 10th., 1903

Dear Washington: I am tremendously interested in the suit against Trotter. Your message was received at Lake George and gave intense satisfaction to the members of the Board present. They feel that your work will be materially helped in the South by reason of the attack upon you. I should watch carefully for a revulsion of feeling in Boston, and not have it appear that there is any persecution of "free thought," but that the position of your friends is held simply because of the vicious interference with the meeting. Yours very truly,

W H B Jr.

TLI Con. 249 BTW Papers DLC.

From William Henry Baldwin, Jr.

N.Y. [City] Aug. 10th., 1903

Dear Washington: In the course of our talk at Lake George I find that the Southern men state that the negro women in some sections of the South, particularly in the far South, have a great desire to have children by white men, and that mothers bring up their daughters to secure it, if possible. It simply opens up a line of inquiry about which I want to talk with you, and which is very interesting. Yours very truly,

W H B Jr

TLI   Con. 792   BTW Papers   DLC.

From Charles Waddell Chesnutt

Cleveland, O., August 11, 1903

Personal.

My dear Dr. Washington: I should have replied sooner to your private and confidential letter of July 7th, but have been very busy, and could not find time to express myself as I would like to — will probably not do that even here.

Permit me to express my strong disapproval of the conduct of Mr. Trotter and his adherents at your Boston meeting. A man who has a cause, or thinks he has a cause, which cannot be presented, at the proper time and place, in calm and dignified argument, has mistaken his calling as an advocate.

Replying to that portion of your letter in which you invite the expression of my opinion on matters pertaining to the race, I wish to say that I differ from you most decidedly on the matter of a restricted franchise. It is an issue gotten up solely to disfranchise the Negroes, and with no serious intention of ever applying it to any one else. I see nothing at all to justify what you term "the protection of the ballot, for a while at least, either by an educational test, property test, or by both combined." It is a complete acquiescence in the withdrawal of the ballot from the Negro, and his entire deprivation of any representation; it means that you are willing, in your own State and county, to throw yourself upon the mercy of the whites, rather than to claim your share in your own government under a free franchise. You may reply that you would have to do it anyway. But you need not approve of it, thereby tying the hands of the friends of the race who would be willing and able to cry out against the injustice. The little handful of colored voters registered in Alabama, for instance, cut no figure in the general result of an election. The State of Mississippi, where the ballot is "protected" in the manner you approve of, has just nominated a governor[1] and a U.S. Senator[2] on an anti-negro platform. The world is not having long to wait nor much need to watch, to see how the white South, under the policy of non-interference, is carrying out its "sacred trust" — I doubt whether "sacred" is quite the word for a trust which was acquired by highway robbery of another class. Your qualification that "whatever tests are required, they should be made to apply with equal and exact justice to both races," would be all right if we could see or hope for any disposition on the part of even a decent minority of Southern white men to apply these tests fairly. I for one prefer to wait until I see this disposition before I will agree that the ballot should be "protected" by restrictions which have but one purpose and can have but one result — to deny the colored race all representation. Such a restriction could never be fair so long as there remained any disparity in the condition of the races, so long as there was any race question in Southern politics; and therefore it could never be fair in your lifetime or mine.

Nor do I think it the part of policy to dwell too much upon the weakness of the Negro race. That their condition should be lowly, in view of their antecedents, is entirely natural, and scarcely calls for any lengthy disquisitions. It is altogether contrary to the spirit of our institutions and to the Constitution to pick out any one class of people, differentiated from the rest by color or origin or anything else, make some average deduction concerning their capacity, and then proceed to measure their rights by this standard. Every individual Negro, weak or strong, is entitled to the same rights before the law as every individual white man, whether weak or strong; nor is there any good reason in law, in morals or anywhere else, why the strong Negro should have his rights and opportunities measured by those of the weak. I think that by recognizing and dwelling upon these distinctions, and suggesting different kinds of education and different degrees of political power and all that sort of thing for the colored people, we are merely intensifying the class spirit which is fast robbing them of every shadow of right. Let the white man dwell upon the weakness of the Negro, if he will; it is not a matter which you or I need to emphasize. The question with which, in principle, we have to deal, is not the question of the Negro race; what the black race has or has not been able to do in Africa should no more enter into the discussion of the Negro's rights as a citizen, than what the Irish have not done in Ireland should be the basis of their citizenship here. We are directly concerned with the interests of some millions of American citizens of more or less mixed descent, whose rights are fixed by the Constitution and laws of the United States; nor am I ready yet to accept the doctrine that those constitutional rights are mere waste paper. The Supreme Court may assent to their nullification, but we ought not to accept its finding as conclusive: there is still the court of public opinion to which we may appeal.

You speak of Jim Crow work for Negroes at the North; I am unable to think of any colored man in this city, possessed of any art or trade, who cannot find employment and earn a living at it. There are plenty of them in shops and factories, sometimes as foremen, and they are not badly represented in offices and stores. *All* the Negroes down South must ride in the Jim Crow cars. Northern prejudice at least discriminates; Southern prejudice doesn't. I would by no means confound the good Southerners with the bad. Judge Jones is a noble man and worthy of all praise; I only wish he represented a larger constituency. But the white South insists upon judging the Negroes as a class. They themselves must be measured by the same rule, must be judged by the laws they make, the customs they follow and the crimes they commit, under color of law, against the colored people. They seem to me, as a class, barring a few honorable exceptions, an ignorant, narrow and childish people — as inferior to the white people of the North — barring a few of the lower class — as the Southern Negroes are said to be to the whites of that section. I make no pretense of any special love for them. I was brought up among them; I have a large share of their blood in my veins; I wish them well, and first of all I wish that they may learn to do justice. My love I keep for my friends, and my friends are those who treat me fairly. I admire your Christ-like spirit in loving the Southern whites, but I confess I am not up to it.

I have taken occasion in the article which I have written for James Pott & Company, to express my disagreement with you upon the matter of the suffrage. I have done so without heat, and with what I meant to make ample recognition of your invaluable services to the country. If I have not said more along that line, it was because I could not believe that anything I might say would add in any degree to your well won fame. But I believe in manhood suffrage, especially now, and especially for the Negro. And I do not believe in a silent submission to any form of injustice.

I think the feeling with reference to yourself on the part of some colored men, which has resulted in occasional and sometimes very unjust and rancorous criticism — a feeling which seems to puzzle you, and which is not very easily explainable — may grow out of a somewhat obscure consciousness of this fact: No man living in the heart of the South, and conducting there a great institution in the midst of a hostile race, can possibly be in a position to speak always frankly and fearlessly concerning the rights of his people. He is not at liberty to express that manly indignation which is always the natural and often the most effective way to meet injustice. He must choose his words; he must trim his sails; he must apply the salve so soon after the blow, that it takes away all the sting of the lash. I do not believe there is in the United States another colored man, situated as you are, who could have said even as much by way of criticism of the Southern whites as you have said. But I still recognize the limitation. But you Southern educators are all bound up with some one special cause or other, devotion to which sometimes unconsciously warps your judgment as to what is best for the general welfare of the race. Your institution, your system of education, whatever it may be, is too apt to dwarf everything else and become the sole remedy for social and political evils which have a much wider basis. The civil and political rights of the Negro would be just as vital and fundamental if there were no question at all of the education of the Southern Negro. It is not at all essential to the comparative happiness of the race that they should be highly educated in any particular way; they might be happy in comparative ignorance if they had the same education and the same chances as the other people among whom they live. It is the *differences* which make the trouble. Educate them all to a high degree and leave the same inequalities, and as old Ben Tillman is so fond of saying — he occasionally tells the truth by accident — you merely shift the ground of the problem, you do not alter its essential features.

Permit me to compliment you upon the pamphlet on lynching; I do not see that the President's is any more forceful. His letter, in spite of all its noble sentiment, I think unduly magnifies the importance of the crime of rape. It is no worse a crime now than it has always been, and cannot, that I can perceive, deserve any different or greater punishment than it has always had. I do not believe it is any more common than it has always been; and it has only seemed so since the fashion grew up of burning Negroes for it and making display headings in the newspapers upon the subject. In the eye of the law it is no greater crime when committed by a Negro upon a white woman than when committed by a white man upon a Negro woman; and yet from the hysterical utterances on the subject one would be almost inclined to believe that rape committed by a white man upon a white woman was scarcely any offense at all in comparison. It is the rape that is the crime, and not the person who commits it; and it is scarcely less unjust to railroad a man to the gallows without opportunity to prepare a defense and give the public time for calm and cool deliberation, than it is to put him out of the way upon the spot with the rope or the torch.

I wish you godspeed in the conversion of the Southern white people; encourage the good ones all you may, but I think the rest of us, when we can get a hearing, should score the bad ones; it will do them good. Your ability and your influence are so great that I should like to see them exerted always in the favor of the highest and the best things, which are also, in the long run, the wisest and the most successful, though perhaps at times not seemingly the most immediately practical. On this franchise proposition I think you are training with the wrong crowd. I wish that you were in a position to undertake the political leadership of the colored race, or that there were one or two men as able and as honest as yourself to do so. I think we might then reasonably hope that the Fourteenth and Fifteenth Amendments would become vitally operative. Cordially yours,

Chas. W. Chesnutt

TLS Con. 551 BTW Papers DLC.

1 James Kimble Vardaman (1861–1930), governor of Mississippi (1904–8) and U.S. senator (1913–19). An anti-black demagogue, Vardaman was one of the few southern political leaders who publicly expressed distrust of BTW.

2 Hernando De Soto Money (1839–1912) was a congressman from Mississippi (1875–85) and U.S. senator (1897–1911). He was a cousin and close associate of Vardaman.

To Emmett Jay Scott

South Weymouth, Mass., 12 August, 1903

Dear Mr. Scott: I enclose a letter from Sweeney, and a copy of my reply to him. My own opinion is, that he is a dead beat, and I think that the sooner we let him down easily, the better. He has a vile record in Indianapolis. Very truly yours,

B. T. W.

TLI Con. 275 BTW Papers DLC.

To Emmett Jay Scott

[South Weymouth, Mass.] August 13 1903

Please wire me number of our teachers registered as life voters, and number, if any, refused registration.

B. T. W.

TWIr Con. 542 BTW Papers DLC.

From Emmett Jay Scott

Tuskegee, Alabama. August 13, 1903

Dear Mr. Washington: I have this morning very carefully gone through all the clippings that have come to us in re the Boston outrage, and I send the most significant ones representing every section of the country. Trotter and his gang can find no comfort in the reception which their nastiness has received. I hope you will have the time before going to Nashville to read them over. I think it will be cheering for you to do so, in that evidence is revealed that the sober thought of the people of this entire country is with you and your efforts to uplift this people. I have myself received much benefit from reading the various clippings. I have not been surprised at the general attitude at all because I have been convinced, as you doubtless have been, that the sanest men and women of the country are entirely in accord with your methods. Yours truly,

Emmett J. Scott

TLS Con. 272 BTW Papers DLC.

From Thomas Goode Jones

Montgomery, Ala., Aug 17th 1903

Confidential

Dear Sir. You will see shortly in the public prints, organized effort among many prominent men in Coosa & Tallapoosa, to release the Cosbys, who were sentenced to the penitentiary by me for peonage.[1] The arguments they use, are that the evil system there is broken up, that *that* rather than punishment in vengeance is the real purpose — that the men are poor, with helpless and dependent families &c. This is so in every case of punishment for crime — however.

The subject, however, has some other aspects, which touch a larger field, and look to a greater end. The object of all good men now is to lessen the friction between the races & to put the blacks especially on as high a plane as possible. Would or would it not confound those who are filled with low hates, if the representatives of the negro race, should publicly take the ground that it had no desire, now that the system was broken up, for vengeance, or to subject the families of the men who are now in prison, to the suffering that they inflicted on others, and that believing it would redound to the public good, and promote friendship among good men of both races, they would be glad to see clemency extended to them? Would it not confound "negro haters" and their friends to have your people take such a stand? Would or would it not lead to better things? I have not maturely considered the question — but am inclined to think it would. Drop me a line giving your impressions, and if the question assumes practical shape I will then indicate, if you agree, how it is best to notice it. Of course this is written for your own eye only.[2] Yours truly

Thos. G Jones

ALS   Con. 262   BTW Papers   DLC.

[1] A detailed account of the case, and an unfavorable judgment of Jones's "experiment in leniency," can be found in Daniel, *Shadow of Slavery*, 51–53, 61–64.

[2] Despite its confidential nature, BTW forwarded the letter to T. Thomas Fortune, who wrote on the back of the second page: "I think his view of the matter Statesman like and that the action would go far to show other guilty ones that *it is* the peonage system & not the men guilty of it that it is desired to destroy. Fortune."

From Robert Curtis Ogden

Kennebunkport, Maine. August 17th 1903

My Dear Mr Washington. My people in N.Y. have done the needful in stirring up the N.Y. newspapers concerning the Business League as requested by yours 13th inst. I have been on the move considerably of late and did not get your letter until today. It is a matter of very deep regret to me that I could not meet you with Mr Baldwin in N.Y. yesterday. He has told you about our meeting at Lake George and it would have been a great pleasure to me to discuss the questions of our possible future policy with you for while I cannot say positively what it will be I am sure you will find yourself in accord with the action of men so sincere, patriotic, and conscientious as those that make our Board. We are under limitations.

Often I find myself ready to break out but restraint of impulse is the only channel for continued usefulness to our colored friends in the South. The most important point, as I see the case now, is to make the sensible and conservative South speak out honestly and courageously. We may bring that about with patience, we never can by violent attack.

The Union League agitation is to be urged again soon. Very truly

Robert C Ogden

ALS   Con. 270   BTW Papers   DLC.

From William Henry Baldwin, Jr.

[New York City] August 19th, 1903

Dear Mr. Washington: I had Walter Page with me last night at my house, and we talked over matters well up to midnight. It was a very eventful evening. We rehearsed the talk had at Lake George, and I drew him a picture of each one of the men on our Board, of the personal and social ambition of each, and the fact that, with the limitations which they seemed to feel necessary in dealing with these questions in which we are mutually interested, it seems impossible for them to seize upon the larger questions which underlie our work. I think Mr. Page was more impressed with the fact that the Southern Education Board is a mere pigmy, doing only a little part in the work, and that the great question is hardly touched by them; that the things that are on your mind and mine are larger, broader, and need more courageous treatment than the Southern Education Board can possibly give. I pictured to him the present situation, as I see it; that the problem is running ahead of us, and that we have got to go into the field to meet it. He understands clearly my point of view, and I am sure sympathizes with it. He is going to deliver a half dozen lectures in the month of October in North and South Carolina. We talked over his program, and I think you will see plainer words spoken by him than by any person who has yet spoken in the South.

The net result of our meeting was, the conclusion that our Southern Board cannot have Negro representation directly, because of the limitations of which I have spoken, but that the General Education Board should have such representation,[1] and the Southern Board should have a conference with representative Negroes from the North and South at a meeting to be held sometime in the fall.

The other and more important part of our conclusion was, that we must find a way to get the Southern white people to realize their sense of duty to themselves, and as to the exact method of bringing this about, we are not clear.

We also discussed the question of National assistance and both believe that the time has come when this should be proposed in a proper way.

Mr. Page is a very strong man. He has seen Prof. Mims within the past few days, and the Professor told him that he had seen you, and that he was "profoundly impressed" with you.

With affectionate regard to you and your family, I am   Yours truly,

W H Baldwin Jr

TLS Con. 792 BTW Papers DLC.

[1] Baldwin wrote Wallace Buttrick on Aug. 23, 1903: "I do not for a moment think that the Southern Education Board can have a representation of negroes on the Board, but that it should have some close, sympathetic relationship with the negroes is very apparent." He did not mention, however, the General Education Board. He spoke of the Southern Education Board as "merely an incident to the great undertow that is drawing us all in," but expressed his determination to resist the undertow. (Con. 792, BTW Papers, DLC.)

From James Benson Dudley[1]

Greensboro, N.C., August 28, 1903

Dear sir: Enclosed you will find a clipping from the Wilmington Messenger of Aug 27th., which I thought would interest you. We have been trying to show that the rapists of the Race come from that element which is not reached by our churches or by our schools.

This editorial gives strength to the statement recently made in

President Roosevelt's letter, that often it appears to be more the color than the crime that enrages the mob and it also very frankly admits that after all the crime of the rapist and the class of negroes who commit this crime, are not the *primary* causes of Anglo-Saxon hostility: it is the success of the intelligent and progressive negro which seems to be widening the breach between the races.

When I went to my native city of Wilmington in 1898 to see after my family in the disturbed conditions of affairs, I met about a thousand soldiers who were drumming four negroes from the city. They were not the indolent drones or paupers; they represented between thirty and fifty thousand dollars worth of property. In that unfortunate trouble, it was not the insignificant negroes that were disturbed, it was the well-to-do and prosperous ones.

This editorial seems now to be working up a sentiment to openly attack the intelligent and orderly negro in the country, because of his success. If such a sentiment can be made general then the more we succeed the more resentful and dangerous this sentiment will become.

With best wishes, I am, Yours truly,

Jas. B. Dudley

TLS Con. 256 BTW Papers DLC.

1 James Benson Dudley was president of the Agricultural and Mechanical College at Greensboro, N.C. (later North Carolina Agricultural and Technical College) from 1896 to 1925.

To Emmett Jay Scott

South Weymouth, Mass., 29 August, 1903

Dear Mr. Scott: I think it will be well during the next month or two for us to have just as little as possible in the colored newspapers regarding Tuskegee. Very truly yours,

B. T. W.

Do not make any further use of the *cut* from the Traveler at present.

TLI Con. 275 BTW Papers DLC. Postscript in BTW's hand.

To Oswald Garrison Villard

South Weymouth, Mass., 31 August, 1903

PERSONAL.

Dear Mr. Villard: I am very glad that Mrs. Washington and I had the pleasure of seeing your mother[1] and Mr. Garrison on the train as we came from New York Friday evening.

Just now, I confess, my heart is made to feel very serious over the election of Vardaman in Mississippi. The Northern press seems to have given the matter little consideration. It does not, I fear, realize what his election means. The issue was clearly defined, and openly debated for months. Vardaman declared himself against education of the Negro, and Judge Critz,[2] his opponent, declared himself in favor of it. Vardaman won. But one conclusion, it seems to me, can be drawn. The majority of white people in Mississippi oppose Negro education of any character. On the questions pertaining to the ballot, and to lynching, there may be differences of opinion; but on the question of education there should be but one opinion expressed by all intelligent people. In this connection we must bear in mind that Mississippi was the first state to take away the ballot from the Negro, and is now, I fear, to lead in the attempt to deprive him of educational opportunities. If this attempt succeeds, there is but one other step, that of reducing the Negro to industrial slavery through a system of peonage, or something bordering upon it. I have spent a good portion of the day writing letters to friends, trying to impress upon them the seriousness of the Mississippi situation.[3] If Mississippi succeeds, other states will follow. As soon as I can command the time, it is my intention to frame a letter to the public on the subject of education of the Negro in Mississippi. The conditions growing out of the Mississippi election are more serious, I am quite sure, than our friends realize. Now is the time, it seems to me, for strong action and brave words.

We were very sorry that you were not in Nashville. From every point of view the meeting was most encouraging. The letters on the meeting which have appeared in the Post were of great service to us. Very truly yours,

Booker T. Washington

TLS Oswald Garrison Villard Papers MH.

1 Helen Francis (Fanny) Garrison Villard (1844–1928), the daughter of William Lloyd Garrison, was a champion of women's rights and a pacifist. Her philanthropy included donations to black higher education and industrial education at Tuskegee Institute. She also contributed funds to the NAACP.

2 Frank A. Critz, born in Alabama in 1846, was a lawyer and judge in West Point, Miss. In 1903 he was a candidate for the Democratic gubernatorial nomination and forced James K. Vardaman into a runoff election held on Aug. 27, 1903. Vardaman won, however, and Critz returned to the bench until 1910, when he was one of six men who unsuccessfully challenged Vardaman for a seat in the U.S. Senate.

3 In a similar letter to Francis J. Garrison on the same day, BTW mentioned that he had written to members of the Southern Education Board "urging them to speak out and act before it is too late." (Francis J. Garrison Papers, NN-Sc.)

From Francis Jackson Garrison

Boston, Sept. 1, 1903

Dear Mr. Washington: I am just in receipt of your letter of yesterday, and share your concern about the success of Vardaman in Mississippi. It is certainly most ominous. That such a man should be saddled on the State for four years is discouraging enough, and, as you say, there is danger of the evil example being followed by other States, just as the "Mississippi plan" of 1875 was copied by State after State. I am glad that you are prodding the members of the Southern Education Board. If they do not act promptly, and if they cannot concentrate opinion and compel vigorous action by the better elements of the South, the danger of further retrogression will be great. A strong word from yourself to the public will also have great weight and power now, and I believe will also have its influence on the southern whites who have consciences.

I am shocked this morning by the dispatch from New Orleans announcing the murder of your friend Planving,[1] simply for urging the negroes to acquire land and become independent. It remains to be seen how soon such atrocities are going to react on the scoundrels commiting them, and arouse the moral sense of the country. You have perhaps seen the contemptuous, and at the same time cowardly, reply of Grover Cleveland to the questions sent him by the New York Evening Post touching the disfranchisement question.[2] When I read his speech at your New York meeting, I said at once that it was a fresh bid for the presidency, and I have been more than ever satisfied of it by all of his subsequent utterances. I therefore felt that your reception of and response to his speech at that time was too cordial and undiscriminating, since he clearly indicated his personal feeling as to the inferiority of the negro. I pray that this reaction may not become a prairie wildfire which will lead to further assassinations and the destruction of schoolhouses, for I realize, as I am sure that you do, that even Tuskegee and the other schools rest on a powder magazine, and may not be exempt from the consequences of the explosion possible if the trains which are now being laid by the Mississippians shall be ignited, but the time has come for plain words and plain warnings to the country. Let me beg of you not to unduly expose yourself away from the great centres. Holding the position which you do, it is incumbent upon you to observe a proper caution in your movements, but having done that, one can only trust himself to the over-ruling powers.

I do hope that your trip abroad will not be spoiled by this, but that I may hear speedily that it is all settled and that you are afloat.

I have your note about the portrait of my father, and will attend to the matter as soon as I can. It so happens that I have nothing now suitable for framing, and I shall have to have one of his portraits enlarged and reproduced.

I was glad to hear of you through my brother and sister, last Friday. I see by this morning's paper that Mrs. Washington was in Cambridge yesterday. With warm regards to you both, and with unshaken confidence in the ultimate triumph of right and justice, I am   Faithfully yours,

Francis J. Garrison

P.S. I am surprised and sorry to hear that the Governor of Tennessee failed to address your meeting at Nashville. The papers stated that both he and the Mayor spoke.

TLS   Con. 249   BTW Papers   DLC.

1 L. A. Planving, a carpenter and principal of the Pointe Coupee Industrial College near New Roads, La., was shotgunned from ambush on Aug. 28. In his last speech Planving had urged blacks to acquire land, and said that eventually they would have white people working for them. The New Orleans *Times-Democrat* reported that citizens of the area knew the identity of the murderers, but that it was unlikely that anything would be done to prosecute them. (New Orleans *Times-Democrat*, Aug. 31, 1903, 3.)

2 The editors of the *Evening Post* asked several leading Democrats if Congress had

any duty to stem the tide of disfranchisement in the South, whether or not other constitutional guarantees would also be eroded, and how long it would be before other minorities, such as northern immigrants, might lose their voting rights. Grover Cleveland replied that he was not willing to take time from his vacation to answer the questions. (New York *Evening Post*, Aug. 28, 1903, 1.)

From William Henry Baldwin, Jr.

N.Y. [City] September 2nd., 1903

My dear Mr. Washington: Thank you for your letter of 31st ult. I am so glad you wrote me fully and so frankly. Do not worry about Vardaman. Remember that the best people oppose him. I say do not worry, simply because I have absolute confidence that they are about twenty years too late to begin the campaign which you fear. Do you not remember how I used to talk with you away back urging haste in your work, so that the ideal and the example might be set for the education of all of us? Every speech you have made in every little country town, as well as in every City, will bear its fruit just as soon as the issue becomes clear. The same spirit that met the situation thirty-five years ago will meet this situation just as soon as the issue is clearly defined. Certainly the Southern Education Board should be heard.

I am much impressed with the importance of issuing a letter which will have a bold, courageous ring. I believe it is a great opportunity for you.

There will be a meeting of the special committee of Messrs Murphy, Buttrick and Shaw, and the calling together of the full board about the first week in October for purpose of increasing its membership, and to suggest new methods of procedure. You will be back from Europe by that time, feeling fresh and rested, and your counsel and wisdom will be of great importance to us. I shall want to find out just what you think would be wise, and that will be my position whatever it may be.

I am hoping and expecting to see you and Mrs. Washington on Friday and Saturday. Faithfully yours,

W H Baldwin Jr

TLS   Con. 249   BTW Papers   DLC.

From Joseph Oswalt Thompson

Birmingham, Ala. September 3, 1903

Dear Doctor: I had already written my brother[1] when I received your letter. I am writing by today's mail to Judge Jones,[2] Colonel Wiley[3] and my brother, enclosing him your telegram. I have written Mr. Hare suggesting that he get a petition signed by the citizens of Tuskegee to the Educational Committee requesting that the Wood bill[4] be defeated. Judge Jones has a great many friends in the Legislature and if I were you I would write him direct. I will also get Judge Roulhac to go to Montgomery in regard to the matter.

If you have any further suggestion please command me. Your friend,

Jos. O. Thompson

TLS   Con. 279   BTW Papers   DLC.

[1] Charles Winston Thompson.

[2] Thomas G. Jones wrote to Thompson on Sept. 4, 1903, that he had already anticipated the request to help defeat the Wood bill. "There is no danger of its passing," he said, "and I doubt very much if it ever gets out of the committee." (Con. 262, BTW Papers, DLC.)

[3] Ariosto Appling Wiley (1848–1908), a lawyer in Montgomery, served in the state legislature from 1882 to 1898 and in the U.S. Congress from 1900 to 1908.

[4] John Richard Wood (b. 1860), a lawyer and representative of Macon County in the Alabama legislature (1894–97, 1902–4), sponsored a bill to tax Tuskegee Institute as a profit enterprise because it made some goods for sale at its industrial shops and farms. BTW and his white supporters succeeded in blocking the measure.

From J. W. Adams

Montgomery, Ala   Sep 5th. 1903

Committee Reports unfavorable on Wood Bill am Doing all I can.

J. W. Adams

HWSr   Con. 248   BTW Papers   DLC.

William Henry Lewis to Melvin Jack Chisum

Boston, September 5, 1903

Dear Mr. Chisum, Will you go to a Notary Public at once and have an affidavit drawn up containing *all the facts* obtained by you in your recent investigation.[1] *Please be explicit as to what was said and done on each particular occasion by each individual.* I do not now recall whether you said some one went to Cambridge with you or not to see the church where the demonstration was to take place, but if there was such person please give his name, and oblige, Yours hastily,

W. H. Lewis

TLS   Con. 265   BTW Papers   DLC.

[1] Chisum's report of a plan by W. M. Trotter and his adherents to disrupt a BTW meeting in a Cambridge church was not made public. Washington used it privately to convince some of his critics of Trotter's unscrupulousness, until it mysteriously disappeared from his files. It was, however, the basis for a draft article by E. J. Scott. (See "Trotter and Trotterism," undated [1905], below, vol. 8.)

To William Henry Baldwin, Jr.

[Tuskegee, Ala.] Sept. 9, 1903

Dear Mr. Baldwin: There are two matters referred to in your previous letters to which I have not replied. First, regarding a report of my work to the Southern Education Board. I shall send a brief report soon though I have taken pains to keep both Mr. Peabody and Mr. Ogden informed as to the nature of the work. I confess to you personally that I have found it difficult to bring myself to the point where I could feel it proper to make a written report to a body which did not feel that it could afford to have me personally present at a meeting in order that I might make a report in the same way that the other officers made theirs, but this is a matter of comparatively little importance. I presume my report should be addressed to Mr. Ogden.

Second; You wrote me about the feeling of yourself and others regarding Mr. Penney's connection with the school. For some time I have felt with you that he was not the strongest person for the work he is doing, but one thing that has rather influenced us in keeping [him] is that the Misses Stokes, who very largely support the work under him, seem to like him very much and I fear that they would be greatly disappointed were he replaced by someone else, still I shall keep in mind trying to make some kind of change at the end of the present year.

So far as I can now secure information, there seems to be no possibility of the Legislature opposing[1] the bill withdrawing support from our agricultural department. Yours truly,

[Booker T. Washington]

TLc   Con. 792   BTW Papers   DLC.

[1] He probably intended to write "passing."

To Frederick Taylor Gates

[Tuskegee, Ala.] Sept. 10, 1903

Dear Mr. Gates: I have been at home several days and have looked over the ground pretty well and now feel rather convinced that we have killed the effort, for the present at least, to take the money from the Negro schools in Alabama. This state of affairs, however, leaves the Board, it seems to me, free to act in a much more dignified and perhaps wise way than it could have done had it been acting under seeming pressure, and I very much hope that at the proper time the Board will see its way clear to help in a generous way some more of the white schools in Alabama. Such action would have a very good effect. I have written practically the same thing to Dr. Buttrick. Yours very truly,

[Booker T. Washington]

TLc   Con. 193   BTW Papers   DLC.

To Timothy Thomas Fortune

[Tuskegee, Ala.] Sept. 10, 1903

My dear Mr. Fortune: I was very sorry indeed that I did not have the privilege of seeing you before I left New York. There are several important matters that I want to take up with you.

I hope your health has been restored by this time and that you are feeling in better shape.

I could not get to see the Secretary as I passed through Washington as he was out of the city, neither have I been able to make connection with Gen. Clarkson lately; he seems to be away from home or does not answer my communications.

I am most anxious that the last dastardly attempt on the part of that Boston crowd to disgrace the race be made public in some way. Of course we have the facts that will support our side, but we want to avoid the opportunity of a libel suit if possible. I wonder if you would not be willing to use the enclosed matter editorially in your paper, making such changes as you may deem best. In case you decide to use it, I think it well for you to let our friend, Wilford H. Smith, go over it with you so as to be sure that there is no basis for a libel suit. In case you do use it I hope it will be very soon and that you will put at my disposal 500 extra copies. I will let you know where to send them. If you care to you can have a talk with Chisum and after that perhaps you can better decide what changes to make in the statement. Yours truly,

[Booker T. Washington]

TLc Con. 290 BTW Papers DLC.

To Thomas Ruffin Roulhac

[Tuskegee, Ala.] September 10, 1903

Personal

Dear Sir: Your kind letter of September 3d, which was sent to South Weymouth, has been forwarded to me here.[1] I want to thank you most sincerely and earnestly for your help in the matter of the bill in Montgomery. The efforts of our friends seem to have completely killed the bill so far.

I did not write to you direct to secure your services in aiding the defeat of the bill for the reason that I have an absolute abhorrence of having anyone feel that I have done any service for them with the expectation of receiving a like favor in the future. It was a genuine pleasure to me to be of some slight service to you and I have never regretted my action.

Should the bill come up again I shall let you know. Yours truly,

[Booker T. Washington]

TLc Con. 249 BTW Papers DLC.

1 Roulhac said he would go to Montgomery the next day to see "the men of character and influence in the House" in the cause of "keeping such a bill from ever seeing the daylight again." (Sept. 3, 1903, Con. 249, BTW Papers, DLC.)

From Thomas Goode Jones

Montgomery, Ala., Sept 10th 1903

Confidential
Dear Sir. I have already written you about the Cosbys pardon. It went forward with a favorable recommendation yesterday. I did this because I believe it will smooth the pathway of the races up there, and the fact that a good many of the blacks have joined in it, will put them in the strongest and most favorable contrast to those who think the legal rights of human beings ought to shrink or expand according to their color. If men like you would write the president that the ends of the law having been attained in these cases, the black people would be glad to see the prisoners returned to their helpless families, I think it would give great moral help to those of the whites, who are battling against many vicious prejudices, to do more effective work in the future. I would be glad if you would write the president, though not *as upon suggestion by me,* on the subject. Yours truly

Thos. G. Jones

ALS Con. 262 BTW Papers DLC.

To William Henry Baldwin, Jr.

[Tuskegee, Ala.] Sept. 11, 1903

Personal

Dear Mr. Baldwin: I want to re-emphasize if possible what I suggested to you in our short conversation Sunday night regarding Mr. Murphy. I find that he naturally is not very happy over present conditions. He is chafing under restraint and restrictions, etc. He is the kind of man that really wants to do something. He has burned his bridges behind him. He is receiving in cash much less than he got as a pastor and I fear is really in cramped circumstances financially. The main point of this letter is to suggest that at some time you give him an opportunity to talk with you very frankly and freely about his condition; you will have to urge him to do so. He has no knowledge of my writing this letter.

So far I have been unable to find anyone who was in sympathy with taking away the agricultural fund from this school except the author of the bill. No doubt, however, that he has a few followers but I am quite sure that the whole thing is now completely killed.

I think it would be a great blunder to lose the services of so valuable a man as Mr. Murphy. Yours truly,

[Booker T. Washington]

TLc   Con. 249   BTW Papers   DLC.

From William Henry Baldwin, Jr.

N.Y. [City] Sept. 11th., 1903

Dear Mr. Washington: Your letter of 9th. You are a little in error in reference to your report to the Southern Education Board. As a field agent of the Southern Education Board your report will be received just the same as the report of several others who do not report direct to the Board and who make written reports. Although I sympathize with your feelings the point would not be well taken.

Your reference to Mr. Penney is important. I should not do anything until you consult with the Misses Stokes and have them entirely satisfied.

I do not understand the last paragraph of your letter. I had understood that the Legislature *would* oppose the Bill withdrawing support from your agricultural department. Yours very truly,

W H Baldwin Jr

TLS   Con. 792   BTW Papers   DLC.

To Emmett Jay Scott

Tuskegee, Ala., Sept. 12, 1903

Mr. Scott: I wish whenever you can you would get a short note in the colored papers about the late arrest of Forbes and Trotter.

B. T. W.

TLI   Con. 281   BTW Papers   DLC.

From Timothy Thomas Fortune

Red Bank, N.J., September 14, 1903

My dear Mr. Washington: I thought it best and safest, after all, to have a talk with Mr. Peterson about the Boston conspiracy article,[1] and we reached the conclusion that (1.) the article is too discursive and full of epithets and expletives, which weaken rather than strengthen a statement of facts; (2.) that the facts as stated are not based upon sufficient evidence in our possession, to protect us, in the event of their being questioned; (3.) that a libel is uttered when the facts and circumstances indicated would incriminate certain parties in the public estimation, and that an action would stand and we should in that event have to defend it. When criminal matters or actions have been contemplated and not executed and when judicial cognizance of the same has not been taken, publication or other utterance constitutes a libel.

283

There is grounds for regret that the conspiracy was not allowed to materialize to the extent of incriminating those concerned in it, when a sufficient police in civilian dress could have taken the parties into custody, as the facts of the conspiracy were in their possession.

We donot think it wise to make the publication in the present status of the case. Yours truly,

T. Thos. Fortune

TLS   Con. 290   BTW Papers   DLC.

1 Fortune had written to BTW on Sept. 12, 1903, that he saw nothing libelous in the article and intended to publish it as an editorial. (Con. 258, BTW Papers, DLC.)

To Theodore Roosevelt

Tuskegee, Alabama. September 15, 1903

Personal.

My dear Mr. President: I note what you say regarding the attitude of some of the Boston colored men. I am sorry that the matter has caused you any concern. The occurrence is very much exaggerated, however, as such matters always are by the newspapers. I do not suffer myself to become very much vexed with these people, but I do pity them. I have taken a little time in which to study them from I think a purely unselfish and disinterested point of view.

First: I find that the rank and file of our people in Boston, as is true all over the country, agree with me and support my policy. The opposition in Boston is kept alive and engineered by about a half dozen colored men, most of whom, I am sorry to say, are graduates of New England colleges. At the bottom of their opposition, there is a feeling of jealousy over what they consider my success.

Second: These men, in most cases, have not had to work their way up from the bottom through natural and gradual processes. Their growth has been artificial rather than natural. They have not paid the price for what they have gotten. Hence they feel that I can take the whole colored race and place it in the same artificial position that they themselves are in.

In most cases, someone has taken these men up and coddled them by paying their way through college. At Tuskegee a man works for everything that he gets, hence we turn out real men instead of artificial ones.

Third: When a people are smarting under wrongs and injustices inflicted from many quarters, it is but natural that they should look about for some individual on whom to lay the blame for their seeming misfortunes, and in this case I seem to be the one. It is a responsibility which I have not sought, but since it has come to me, I am willing to do my duty as best I can.

Fourth: As I see the colored people throughout the country, I am convinced that I am safe in saying that no President since Lincoln has ever had their support and love to the extent that you now possess it.

Forgive me for burdening you with so long a letter. Yours very sincerely,

Booker T. Washington

TLS   Theodore Roosevelt Papers   DLC.

From William Henry Lewis

Boston, September 16, 1903

My dear Mr. Washington, Your telegram came while I was absent from the city. I have written Chisum and received letter from him in which he states that the affidavit will be forthcoming. I do not think, so far as I am concerned, that I will use the affidavit just now. I rather prefer to hold it as a club over their heads. Besides I am not inclined to believe absolutely the story of our confidential friend. I think that he has overdrawn it somewhat, and I am not sure that he did not himself make some of the propositions purporting to have been made by others. On the whole I am glad we did not act in a rash and hasty manner on his information.

There is nothing new in regard to the riot cases, they will come up the latter part of the month, except there is this development: McMullen came to me recently and stated that as far as he and

[the] Church were concerned they were willing to let the matter drop and have the cases placed on file. I advised him strongly against that unless and until Trotter and Martin both came to him in person and ask[ed] forgiveness and were willing to apologize, and then it would be time enough *to consider what ought* to be done. He agreed with me, and so the matter stands as before.

Forbes came to me a day or two ago and stated that I was the man in the way, and wanted me to agree to call off the dogs. I told him I did not feel like doing anything of the kind, since neither Mr. Trotter nor Mr. Martin had approached me, and if I did anything without their personal request, they maintaining an independent attitude, I had not the slightest doubt that if the thing was settled they would be gloating over it as a triumph for them.

It may be that they will try the case; if so, I think we ought to have the evidence taken in the lower court so that our witnesses may be as well prepared as theirs.

You have doubtless heard of the arrest of Forbes and Trotter for criminal libel upon one William Pickens. The case comes up tomorrow.

Please let me know when you are to be in New York. When I see you I have another matter I would like to talk with you about. Sincerely yours, etc.,

William H. Lewis

TLS   Con. 265   BTW Papers   DLC.

J. C. May [Wilford H. Smith]
to R. C. Black [Emmett Jay Scott]

New York City, New York. September 18th, 1903

Dear Friend, R. C. Black: I wired you from Boston yesterday signed "McAdoo" informing you that both parties were bound over to await the action of the Grand Jury at the October Term of the court. They were very much disappointed at the decision, as it appears that their lawyer had held out to them the hope that they would be acquitted, because the publication could in no sense be held to be libelous. It appears that he was unable to draw a distinction between matters that might be said of a candidate for office and a person not a candidate. Their being held on this charge has a tendency to chill the ardor of their friends as no one clings to a sinking vessel.

It will be necessary for our mutual friend to stiffen the backbone of Lewis, as regards the church case, as I understood they are appealing to him to be let off on a fine.

Our case yesterday was ably handled, and many important points brought out in our interest for the benefit of the by-standers, which it would take up too much time to write. This I will mention however, that, instead of the name of the paper being "The Guardian" it should be more properly named "The Assassin." The fact also came out in the proof, that the purpose of the sheet was to kill "His Nibs." Please call attention to the items of expense; $25 for myself, and $15 for the other man.

It will be necessary for our man to go back in October to be before the Grand Jury, and also attend the trial. It may be that I can control the matter just as well by correspondence, and my presence will not be required. However, I think the best results can be obtained by my personal supervision of affairs, if the expense item is not too large.

Kindly protect the other matters about which I wrote you, as speedily as possible. Very truly yours,

J. C. May

TLSr   Con. 25   BTW Papers   DLC.

Extracts from an Address
before the National Baptist Convention

Philadelphia. September 18, 1903

The position occupied by the delegates to this convention is a very serious and responsible one. In a very large degree you hold the future of the Negro race in your hands. The Baptist Church is organized on the plan of a republic; it is self-governing. A republic cannot exist without an intelligent constituency, neither can the Baptist denomination make progress without an intelligent ministry and an intelligent membership.

The responsibility resting upon the Negro minister is a peculiar one. He has to perform many duties that the white minister is not called upon to perform. The masses of our people look to the minister for instruction in matters of education, industry and business, and the minister should be prepared to guide our people in these directions. In a very large degree the Negro minister during the last twenty-five or thirty years has been the preserver of peace and harmony between the races; but for the forbearance and patience and the gentle tact of the Negro minister many race riots would have occurred in our country.

. . . .

In a peculiar sense you will find more and more that it will become the duty of the Negro minister to take the unpopular side of many public questions. It requires little courage and backbone and intelligence to glide easily along with public opinion. What we need in an increasing degree is that kind of leadership in the pulpit that is willing to stand adverse criticism, to be misunderstood and even abused for the sake of the right. Our people do not need flattery so much as they need facts.

. . . .

You will find one of the problems that is going to press more seriously upon you for solution in the near future than in the past is the one of employment for our people, especially in the Northern cities. Competition is becoming more and more severe. The Negro who comes to Philadelphia, for example, from the South, naturally finds more severe competition in the matter of industry, but he finds himself surrounded by temptations on every hand and between competition and the temptations a very large proportion of the race is likely to go down unless they are guided carefully and wisely by the ministers. No race of people can make permanent and satisfactory progress unless they have steady, reliable and encouraging employment. We can only hold our own in the world of labor and industry by teaching our people to do a thing as well as anybody else, by teaching them to perform common labor in an uncommon manner. I have been very sorry to note that in the city of Chicago within the last few months 800 or a thousand of our people were turned out of restaurants where they occupied positions as waiters for many years. Their places were taken by men of another race. We must see to it that what has taken place in Chicago does not take place in other parts of the country. In proportion as our people have steady paying employment, in the same proportion is the church supported and will the minister prosper. In every part of this country the white people are organizing and supporting various institutions that give the very best instruction to men and women in all lines of hand work. In the South today I am safe in saying that perhaps ten times as much money is being spent for the industrial education of white men and women as is being spent for the same kind of education for our people. We cannot hold our own in the labor world unless we are constantly taking advantage of every opportunity to improve our selves. We must not only become seekers of positions, but must become creators of positions.

Another phase of life with which the ministers should be deeply concerned is the large number of idle loafing young men that are to be found upon the street corners of every large city. In many cases you will find that these men are supported by the earnings of the female sex. These loafers should have brought to bear such an influence on them that they will be compelled to seek honest, productive work.

· · · · ·

Now is the time for the Negro to seek homes in every part of this country. Land is cheaper now than it will ever be again. We must plant ourselves in the soil and become taxpayers. In proportion as we get hold of property, own our homes and help support the government in the same proportion will many of our difficult problems be lightened. A poverty-stricken race is not a race that is respected and has great influence in the counsels of the nation or in business circles. We must not only be a race of money earners but of money savers. If we make a dollar we must see to it that a portion of that dollar is safely invested for future use. The great test of a race, as of an individual, is to provide today for tomorrow, to do without today in order that it may possess tomorrow. We must see to it that we spend less than we earn, and that nothing is spent on vain superficial show.

. . . . .

Bishop Candler of Georgia, struck, in my opinion, the heart of the race question a few days ago when he said that each race should try to correct the evils among its own people, and that the white race should cease abusing the Negro at long range, and that the Negro at the same time should cease his crossfire at the white man. The Negro minister is in a peculiarly good position to put this advice into practice. The greater proportion of our people live in the South, and I say here what I have said in many parts of the country that, it will be to our interest in every manly, straightforward manner to cultivate the friendship of the people among whom we live.

. . . . .

We must cultivate the disposition of drawing the line between the good and the bad, the moral and the immoral. In some parts of our country the line is too lax and the result is that all of us are classed together.

Less and less each year you will find that little emphasis is being placed upon mere denominational differences and increased emphasis is being placed upon real life.

In the Northern states especially, in addition to his other duties, the Negro minister should speak out in no uncertain tone against the unfortunate habit that I fear is growing, that of bartering away his vote for gain. No people who sell their votes, whether white or black, are worthy of the privilege of the American franchise. In some quarters I very much fear that we are getting a reputation for being ready to part with our votes at almost any cost. Let it be understood among all of our people in every section of the country that a suggestion to purchase our vote is the grossest insult.

Do not understand from the tone of my remarks that I do not appreciate the tremendous progress which the race has made since it became free. This progress has been maintained in the midst of difficulties and discouragements that would have well nigh overwhelmed a less determined race. We are still going forward and intend to go forward with a greater degree of spirit. There is no influence that can permanently discourage or dishearten us. Year by year we are gaining strength and experience and self-confidence that shall make our progress many fold greater in the future years than it has been in the past.

TM Con. 956 BTW Papers DLC.

1 Emmett J. Scott wrote to William H. Baldwin, Jr., that BTW had been invited by the Baptist officials so that "they might in some measure let him know how thoroughly in accord with him they are." Scott said the vast auditorium had not been filled during the convention until the night of BTW's speech, when "a guard of some twenty policemen was required to keep the vast concourse in order. The Philadelphia newspapers report that not less than from twelve to fifteen thousand people were in attendance." When BTW entered the auditorium, Scott reported, "the vast audience arose to its feet and frantically yelled a reception which could not have done less than warmed the cockles of Mr. Washington's heart, as it certainly did mine." (Oct. 10, 1903, Con. 792, BTW Papers, DLC.)

An Article in the New York *Sun*

New York, Sept. 22, 1903

BOOKER WASHINGTON, SEAGOER

BOUND FOR EUROPE ON VACATION. NOT FOR HIS HEALTH'S SAKE

Booker T. Washington came here yesterday morning from Tuskegee on his way to Europe. He is staying at the Hotel Manhattan. It is not on account of his health, however, as has been reported, that he is to take an ocean voyage. He said last night:

"As a matter of fact my general health was never better, but I have had no vacation and a number of my friends have insisted that I take a short trip to Europe. I have yielded to their wishes, but shall return on the same ship I sail upon, and shall not be gone longer than three weeks altogether."

Of the Tuskegee Institute and its prospects he said: "Our term began Sept. 8 with the largest attendance in the history of the school. So great is the desire to enter the school that we have been compelled to refuse admittance to 1,048 young men and women who have applied in the last thirty days."

New York *Sun*, Sept. 22, 1903, 3.

Kelly Miller to Emmett Jay Scott

Washington, D.C. Sept 24th 1903

My Dear Mr. Scott: I have just learned with deep regret of Mr. Washington's state of health and of his trip to Europe for recuperation. I am sure that all colored men of whatever school of belief or shade of opinion will wish him a "bon voyage["] and speedy recuperation.

You have probably seen the article in the Boston Transcript of Sept 18th & 19th, headed "Washington's Policy" and signed "Fair Play."[1] These articles were written by me. It was my aim to be fair and impartial to all sides of the controversy and to suggest the absolute necessity for some common ground. I trust that the plain speaking which I deemed necessary to full and frank discussion of the points in issue will be accepted in the spirit of kindly candor, in which it was employed. Trusting that the great and good work of Tuskeegee will go forward with increasing influence and effectiveness, and wishing you the fullest possible personal success I am Yours truly,

Kelly Miller

ALS Con. 4 BTW Papers DLC.

[1] These articles took a middle position between BTW and his critics. Miller observed that BTW was "not a leader of the people's own choosing" and that "few thoughtful colored men espouse what passes as Mr. Washington's policy, without apology or reserve." On the other hand, he noted that the radicals lacked organization, leadership, and constructive achievements. He concluded: "The Negro's lot would be sad indeed if, under allurement of material advantage and temporary easement, he should sink into pliant yieldance to unrighteous oppression; but it would be sadder still if intemperate insistence should engender ill will and strife, when the race is not yet ready to be 'battered with the shocks of doom.'" The essay is reprinted in Hawkins, ed., *Booker T. Washington and His Critics.*

From Emmett Jay Scott

Tuskegee: Oct 1/03

Dear Mr. Washington: I write to ask if it will be possible for you to arrange — in any way — with the Southern or the General Education Board whereby I may do for colored newspapers what Dr Dabney and his assistants do for white newspapers — namely, the preparation of items which shall tend to preserve interest in the various reforms these boards are seeking to promote! I sh'd be especially grateful if I c'd do some such service for say $35 per month, or even more if possible.

I must really earn more money *in some way*, than I am now earning. I can say with entire truthfulness that now I do more actual work for the school, and touch many more outside interests than anyone connected with the school, *but on this I make no plea!* I am content to do my level best in every way that I can — and fully recognizing the limitations of the school's resources I c'd not hope for any further increase from it — or from you — but if this outside resource could be reached I sh'd be most grateful for whatever you sh'd do. Yours sincerely

Emmett J. Scott

ALS   Con. 249   BTW Papers   DLC.

Wilford H. Smith to Emmett Jay Scott

New York   Oct 10th [1903]

Trotter Sentenced to thirty days church Case — Trotter and Forbes indicted libel Case.

Smith

HWSr   Con. 542   BTW Papers   DLC.

Emmett Jay Scott to Laura Anna Knott

[Tuskegee, Ala.] October 15, 1903

Dear Madam: Miss Portia Washington graduated at the Tuskegee Institute with the class of 1900, and so I am sending you a catalogue of the institution for that year that you may see precisely the studies

293

she had here.[1] It is difficult to check your credential blank in the light of our arrangement of studies, and so I send the following explanation: For instance, Miss Washington spent one year in taking our course in psychology; this study is put down in the catalogue as Mind Study. She also had general history, in which was included ancient, medieval and modern history. The school being an industrial school, some of the academic studies are classed as industrial corollaries, for instance, as in Miss Washington's case, the student having dressmaking as industrial study would have geometry as the academic corollary but would perhaps not have physics nor chemistry, but in Miss Washington's case she took the chemistry as well, doing double work. In mathematics she had both algebra and geometry, Wentworth's publications being the textbooks. For English, as you will note by the catalogue, American and British Classics were used for the foundation of grammar, rhetoric, composition and literature. There was supplemental work as well. We have no course in Latin, Greek, French or German, but Miss Washington had German under a private tutor, one of our instructors.

I shall be greatly obliged if you will, after checking this catalogue, return it to us as it is from our files. Yours truly,

[Emmett J. Scott]

TLc   Con. 263   BTW Papers   DLC.

[1] Laura Knott had requested a listing of Portia's school work at Tuskegee in order to determine the requirements necessary for her to graduate from Bradford Academy. (Laura Knott to Emmett J. Scott, Oct. 8, 1903, Con. 263, BTW Papers, DLC.)

To Clarence Hamilton Poe[1]

[Tuskegee, Ala.] October 17, 1903

My dear Sir: In further answer of your favor of September 29th, which came to Tuskegee during my absence on a short vacation trip in Europe, I write to say that the statement has been made by us, and is true, that not one of our graduates has ever been sent to the penitentiary for a crime. The school has never undertaken to say that no student who has ever attended the school has been sent to prison, but our claim is that no sudent who remains at the school long enough to take its course of study has ever been thus treated. Further I would say, that it is not true at all that the two men referred to in the enclosed clipping were even students, much less graduates of this institution. How far our graduates are earning an honest living, the printed matter I have sent you amply testifies. I would be pleased to know that the printed matter sent you some time ago reached you. Very truly yours,

[Booker T. Washington]

TLc   Con. 249   BTW Papers   DLC.

[1] Clarence Hamilton Poe (1881–1964), born in Chatham County, N.C., began writing articles for the *Progressive Farmer* when he was fourteen years old. He became editor in 1899, and in 1903 he purchased the magazine and headed the Progressive Farmer Co. for fifty years. Poe was a segregationist who even advocated residential segregation in the rural districts. He did, however, work to disprove the popularly held belief that educated blacks committed more crime than the uneducated. Poe opposed the movement to divide school funds along racial lines not on the basis of racial justice but because it would be inexpedient for whites to lose control of the direction of black education. (*Outlook*, 71 [Aug. 23, 1902], 1010–13.) Poe championed the universal educational campaign of Gov. Charles B. Aycock, and in 1912 became Aycock's son-in-law. In 1913 he led an educational movement to upgrade rural white schools after the 1910 census revealed North Carolina to be highest in white illiteracy and lowest in per child expenditure for education.

From Samuel Edward Courtney

Boston, Oct. 18th 1903

My dear Mr. Washington, I have just sent to the Editor of the Atlanta Constitution yesterday's "Boston Guardian" which contains a letter from "Prof. Towns"[1] of Atlanta University, expressing sympathy &c for the *"rioters"* Trotter & Martin. It is a weak dirty letter from a man like Towns to Trotter, evidently intended to be strictly private, but like others in the same Column, "too good to keep out of the Guardian."

I also sent the Constitution the account of the sentence given by Judge Sherman[2] which appeared in the Boston Globe of Oct. 9th. Should the Constitution take up the letter, Towns will think Trotter indiscreet, if not *Crazy*.

Pickens' case will come up soon. It looks as if Forbes & Trotter will have a chance to spend a few months in Penitentiary for the "good of *their* cause."

Received your card from Paris was glad to get it, am delighted to hear you had a pleasant trip & returned much rested. With Kindest regards. Very truly yours —

S. E. Courtney

ALS Con. 253 BTW Papers DLC.

1 George Alexander Towns (b. 1870), a graduate of Atlanta and Harvard, taught at Atlanta University for many years after 1900. His letter of sympathy to Trotter, who published it in the Boston *Guardian*, was a source of embarrassment to President Horace Bumstead, for many of the school's white donors and supporters were admirers of BTW. "When you told Mr. Trotter that he was going to jail for a principle, you obscured the fact that he had done anything worthy of punishment," Bumstead wrote Towns. (Nov. 14, 1903, quoted in Fox, *Guardian of Boston*, 62.)

2 Edgar Jay Sherman (b. 1834), judge of the superior court of Massachusetts.

R. C. Black [Emmett Jay Scott]
to J. C. May [Wilford H. Smith]

[Tuskegee, Ala.] October 19, 1903

Dear Friend: Have made note of your letter from your Boston attorney. Under all the circumstances, perhaps it would be well to agree to Lewis' suggestion to have the cases nolle prosequi.

I think it well in agreeing to this proposition, however, to insist upon the following:

1. That retraction be published in three successive issues of the paper.

2. That you specify the character of type to be used, display type, I would suggest.

3. That insistance be made that the retraction be published on front page, top of column.

Further, I would suggest that you insist that it first appear before Trotter comes out of jail. If you do not get it in this week's issue, insist that it be in the following issue, which will be before he is released. I understand that it is your purpose personally to draft the retraction, and I hope you will make it as strong and as broad in its sweep as possible.

Let me know of the course of events as they develop. Yours truly,

R. C. Black

4. That they pay ½ or all of the costs of suit!

TLSr Con. 25 BTW Papers DLC. The fourth item, added as a post-script, is in Emmett Scott's hand.

To Theodore Roosevelt

Tuskegee, Alabama. October 20, 1903

My dear Mr. President: In order that you may be kept informed as to the attitude of the colored people regarding your administration, I take the liberty of sending you the names and addresses of the 178 Negro newspapers published in this country. As I have indicated, all of these papers, except 5,[1] heartily support your policy. The opposition or uncertainty of this 5 is not in the long run hurtful since it serves to keep the papers which favor you more earnest in their support. Very truly yours,

Booker T. Washington

TLS Theodore Roosevelt Papers DLC.

[1] The black newspapers listed as "opposed" to Roosevelt were the Washington *Bee* and the Boston *Guardian*, and those listed as "uncertain" were the Jersey City *Appeal*, the Chicago *Conservator*, and the Cleveland *Gazette*.

To Clarence Hamilton Poe

[Tuskegee, Ala.] October 20, 1903

My dear Sir: In my letter to you a few days ago, I meant to have stated that neither of the three boys hanged in this county ten years ago were ever enrolled as students in our catalogue. I think one of them attended for a short time the small public school in the town of Tuskegee, but was not connected with this institution. Very truly yours,

[Booker T. Washington]

TLc   Con. 249   BTW Papers   DLC.

To Robert Curtis Ogden

[Tuskegee, Ala.] October 20, 1903

Dear Mr. Ogden: In connection with our conversation when I last saw you, I think I ought to say to you that I have evidence which is indisputable showing that Dr. Du Bois is very largely behind the mean and underhanded attacks that have been made upon me during the last six months.[1] This, of course, is for your own personal information. Very truly yours,

[Booker T. Washington]

TLc   Con. 249   BTW Papers   DLC.

[1] It is doubtful that BTW had such evidence. At the time of the Boston Riot, Du Bois was en route to Boston by coastal steamer, after teaching in the Tuskegee summer school. By a previous arrangement he stayed at Trotter's home for the remainder of the summer. Du Bois also stated that, while he could not approve of Trotter's methods, he sympathized with Trotter as a victim of Washington's persecution after the riot. These facts may have seemed to BTW to justify his charge against Du Bois.

To William Henry Baldwin, Jr.

[Tuskegee, Ala.] October 20, 1903

Dear Mr. Baldwin: I write you regarding the trouble among the students which occurred September 28th.[1] For the last three or four years, there has been an increasing desire on the part of the students and their parents to have additional opportunity to learn trades. Our night school students have been well provided for in this respect, but the day school students felt that they were not given sufficient opportunity to learn trades. With the desire to meet this condition, during the summer we decided to have the day students work at their trades, or other industries during half of the day, and spend the remaining portion of the time in the class-room. In trying to adjust matters to this new condition, I think I am safe in saying that the students were crowded pretty hard both in their studies and in their industrial work. The attempt was made on the part of the heads of the literary department to get as much out of the students as possible, and the same was true regarding the heads of the industrial departments, and between the two, the students had little time left. I realized before I left for Europe that the system was far from perfect and would have to be changed from time to time as experience justified it, and with this in view, I called the teachers together once or twice before leaving and asked them how the new system was working. Each time, the teachers reported that it had not been tried sufficiently long to enable them to pass upon it intelligently, and so, nothing was done about making a change or modification before I left. When I had been gone for a week or ten days, the pressure became pretty hard upon the students, and a few strong ones took advantage of the dissatisfied condition of the rank and file, and led them into an open rebellion. The whole thing was most carefully planned and executed. The young men marched from the breakfast table to the Chapel and locked themselves in the Chapel, and declared that they would not work or study until a change was made. Mr. Logan and the other teachers refused to treat with the students, however, until they had dispersed and gone about their duties. After the students had obeyed in this respect, a modification was made in the rules. The result is, so far as I can get hold of the facts, about 47 students left the school during the week that the disturbance was most active. Up to the 16th of October last year, we enrolled 1362 students, and for one cause or another 54 left the school. Up to the corresponding date this year, 1382 have been enrolled and 103 have left. In each case, the number of students leaving includes those who could not pass the required examination, who were too small, or were physically weak, as well as those who were sent away for misdemeanors, and those who left of their own accord because of some dissatisfaction, or on account of sickness of themselves or their families.

I have not written you, or any of the other Trustees, earlier about the matter, because I wanted to take a few days in which to study the whole situation.

The student body is now quiet and satisfied, but I am taking up the whole system with a good deal of care, with a view of still further perfecting it. Of the 47 students who left, I find that few of them were in our higher classes, and in a good many cases they were students who had unsatisfactory records and would perhaps have been dropped out in the natural course of things either at the end of the month, or at the end of the school year. One would not miss from the Senior Class the small number that left who belonged to this class.

In studying the whole matter, I do not see how our teachers could have acted more wisely under the circumstances than they did. I think if I had been on the grounds, I could have nipped the matter in the bud, and there would have been no outbreak, but since I was not here, I do not see how anyone could have managed the affair more carefully, wisely and patiently.

I shall be very glad to have any suggestions or advice from you bearing upon the subject about which I have written. Very truly yours,

Booker T. Washington

TLcSr BTW Folder ViHaI. This copy was sent to Hollis B. Frissell. The same letter was sent to Robert C. Ogden, Oct. 20, 1903, BTW Papers, ATT.

[1] On Sept. 6, 1903, the Tuskegee faculty approved drastic schedule changes designed to increase the time students spent working at their trades. Several teachers expressed fear that the new schedule would not allow students sufficient time each day for study. (Minutes of the General Faculty Meeting, Sept. 6, 1903, Con. 1013, BTW Papers, DLC.)

A widespread and occasionally bitter protest culminated in a three-day general strike of the students on Sept. 27–29. The protest also divided the faculty, some of whom sympathized with the students. In one incident the assistant to the commandant, Capt. George A. Austin, was stabbed by a student. (Minutes of the Executive Council, Oct. 19, 1903, Con. 1005, BTW Papers, DLC.) BTW's first impulse was to quell the rebellion by seeking out the leaders, but Margaret Washington pointed out that the rebellion was so general that it would be impossible to determine the leadership. The council also passed a regulation prohibiting student meetings without the approval of BTW, but the rule was not announced during the troubles for fear of inciting further disturbances. (Minutes of the Executive Council, Sept. 29, 1903, Con. 1005, BTW Papers, DLC.)

To Alva Fitzpatrick[1]

[Tuskegee, Ala.] October 21, 1903

Dear Sir: I have just given directions to have the Montgomery Daily Evening Times sent to this school regularly. I am very glad to see your name attached to this paper.

In this connection, may I be permitted to make a suggestion. As a pure matter of business, to say nothing of the amount of good that could be accomplished, I have been wondering why some daily paper in the South did not give more attention to the better life of the Negro. Nearly half the population of Alabama is colored people, and over half the population of Montgomery County, I think, is colored. There is a great field among these people for the circulation of a paper that will treat them justly, and will give from time to time news of a character that will encourage them, instead of making prominent all the criminal matters pertaining to the race. Now, in making this suggestion, I am perfectly aware of the fact that should your paper, or any other paper, go too far in the direction I have indicated, it would be called a "nigger paper," and thereby lose circulation and influence among the white people. I believe however, that a paper can have a large circulation among the colored people by reason of its fairness to them, and at the same time, keep its influence and circulation among the white people. You have a great field before you in this direction, and I hope that you will at least investigate the suggestion I make.

I wish that you might quietly, if you think well of it, talk the matter over with such colored men as J. W. Adams, H. A. Loveless, Dr. Dungee, Nathan Alexander, and others. Yours truly,

[Booker T. Washington]

TLc   Con. 249   BTW Papers   DLC.

1 Alva Fitzpatrick was a prominent Montgomery editor and businessman. He was an officer of two Montgomery building and loan associations, editor of the Montgomery *Times*, and later an officer in a soap-manufacturing company. In 1916 he was editor of the *Alabama Democrat*.

To William Henry Baldwin, Jr.

[Tuskegee, Ala.] October 21, 1903

Dear Mr. Baldwin: Within the next few days, a colored man by the name of Melvin J. Chisum, will be likely to call to see you. So far as I can learn, Chisum is a good, earnest fellow with the best of intentions. I do not know just what his mission will be, but I know he is trying to publish a magazine in New York, and I think has found it rather hard sailing. I rather suspect he wants you to give him a little lift in that direction. If he had the proper amount of capital with which to operate, I believe he would publish a very good paper. I know, however, that you have a good many calls. Yours truly,

[Booker T. Washington]

TLc   Con. 792   BTW Papers   DLC.

From William Henry Baldwin, Jr.

New York   Oct 21, 1903

B. T. W. I see Prest. — at lunch on Tuesday 27th. Write me points you have in mind. Either here, or to some Washington hotel, advising me where. What do you say to Peabody's reference to Kelly Miller letter.[1]

B.

ALI   Con. 792   BTW Papers   DLC.

1 Probably a reference to Miller's critique, "Mr. Washington's Policy." See Miller to E. J. Scott, Sept. 24, 1903, above.

To Randall O. Simpson

[Tuskegee, Ala.] October 22, 1903

Dear Sir: Your kind letter of October 17th has been received, together with the paper referred to. I thank you very much for writing me and for calling my attention to the matter. I would say that I make a rule not to deny charges that are made against me or the school. I very seldom deviate from this rule. In the first place, I find that unreasonable charges usually take care of themselves if only a little time is permitted to elapse. In the second place, if I were to make a practice of denying charges, a good part of my time would be occupied in that way. If a charge is made to-day and I deny it, and another false one is made tomorrow and I fail to deny it, people will reason that because I denied the first and failed to deny the second, that the second is true, and so I should be in continual controversy and hot water.

I am very glad to answer the questions that you suggest. By this mail, I send you a marked copy of my annual report which has just come from the press. In the first paragraph, I make the statement that no graduate of this institution has ever been sent to the penitentiary. That statement is made upon a careful record kept of our students. I have never made the assertion that no student has ever been convicted of crime, but, that no graduate has ever been convicted of crime, and by that I stand. Some ten years ago, three boys were hanged in this county. I have carefully looked over our catalogues and cannot find the name of either one of these boys in our catalogue, and that is proof that they never attended this school. I have the impression that one of them did attend for awhile the public school. Several of our undergraduates have been in the courts of Tuskegee for various crimes, but in most cases I think it will be found that these students have been taken into the courts either by our teachers, or by myself. We have always pursued the policy of working in co-operation with the county officials and do not have our students feel that we would hide crime for them, but have, in every case, when we thought the seriousness of the crime demanded it, had the students arrested ourselves and turned over to the officers.

As to what our graduates are doing in Macon County, I think that question is fully answered in my World's Work article[1] which I send you. I also send you a marked copy of The Outlook containing a record of what our graduates are accomplishing in Montgomery.[2]

I hope that I have answered all of the questions asked of me. If I have not, please be kind enough to let me know, and I shall endeavor to give further information. I do not think it wise, however, for you to quote me directly in refuting these charges, but you can use this information in any way that you desire. Very truly yours,

[Booker T. Washington]

TLc Con. 261 BTW Papers DLC.

1 BTW, "The Successful Training of the Negro," *World's Work*, 6 (Aug. 1903), 3731–51.

2 *Outlook*, 74 (July 18, 1903), 689–90. *Outlook* responded to the charges of Gordon Macdonald that Tuskegee graduates in Montgomery were generally shiftless by sending an investigator of their own, who found them to be productive and active citizens. See Gordon Macdonald to the Editor of the Washington *Post*, ca. Apr. 28, 1903, above.

From Alva Fitzpatrick

Montgomery, Ala., Oct. 22nd '03

My Dear Sir: I have your esteemed favor of 21st advising me of your subscription to the Evening Times & I thank you very much for your proof of appreciation of the paper.[1] The Times was started under modest circumstances "to feel our way." Its reception by the public has been a most agreeable surprise & we find that in order to take care of our patronage we will have to enlarge our facilities which we are preparing to do. We are going to buy a larger press, put in machines and adopt features that will greatly improve the paper.

I value most highly your suggestions regarding attitude towards the Colored race. You may be assured that my policy on this question will be one of liberality and strong friendship. The paper will voice my long cherished opinions on the question. As soon as I am able to get things organized & mapped out, my purpose is to have a good space regularly appropriated to discussions of such topics as will appeal to those interested in this, to me, one of the greatest of subjects. I've gone already far enough on this line to decide me to invite from leading Colored men of the state a contribution to thought on this inquiry: "What are the best means to employ to further advancement of the highest interest of the Colored race in the state, and the South?"

I should esteem it a privelege to have you write me the first, of what I desire to be a long series of articles on this topic and also to have your opinion on it as a text for the promulgation of ideas; also any other opinion with which you may favor me by way of suggestion on this department feature of the paper. I would be glad to have you write me this paper as soon as convenient. I propose to accompany these pieces with editorial comment and to bring the subject squarely before the people.

I shall see, also, Adams & Loveless and talk with them on the subject.

It is the purpose of Mr Stern[2] to visit you soon and I would be glad to have you talk with him fully on the subject. Mr Stern is my associate & you will find him a most agreeable gentleman and one thoroughly in accord with me in his ideas and convictions on general subjects. Sincerely yours

Alva Fitzpatrick

ALS Con. 268 BTW Papers DLC.

[1] BTW sent W. H. Baldwin, Jr., a copy of the letter, remarking: "We need such a paper in the South to aid our educational efforts and to show the more encouraging side of the Negro's life." (Oct. 24, 1903, Con. 792, BTW Papers, DLC.) In November he sent Joseph B. Stern letters of introduction to Baldwin and Robert C. Ogden. (Nov. 7, 1903, Con. 268, BTW Papers, DLC.)

[2] Joseph B. Stern was publisher and general manager of the Montgomery *Times* beginning in 1903.

To Robert Curtis Ogden

[Tuskegee Ala.] October 23, 1903

My dear Mr. Ogden: Much earlier than this I meant to have sent you a brief report indicating something of the work that I have been doing during the past year as one of the Field Agents of the Southern Education Board.

First. Just as far as I can spare the time for it, I have kept up the work of visiting various Southern States and talking to the teachers and the masses of the people with a view of helping them to improve the public schools. An example of this kind of work is my going to Florida last February and speaking to the masses of the people, white and black, at night, and meeting the principal teachers of the state the following day. The traveling expenses of the colored teachers were paid out of the fund received from your Board. Practically the same plan was followed in Louisiana, where I held a most successful meeting last October, except I did not pay the expenses of the teachers, the meeting in that case was gotten up by Dr. Alderman. I am just on the eve of going to North Carolina for similar kind of work.

Second. During some portion of the year I have kept a man employed who has made a special and direct effort to show the colored people in this county especially, how to build and improve school houses and to lengthen the school term.

Third: I have spent during the year about $200 through Mr. C. W. Hare in helping educational rallies and meetings among the white people in Macon County. I thought it wise to do this because it is most important to show, in a county where so much stress is laid on the Negro, equal interest in the education of the white people.

Fourth. I have pursued the plan of putting printed matter as widely as possible, bearing upon the improvement of the public schools, into the hands of the teachers and masses of the people.

If you desire it, I could go more into detail in showing just what I have attempted to accomplish. To me, the most satisfactory part of the work has been the meetings held in large centers where both races could come together and hold a free and frank discussion of conditions and the duty of each race towards the other. I hope to do very much more of this work in the future than I have been doing in the past. Yours truly,

[Booker T. Washington]

TLc Con. 33 BTW Papers DLC.

To William Henry Baldwin, Jr.

[Tuskegee, Ala.] October 23, 1903

Dear Mr. Baldwin: In my previous letter to you regarding the rebellion of the students, I fear I gave the impression that the disturbance was caused by reason of their opposition to any industrial work. If I gave such an impression it was not correct. I have looked more thoroughly into the matter, and I am quite sure that there is no feeling against any form of labor. The outbreak was occasioned by reason of the fact that the students felt that they were required to devote too much time to both indusrial work and studies with too little time for preparation, and I am rather inclined to think that there is a good deal in this view of the case. I am, however, working upon the schedule daily and hope to have it adjusted within a few days. Yours truly,

[Booker T. Washington]

TLc   Con. 792   BTW Papers   DLC.

To Samuel Edward Courtney

[Tuskegee, Ala.] October 23, 1903

My dear Dr. Courtney: I have your note of October 18th, and thank you heartily for it. I shall carefully watch the Constitution to see if it makes any reference to Towns' letter. I have no doubt, as you suggest, that it was intended to be strictly private but it was too good to keep out of the Guardian. I do not believe that the authorities of Atlanta University will find themselves greatly pleased with the sympathy expressed by this teacher for so riotous a crowd as Trotter and his gang.

With sincere good wishes, I am, Very truly yours,

[Booker T. Washington]

TLc   Con. 253   BTW Papers   DLC.

To Isaac Newton Seligman

[Tuskegee, Ala.] October 23, 1903

My dear Sir: Sometime ago in a letter to me, you said you would like to keep a little money here that might be used to help pay the personal expenses of students who were too poor to help themselves or who were especially unfortunate. You will perhaps recall that you gave me a sum of money to be used in this way about a year ago and I reported to you on the use of it. I have very seldom handled any money that has given me such genuine pleasure and at the same time I felt was made to do more good than was true of the sum you gave me. In most every case it was used to help students who had done everything they could to help themselves and had gotten to the limit and the money came to them as a complete and overwhelming surprise. Yours truly,

[Booker T. Washington]

TLc   Con. 274   BTW Papers   DLC.

To George F. Richings

[Tuskegee, Ala.] October 24, 1903

My dear Mr. Richings: The thing I wanted to talk over with you is the possibility of your giving a series of meetings of the kind you always give in practically all the colored churches of Chicago and vicinity. Some busy-bodies for sometime have been making a special effort in Chicago to work up a sentiment against me personally and against the institution, and I am very anxious that in your own calm but convincing way you give the masses of the people an opportunity to see just what we are accomplishing. If you could see your way clear to do this we shall be willing to pay you $10 for each church that you visit and will pay the money on receipt of a report from you.

Enclosed I take the liberty of sending you a copy of my last report which has just come from the press. You may find some valuable data in the report.

Of course if you decide to go to Chicago, I desire you to do so just as soon as possible. Yours truly,

[Booker T. Washington]

TLc   Con. 273   BTW Papers   DLC.

From William Henry Baldwin, Jr.

N.Y. [City] October 24th., 1903

Dear Mr. Washington: I have your letter of 20th., about the trouble among the students.

My first impression was, that I was mighty glad to see that a body of negroes had the courage to revolt against conditions which they thought were unjust.

As to the rest of it, I do not believe that any trouble would have occurred if you had been there.

Next, although the teachers probably thought that they were acting wisely, I am inclined to feel something wrong was done or else the boys would not have taken such a decided stand. There was probably *something* done, or *undone* which if a similar case should arise would not be tried again. Therefore, if this is so everybody has learned a lesson.

I should like very much to talk it all over with you. There is always some *little* thing that causes strikes and troubles, little things get magnified into big things, and you will find some fault some where on the part of the teachers, or else my experience in other similar cases belies my judgment.

I am expecting to see you here pretty soon. Faithfully yours,

W H Baldwin Jr

TLS   Con. 792   BTW Papers   DLC.

From Edward Augustine Benner

Wellesley, Mass. Oct. 24, 1903

My dear Dr. Washington: I am very glad to report a great improvement in Booker's spirit and way of going to work. He seems to have acquired more manliness and feeling of responsibility. I hesitate to express to you all that I think I have observed, but I have more hope of a good year than I anticipated for him. It may be that he will not do brilliant work, but if his industry and loyalty hold out, he will make such advance as will gratify you more than a large pile of brick and mortar for Tuskegee.

I trust you have been much benefited by your brief Atlantic trip. Yours very truly,

Edw. A. Benner

ALS   Con. 249   BTW Papers   DLC.

From Roscoe Conkling Simmons

Mound Bayou, Miss. Oct. 25 1903

My dear Uncle: I have intended to write you for some time, but I have been quite engaged in moving Mr. Montgomery's headquarters from Jackson, and in addition, this is the fall of the year and our people are busy harvesting crops and making yearly settlements.

I am so happy to know that you are back to the country. You move around at such a speed that no one can keep track of you. I trust the time will soon come when you can stay at home more. I know you had quite a delightful trip. I don't suppose you are really anxious to get on any more flesh.

The state schools are crowded to the doors, and can accommodate no more. I am told by the older people that such a rush to the schools has never been so noticeable. I think this is due to the fact that our men and women are of the opinion that Vardaman means to curtail the educational provision for their children. A large number are leaving the state, especially is this true of the eastern section of the state, Noxubee and Monroe Counties are very prominent in this respect. Politically our people are very much wrought up. They are seemingly bent on Edgar Wilson's decapitation, and since Mr. Wilson gave out that you had nothing to do with appointments, no more than any other "Nigger" they are viciously inclined toward him. They are solidly for the President, you can hardly find ten coloured men in the state who are opposed to the President's nomination, but they are determined to show the President that Mr. Wilson is very much disliked and that a mistake has been made in the state.[1]

If you think about it long enough please mention to Aunt Margaret that I would feel very much accommodated if she will bring to your attention the matter about which I wrote her some days ago.

I hope you are well and the school is prosperous. Mr. Bedford spent two days with me this week. It might be of interest to you to have him tell you something of the situation in the state.

With much love for you and Aunt Mag. Affectionately your nephew

Roscoe

ALS Con. 277 BTW Papers DLC.

[1] Simmons wrote Emmett Scott on the same day expressing his disgust with racial politics in Mississippi and stating that "Mr. Wilson is a bad man, the very worst white man in the state...." Simmons said that if political appointments were left in Wilson's hands it would "deprive us of all connection with the government, as we have none with the state." (Con. 261, BTW Papers, DLC.) BTW responded by cautioning Simmons about "putting too much confidence in every rumor that you hear without your being sure that it is confirmed or based on facts." He told Simmons that Isaiah Montgomery's resignation "was in the hands of the President and had practically been accepted before Mr. Wilson knew that there was any irregularity in his office or any charges brought against him." (BTW to Simmons, Nov. 8, 1903, Con. 277, BTW Papers, DLC.)

To William Henry Baldwin, Jr.

[Tuskegee, Ala.] October 26, 1903

Dear Mr. Baldwin: There are about fifteen colored people who practically control the public sentiment of the Negro race, and I have thought it over pretty carefully for sometime and have come to the conclusion that it would be a good and helpful thing if we could have a meeting in New York City during the first week in January, 1904, lasting three days, when we might quietly take up all the interests of the race and agree as far as possible upon policies to be pursued. Of course the meetings would be wholly private. I mention New York as the place of meeting because that is the only city where a meeting of that character could be held without it getting into the newspapers. What do you think of the plan? I have talked it over with some of our best colored people and they agree with me as to the wisdom of the meeting. Your truly,

[Booker T. Washington]

TLc Con. 792 BTW Papers DLC.

To Peter Jefferson Smith, Jr.

[Tuskegee, Ala.] Oct. 27 [190]3

My name was used too much in The Citizen last week. Do not let it appear if possible this week. Avoid controversy with Trotter and his crowd.

W.

TWIr Con. 542 BTW Papers DLC.

To Robert Todd Lincoln

[Tuskegee, Ala.] October 28, 1903

My dear Sir: Enclosed I send you a copy of a dispatch sent out from Nashville Monday night, regarding the Pullman car accommodations for colored people in the South. I very much hope that there is no foundation for those statements. Ever since its existence the Pullman Company has treated the colored people with the greatest justice and educated and refined colored people in the South have absolutely nothing to depend upon but the Pullman car. I believe that if your company does not yield to temporary and local pressure, matters will soon straighten themselves out and everything will go on smoothly as it has been going in the past. You have no idea what a great injustice will be done our people and what suffering will be caused if your company were to yield to the wishes of some of the more prejudiced and narrow-minded people.

If you contemplate taking any serious action, I wish at least that you would permit me to be heard by you before such action is put into operation. Very truly yours,

[Booker T. Washington]

TLc   Con. 249   BTW Papers   DLC.

To William Henry Baldwin, Jr.

[Tuskegee, Ala.] October 28, 1903

Dear Mr. Baldwin: Enclosed I send you clipping from Tuesday's Constitution which explains itself.[1] I can hardly believe that such action will be permitted. It will be almost the last straw in the direction of breaking the camel's back if such an outrage is committed. I cannot conceive of how I could do my work in the South and be compelled to sit up in a jim crow car night after night. My special purpose in writing you is to ask if you will not get at the bottom of this matter and find out whether or not there really is to be a meeting of the Pullman car agents in Chicago, and whether or not they purpose to take serious action. I also suggest that you could help very much in the matter perhaps by reaching directly Mr. Lincoln and the Directors of the Pullman Company. I think if strong pressure were brought to bear on Mr. Lincoln and the Directors on the part of strong men in New York, that they would not yield. I am sure that if we can pass through this temporary and local excitement, matters will go on quietly as they have been going in the South in reference to the Pullman cars. It is a matter that means more to us than you can conceive and any help you can render us I am sure will be greatly appreciated. Very truly yours,

[Booker T. Washington]

TLc   Con. 792   BTW Papers   DLC.

[1] The Atlanta *Constitution*, Oct. 27, 1903, 1, reported that blacks would be barred from using the same sleeping cars as whites in Tennessee. The newspaper stated that the action came from Gov. James Frazier of Tennessee, who was returning to Nashville in a Pullman car and found five blacks using the same car who "monopolized the porter's time and otherwise made themselves obnoxious to white persons."

313

To Judson Whitlocke Lyons

Tuskegee, Alabama. October 28, 1903

My dear Mr. Lyons: You will perhaps recall that about the middle of last February I addressed you a letter concerning a private conference to be attended by about fifteen or eighteen of our most prominent men, representing various sections of the country and various race interests, for the purpose of considering quietly all the weighty matters that now confront us as a race. The meeting was not called at the time hoped for in my last correspondence for the reason that there was delay and some disappointment in providing funds for the expenses of the meeting. That feature has now been provided for in a way that will not make those who attend the conference feel obligated to any individual or organization and leave them free for open and frank discussion.

I very much hope that you can now see your way clear to attend such a conference in New York City to be held, if possible, on the 6th, 7th and 8th of January, 1904.

The value of such a meeting will consist very largely in everything connected with it, even the fact that there is to be such a meeting, being kept absolutely from the public for the present, and I wish to enjoin upon you the importance of nothing being said concerning it.

I very much hope that you will feel it to be your duty to throw aside all other engagements, for the purpose of attending this meeting, which, I believe, is going to be the most important, serious and far-reaching in the history of our people. Other matters can wait. The things to be considered by this gathering I think cannot wait longer. The recent action taken by the Governor of Tennessee in relation to Pullman car accommodations for colored people is but one of the signs which show the importance of such a gathering as we contemplate. Yours truly,

Booker T. Washington

TLS DHU.

To William Edward Burghardt Du Bois

Tuskegee, Alabama. October 28, 1903

Dear Dr. Du Bois: The enclosed is a copy of a letter[1] which I have sent out to all the parties mentioned in our previous conference, and I hope very much it will have your approval. If for any reason you think any changes should be made in the personnel of those invited, I wish very much that you would say so. Yours truly,

Booker T. Washington

TLS W. E. B. Du Bois Papers MU.

[1] In the Du Bois Papers, MU, is a copy of BTW to Abram L. Grant, Oct. 28, 1903, identical to the letter to Judson W. Lyons of the same date, above.

From Archibald J. Carey[1]

Chicago, Oct. 28 1903

My Dear Sir: You have perhaps seen or heard of the relentless tirade which certain men are waging against yourself and your work in this city. There are those of us, however, who stand as firmly by you as ever. I have taken occassion to remark from my pulpit here in Chicago, and on the floor of our annual conference in Des Moines, Ia and Richmond, Ind. that "I am prepared to stand for Mr. Washington, alone, if need be, against all Chicago; because of my implicit confidence in the man, in his methods and the ultimate triumph of the principles for which he contends." And I am indeed happy to assure you that the rank and file of our people believe sincerely that no man has the interests of the race at heart more than yourself and for this reason they are pained at this needless assault.

Now certain friends of yours have conferred together with myself and we have thought of the following plan as an offset and as an opportunity for the Chicago colored citizens to put themselves on record in a fair light. The plan has the hearty endorsement of Bishop Grant, Editor Hinman of the Inter-Ocean et al.

On Thursday Dec 10. (if this date meets your convenience or some date in Dec other than Monday, Wed. or Thursday, because those are drill nights at the armory) The several lodges of K. of P. will have a prize drill at the 1st Reg. Armory under the auspices of Quinn Chapel. We expect the Gov. his aides and any number of distinguished citizens. The Governor to make a brief address, one other short speech and we write to ask if you will kindly be present and deliver the address of the evening.

Bishop Grant hopes to see you soon and urge upon you to accept. Your friends here are anxious for you to come, and join me in this request. Thursday Dec. 10 or any Thursday in that month best suited to your convenience.

With prayers & best wishes for your continued success. I remain yours faithfully

A. J. Carey

Kindly inform me at your earliest opportunity.

ALS   Con. 550   BTW Papers   DLC.

1 Archibald J. Carey (1868–1931) was the pastor of Quinn Chapel A.M.E. Church in Chicago, the oldest black church in the city, from 1886 to 1909. Born in Georgia, where his parents had been house slaves, Carey was educated at Atlanta University. Both at Quinn Chapel and after 1909 at the Institutional Church and Social Settlement he used his pulpit to promote black social welfare programs and improved race relations. He was also active in partisan politics. Though a Republican, he occasionally supported local Democratic candidates. In 1914 the Democratic Mayor Carter Harrison appointed Carey to the motion picture censorship board, where he succeeded in banning the anti-black film, *The Birth of a Nation*, in 1915.

From James Carroll Napier

Nashville, Tenn., Oct. 28th. 1903

My dear Mr. Washington: I have just had an extended conference with Gov. Frazier. He disclaims any intention to wrong the colored people or to curtail their rights and privileges. On the other hand he asserts that he wishes to do all in his power to encourage and help them to elevate themselves. He says that his recent action was not based upon any prejudice or ill feeling, but wholly upon a desire to see that the statute which provides for separate and equal accommodations for the races shall be impartially executed. He also says that he would be as quick to make complaint against any failure to give the colored people what they are entitled to under the law as he was to make the one above referred to. He does not think that his action will have a tendency to exclude colored people from sleeping coaches but only to force the Rail Road and Sleeping Car Companies to furnish separate and equal accommodations to each. I asked him particularly about the conduct of the people complained of on September 26th. last. He said he had no criticism to offer other than that their presence in the car was a violation of law.

After talking with you yesterday I sent a telegram to Mr. Lincoln, a copy of which I enclose herewith.[1] I am sure that what you have done will have its influence with him and the action to be taken at the meeting now being held in Chicago.

I do not think that this agitation will affect us very seriously. It will, however, embolden the prejudiced agents in their efforts to circumvent our endeavor to ride as freely in sleepers as we have done heretofore unless the Chicago meeting positively prohibits them from doing so. This I hope the meeting will do. Mr. Cranberry the local attorney of the Pullman Company here claims that our statute does not apply to sleepers operating in the State and in this view I concur with him.

I hope that you will not cease your efforts to counteract this movement against us. All our people are greatly wrought up over the matter and consider this stroke as being more directly aimed at the intelligent and respectable negro than anything else that has heretofore been done.

Mrs. Napier joins me in warmest remembrances to both you and Mrs. Washington. Very truly and sincerely yours,

J. C. Napier

TLS Con. 269 BTW Papers DLC.

[1] Napier enclosed an undated copy of a wire to Lincoln: "To exclude colored people from Pullman coaches would entail upon them the greatest wrong, injustice and humiliation. In the name of your revered father we ask that you use your great influence to avert this calamity and prevent additional oppression."

From Henry Hugh Proctor

Atlanta, Ga., Oct. 29, 1903

My dear Mr. Washington: Have sent telegram to Mr. Lincoln. Bishop Turner signed it. We are also sending letter. Bishop is also sending one.

We are arranging for a meeting of about twenty leading colored men to meet you here Saturday night.

If desired, it is possible we can get a private hearing with Commission.

I will meet you at the afternoon train Saturday. Wire me. Yours truly,

H. H. Proctor

ALS   Con. 270   BTW Papers   DLC.

From Emmett Jay Scott

[Washington, D.C.] Oct 30, 1903

My Dear Mr Washington: I am at a Colored hostelry & they have no ink, so you will excuse the pencil!

I have seen Cooper. He seems to have everything well in hand & I believe the paper will come out regularly hereafter. He claims that the lawyer he has retained in the Barnett suit has been bleeding him for all the ready money he could command & that that has interfered to prevent getting the paper out regularly. He did get out last Saturday but not the week before. None of our copies reached Tuskegee however before I left. I said *absolutely* nothing to Cooper that w'd give him the chance to fall back on us — as he w'd do if he knew we were unduly concerned as to the preservation of the *Colored American!* He says there is not the slightest chance for the paper to "go by the board" — or get out [of] his hands! The grand jury has not indicted him but may. He seems a bit scared — but claims that Terrell & all say he will not suffer! If Cooper can be diplomatically assisted — only in his emergencies it will be best — &

certainly he ought not be allowed to feel he can fall back on us "for a lift" whenever the fancy strikes him.

I have not been able to penetrate much as to the Sociological Congress! I have talked with many but there seems to be no well defined idea as to just what it is to be. I have not seen Lawson — nor Kelly Miller yet — but shall *today sure!* Yesterday was a busy day — I saw Adams — Terrell, Cooper — McKinlay — & the President! As for Adams. He must be dropped, such wobbling I never saw. He is scared to death & pressed me to declare what he ought to do. I refused any comfort, telling him to decide himself. He is afraid of Morris & the whole Chicago gang & tried to push it up to me that all of Chicago is against us — that you have made mistakes — *etc — etc.* I called for specifications & he fell down miserably. Terrell & McKinlay are disgusted with him. I cannot write of his interviews with them & his cowardice — but I'll repeat it all when I come & you'll feel the disgust that I do!

I went to White House at 1 o'clock. Mr Loeb[1] admitted me immediately. He did not seek to have me tell him what I wanted or anything & was most kind. The President gave me 20 minutes in his private office. I went over everything possible. To start, let me say he is a[s] staunch as ever — as overwhelmingly enthusiastic over you as ever! He says that the whole gang at Boston (he said gang) has given up trying to scare him — or influence him as regards yourself. That he was glad to have the colored newspapers sent — but that I was asking him to draw the color-line as regards reading them since he reads no newspapers! That he feels you have the situation well in hand — & he trusts our assurances! As to Abyssinia! He jumped at it & said he'd do it — said we ought to get the best possible man — some such man as Durham (& praised Durham greatly) — I told him you'd rather have it go to a white man rather than have a "cheap" colored one go! He thought that was good! Said he'd appoint the Haytian Commission & thanked you for mentioning it. He wants to know when it is to be — & asks that you write him. Told him we would. Says he'll see you anytime you call. He knows nothing of Morris (of Chicago) or the scheme mentioned by Lawson.

I spoke of Fortune! Told him of your letter to Fortune — etc — also of Fortune's fighting & others getting glory. I told him of muddle in regard to his accounts. He asks that you write him about it when Shaw returns & says he'll take it up personally. He says tho'

319

that he has "but little influence with this administration in financial matters" etc! This was a quotation from Lincoln & when I laughed & put it up to Lincoln, he said that if it was not true he'd want to chop heads off — because even he c'd be wrong. He took a fall out of lily whites — La. Texas & Ala. I congratulated him for you — on his 45th anniversary & it seemed to please him very much!

I'll go after the Sociological business at once & will write you fully. Go to Baltimore tomorrow! Yours sincerely

Emmett J. Scott

ALS   Con. 249   BTW Papers   DLC.

1 William Loeb, Jr. (1866–1937) became Theodore Roosevelt's private secretary in 1899, assistant secretary to the President from 1901 to 1903, and secretary from 1903 to 1909. From 1909 to 1913 he was collector of the port of New York and then vice-president of the American Smelting and Refining Co.

From Charles Waddell Chesnutt

Cleveland, O., Oct. 31, 1903

My dear Dr. Washington: Replying to your favor of Oct. 26th, in which you make inquiry concerning the letter addressed to you by Rabbi Moses J. Gries[1] of this city, (which I return) I would say Mr. Gries is pastor of the leading Jewish congregation of Cleveland, (and a very fine man,) and that the lecture work concerning which he writes you is that of the Temple Course, which is a lecture course carried on under the auspices of the Temple congregation. They present talent of various sorts; among their oratorical attractions are Thomas Dixon,[2] Russell Conwell[3] and others. Elbert Hubbard[4] has lectured to them, and Mayor Sam Jones[5] of Toledo, and other distinguished men. I have appeared before them myself, but local talent cuts no great figure in such affairs.

The congregation is made up of Jews, and while a great many people of other creeds patronize the lecture course, I do not imagine there are among them many persons of considerable wealth and social influence, though of course a few such people might be attracted by the presence of a distinguished speaker who could not be heard elsewhere. And Jews, you know, have many charities and philanthropic enterprises of their own, which I imagine require the bulk of their resources available for such purposes.

I read your article in the October "Atlantic," and I agree with it perfectly so far as it preaches the doctrine of labor, patience, and industrial training. I disagree with it most pointedly where, even by inference, the registration of the twenty-five teachers of Tuskegee or even the twenty-five hundred colored voters in Alabama is accepted in lieu of the 180,000 votes to which, under manhood suffrage, the negroes of Alabama would be entitled. I commend to your consideration the editorial in the "Independent" of this week, which expresses my views upon your work exactly. I had the pleasure of meeting Dr. Ward, the editor of the Independent, here a week ago, while he was in attendance upon the American Missionary Association Convention; I was invited to lunch with him at the residence of an acquaintance, but was unable to be present, and though I met him afterwards our interview was very brief, and did not touch upon your work. However, he evidently thinks upon the subject just as I do. To my mind it is nothing less than an outrage that the very off-scourings of Europe, and even of Western Asia may pour into this Union almost by the millions annually, and be endued with full citizenship after a year or two of residence, while native-born Americans, who have no interest elsewhere and probably never will have, must be led around by the nose as members of a "child race," and be told that they must meekly and patiently await the result of an evolution which may last through several thousand years, before they can stand upon the same level of citizenship which any Sicilian, or Syrian or Turk or Greek or any other sort of European proletary may enjoy in the State of Alabama.

The article in Pott & Co.'s book is the only thing I have published for a year or two, my time having been mainly absorbed in the somewhat prosaic task of earning a living along other lines; but I hope to do better in the future. I hope that you enjoyed your trip to Europe, indeed I do not see how a man of breadth and culture could do otherwise. My daughter, Ethel, whom you know, has become within a month the mother of a fine boy. She and the child are doing well. Please give my regards to Mrs. Washington and believe me, Cordially yours,

Chas. W. Chesnutt

TLS Con. 551 BTW Papers DLC.

1 Moses J. Gries (1868–1918), a graduate of Hebrew Union College and the University of Cincinnati, was rabbi of Tifereth Israel in Cleveland from 1892 to 1917.

2 Thomas Dixon, Jr. (1864–1946), born and reared in North Carolina, was a Baptist minister, lecturer, and author. He wrote several racist novels, including *The Leopard's Spots* (1902) and *The Clansman* (1905). Much of the motion picture *The Birth of a Nation* (1915) was based on *The Clansman*.

3 Russell Herman Conwell (1843–1925), a Baptist clergyman who revitalized Grace Baptist Church in Philadelphia, founded Temple University, and was well known for his lecture "Acres of Diamonds," which he delivered more than six thousand times.

4 Elbert Green Hubbard (1856–1915), printer, editor, and lecturer, published *The Philistine*, a monthly magazine of common-sense philosophy, from 1895 to 1915. His monthly sketches, *Little Journeys*, including one on Tuskegee, eventually filled fourteen volumes. In 1899 he wrote *A Message to Garcia*. He was a victim of the *Lusitania* disaster.

5 Samuel Milton ("Golden Rule") Jones (1846–1904), a Toledo industrialist, was a reform mayor of Toledo from 1897 to 1904.

From Emmett Jay Scott

Windsor Hotel Philadelphia Nov. 1/03

My Dear Mr. Washington: As I wired you last night — I have seen both Hawkins[1] (of the Lancet) and Murphy[2] of the Afro-American. I spent 3 straight hours with Hawkins. He is the recalcitrant and am flattering myself that I pulled him around good & hard. He had all of the usual vague, indefinite, half-baked opinions to unload. I held him to the record & asked in every case for specifications! I utterly confounded him & appealed to his reason on the issue presented. He is in many ways a fine fellow & well worth holding onto. He confessed when we parted that he had new light & warmly praised my presentation of the cause, remarking as to the sincerity of it all, etc., etc., all of which while flattering is interesting mostly because it seemed to mark conversion! He is well-educated — is a lawyer & has the paper on the side. He asked me when we parted to be his guest at his home at night & I went. He had a party of lawyers, doctors, teachers etc., to come in to meet me & seemed in every way anxious to be agreeable. He is agreeable as to the lecture — (under both auspices) but Murphy is not enthusiastic & so I want to leave it open till I return so as to tell you what I think it best that we do — I am sure I can straighten it out to the entire satisfaction of all concerned! As for Murphy: he is for us — good & strong & was only chagrined in the Lecture matter. The other fellows have dubbed him a ["]Washingtonite" & I think he'll stand up bravely & well. He is to come there early in January returning from Florida. He is going down to the Conferences to be held by *Bishop Handy* & so I got a chance to enter & press home an invitation that he come by & I think he will, & also that we shall lose nothing by his visit.

I have not seen Mr Durham yet tho' I wired him I was to be here today. He may be out of town, but I am just going to look him up. I shall press the New York matter, as hard & fast as possible & return as early as I can. I hope for some measure of success in that *Age* matter & hope I shall please you by effecting an arrangement that will be satisfactory. Yours very sincerely

Emmett J. Scott

Mr Hunt has my New York address!

ALS Con. 249 BTW Papers DLC.

1 William Ashbie Hawkins (b. 1862) was a graduate of Morgan College in Baltimore (1881) and Howard University Law School (1892). A lawyer in Baltimore, he took an active role in cases involving the rights of blacks. At various times he was editor of *Education Era, Lancet, Cambridge Advance*, and *Spokesman*. Hawkins was a leader of anti-Washington sentiment in Baltimore.

2 John Henry Murphy (b. 1840) was in the feed and produce business and then worked as a "house decorator" for twelve years before entering the printing business in 1890. In 1899 he purchased the Baltimore *Afro-American* and served as president and general manager. The *Afro-American* was a pro-Washington newspaper, although it usually was neutral toward the Tuskegean's critics.

To John Cowles Grant

[Tuskegee, Ala.] Nov. 2, 1903

Will you be kind enough to find out if I and two or three other colored men from South can have private interview with Robert T.

Lincoln on November twelfth or thirteenth either in Chicago or New York. Please telegraph answer my expense.

Booker T. Washington

TWSr   Con. 542   BTW Papers   DLC.

To James Carroll Napier

[Tuskegee, Ala.] Nov. 2, 1903

My dear Mr. Napier: We had a meeting of about twenty gentlemen in Atlanta night before last and took up fully the recent developments in regard to sleeping cars. One of the results of the meeting was the appointing of a committee including Mr. Rucker, Mr. Proctor, Dr. Du Bois and myself to go to Chicago and have an interview with Robert T. Lincoln. The meeting also instructed me to invite you to accompany the committee to Chicago, and this I very much hope you can consent to do. Our present plan is to be in Chicago on the 12th or 13th of November. I have today telegraphed to Chicago to see if we can have an interview with Mr. Lincoln on these dates either in Chicago or New York, wherever he should happen to be.[1] Yours truly,

[Booker T. Washington]

TLc   Con. 268   BTW Papers   DLC.

[1] The next day S. Laing Williams wrote BTW that he had tried to see Robert T. Lincoln in Chicago to arrange for an interview but that Lincoln had refused to see him. Through his secretary, Lincoln said that a conference with blacks might do more harm than good. He also stated that he had received a large number of letters from blacks all over the country and that he was fully aware of their opinion in the Pullman car matter. (Nov. 3, 1903, Con. 249, BTW Papers, DLC.)

To James Sullivan Clarkson

[Tuskegee, Ala.] November 3, 1903

Personal

My dear General Clarkson: I have just heard that there is an effort being made, mainly by the business men of New York, to have a

permanent and separate Minister sent to San Domingo. You know
Powell now acts for both Haiti and San Domingo. In case this plan
is carried out, would not this be a good position for our friend Fortune? It was through Fortune's influence a few days ago that the
colored people in their state convention in New Jersey endorsed
the President strongly. He is constantly doing this kind of work.
He breaks out in a wrong way once in a while in his paper, but he
can be controlled and is always open to reason. Yours truly,

[Booker T. Washington]

TLc   Con. 252   BTW Papers   DLC.

To Hollis Burke Frissell

Tuskegee Alabama. November 3, 1903

My dear Dr. Frissell: You do not know how very grateful I am to
you for your kind letter of recent date and how much your words
encourage and strengthen me. I appreciate what you have done and
what you say thoroughly.

I shall be most willing to speak at the meeting in February which
you suggest, only it is important that the date be fixed definitely as
soon as possible so it will not conflict with other engagements. You
speak of a general meeting. I do not know exactly to what this refers.
I hesitate to place my opinion by the side of yours, but I do feel that
a meeting definitely in behalf of Hampton would accomplish more
than a meeting that had no special object in view. Hampton is a
large enough institution around which to center the general discussion of Southern Interests.

I think such a letter as you suggest to the Boston Transcript would
be most helpful in many directions and I hope you will write it.
I often find myself, among other colored people, becoming rather
tried with Kelly Miller. The trouble is no one ever knows where
to find him, he tries to place himself on all sides and keep in favor
of all parties. If he could overcome that weakness I think he would
become a great power.

It is a little difficult to analyze the opposition that has manifested itself to me in some quarters among the colored people. So far as I can get hold of it, I think in the first place a large proportion is due to jealousy or envy, and then a few others who have ambitions in political directions feel that the President consults me pretty generally in regard to offices and other matters pertaining to the colored people; in a word they feel that I have his confidence and that he depends upon me, and I am quite sure that in one or two cases the attacks which have been made have been carefully planned with a view of trying to scare the President and make him feel that he must either drop me or he will lose the support of the colored people. I have not failed to make my position entirely clear to the President and have told him in so many words, that if at any time his relations with me were calculated to weaken himself or hurt his own interests I wished him to consider what would be best for him first, but I am glad to say that he has shown himself even stronger than I suspected in this regard. He has paid absolutely no attention whatever to the criticisms and I do not believe intends to. He understands the animating causes of the whole outbreak and seems to depend upon me more and more now every day. Throughout all the agitation it is most encouraging to note that the rank and file of our people see matters clearly and correctly, and no man could ever have his hands held up more strongly and loyally than my hands are held up by the masses of our people. The opposition centers mainly among a few in Boston, Chicago and Washington and has back of it one of the two causes to which I have referred.

I shall read with interest your editorial in the Southern Workman. Yours very truly,

Booker T. Washington

I am sure that much of the opposition has its origin in Atlanta University, although I have always been kind to them there or attempted to be.

B. T. W.

TLS   BTW Folder   ViHaI.   Postscript in BTW's hand.

To John Stephens Durham

[Tuskegee, Ala.] November 3, 1903

Dear Mr. Durham: I have your note written from New York. What you say regarding Santo Domingo is important. If you get hold of any further information regarding that point, please be good enough to notify me at once, even by telegram if necessary.

I was intending to write you a letter to-day to say that I have put the matter of Abyssinia before the President and he is enthusiastic over the suggestion of recognizing it as a nation, and was equally enthusiastic over your name in connection with the mission. He praises you very highly. I do not know in detail just what has to be done in order to put the thing upon a working basis, but I am planning to see the President in person within the next two weeks, and will know a little more than I do now. I wanted to get this information before you sail in the hope that your trip may be delayed at least long enough for us to have a consultation. If you can meet me in Washington, I suspect it will be better.

I do not think you will find Abyssinia an unhealthful country. I have always heard the contrary opinion expressed.

I think your opinion of Mr. Wharton[1] is very good and I would use it to the fullest extent. I also think it wise for you to see Senator Aldrich[2] as he has suggested.

I am not sure just what day I shall be in Washington, but think it will be near the middle of the month. Yours truly,

[Booker T. Washington]

TLc Con. 249 BTW Papers DLC.

[1] Joseph Wharton (1826–1909) of Philadelphia was a wealthy zinc, nickel, and steel manufacturer and a founder of Swarthmore College and the Wharton School of Finance and Commerce of the University of Pennsylvania. A patron of Durham, he had recently written Senator Nelson W. Aldrich urging that Durham be considered for more important work than he was doing with the Spanish Claims Commission. (Durham to BTW, Oct. 28, 1903, Con. 256, BTW Papers, DLC.)

[2] Nelson Wilmarth Aldrich (1841–1915), financier and U.S. senator from Rhode Island (1881–1907), was one of a coterie of four or five who dominated the Senate in the early years of the twentieth century and sought to block progressive reforms.

To William Pickens

[Tuskegee, Ala.] November 4, 1903

Personal

My dear Mr. Pickens: I thank you very much for sending me a copy of your letter to Dr. Beard. I was a little curious to know what subject Dr. Beard's letter to you covered. It seems to me that on the whole you have pursued the wisest course in permitting these men to make an apology and thus teaching them a lesson which I hope will be a benefit to them in the future. I am sure you cherish no personal grudge against them but wanted to teach them to be decent because of its beneficial effects to the race as well as to yourself. Personally I have not the slightest feeling of resentment against these people who seem to make me the continual object of their attacks. I have great pity for them. I hope they have learned a lesson which will do them some good.

I shall hope to see you when I am in the North again. Yours truly,

[Booker T. Washington]

TLc Con. 261 BTW Papers DLC.

To Emmett Jay Scott

Tuskegee, Alabama. Nov. 4, 1903

Dear Mr. Scott: A magazine is to be issued in Atlanta called "The Voice of the South," December 1st or January 1st. The thing is under the control of J. L. Nichols & Co., Naperville, Ill., and considering the fact that they have agencies established all through the South it is my opinion this magazine is going to be a power and successful from the start. A colored man by the name of Hopkins,[1] whom you will find in the Atlanta office of Nichols & Co., is to be in general control of the magazine, and a young man from Richmond[2] is to edit it. I am very anxious that you have a good confidential talk with Hopkins and be very sure that we get an influence with this magazine that shall keep it working our way or at least not against us. Hopkins seems to be a very sensible fellow, but we want to be sure that he does not get under wrong influences, which is very easy to be done at Atlanta. Yours truly,

Booker T. Washington

TLS Con. 275 BTW Papers DLC.

1 John A. Hopkins was an agent of J. L. Nichols and Co. while a student at Virginia Union University. When the Nichols executive John A. Hertel visited the campus in 1903, Hopkins introduced him to J. Max Barber. Soon after graduation in 1903 Hopkins joined the Nichols staff as head of the Negro department at Atlanta.

2 Jesse Max Barber, born in Blackstone, S.C., in 1878, was educated at Benedict College and Virginia Union University, where he graduated in 1903. From 1904 to 1907 he edited the monthly *Voice of the Negro*, the best black magazine of the period. BTW arranged for his secretary, E. J. Scott, to be an associate editor, and sought to dominate its editorial policies. Barber made his magazine a forum for the whole range of black opinion on every topic of interest to the race, but he made clear in his editorials that he favored the views of BTW's critics, and he was one of the founders of the Niagara Movement in 1905. In an effort to control Barber, Scott resigned from the magazine in protest and BTW privately secured from the Nichols executives, who had published two of his books, promises to moderate Barber's editorials. During the Atlanta Riot in 1906, Barber telegraphed an account to a New York newspaper, but when a telegraph operator revealed his name to white vigilantes, threats on his life forced him to flee to Chicago.

There he attempted to continue his magazine, which had reached a circulation of 12,000, but he was unable to secure financial backing. Through BTW's private intervention Barber also lost positions as a newspaper editor in Chicago and teacher in Philadelphia. Seeking a career in which BTW could not hound him, he worked his way through dental school and set up a practice in Philadelphia. During World War I he was president of the Philadelphia branch of the NAACP, and in the twenties and thirties there were occasional echoes of his earlier militancy.

To Wilford H. Smith

[Tuskegee, Ala.] November 4, 1903

Personal

Dear Mr. Smith: I have been glad to see the enclosed correspondence from Mr. Converse,[1] and also I have noted the apology to Mr. Pickens published in the Guardian. I note however, that nothing is signed on the part of Trotter. What about that side of the case? I shall talk the whole matter over with you when I see you. Yours truly,

[Booker T. Washington]

TLc   Con. 277   BTW Papers   DLC.

1 John W. Converse (b. 1848), a white Massachusetts lawyer residing in Somerville.

To Margaret James Murray Washington

Tuskegee, Alabama. Nov. 4, 1903

Mr. Washington would be pleased to have Mrs. Washington go driving with him this afternoon at a quarter of five.

HL   Con. 866   BTW Papers   DLC.   Margaret M. Washington replied on the invitation: "I can not go. Am not well enough to go behind those horses. M."

Kelly Miller to William Edward Burghhardt Du Bois

Washington, D.C. Nov 4 1903

Dear DuBois: Yours received this day — Of course Prof Booker T. has notified you of the date for the New York Conference (Jan. 6th, 7th, 8th). Our local conference I fear is almost a matter of "help me Cassius or I sink." I am glad that Mr. W. will be present. It will give weight and currency to the movement. I do not think that the conference can be stampeded by his presence. I shall stand uncompromisingly opposed to the endorsement of any individual or his platform.

Roscoe will also be here. You should come by all means. Will you come if free transportation can be procured?

I was both glad and sorry to see your Guardian letter — glad for the sympathy expressed for as sincere a man as there is in the race; but sorry in that I feel sure your expression will be misjudged.

I am sending you a list of my fugitive articles — also list topics suggested for conference. Yours truly

Kelly Miller

ALS   W. E. B. Du Bois Papers   MU.

To William Edward Burghardt Du Bois

Tuskegee, Alabama. November 5, 1903

Dear Dr. Du Bois: Replying in part to yours of November 3d, I want to get your opinion on the question as to whether or not either Bishop Turner or Bishop Holsey[1] should not properly be included in our New York conference. Both of these men represent in a way the John Temple Graves idea and that is an element which I wonder if it is safe for us to ignore if we wish to have all sides of the question fairly and honestly considered.

I will write you later about the other suggestion raised in your letter.

In looking over the list I find that we have no representative from the state of Texas. Texas is so large within itself that I have been wondering if that section of the country should not be represented, in that case have you any one to suggest? I think you know R. L. Smith, a graduate from Atlanta University, and a man who has done excellent work in many directions in Texas. In case you decide to have some one from that state I can think of no one who is more representative in his character. Perhaps you know some other person.

I have been telegraphing trying to make arrangements for our reception in Chicago ever since I reached home, but up to the present time nothing is very satisfactory. Mr. Lincoln is evidently waiting for some developments in the South or trying to hedge. The last telegram wanted to know the names of the committee and parts of the country that they represented and the object to be covered

331

by the conference. This information I telegraphed day before yesterday, but still no answer. Yours truly,

[Booker T. Washington]

It may be, however, that the company is holding out in our
favor and is trying to avoid seeing committees in order to not
attract attention and thus not stir up the South to any great extent.

TL   W. E. B. Du Bois Papers   MU.

1 Lucius Henry Holsey (1842–1920), the son of a slave mother and her white
owner, was ordained in 1867 as a minister in the Georgia conference of the Methodist
Episcopal Church, South, and three years later was a delegate to the first conference
of the Colored Methodist Episcopal Church which resulted in the formation of the
C.M.E. Church as a separate body. Holsey became bishop in 1873. In 1904 he was
elevated to senior bishop. Holsey, who had no formal education, was a gradualist
on matters of racial advancement and generally supported BTW. By the end of the
century, however, Holsey's disillusionment with racial progress led him to propose
a semi-independent black state in America in order to assure the survival of the
race.

To Timothy Thomas Fortune

[Tuskegee, Ala.] November 5, 1903

My dear Mr. Fortune: I do not think I have had time to express
to you fully my own relations to the effort of some parties to reorganize and enlarge the Age. The matter was brought to my attention forcefully when I was last in New York, and I told the
parties that I would permit Mr. Scott to serve in the way of giving
advice and also in cooperating in any way that might bring about
the desired result. The whole matter I would have explained to
you had I had the opportunity of a consultation. My interest in the
whole scheme centers here: There is a very rare and great opportunity in this country for a strong national paper representing our
race. Somebody is going to occupy that field within the near future.
The only question is whether we shall occupy it or permit our
enemies to do so. Of course when it comes down to the pure matter
of business which centers around you and Mr. Peterson I cannot

attempt to advise; no one knows the business so well as yourself and its value to you. Yours truly,

[Booker T. Washington]

TLc   Con. 290   BTW Papers   DLC.

To Timothy Thomas Fortune

[Tuskegee, Ala.] November 5, 1903

My dear Mr. Fortune: I am in receipt of your kind letter of October 31st. I do not now make any decision pro or con regarding your suggestion to write an open letter defining my position on industrial and higher education and of political disfranchising. I simply raise a question for your consideration. Would it be possible for me to place myself on record in any more forceful and plain manner than I have already done in my books, "The Future of the American Negro" and "Up from Slavery"? I have discussed fully every one of these questions in these two volumes, and have more recently discussed fully the subject of industrial education in the October number of the Atlantic Monthly. You will note that not one of the papers that are opposing me has dared to print a single line from the Atlantic Monthly, neither did these papers print my Louisville address. They systematically avoid publishing anything that defines my position on all these vital questions. Another consideration is, would they not raise a great whoop and yell and say they had gotten me scared and had put me to explaining? If I felt that there was any widespread honest ignorance as to how I stand on all these questions I confess I would not hesitate about complying with your request, but the papers that are against me would not in the least be affected by anything that might come from my pen, they would be just as bitter as they now are. My only concern is that my friends shall not be placed in a weak or awkward position. Would not the enclosed marked utterance from me answer your purpose? Understand I do not throw aside your suggestion. You may be right and I may be wrong. I only want to get all the light on the subject I can get before acting.

Now in regard to the January private conference, you must be present by all means. I have not told you before, but some of the parties who have been asked to meet in the conference have made a special fight against your being invited. The absurdity and ridiculousness of it has exasperated me. Objection has been made by men whom you have helped make powerful and useful. For you not to be present would place me in rather an awkward position.

I have some pretty good evidence to the effect that the Boston paper is about to fall to pieces and that there is a disagreement between the main people connected with it. Yours truly,

Booker T. Washington

TLS Con. 261 BTW Papers DLC.

To Stephen Frink Dana[1]

[Tuskegee, Ala.] November 5, 1903

My dear Sir: Your kind letter containing your check for $500 for the benefit of our institution has been received, and I send you enclosed our Treasurer's receipt for same.

Since this institution was started in 1881 I have received many donations from a good many sources, but I wish to assure you that no gift of money has come that has given me such genuine pleasure and such a pleasant surprise as your generous gift. I prize it all the more because you knew me when I was a boy in the Kanawha Valley. I also recall that your firm has been the cause of helping many of our people to get upon their feet in West Virginia.

We have quite a number of West Virginia People here in the institution, some in the capacity of teachers and others as students. We have several who used to work for the Campbell's Creek Coal Co. My brother, J. H. Washington, is the Superintendent of Industries, and the others perhaps you would not recall.

I hope at some time you can see the work which we are trying to do here.

By this mail I send you a copy of my book, "Up from Slavery," which I hope you may find time to glance through. Yours truly,

[Booker T. Washington]

TLc Con. 255 BTW Papers DLC.

¹ Stephen Frink Dana, born in New York in 1836, moved to Kanawha County, W.Va., in 1865 and founded the Campbell's Creek Coal Co., which by 1900 had become the largest producer in the area. He was also president of the Kanawha and Ohio Transportation Co., which owned steamboats, barges, and a railroad used to haul coal to Cincinnati. Dana lived in Cincinnati after 1875. He contributed occasionally to Tuskegee for a number of years. In 1914 he wrote BTW: "When I think back of the time when you and I lived on the Kanawha River, and I saw you running around doing errands, I wasn't looking very closely at you, but you seemed to be a nice little boy who always kept out of trouble, and looked for something to do. But now when I know what you have done I realize that you are doing some of the best work to be done in the United States." (Dec. 1, 1914, Con. 769, BTW Papers, DLC.)

To Henry Hugh Proctor

[Tuskegee, Ala.] November 6, 1903

Dear Mr. Proctor: On reaching home on Monday, I telegraphed to Chicago with a view of having a time set when our committee would be received by Mr. Lincoln. I stated that either the 12th or 13th would be convenient. The next day I received a telegram in reply asking the names of the committee, the parts of the country they represented, and the object to be covered by our conference. I immediately telegraphed in reply this information. Up to the present time I have received no answer to my last telegram.

In the meantime I have received a letter from Mr. S. Laing Williams, a copy of which I enclose. I rather think that this letter throws a great deal of light on the whole subject, and I doubt very much whether our committee will secure a hearing. As individuals none of us I think, would have any trouble in being received by Mr. Lincoln, but it is evident for some reason he means to avoid receiving any committee. I do not think that Mr. Lincoln's action in this regard is to be taken as unfriendly or unfavorable; I rather think that he is trying to avoid stirring up the question as much as possible, and that he fears if it were known that we are pressing the matter in Chicago that a back fire might be started by the Southern people. Neither do I think that any decision has been reached by the company, otherwise I think Mr. Williams' committee would have been so informed. It is evident that the many letters and telegrams which have been sent to Chicago on the subject have done good, and I advise that in every way possible this agitation be kept up. I have talked with Dr. Du Bois through the telephone this morning, and both he and I are of the opinion that under the present circumstances it would be useless to go to Chicago unless we get a definite reply as to an audience.

Will you be kind enough to show a copy of this letter to the other members of the committee? I have sent a copy direct to Dr. Du Bois.

Enclosed I return the petition or letter addressed to Mr. Lincoln which I have signed. You and the other members of the committee can do as you think best about forwarding this if it is not taken by the committee. Yours truly,

[Booker T. Washington]

TLc   Con. 261   BTW Papers   DLC.

To Whitefield McKinlay

[Tuskegee, Ala.] November 6, 1903

My dear Mr. McKinlay: I thank you very much for your interest in taking measures to see that the work of the Sociological Conference is kept on high ground and under the control of proper people.

I wish to say this in regard to my attendance. I am trying to arrange to be present, but the recent sleeping car agitation in Tennessee has thrown new duties and responsibilities upon me rather suddenly. We held a meeting in Atlanta a few days ago and I was appointed on a committee with three or four other gentlemen to go to Chicago and see Mr. Lincoln in regard to the enforcement of the new law. It may be that Mr. Lincoln will name a date for our reception which will prevent my attending the Washington conference, and between the two I believe you will agree with me that the Chicago matter is the more important since matters will get into a bad shape if we wait. In case however, I find myself in a position to attend the Washington conference I very much prefer to attend in a private capacity and not feel that I have got to make a public address. Of course I should not mind speaking in the private meetings, but for one to be constantly under the strain of speaking in public is a constant wear and tear, besides I was wondering if I could not accomplish more good in the private conference than by public utterance. Yours truly,

[Booker T. Washington]

TLc. Con. 267 BTW Papers DLC.

To Timothy Thomas Fortune

Tuskegee, Alabama. November 7, 1903

My dear Mr. Fortune: My present plan is to leave here tomorrow morning, stopping in Washington for one or two days, and from there I go to New York where I shall hope to see you. Jesse Lawson has been doing his best to get me to take some prominent part in his Sociological Conference, but so far I have rather kept out of it, but I think it well on the whole to look in upon it and especially be present during the first day and see that no harm is done to our friends. Of course next year being a Presidential one, every effort possible is going to be made to get the control of the Afro-American Council out of your hands and we must watch matters at every point.

I have not read carefully the South Atlantic Quarterly but am planning to do so. I have read extracts from it however, and Prof. Bassett's article has stirred up a hornet's nest in the South, especially in North Carolina. Perhaps you have seen something of the criticism aimed at him. There is one thing, however, that is becoming more and more noticeable, and that is the serious people in the South give very little attention to these foolish newspaper criticisms of such a man as Bassett. His statements are in keeping with yours in the introduction to "Black Belt Diamonds," and I rather think he must have read your introduction. Yours truly,

Booker T. Washington

TLS   Con. 261   BTW Papers   DLC.

To Judson Whitlocke Lyons

[Tuskegee, Ala.] November 8, 1903

My dear Sir: I am in receipt of your letter of recent date, and in reply I would say that I cannot understand how a private conference, composed of a few of our leading men, could in any way endanger party success. Practically every man who will be present is a worshiper and supporter of Mr. Roosevelt, and none more so than myself. No man in the country, however, would honor us more quickly for not only considering matters that might come within the strict boundary of party interests, but for taking up at the same time the larger interest of the entire race, than would President Roosevelt, so that whatever is done by the meeting will be of a character I am sure that will have his complete confidence and good will. It will be impossible for me or any other individual to say in advance just what questions will be considered and what left unconsidered. The main point of this letter, however, is to say that we wish to have all sides of race interests represented and wished you to be present to represent the political interests. If, however, you cannot see your way clear to be present we should like to know now so that we can select some one else to represent the political side of our life. Yours truly,

[Booker T. Washington]

TLc   BTW Papers   ATT.

To William Edward Burghardt Du Bois

Tuskegee, Alabama. Nov. 8, 1903

Dear Dr. Du Bois: Please be kind enough to let me have your opinion of the following matters just as early as possible as time is pressing:[1] Of course the main object of our New York Conference is to try to agree upon certain fundamental principles and to see in what way we understand or misunderstand each other and correct mistakes as far as possible. I agree with your suggestion that in Chicago, for example, we ought to have as far as possible, all shades of opinion represented. I have no objection to inviting either Dr. Bentley or Mr. Morris. Which one do you prefer? Of course we could not invite them both. In this same connection I think that we ought to have W. H. Lewis from Boston as we could only get at both sides of New England thought by having him or some such man, as well as Mr. Morgan. The more I think of it, the more I feel convinced that Dr. J. W. E. Bowen ought to be present. He represents a very large constituency and I have found him on all questions a pretty sane man. I have already written you as to your opinion about either Bishop Turner or Bishop Holsey. Of course we must avoid having the conference too large and too expensive. Do you really think that Dr. Grimke would represent some idea or element that would not be represented by somebody else already invited? Please think of this and write me. As to Fortune; we may or may not agree with a great many things that he does, but I think there is no question but that he influences public opinion in a very large degree. We must make an especial effort to drop out of consideration all personal feelings, otherwise the conference will be a failure from the beginning.

So far in making up the conference, I fear it has one especially weak point which should be strengthened if possible. We should bear in mind that the bulk of our people are in the South and that the problems relating to their future very largely surround the Southern colored people, and we should be very sure that there is a large element in the conference who actually know Southern conditions by experience and who can speak with authority, and we should not have to depend too much on mere theory and untried schemes of Northern colored people. Yours truly

Booker T. Washington

TLS   W. E. B. Du Bois Papers   MU.

[1] Du Bois replied, insisting on seeing the final list of those invited before deciding whether to attend. Undated note, Aptheker, ed., *Correspondence of W. E. B. Du Bois,* 1:54.

An Extract from the Proceedings of the Washington Conference of the National Sociological Society

Washington, D.C., November 10, 1903

PROF. L. P. MOORE suggested that some one give setting to the topics to be discussed, and PROF. MILLER took up the next topic, "Race Harmony," "Problems of the City Negro," and "Rape and Lynching," proceeding to give direction to the discussions to follow.

[Prof. Booker T. Washington had entered the church while Rev. A. M. Green was speaking, and was greeted with prolonged clapping of hands.]

PROF. KELLY MILLER:

Mr. Chairman: I notice that the great Tuskegeeian, Prof. Booker T. Washington, has entered the house, and I move you that unanimous consent be granted him to speak on any subject agreeable to him.

Consent was granted, and Prof. Washington spoke as follows:

PROF. BOOKER T. WASHINGTON:

My remarks will be very few and very short.

For once I want to have the privilege of listening and not talking. In fact, as I grow older I sometimes have the feeling that if I had listened more and talked less I would have accomplished more work than I have accomplished. I came here at the cost of much precious time, away from many pressing and important duties, and if I do not stay to the finish of your Conference I hope that you will not consider that I am not deeply interested in what you are doing; it will be because I am forced to go away for interests especially pressing us in certain sections of the South. I am very glad that this Conference has been called, and I hope that we will learn more and more, as the years pass by, that no one organization, no one institution, no one individual, can represent all the interests of the race.

We need organizations, both national and local in character, in order that all the issues of the race may be reached and may be emphasized, and I hope that through such an organization as this that the lesson of organization will be more and more emphasized. We are all trying to reach the same end. We may travel, for a time at least, on different lines, but the goal is the same. You can do a certain work in this organization if you follow the suggestions which have been outlined and emphasized in the printed matter concerning it, a work that perhaps no other organization can do. There are three or four others that can do a work that this organization cannot do, and it is only through the various organizations, as I have said, that all sides of race issues can be emphasized and properly represented. That Mr. Lawson, or another, may not belong to all of these organizations should not be taken to indicate that he is not as deeply interested in the problems of those organizations as those in them. I repeat that you have a work to do in this organization that is not being done by any other, and a work that will redound to the great good of the entire race. I am glad that we are getting to the point where we can talk without regard to denomination, without regard to political parties, and discuss our race interests in a large and broad sense, as I see we are doing here this evening.

Now, there are two things that I want to say before I finish. One is that I hope you will always bear in mind that the great body of our people live in the South. There are eight millions and more of us down there, and the problem is there. If you can help us to bear our conditions, I hope you will keep in close touch and sympathy with those who are striving for better conditions right there in the South. There are some who, at all hazards, mean to remain there. If they suffer, they mean to remain there — right there in the heart of the South — as long as the bulk of our people are there. It is comparatively easy for you in these atmospheres to discuss the problem, but do so always with a view of looking not to your own interests, but to those of the larger masses of our people in the South.

In the discussion of these questions it seems that we should bear in mind that agitation, as one gentleman said a minute ago, should have a very large and important part. That is proper. The condemnation of wrong should always have a very large and important place; the demands for rights withheld should have a large and important place; but a very large place in all of our discussion and in all of our efforts should be given to something that is constructive. Now, some of us live in the section of the country where we hear of these wrongs. We eat them for our breakfast, for our dinner, for our supper. We live on them day in and day out. Some of them we know pretty well. Along with the condemnation I hope that such a thoughtful body as this will turn its attention more and more in the constructive direction. What we can construct, what we can project, is what will bring us relief. I have great hope when I see such an intelligent and conscientious body doing something in this high-reaching and constructive period.

Question — By REV. HARVEY JOHNSON: I believe what you say, that we must construct; we must do, if we can convince the people who are opposed to us that we can do. Have we not constructed something? Something that is operative. Has that construction effected or accomplished the end in view? Do you note any tendency on the part of the Southern white people to accord you justice on the score of the great, great work that you have accomplished in Alabama, or to accept you and yours and me and mine in this section more than before, because of that construction?

PROFESSOR WASHINGTON: We have got to do our duty. In a great many cases you have got to wait patiently for results. If we keep on doing our duty, whether we see immediate results or not, the results will take care of themselves.

Proceedings of the Washington Conference on the Race Problem in the United States under the Auspices of the National Sociological Society, Washington, D.C., November 9, 10, 11, and 12, 1903 (Washington, D.C., 1904), 141–44.

To Emmett Jay Scott

Hotel Manhattan   New York City. Nov. 11th, 1903

Dear Mr. Scott: You may be interested to know that I have just learned by telephone from Dr. Courtney that the Trotter-Forbes gang have fallen out among themselves, and are likely to go to pieces. Forbes and Trotter do not speak. The whole thing occurred over the Pickens apology. Forbes has placed his part of the ownership in the "Guardian" in the hands of Wm. H. Lewis to be disposed of, without the knowledge of Trotter and his crowd. I shall write more fully later. Very truly,

Booker T. Washington

TLS   Con. 249   BTW Papers   DLC.

From Emmett Jay Scott

[Tuskegee, Ala.] Nov. 11, 1903

Courtney Wires can buy half interest Guardian fifty each and three hundred obligations.

E. J. Scott

TWSr   Con. 542   BTW Papers   DLC.

To Richard W. Thompson

[New York City] November 12, 1903

Dear Mr. Thompson: I hand you herewith an item which you may be able to use in some of your matter. I would also call your attention to the apology made by Trotter and Forbes so as to prevent wearing stripes. The move in this matter was made by Lewis and other of our friends who interceded to prevent these men from being tried if they should make ample apology, as they have done.

The apology I find, was written out by Pickens' attorney and inserted by them without any change. I send this information as you may care to use sometime as rebuttal of their story that they have been glad to make the apology because Pickens has recanted or some such drivel as that. See last issue. You will know, of course, how to riddle that kind of contention on their part. Yours truly,

[Booker T. Washington]

TLc Con. 279 BTW Papers DLC.

From Emmett Jay Scott

Tuskegee, Alabama. November 14, 1903

Dear Mr. Washington: What you say regarding the Trotter-Forbes imbroglio is very interesting. It would certainly be very interesting for Trotter to wake up some morning and find that the other half interest is in the hands of some special ones of our friends.

You have written nothing with regard to your Washington visit. I am wondering if it was satisfactory. I take it that your interview with the President was as satisfactory as mine with him was. Yours truly,

Emmett J. Scott

Mr. Bruce tells me that my judgement of the Congress was correct!

TLS Con. 274 BTW Papers DLC.

To Warren Logan

Hotel Manhattan New York City. November 18th, 1903

Dear Mr. Logan: Please ask Mrs. Lee[1] to have the students well drilled in the singing of Dixie, as well as of the Star Spangled Banner, for the occasion of Mr. Peabody's visit. I mean that the old words to this song should be sung. Very truly yours,

B. T. W.

TLI BTW Papers ATT.

1 Jennie C. Lee taught vocal music at Tuskegee Institute from 1903 until after BTW's death.

To Emmett Jay Scott

Hotel Manhattan   New York City. November 18th, 1903

Dear Mr. Scott: You may be interested to know that Mr. Fortune and I had a long conference today with Hayes. It is thoroughly agreed that Fortune is to attend with several of his friends the Suffrage League at Washington, and by working in sympathy with Hayes, control the delegate body. Gen. Clarkson has been most kind in helping us to find ways to transport Fortune's friends to Washington.

Mr. McKinlay states in a letter which I have just received from him that Corrothers wishes to see me, and I have invited him to come to New York.[1] Hayes thinks that he can control Chase, and with that element disposed of, we have only to fear the Boston and Chicago delegations, neither of which we are sure will appear.

Adams[2] has been in New York for two or three days, and has been all the time at the heels of Fortune or myself. I greatly fear that his mind is unbalanced, or will quickly become so. He now begs that you do nothing about his resignation, but allow him to remain in his office in the league. I told him that I would put the matter before you.[3] Very truly,

Booker T. Washington

TLS BTW Papers ATT.

1 Scott wrote BTW: "As to Corrothers, I do not think the man is worth paying any attention to. There is one thing which I have wanted to say for some time, and that is, I think we are making too many of these small fellows feel that they are important and that they are being considered as important factors when they are, as

a matter of fact, but infinitesimal nothings." (Nov. 21, 1903, BTW Papers, ATT.)

2 Cyrus Field Adams.

3 Scott replied: "Poor Adams! I do not know what to think of him. He has absolutely no manhood of the real kind. I have a letter from him which I herewith attach in which he tells me that after consultation with you, he has decided to agree to withdraw his resignation. He has wobbled so thoroughly and so completely that I have lost all the real respect I had for him. A man who cannot stand by his friends when he should do so, is hardly a man to be trusted again." (Nov. 21, 1903, BTW Papers, ATT.)

J. W. Adams to the Editor of the Chicago *Conservator*

Montgomery, Ala., November 21, 1903

My Dear Sir: Once or twice I have seen extracts quoted from your paper criticising the course of Booker T. Washington.

If you will excuse the personal reference given, I want to say that I am a colored merchant and have lived in Montgomery practically all my life, and if you wish to find out about my business standing and character I can refer you to any of the banks in the city of Montgomery. I have not only taken an interest in my business, where I employ six colored clerks, but I have also taken an interest in the public affairs of the state and in everything that would tend to advance the interests of the colored people. I am now one of the bondsmen in the case of a colored man who has appealed his case to the U.S. Supreme Court because he was disfranchised through the operation of the new constitution. We have sent up to the U.S. Supreme Court three cases looking towards annulling the present constitution, and I have contributed and taken an active interest in all three of these cases. I state this only to have you know that I am interested in the political life of our people as well as in the business and educational life.

I have known Mr. Washington intimately and his work for practically twenty years, and there are a few things which I ought to say for the benefit of those who perhaps do not understand the work he has done and is doing, as we here in Alabama understand it.

In the first place, you who reside in the North say that you have no problems in that section of the country and that the only problem that exists regarding the Negro is the one in the Southern States. Granting that this is true for the basis of our argument, is it not a fact then that since your desire is only to help us that we should be consulted, and is it not a further fact that we are most likely [to] know more about our condition and needs than those residing a thousand miles away from us? If this would seem to be true, you can only find out about our actual condition and our actual needs by keeping in close touch and sympathy with the leading colored men of the South.

I do not believe you can help us very much by misrepresenting our leading men. I feel perfectly aware of the fact that there is a certain class of colored people who will never forgive Mr. Washington for having DONE something instead of spending his time in mere talk as to what he meant to do. The majority of our leaders have spent their lives in mere talk, and when they died the race was little better off than it was before. In the case of Mr. Washington, he has already built a monument in the shape of an institution having over a million dollars worth of property and has sent out thousands of educated men and women to help the race.

Mr. Washington is different again from most of the leaders of our race in that he remains here with us in the South. Many of the men whom we have elevated at the risk of our lives to positions of honor and trust have moved out of the South as soon as they have reaped all the honors that we could bestow upon them, and now reside in Northern states, or in the District of Columbia. Mr. Washington remains with us and bears whatever burdens we have to bear.

Another thing for which we feel sure some of the so-called leaders will not forgive Mr. Washington, was his ability in securing the single gift of $600,000 for his institution and for the benefit of the race. Many of us in the South felt that this would call down on his head the anathemas of scores of would-be leaders, & we have not been disappointed.

Some people in the Northern States are fond of referring to Mr. Washington as a "coward." It is to be noted, however, that some of the people who call him a "coward" are not brave enough themselves to remain in the South when danger seemed to threaten them. It is very easy for one to remain a thousand miles away and call someone a "coward" who is in the midst of the conditions from

347

which they fled. It is also easy and requires no courage for one living in Chicago, or Boston, for instance, to give advice to the colored people at the South. It is easy, in loud voice and emphatic tone to tell us what we should do in order to protect our "manhood." If these people want to prove that they have more "manhood" or more courage than we have, the thing for them to do is to come into the heart of the South and prove their courage. If they are not brave enough to come here and make their speeches and "demand" their rights in the way that they are advising us to do, their abstract talk and abstract advice mean very little to us. We want leaders who will come here and live among us and be brave at the same time. The colored people who live in the South are not the cowards that you think we are. Has there ever been a case in the history of the South when any one individual was compelled to stand for months severe condemnation and criticism because he accepted the invitation of the President of the United States to dine with him as was true in the case of Mr. Washington? If he was a "coward" then would have been the time to prove his cowardice, but instead of acting cowardly he stood up without flinching in the face of this wholesale denunciation and criticism.

While we have lost in many respects many of our political rights, we still have something in this regard that we can pin to. In Alabama we have two colored men holding high Presidential offices. In Illinois, I think you have none. In Georgia two colored men hold the most important political offices in that state. Our people are equally well represented in Florida and in Louisiana, to say nothing of other states. If we were the cowards that you think we are, we could not be so well represented even in the holding of public offices.

Another charge that is often brought against Mr. Washington by a few colored people is that he is friendly with the Southern white people. This is a very plausible charge, but we of the South have long since learned that we can retain our manhood and self-respect and still be friendly in many cases with the white people by whose side we live; this is the only sensible course, we feel, for any race to pursue. We can live in friendship with the white people and still demand our rights as citizens, and this we intend to do, as the cases we are carrying to the Supreme Court prove.

There has never been an important crisis in the history of the race in the South during the last fifteen years in which Mr. Washington has failed to put himself bravely and strongly on record against injustice. When the state constitutional convention in Louisiana was in session, he addressed that body, protesting in strong terms against the discrimination against the colored people which the new constitution would permit. He did the same thing when the attempt was made to pass a similar constitution in Georgia, and still later in the case of the Alabama State Constitutional Convention. On three different occasions within recent years he has spoken out in strong and brave words against the deplorable habit of lynching. It is true that Mr. Washington is not talking on these subjects all the time, and if he did his words would have no more weight than the words of many of his critics. When the proper occasion arises he always places himself on record.

It is perfectly well understood that it is due to Mr. Washington's influence and efforts more than anything else that the Lily White movement in this state which started so vigorously a few months ago and threatened to spread over the whole South, was completely checked and crushed out. If Mr. Washington had done no more than this to show his interest in the public life of the colored people the race would be justified in continually praising him. There has never been, since the war, such a crucial test of the race as that presented by the Lily White movement, and we who reside in the South and know the facts, the real facts, know to whom to give credit for crushing this movement. And all of us here understand perfectly that in connection with the rebuke to the Lily Whites, Mr. Washington made the statement which a few have tried to distort, that even the new state constitutions made by the Democrats seemed to put a premium upon intelligence, character and property, & that they, the Lily Whites, were trying to go further in their efforts to disfranchise the Negro than the Democrats were through their new state constitutional conventions.

Some of Mr. Washington's critics pretend to be greatly offended because of his insistence upon industrial education as well as literary and religious[1] training. The Tuskegee Institute is not the first nor the only industrial school. There are dozens of industrial schools in the South, mostly conducted, however, by white people. If industrial education is so harmful why do not some of these people who criticise Mr. Washington attack these industrial schools conducted by the white people instead of concentrating all their force upon one man; and why is it that so many of the other schools pretend to have industrial departments when it serves their purpose? The people cannot be deceived. We understand perfectly well that these attacks grow in a large measure out of a feeling of jealousy because of Mr. Washington's recognition and success, and at all hazards we at the South mean to stand by and support him, and we are glad to say that practically all the Northern people, except at a few centers here and there, are supporting him in the same way.

[J. W. Adams]

TMd BTW Papers ATT. Editorial changes in Emmett Scott's hand. An earlier draft, dated Oct. 26, 1903, in Con. 254, BTW Papers, DLC, also contains corrections in Scott's hand, indicating that Scott was the author of the letter. It was reprinted in the Indianapolis *Freeman*, Dec. 5, 1903, 1, 4.

1 "Literary" in the draft, but changed to "religious" in the published version.

From Emmett Jay Scott

Tuskegee, Alabama. Nov. 23, 1903

Dear Mr. Washington: I have no reason for suspecting that there is any extreme drinking of whiskey or other liquors on the school grounds. I have heard one or two rumors of indulgence of certain persons, but these rumors are not well defined nor can they be well proved so far as I know. If there was any such widespread indulgence more than likely I should have been able to discover it. Yours truly,

Emmett J. Scott

TLS BTW Folder ViHaI.

Timothy Thomas Fortune to Emmett Jay Scott

Red Bank, N.J., November 25, 1903

My dear Scott: Your letter of the 23rd instant[1] was received, and I am glad as usual to hear from you, but I am always distressed because you have so much to do and so little time and opportunity to take the small pleasures incident to life.

Why, no; I had no intention of publishing the statement about the rumpus in the school. I wanted the facts in case it became necessary to say anything about it, as the notice from the California paper I sent you was the first I had heard of it. Such things happen in schools all the time, and have no significance beyond those immediately concerned.

Yes; for the two weeks he was in the city I saw much of the Wizard and we considered some things and planned others, but what it will all come to is another matter.

I am very much amused at the seriousness with which you take the Boston Guardian libel matter. There is nothing in it whatever. I caught Peter Smith in Mr. Washington's room and began to bully and badger him about the Boston gang and insisted that they had libeled me and that I was going to go for them. He took it very solemnly. Wilford Smith went to Boston the same evening, and so the whole Boston push got the idea, as the Wizard would say, that I was going to do 'em. The Guardian came out current showing in a long wail why I should not prosecute them. And the rogues have begun to run all along the line, simply because we forced their bluff and made them show down. No; I have had no intention of prosecuting the gang at this time.

The Age reorganization matter is still indeterminate.

Some day I shall get down to Tuskegee again. Travel in the South is so disgusting that a gentleman never likes to undertake it.

I expect to go [to] Washington about December 1 and remain until the 15th. There will be much there to do, and what is done will determine many things for the future.

I am working very hard, but as my health is fair and bank account damned low, I suppose I should be happy. And the family are all well and join me in love to you and yours. Yours truly,

T. Thos. Fortune

TLS BTW Papers ATT.

1 In Con. 258, BTW Papers, DLC.

From Edward Elder Cooper

Washington, D.C., Nov. 25, 1903

Dear Mr. Washington: I presume you are very busy, too much so to be annoyed with a letter from me, and yet

> "A little nonsense now and then
> Is relished by the wisest men."

I am publishing in this week's Colored American a letter from my Memphis correspondent, a Mr. Turner.[1] He is a good agent, but is inclined to be cranky, is down on the mulattoes, although he has a mulatto wife, is a letter carrier by profession, and a fourth edition of Ida B. Wells. He is a clever fellow for he has obtained a weekly circulation of about five hundred copies each week for Memphis, for The Colored American. He is a great admirer of Prof. Du Bois and in an article which I have printed this week, I can see the fine Italian hand of Du Bois all the way through it. They made several thrusts at you and to have published the letter, as it was written would have kept it from going through the mails, under the rule of *obscene literature.*

I have cut all of the poison out of the article, and will send you an extra copy tomorrow night. The point I want to make is that a great many people are over rating Du Bois. He is a small fellow, and will do a little trick. He is soon to start a paper from Atlanta to be known as "The Black American." In this he hopes to array the full blooded Negroes, as he terms them against the mulattoes. It will please a certain class of whites and a certain class of Negroes no doubt; but like the Irish agitators in Ireland they could not write down just what they wanted, if they were given paper and pen and ink. I will send you the manuscript if you would like to see it. It is typewritten and you will see what I have cut out. The part that is cut out is what will interest you. I hope you are getting along alright, and if I had thought of it, I would have written you to send Mrs. Cooper a big fat Thanksgiving turkey. It is too late now, so don't bother yourself. Did you get the paper I sent you last week? With best wishes, I am, Yours sincerely,

E E Cooper

TLS   Con. 550   BTW Papers   DLC.

1 William M. Turner, a Memphis postal employee writing under the pseudonym Brom Bones, criticized teaching black children that white skin and straight hair were the natural characteristics of humans. He pleaded for race pride and urged blacks to teach their children their black heritage proudly. "We must respect ourselves before expecting others to respect us," he wrote. "I have a daughter, and loving her as I do, I would rather see her burnt to ashes than to see her following the pathway of a large number of half breed women, who are too white to be Negroes and not white enough to be white." (Washington *Colored American*, Nov. 28, 1903, 1–3.)

To Samuel Edward Courtney

Hotel Manhattan   New York City   November 27th, 1903

Dear Dr. Courtney: I advise that you be very judicious in your dealings with Forbes, as it is quite possible that he is playing the part of a possum. Very truly,

[Booker T. Washington]

TLc   Con. 253   BTW Papers   DLC.

From John Andrew Kenney

Tuskegee, Ala. Nov 27–03

My Dear Mr. Washington. Your letter of recent date was duly received, and was given serious consideration. I have deferred answering in my effort to arrive at a definite conclusion. Up to present I am unable to express a definite opinion as to whether the cases of typhoid which we have had are due directly to conditions here present.

From June 6th to present date we have had thirteen cases of typhoid fever including the four cases which are now in the ward. Some of these cases have been mild, others quite severe. Previous to June 6th there had been only one case, which was in last December making fourteen cases in twelve months. Of this number we lost four. A pretty high mortality. One of the mildest cases we have lost, and one of the severest, showing how treacherous is this disease.

Conversation with Dr. Johnston shows that he has had fifteen cases or more during late summer and early fall. None of his cases were in the school community. They were in the town and county. So the disease is not located among us. Nor is there an epidemic. The cases are what we term sporadic, one here and there.

Now, as to the cause — typhoid fever is produced by a specific germ, and it is conceded by all authorities that this germ must be present to produce the disease. The most usual source of infection is the drinking water. I have tried in a general way to locate the cause. I examined the wells, and suggested that they be cleaned. Which was done and which in fact has been done periodically. I questioned those patients infected as to the source of their water supply. They all drank from various sources. Some of them had been among us only a short while, giving the suspicion that they came among us bearing the germs in their intestines and they matured during their short stay here. Others have been with us so long a time as to leave little doubt that they were infected here. This is true of the majority. Some state positively that they have not been off the grounds in several months.

Now, my previous training and present apparatus will not permit me to locate the special germ, nor does my time permit me to search for it intelligently, but we have sufficient reason to question our water supply. While I have no reason to express a positive opinion that some special well or cistern here is infected, I do believe firmly that some of our water does help prepare the soil in our bodies for the reception of these germs. The taste and smell are often questionable, and examination shows entirely too much organic matter present.

I am sure Prof. Carver will pardon my use of his name in saying that on a miscroscopical examination he found an over-abundance of little germs which act as predisposing or exciting causes to intestinal disorders. His specimen, was I think, taken from the tank. Of course this does not show that typhoid fever is present. The water might be so full of germs as to solidify it, without producing typhoid, but it does show that the water is below the standard in purity.

We have too much surface drainage and the imperfect system of earth closets, and open wells. We can never hope to have an unquestioned water supply till these evils are remedied. An example: All the sewage and waste water from Rockefeller Hall is turned free in the woods to find its way by a sluggish lazy route into a little ditch within a few feet of the school's reservoir. This drainage thoroughly impregnates the soil before it enters the ditch which usually contains no water where it must seep away in the soil or evaporate. The odor in the woods on passing tells its tale. 'Tis dangerous to have human dejections emptied any where near a well or water supply as is true in this case.

I shall continue to study these conditions and notify you promptly of any out break or considerable increase.

I may have to ask that an experienced chemist and bacteriologist be supplied with samples of our water for thorough investigation. Yours with great respect.

Jno. A. Kenney

ALS Con. 263 BTW Papers DLC.

Emmett Jay Scott to Richard W. Thompson

[Tuskegee, Ala.] Dec. 1, 1903

Dear Thompson: The Wizard is just home today and I have taken up your matter at once. If you will ratify the suggestion, I can arrange at once to have $12 per month sent you regularly by the Treasurer. Please let me know how this strikes you. This is all that the Wizard feels that he can afford to appropriate for this purpose at this time. Yours truly,

[Emmett J. Scott]

TLc BTW Papers ATT.

To William Henry Lewis

[Tuskegee, Ala.] Dec. 3, 1903

My dear Mr. Lewis: I am very grateful to you indeed for seeing Mr. Barnett[1] and getting me released from the Cambridge engagement. It is a great relief I assure you.

355

I had already taken up the matter of your sister, and Mr. Bruce has written her regarding the possibility of her being able to do primary work. If she can do it I think we can give her a position.

The only thing in the way of inviting Forbes is this: Du Bois is very sensitive on the question as to who shall be invited, in fact I very much fear he is trying to find an excuse to absent himself, and I have the feeling rather strongly that if Forbes is invited since he has made a break with Trotter that Du Bois will object, for he does not object to saying that we are trying to pack the conference with people who are thinking in a certain direction. I shall talk this phase of the question over with you when I see you. Yours truly,

[Booker T. Washington]

TLc   Con. 265   BTW Papers   DLC.

¹ I. D. Barnett.

To Timothy Thomas Fortune

[Tuskegee, Ala.] December 3, 1903

My dear Mr. Fortune: I have received your kind letter regarding the progress you are making in reference to the Washington meeting and am very glad to hear what you are doing. There is one point, however, I want to press with a good deal of emphasis, and that is that you make no effort beyond securing the few men who are absolutely necessary for its control. Of course if Hayes can get the other people there in response to his own efforts, it will be your plan to work in cooperation with him and with them, but you ought not to take the burden of securing men who could not come but for your efforts, aside from those we have decided upon.

I shall be passing through Washington next Sunday night. Yours truly,

[Booker T. Washington]

TLc   BTW Papers   ATT.

To William Henry Baldwin, Jr.

[Tuskegee, Ala.] December 3, 1903

Dear Mr. Baldwin: I write you regarding the sleeping car business. I am very glad to have seen your last letter. I find it is quite necessary to go ahead in the matter and have Mr. Cravath[1] give us his opinion upon the subject.

I have learned of three different cases lately where the Pullman car people have either refused or avoided selling sleeping car accommodations from Cincinnati to colored people. In one case a woman bought or attempted to buy, a sleeping car ticket in Cincinnati to some point in Tennessee, and it seems that the agent didn't know she was colored until he had sold the ticket and he saw her talking with some colored people and therefore supposed she was colored; pretending that there was some mistake regarding the ticket, he secured it from her and returned the money. In another case a colored minister bought a ticket and got upon the car and the conductor tried to get him to go out, but knowing his rights he refused, and the result was that they let him ride from Cincinnati to Atlanta, Ga., in the drawing room at single berth rates. Dr. Mason, the Secretary of the Freedmen's Aid Society in Cincinnati, a very intelligent and level-headed colored man, says that one of the Pullman car ticket agents in Cincinnati has told him that he has received instructions not to sell tickets to colored people. Yours truly,

[Booker T. Washington]

TLc Con. 792 BTW Papers DLC.

[1] Paul Drennan Cravath, born in Berlin Heights, Ohio, in 1861, was the son of Erastus Milo Cravath, president of Fisk University. A leading New York lawyer, Paul Cravath was a trustee of Fisk, and he and BTW later worked together closely in a fund-raising campaign for Fisk. In 1911 he was involved in behind-the-scenes legal negotiations of the trial of Henry A. Ulrich for assaulting BTW in New York.

Richard W. Thompson to Emmett Jay Scott

Jeffersonville, Ind., Dec. 4, 1903

Personal.

Dear Scott: The terms suggested are accepted, with thanks for kindly interest manifested by you in the matter. To avoid any possible hitch, let me ask that you tell me specifically just what you want done, line of thought most helpful to the cause, and methods most likely to produce satisfactory results. Say it now, and it will be all over! I can handle five papers for anything in the Wizard's interest — Kentucky Standard[,] Freeman, Advocate, Citizen and Colored American. I can't hear from Moody, of Chicago Monitor, any more. Don't think he cares for a letter, but will accept any note from time to time. It might be well to send me papers of various kinds, when containing information of value. You might also state at what point or date you wish month to begin. I shall endeavor to give you a service that will justify the outlay mentioned. All matters, of course, are in the strictest confidence. I do not think any one regards me as being in the employ of the school as my policy for eight years has not undergone the slightest change with reference to Mr. Washington and his work.

I am sending you under another cover a copy of the Jeffersonville Daily Star (White) containing a pretty fair review of my speech at Wesley Chapel, G. W. Langford's church. Mr. Washington could not have failed to have been inspired by the cordiality with which Tuskegee's story was received, had he been present. Did you find a litho for Langford. He saw mine at my house and wanted one. A business league has been organized here, and delegates will be sent to Ind'p'l's. Public meeting on 14th. If you are sending Mr. Washington's latest pamphlet "Successful Training, etc." from "World's Work," I should be glad to have one.

I assume there is nothing in the rumor that Fortune intends to sue Trotter for libel. The Washington Record, under Cromwell's influence, is a copperhead sheet. Can't Manly control the policy of his paper. It has no good blood for Tuskegee. Hershaw writes me of Cromwell and his anti-Washington sly digs. H. thinks the literaries will discuss B. T. W. on the same old lines. Shows no signs of conversion himself. Toomey is at Second Baptist now. He is my friend,

and can be trusted to carry out any plan that might be deemed helpful. Hershaw says Mr. W. spoke at a disadvantage before the Sociological to-do, attributing his "defensive" attitude and lack of "usual
confidence" and "vigor of statement" to "unsympathetic environment." Thinks Mr W's acquiescence in / if not actually inspiring /
the conviction and jailing of Trotter a tactical blunder. I give you
this as Hershaw represents the enlightened officiousness of the anti-
crowd and you can get a further idea of their line of talk. Things
are all right over this way. Yours,

R. W. Thompson

ALS BTW Papers ATT.

To Francis James Grimké

[Tuskegee, Ala.] December 5th, 1903

Dear Dr. Grimke: I have your letter of recent date. I very much
hope that you, yourself, will attend the conference as I do not think
any one taking your place can be of the service that you would.

In regard to your brother; there are one or two considerations
which I wish to call to your attention. First; you will note that he
resides in Boston, and we have already invited two persons from
that city; this, it seems to me, would give Boston an undue representation. Second; in politics I understand that he is a Democrat,
and you will note that we have already invited one prominent
Democrat[1] from the West. Of course we have had to keep in mind
two things; first, not to make the conference too expensive, second,
not to have it too large to be so unwieldy that it will be a mere
forum of discussion rather than a quiet[,] confidential, serious,
heart to heart talk.

I will take up with Dr. Du Bois the name of the other persons
that you suggest. All of them are good men and I wish there might
be no hesitation in inviting them. Yours very truly,

[Booker T. Washington]

TLc BTW Papers ATT.

[1] Fredrick L. McGhee.

From Horace Bumstead

Roxbury, Mass., December 5, 1903

Personal.

My dear Dr. Washington: I am directed by the Executive Committee of our Trustees to transmit to you the enclosed copy of a minute which they have unanimously adopted in regard to a letter written by our Professor Towns and recently printed in the Guardian newspaper.[1]

I hardly need tell you that this is one of the most painful incidents that we have ever had to deal with. Our effort has been not only to set the University right, but to mend the matter with as little injury as possible to all the interests concerned. For this reason, while you are at liberty to make such use of this minute as you deem wise, we think you will agree with us that nothing would be gained, and that further unnecessary injury might be wrought, from its publication in the newspapers.

I feel moved to add a word personally in regard to Mr. Towns, whom I have known well for some eighteen years, and whom I think you also know to some extent. What I wish to say is that this letter is entirely out of character for the man and by no means represents his dominant spirit and temper. On the contrary, he is one of the most lovable of men, kindly and courteous in spirit and faithful and conscientious in the discharge of duty. In view of this, his recent letter is a matter of great amazement and sorrow to me personally. But I cannot resist the conviction that he wrote it under the influence of unusually strong feeling, and that he is sincere in his acknowledgment of error and expression of regret. Yours very sincerely,

Horace Bumstead

TLS BTW Papers ATT.

[1] The minutes recorded the "great astonishment and profound regret" of the Atlanta University trustees that the Towns letter was published. The trustees considered the references to BTW "intemperate and discourteous" and denied that the letter represented the "teaching or spirit of the University." (BTW Papers, ATT.)

To Timothy Thomas Fortune

[Crawford House, Boston] December 8th, 1903

PERSONAL.

Dear Mr. Fortune: Since seeing you in Washington I have thought considerably about a part of our conversation, and am now convinced of one or two things.

In the first place, I do not think it wise for me to give my personal consent to anything which would seem to recognize Trotter in any capacity whatsoever, as temporary chairman, or otherwise. In the first place, he would work the press industriously and spread the news throughout the country of such an election, which would endorse his leadership in breaking up the Boston meeting, and his condemnation of myself. Secondly, such an election would give him an opportunity to make a speech, in which he would condemn me in his usual manner, and which would also get into the press. Thirdly, any set of men or any convention which would elect a man like Trotter to the position of temporary chairman could have no permanent influence in condemning me; in fact, it would help me to be condemned by a set of men who would so far forget themselves as to elect Trotter temporary chairman or anything else.

These matters I submit for your earnest consideration. I shall be here at the Crawford House Tuesday and Wednesday, and shall be in New York at the Manhattan on Thursday the tenth, and perhaps a few days longer. Yours very sincerely,

[Booker T. Washington]

TLc BTW Papers ATT.

To Timothy Thomas Fortune

Crawford House   Boston, Mass. December 9th, 1903

PERSONAL.

Dear Mr. Fortune: I have just received your telegram, and am sorry that you cannot come to New York tomorrow. The gist of what I wished to say to you is this, and I beg that you will think about it seriously.

First, in the matter of Trotter, I have already expressed my opinion.

Second, with my present information, I think that it would be a mistake for you not to stand by Hayes, and keep in close touch with him, according to the promise made in his presence. It would hurt very much if an opportunity should be given Hayes to say that you went back on him. The influence of a broken, or seemingly broken, promise would last for many months; but the influence of a seeming defeat would be temporary. In my opinion, it pays to let our friends and our enemies know that promises are to be kept sacred, whether keeping them places one on the winning or losing side.

Third, since you are President of the Afro-American Council I believe that it would be a mistake for you to accept the office of permanent chairman, or any other office in the Suffrage League, if you have to make the least effort to secure such office through your friends. If the office came through unanimous choice, that would be another matter; but for you to make an effort to secure such office would say plainly to the world that you are trying to control not only the Afro-American Council, but also the Suffrage League, for your own personal interests. My opinion is, that you would be a much bigger man, and a more potent factor if you would act throughout the entire meeting as a peace-maker, and a disinterested party, rather than as an aspirant for office. In other words, I think that you would do wisely to carry out our original program, agreed upon when Hayes was present, to help make the Suffrage meeting a success, rather than try to monopolize anything. By following the plan I am suggesting I believe that you will come out with flying colors, and with the good-will and confidence of everyone. In a word, I believe that you can accomplish your wishes more satisfactorily by placing your friends in office, than by accepting office yourself. I think it would be wise for you to act as a disinterested party throughout the entire meeting, ~~and to be in Washington ostensibly to look after your Philippine report, and to attend the Suffrage meeting.~~

I beg that you will consider these matters very seriously. I shall probably be in New York both Friday and Saturday. Very truly yours,

[Booker T. Washington]

TLc BTW Papers ATT.

To William Henry Baldwin, Jr.

Crawford House   Boston, Mass. December 9th, 1903

Dear Mr. Baldwin: I was very much gratified as I came up on the train this week to note that the Southern people on the train, including several Congressmen from Georgia, Alabama, and Mississippi, endorsed almost without exception, the action of Trinity College in refusing to accept the resignation of Prof. Bassett. One Atlanta man went so far as to say that the day of ostracism in the South on the account of freedom of speech is past.

I hope to see you in New York. Very truly yours,

[Booker T. Washington]

TLc   Con. 792   BTW Papers   DLC.

From Francis James Grimké

Washington D.C. Dec. 9th, 1903

Dear Mr. Washington: Your last letter was duly received. I write to say (1) that my brother is not a democrat and never has been. He is what is known as a Mugwump or Independent in politics. (2) that in case I attend the conference in January, I will defray my own expenses. Yours truly

Francis J. Grimké

ALS   BTW Papers   ATT.

From Whitefield McKinlay

Washington, D.C. 12/9/03

Confidential.

Dr Mr. Washington: Under no circumstances give one cent to defray expenses of the Suffrage Convention which will convene here next week. Nor should your name be allowed to be used in connection with it, as I am afraid it will result in a scandal. There are already rumors afloat, which are unpleasant to hear. I telegraphed you at Tuskegee hoping to see you when passing through. Very truly

W McKinlay

ALS BTW Papers ATT.

From Emmett Jay Scott

Tuskegee, Alabama. December 10, 1903

Dear Mr. Washington: I have been to Atlanta this week to confer with Dr. Bowen and the Nichols representatives with reference to the magazine. We seem to have reached an amicable understanding all along the line, and this is very pleasant and satisfactory to say, I assure you. Dr. Bowen I find particularly satisfactory. He more than ever before, is in accord with Tuskegee and its work, and was particularly anxious that you [be] represented in the first number, also to have your photograph in this first number, saying that a man so prominent should have his photograph accompany his article although it is not the purpose to do this with all the articles that appear. I am to edit one of your articles which has already appeared for the first number. Our understanding seems to be thorough and complete in every particular, and I believe that the Nichols people really mean business. The present purpose is to get the magazine out by January 1st. I have made up a lot of advertising matter and am otherwise working with them to their satisfaction.

Going up I was in a wreck, but aside from a shock sustained no injuries. The three Pullman cars and dining car were entirely wrecked. Yours very truly,

Emmett J. Scott

TLS   Con. 274   BTW Papers   DLC.

To Whitefield McKinlay

Hotel Manhattan. New York City. December 11th, 1903

PRIVATE AND CONFIDENTIAL.

Dear Mr. McKinlay: I have received your letter, but hardly know what it means. I have acted wholly upon your suggestions in this matter, and upon nothing else. I arranged a conference between Fortune and Hayes, and they agreed in my presence to work in harmony with each other, and try to have a successful, friendly meeting, instead of a fight between the Council and the Suffrage people. It is understood that Fortune is to act in cooperation with Hayes to make the meeting a success, and to recognize that Hayes and his friends have the right of way.

I have not spent, and do not intend to spend, one cent toward paying the expenses of delegates to any meeting. All kinds of propositions, looking toward a bargain of some sort, are constantly made to me, but I have steadfastly refused to consider them, and shall continue this course in the future. I am often surprised to learn about the tremendous amount of money I possess. If I were spending one-tenth as much money as I am often given the credit of spending, I should have to be a millionaire several times over.

Hoping to see you soon, I am, Very truly yours,

[Booker T. Washington]

TLc   BTW Papers   ATT.

From James Carroll Napier

Nashville, Tenn., Dec. 11th. 1903

My dear Mr. Washington: My acquaintance is so limited in New York that I have taken advantage of your suggestion of the 5th. instant and written Mr. Anderson to secure me a suitable place to stop during the conference. I thank you for your suggestion.

I would be glad to have you give me an outline of the programme, the matters to be discussed at the meetings and the method of procedure.

I think that the time has come when we should take a bold stand in favor of law and order and insist on their rigid execution as applied to the Negro whether in his favor or against him. The method of ignoring all laws and parts of laws, from the provisions of the Constitution of the United States to the very smallest town ordinance which tend to the elevation of the Negro, ought and should be abandoned. The same may be truthfully said of every custom and usage that tends to the recognition of his respectability and manhood. There is a disposition to change all these and make them to operate against him. Can we not do or say something to convince the people of the Country that law is *law* and that the provisions and statutes, which appertain to the elevation of the Negro, are just as sacred and as much entitled to strict observance as any other? I am mindful of the fact that these are very delicate matters with which to deal and that while we fight from the front we must be watchful lest an attack be raised from the rear. We must look to your wisdom and leadership to guide us over these places.

A most respectable colored citizen applied at the ticket office of the N. C. and St. L. Ry. in this City a few days ago for a berth in a Pullman Sleeper. He was flatly refused and was told by the agent that he had orders to sell no berths to colored people. It strikes me that this is an excellent case for the attorneys who have been retained by Mr. Bliss[1] to look after such matters. I shall tell you more of it when we meet and I trust that the attorneys may see fit to take it up.

Hoping that the conference may be well attended and that its deliberations may result in great good for the cause of humanity and the advancement of the Negro's interests throughout the Country, I am, Very truly yours,

J. C. Napier

1 Possibly Cornelius Newton Bliss.

TLS   Con. 269   BTW Papers   DLC.

From George F. Richings

Chicago Ill   Dec 12th 1903

Dear Mr Washington   I am sending you under another cover some Chicago papers with marked articles. I am very much pleased with the result of this last weeks work. I am getting up quite an interest among the people at large. I am finding out in a quiet way who are for you and who are not, among the pastors. Rev Thomas at whos[e] church I was Wednesday and Thursday nights, I found was not where I had hoped to find him regarding you, but he said publicly when I had finished that he was weak on you but he would not have missed the splendid way in which I illustrated your school, for he sait [said] it would show his people what a wonderful work a colored man had done, and of all places said he, where we need stir[r]ing up as to what our great men have done is right here in Chicago. One man at Quinn Chapel came up and said "that the pictures from Tuskegee was worth a dollar, and he says I know now that Ed Morris, and John Jones, and a lot of the would be politicians have been lying on Mr Washington." I think when I have finished the Chicago churches, you had better let me go for a week to Springfield Ill, for Mr Morris, and Jones I am told held a big mass meeting out there against you and the Institution. Tomorrow is our mens meeting at Quinn Chapel. We have given away 1000 tickets. I shall make Tuskegee a big part of that lecture. I sent Mr Logan as he requested bills and statement for work done up to now. I am glad to tell you that I am having more people at my lectures than I hoped for when I came, but I am giving the churches a good chance to make something out of the lectures, in order that they work harder to get out larger numbers. I am   Yours Very Truly

G. F. Richings

ALS   Con. 273   BTW Papers   DLC.

From Robert Heberton Terrell

Washington, D.C. December 13, 1903

My dear Mr. Washington, Your telegram received. We were in conference on the Suffrage Convention matter when it came. Gov. Pinchback McKinlay, Dancy and I have been working hard for a week or more to ward off anything like a foolish or indiscreet expression from it. I say frankly that we are at sea as to what it will do on account of the composition of the body. A gentleman who is a delegate called to see me tonight and told us all that happened in the private meeting held by the Committee yesterday. Chase denounced Corrothers and Corrothers denounced Chase. Other things of similar character happened. Our friends will insist on an endorsement of the President and no mention whatever of your name, one way or the other. I don't know whether they will control matters or not. There are so many grafters and boodlers in the Convention that a man cannot tell what will happen. One of my friends has prepared the address. He is not a member of the Convention. It may be changed in some particulars. Nearly all the preachers here are delegates. I shall watch matters very closely. I am urging Hayes for President. He seems to be the best man for us. The leading spirits of the meeting are begging some one to purchase them. I wouldn't give them a nickel.

I am having the pension matter looked after. Yours truly,

R. H. Terrell

ALS   BTW Papers   ATT.

To William Edward Burghardt Du Bois

Hotel Manhattan, New York City. December 14th, 1903

Dear Dr. Du Bois: Enclosed I am sending you a copy of the opinion of Mr. Cravath upon the Pullman Car question.[1] Another step in this direction will soon be taken. I wish that you would be kind enough to let all the Atlanta members of the Committee see the opinion. I have sent a copy direct to Rev. Proctor. Very truly yours,

[Booker T. Washington]

TLc   Con. 256   BTW Papers   DLC.

[1] BTW and William H. Baldwin, Jr., sought legal advice from Paul D. Cravath of New York. Cravath replied that the law clearly provided for separate but equal accommodations. In the absence of separate coaches, Cravath thought that blacks should be admitted to the white coaches, and if any state statute was passed excluding blacks from sleeping cars it would be unconstitutional. (Dec. 9, 1903, Con. 867, BTW Papers, DLC.)

From Robert Heberton Terrell

Washington, D.C. December 14, 1903

Dear Dr. Washington, The Suffrage Convention opened today. The session had hardly begun before a row was precipitated and a split became imminent. I am informed that the spirit of the meeting seems to be in favor of Hayes for its permanent Chairman. I expect nothing whatever in the nature of good to come out of the meeting. The Convention has been made possible through the influence of Chase and Trotter, and what can such spirits accomplish that will be helpful to us?

I enclose a clipping from the Evening Times. Yours truly,

R H Terrell

ALS   BTW Papers   ATT.

To Horace Bumstead

Crawford House, Boston, Mass. December 15th, 1903

Dear President Bumstead: Please pardon me for my tardy reply to your letter of December fifth. I have been on the road to such an extent that I have hardly had time before now to answer.

I am grateful to the Executive Committee for the action it has taken, and see no reason why the matter bearing upon Prof. Town's letter should go any farther. I hope that all parties will now consider the matter closed. Very truly yours,

[Booker T. Washington]

TLc BTW Papers ATT.

Emmett Jay Scott to Jesse Max Barber

[Tuskegee, Ala.] December 16, 1903

Dear Mr. Barber: I am sorry the article was so late in reaching you. I thought that I was sending it in plenty of time.

As you say, I did not understand your relations with the Nichols people, and I am glad all the more for that reason that I made the trip to Atlanta for the conference which we had. You are entirely wrong, however, in suggesting that I have any idea that you were a "cheap secretary or proof reader," first of all because a man is a secretary does not give the idea that he is a cheap man. You will see that I have in mind a very delicate personal reference; I consider my place as Mr. Washington's secretary as honorable as any place held by any black man in the country; the emolument that goes with it is as liberal as that received by black men in this country. I say this to you simply and solely because of the intimation which your letter carries. Mr. Hopkins had spoken so highly of you to me that I knew you must be a man of strong parts or you would not be associated as you are in the publication of this magazine.

It was my purpose when I should make up the review, to send it to all of the newspapers in the country published by colored men.

If this is not agreeable I shall be glad to have you advise me to that effect.

With sincere good wishes, I am, Yours very truly,

[Emmett J. Scott]

TLc   Con. 249   BTW Papers   DLC.

From Andrew M. Bush, Frederic S. Monroe,[1] and Edwin B. Jourdain

New Bedford, Mass. December 17, 1903

Dear Sir: The frequency with which the advertisement of your lecture on "The Elevation of the Negro in the Black Belt of the South" has appeared during the past week ensures you a large audience, and we take the opportunity to ask you to give to that audience, the race and country, your reasons for some of the apparent inconsistencies of your attitude anent the civil and political rights of the colored American.

We appreciate most fully your service to the race in constructing the large and costly plant at Tuskegee, but are most actively and earnestly opposed to some of your methods of winning support. And we want to put the question fairly: do you believe it necessary for the support and maintenance of Tuskegee that you should bow subservient to unreasoning and senseless southern prejudice and opposition to the civil and political rights of black Americans?

Do you believe it serves to elevate the Negro, when you not only fail to speak out in condemnation of such unjust and humiliating proscriptions as "grandfather" clause suffrage provisions, and "jim crow" car laws, but actually seek to find something good to say about them?

Do you believe the real or fancied interests of Tuskegee and its 1500 (or, even if it were 15,000) students, justified your absolute refusal to utter one single word of condemnation on the occasion of several particularly horrible and atrocious outrages in the south?

Do you know that Collier's Weekly (with a circulation all over this country and in England) on August 29, 1903, editorially said:

371

"Miss Anna Dorsey gives truest pictures of Negro life the platform affords, on high authority of Booker T. Washington," and proceeds to say that Miss Dorsey pictures to them a people ". . . gently and happily barbaric . . . with sufficient food, drink and warmth the Negro is happy, come what may. . . . The women are without chastity . . . as long as black women are of such easy virtue, their sons can hardly be checked in their most unmanageable crime," and continued, "Her view of essential Negro character becomes doubly important when it is accepted as truth by the man whose opinion weighs most."

Have you sought either through Collier's Weekly itself, or from the public platform to contradict or deny the endorsement attributed to you, of such a wholesale, damnable, blackening slander against the women of our race?

Do you not believe that a man whose opinions are accepted as authoritative on race matters owes a higher duty to the 10,000,000 people of his race, than any he may owe the 1000 or 10000 students in one school or a dozen schools?

Don't you know that Secretary of the Navy William H. Moody[2] (one of the staunchest friends of the Negro, and of law and order, in public life today) has said that he was greatly handicapped in his efforts to investigate and check lawless violence against the Negro, because of your failure to speak out in protest against such outrages; members of Congress saying they did not see why they should be concerned, if you were not?

Do you consider the American Negro more, or less than a man, when you say that he has no occasion to find fault with treatment and conditions which no other race in our great composite citizenship would accept without the most strenuous and ceaseless protest and opposition?

Do you accept that most specious and pernicious doctrine — that the dollar makes the man — when you advise the Negro not to oppose those who are seeking to strip him of every vestige of civic manhood, but to devote his energies to acquiring property and wealth?

Don't you know that every institution of learning of eminence in the country today is seeking to instill into its youth the idea that man is inestimably superior to mere material progress; superior to money; that the development and elevation of man in mind and body is the supreme work for society?

Do you believe you can cure the Negro of his petty vices and weaknesses by comically portraying these weaknesses for the amusement of white audiences? Have you forgotten that though the Negro may steal chickens, the white American stole human beings? That though there may be black brutes who despoil white women, that there were, and still are white brutes who despoil black women, and that both are equally monsters, equally deserving the extremity of legal vengeance?

Undeniably a large portion of white Americans like to hear anything derogatory of the Negro; it eases their conscience for the wrong they have done him. Depreciation of the Negro was a part of the slave holders stock in trade; and it is the principal means relied on by those who seek today to force the race into a position of civil and political serfdom; by it they hope to alienate public sympathy and silence opposition. But do you think in coming years posterity will speak kindly of the man or men, who have bartered their heritage for a mess of pottage, and bequeathed to them a battle this generation should have fought, with an enemy who will be entrenched by years of uncontested adverse holding?

According to the figures submitted by Tuskegee, Hampton, Claflin, Atlanta and numerous other schools to the Seventh Atlanta Conference in 1902, there are about 10000 children in Negro Industrial Schools in the south, and of this number Tuskegee had 1180. Out of 21 schools reporting over 2000 students learning trades, i.e. actually enrolled in classes in carpentry, brick laying, plastering, painting, iron and sheet metal working, forging and machine shop work, Tuskegee ranked third with 161 students so enrolled, Claflin being first with 345 pupils enrolled. Tuskegee reported about 150 trade graduates, of whom 32 per cent worked at trades and 19 per cent taught trades. Hampton reported 217 trade graduates, of whom 51.5 per cent worked at trades, and 12 per cent taught. Claflin reported 98 trade graduates, of whom about 47 per cent worked at trades and about 14 per cent taught. By the same report it appeared to cost as much to run Tuskegee a year as it did to conduct the whole southern work of the Freedmen's Aid and Southern Educational Society with their 43 schools, 413 instructors, and 10146 pupils.

If Hampton and Claflin could exist and make as good and a better showing than Tuskegee, in trade school graduates, and if the other schools could exist with their 10000 pupils and 2000 actual trade students, without giving a quasi endorsement to unfair suffrage laws and jim crow cars, why is it necessary for Tuskegee to furnish aid and comfort to the enemy in order to graduate 150 trades students?

Do you believe that private philanthropy can supply even half of the unschooled children of the south with schools?

After more than twenty years of existence and growth, Tuskegee the most liberally supported school for Negroes in the country can only accommodate about 1500 students, and has to turn away about 1000 would be students. Does not this fact demonstrate the utter incompetency of private philanthropy as an adequate means of providing schools?

The twelfth national census in 1900 showed a school population of over 3,000,000 Negroes in the south. Of this number only about 30 per cent (less than one third) were in school, and most of them received only from one to three months schooling. In your own state of Alabama, only about 22.8 per cent were in school in 1900.

Is it not evident that national aid to southern education is absolutely necessary if adequate school facilities are to be offered the children of school age, and that a compulsory attendance law is necessary to secure proper results? Is it not the government's duty to give the Negro youth today that opportunity for knowledge and self development which she helped rob him of? This is what we are striving for.

In behalf of the Union League

Andrew M. Bush
Frederic S. Monroe
Edwin B. Jourdain

TLS   Con. 261   BTW Papers   DLC.

[1] Frederic S. Monroe was secretary of the Union League of New Bedford, Mass.

[2] William Henry Moody (1853–1917), a congressman from Massachusetts (1895–1902), was Secretary of the Navy (1902–4), Attorney General (1904–6), and Associate Justice of the U.S. Supreme Court (1906–10).

From Pinckney Benton Stewart Pinchback

Washington, D.C., December 17, 1903

My Dear Doctor: I have just been consulting with our friend Mack[1] in regard to the subject matter of your telegram to him. I do not see the necessity of making any explanation to the President in regard to the so-called Suffrage Convention recently held here. While there were some decent men in it, it turned out to be just what I predicted it would in my letter to you. Its proceedings from start to finish were disorderly and undignified, and it finally went to pieces because certain disreputable elements could not control its proceedings. Very luckily for the race at large the press of this city dealt leniently with it and saved us from what came near being a national disgrace. I am not in favor of a delegation visiting the President for another reason, viz: he has been deluged with negro delegations in the past few weeks and I think he is entitled to a little rest. If, however, you have anything specific that you wish to attend to send us an outline of it and we will attend to it at once. Yours very truly,

Pinchback

(DICTATED)

TLS   BTW Papers   ATT.

1 Whitefield McKinlay.

To Timothy Thomas Fortune

Crawford House, Boston, Mass. December 18th, 1903

PERSONAL.

Dear Mr. Fortune: Please say nothing else in the Age about the suit against the Guardian for libel. If you do, you will seriously embarrass Lawyer Smith, and place him in an awkward position. I will explain when I see you, but hope that you will let the subject rest until then. Mr. Smith seems able to bring matters to a head soon in a quiet way. Very truly yours,

[Booker T. Washington]

TLc BTW Papers ATT.

Emmett Jay Scott to Wilford H. Smith

[Tuskegee, Ala.] December 19, 1903

My dear Mr. Smith: I was in Montgomery yesterday and learned something which I thought I would pass on to you. An attorney who was implicated, told Mr. Adams yesterday of the conspiracy to do you harm when you appeared in court in the John [Dan] Rogers case sometime ago. It was the plan, he said, for one attorney to grab you, another to search you, and another to strike you with a chair, but that some one whispered it to Judge Thomas[1] and he arose in court, suspending proceedings at once to say that any attempt to offer you a discourtesy would be followed by confinement in jail for five days. You may remember some such instance; if you do, that was the reason for the judge's statement. I understand that there is very great feeling against Judge Thomas because of his stand in the matter.

I am going to make a desperate effort to be in Washington when you appear before the Supreme Court January 4th. If possible I wish to reach there the night of January 3d so as to be present at the argument. Will you let me know what time in the day on the 4th you will most likely speak.

Can you have Miss McAdoo send me some data respecting yourself and any information I could use in a special article for the New York Evening Post to appear about the time of your appearance before the Supreme Court. Such an article I am quite sure, will do good. It ought to do good any way. Yours truly,

[Emmett J. Scott]

TLc BTW Papers ATT.

1 William Holcombe Thomas (b. 1867) practiced law in Montgomery from 1892 until he was elected judge of the city court in 1901. Thomas secretly aided BTW in pushing the Alonzo Bailey case to the U.S. Supreme Court. (Daniel, *Shadow of Slavery*, 68–71.) In 1910 Thomas returned to private law practice until 1915, when he was appointed associate justice of the Alabama Supreme Court. He was the author of several books and articles on law, history, and religion.

To Emmett Jay Scott

[Tuskegee, Ala.] December 26th, 1903

Dear Mr. Scott: In connection with the reorganization of the New York Age, I hope you will keep in mind the following points.

1. The name of the paper should indicate the interests of the paper, as, for example, The Black American and New York Age.

2. It should definitely be understood that the policy of the paper is to be distinctly constructive, and that it should not be the medium of whining, complaint, and condemnation.

3. There should be a weekly summary of news bearing upon the interests and affairs of the colored people, but no summary of general news, which has already been secured in better form in the white press, will be needed. Very truly,

B. T. W.

TLI   Con. 550   BTW Papers   DLC.

To John Henry Washington

[Tuskegee, Ala.] Dec. 26, 1903

Mr. J. H. Washington: The following matter I wish you to give immediate attention to today. The exposure to girls and lady teachers of the girls water closet is something disgraceful, and I wish you would take hold of the matter at once and arrange so that the boxes and general back part of the water closet can be shielded from view of the lady teachers and girls passing to and from the chapel.

[Booker T. Washington]

TLc BTW Papers ATT.

To James Sullivan Clarkson

[Tuskegee, Ala.] December 26, 1903

Personal

My dear General Clarkson: When I see you again I want to go over the matter of the preparation of some kind of plank for the national platform covering the following points: First, putting the party on record as regarding the Lily White movement in the South. Second, as to the enforcement of the 14th and 15th amendments.[1] Something strong will have to be said on both of these questions and it will take the wind out of the sails of Hayes and the Suffrage crowd if they can be anticipated in this matter. Yours truly,

[Booker T. Washington]

TLc BTW Papers ATT.

[1] Clarkson replied: "I agree with you that something very strong will have to be said on behalf of these questions. . . . The party cannot flinch nor evade its plain duty next year on these vital and human subjects." (Dec. 29, 1903, Con. 19, BTW Papers, DLC.)

To James Sullivan Clarkson

[Tuskegee, Ala.] December 26, 1903

Personal

My dear General Clarkson: It was rather amusing the other night as I came through Washington, to hear of the experience that the colored ministers of Washington are now having, I mean those who did not vote to endorse the President in the recent suffrage convention. Their congregations are giving them all kinds of trouble; in one case it is stated that the minister will have to resign, in another the minister was so set upon by hundreds of members of his congregation that he had to deny any connection with the suffrage meeting, in fact the joke is it now seems hard to find a colored minister in the whole District of Columbia who will admit that he even attended the suffrage meeting. Yours truly,

[Booker T. Washington]

TLc BTW Papers ATT.

To James A. Cobb[1]

[Tuskegee, Ala.] December 26, 1903

My dear Sir: Mr. Whitefield McKinlay has told me of your splendid efforts before the recent meeting held there, to vindicate President Roosevelt, if he needed such vindication. It seems to me a fair thing to say that any black man who has any feeling of opposition to President Roosevelt is indeed a queer individual. I thank you as one who admires the President greatly for what you did in the direction mentioned. Yours very truly,

[Booker T. Washington]

TLc BTW Papers ATT.

1 James A. Cobb (1876–1958), born in Arcadia, La., was the son of an ex-slave and a white Louisiana lawyer and landowner. His mother became a servant at her former owners' boardinghouse, and she sent her son to a rural school in which he was the only black student. After a secondary education at Straight University, he attended Fisk and Howard University Law School. He worked as a Pullman porter to help pay his expenses. Cobb was admitted to the D.C. bar in 1901. He was a supporter of Theodore Roosevelt and BTW. From 1907 to 1915 he was a special assistant U.S. attorney, and he held a municipal judgeship in the District of Columbia during the Coolidge and Hoover administrations. Cobb was a director of the NAACP, and as a leading Washington attorney, he was counsel in several important NAACP legal actions in Washington. Cobb also was a professor and dean at Howard University Law School.

To J. M. Harris

[Tuskegee, Ala.] December 26, 1903

Dear Sir: I understand from some of our teachers who wish to take policies in your company, the U.S. Casualty, with headquarters at 141 Broadway, New York, it is the policy of the company not to issue policies to colored persons. I wish to say to you that your company does a real injustice if it enforces such a rule as this against the teachers of this institution. As you know, the health conditions here are satisfactory from every point of view. The health of every student as well as every teacher is protected in every possible manner. Also the habits of these teachers are satisfactory, otherwise they would not be in the employ of the institution, as none are employed except those who represent in every possible way the highest development of the race. If you can arrange to have policies issued to such of our teachers as desire them, I think it will be to mutual advantage. Yours truly,

[Booker T. Washington]

TLc   Con. 249   BTW Papers   DLC.

To Timothy Thomas Fortune

[Tuskegee, Ala.] December 27, 1903

Dear Mr. Fortune: I wish you would wire S. Laing Williams at once asking him to acquaint himself with proprietorship of the Chicago Conservator as it will be helpful. He can come to the Conference in January primed with this information, at which time we can go over it. I am writing this letter on Sunday and so am not able to put in check to cover telegraphic account, but shall send this on Monday. Yours truly,

[Booker T. Washington]

TLc   BTW Papers   ATT.

To Theodore Roosevelt

[Tuskegee, Ala.] December 28, 1903

My dear Mr. President: On the 6th, 7th and 8th of January, we are to have a private conference in New York City, composed of twenty-five leading colored men gathered from all sections of the country. They will represent the educational, political, moral and sociological forces at work for the elevation of the race, and the conference will be composed of those who agree as well as those who disagree on important matters and we are hoping to make it a means of accomplishing a great deal of good for the race.

I shall call to see you on the afternoon of January 5th with the hope that you may have some suggestion to put before the conference. Yours very truly,

[Booker T. Washington]

TLc BTW Papers ATT.

To Carl Schurz

[Tuskegee, Ala.] December 28, 1903

My dear Mr. Schurz: I spent a portion of Christmas Day in reading your article in McClure's Magazine,[1] and must say to you what I have just said to Mr. Baldwin in a letter, that it is the strongest and most statesmanlike word that has been said on the subject of the South and the Negro for a long number of years, and I want to thank you most earnestly for the article. I earnestly hope that it will have a large circulation in the South. McClure's Magazine is read a good deal by Southern white people, and I hope the results will be very far-reaching. Yours very truly,

[Booker T. Washington]

TLc Con. 274 BTW Papers DLC.

[1] Carl Schurz, "Can the South Solve the Negro Problem?" *McClure's Magazine*, 22 (Jan. 1904), 258–75. Schurz reviewed southern attitudes toward blacks since Reconstruction and concluded that the disfranchisement movement was an unconstitutional attempt to thwart racial progress. He termed certain southerners as

"reactionists" who wanted the racial problem left in their hands so they could reduce blacks to a state of serfdom. He called on the "many enlightened and high-minded men and women" of the South to organize to fight against race prejudice by a campaign of education. He believed the racial problem would only be solved by a fair observance of the law and the elimination of lawlessness and ignorance of both blacks and whites.

To Edward Henry Clement

[Tuskegee, Ala.] December 30, 1903

My dear Mr. Clement: Enclosed I send you marked clippings which present a very interesting case. It is that of a colored man who was lynched or murdered at Pineapple, Ala. The lynchers murdered or burned the colored man, and then to hide their crime set fire to the prison, but the flames extended from the prison to the business portion of the town and as a result nearly the whole of the business section of the town was burned. The white people are now in quite a state of indignation and are making every effort possible to have the lynchers brought to justice. It is a very interesting case as it shows the final results of mob violence. Of course one wonders if the same indignation would have been shown if the property of the white people had not been burned. Yours truly,

[Booker T. Washington]

TLc Con. 253 BTW Papers DLC. BTW sent a similar letter to Oswald Garrison Villard, Jan. 1, 1904, Con. 295, BTW Papers, DLC.

To William Henry Baldwin, Jr.

[Tuskegee, Ala.] Dec 30 1903

If needed can you let me have one thousand dollars to use in connection with New York conference expenses until February. Answer.

Booker T. Washington

HWSr Con. 792 BTW Papers DLC.

To Whitefield McKinlay

[Tuskegee, Ala.] Jan. 2, 1904

My dear Mr. McKinlay: In answer to your telegram, I have just sent Dr. Grimke a telegram which reads as follows: "If you cannot attend New York conference shall be glad to have you invite your brother to take your place under same conditions which you were invited."

I confess to you I have sent this telegram very much against my own personal wishes and sense of what is right and proper, because I do not feel that Archibald Grimke has ever done anything to entitle him to membership in such a body. In the second place, he represents a noisy, turbulent and unscrupulous set of men to such an extent that I cannot feel that he would enter into the serious and far-sighted deliberations of such a conference in the way that we plan to enter into it. I wish, however, directly or indirectly, you would say to Mr. Grimke that the conference is called for a serious purpose and not for the purpose of airing personal grievances or entering into a scramble, and that if he attempts to have the same kind of "nigger meeting" that was had in Washington a few days ago, it will be much wiser for him not to go to New York. Those composing this conference are determined to have a quiet, dignified and high-toned deliberation and will submit to nothing that is not in keeping with this policy. Aside from this view of the case, I have invited at the suggestion of others one or two other persons who are bitterly opposed to me, and after receiving these invitations they had such a low sense of honor that they gave the details of my letter out to the public press, this is notably true in Boston and Chicago. I have laid aside my own personal feelings in several other cases, as in the case of Mr. Grimke, and have invited him with the hope that good shall be accomplished. It should be the earnest effort of every individual attending this conference to keep the good of the race uppermost and sink everything else. I do not overlook the fact that within the last few months Mr. Grimke has c[al]led me a traitor and has applied every other epithet that he could think of to me with a view to injury, all this, however, I waive aside for the sake of the larger good that I hope will come, but I repeat I hope you will impress upon him that we are not going there for a scramble but for a dignified earnest endeavor to help the race. Yours truly,

[Booker T. Washington]

TLc Con. 258 BTW Papers DLC. A similar but less candid letter went to W. E. B. Du Bois on the same date, Con. 287, BTW Papers, DLC.

To Peter Jefferson Smith, Jr.

[Tuskegee, Ala.] Jan. 3, 1904

My dear Mr. Smith: This week's issue of the Colored Citizen shows evidence of much improvement. My name appears too often in Mr. Thompson's correspondence. The letter of your Washington correspondent is good. I expected to have seen a long letter from New Bedford; it is hardly what I expected. Yours truly,

[Booker T. Washington]

TLc Con. 19 BTW Papers DLC.

Margaret James Murray Washington to Emmett Jay Scott

Tuskegee, Ala. Jany 5 1904

Telegraph me how and where Mr Washington is.

Mrs Booker T Washington

HWSr Con. 553 BTW Papers DLC. Received at the Hotel Manhattan, New York City.

Summary of the Proceedings of the Conference at Carnegie Hall

New York City   January 6th, 7th and 8th, 1904

It is the sense of this conference

1.   That the bulk of the Negro race should be encouraged to re-

main in the South, and especially in those sections where the present physical domination must ultimately bring political and civic equality; and that every effort should be made to uplift and develop them in their present domicile.

At the same time, under favorable circumstances, individuals may properly be encouraged to take advantage of the more liberal conditions of the North and West.

2. That in a democratic republic the right to vote is of paramount importance to every class of citizens and is preservative of all other rights and interests. The Fourteenth and Fifteenth Amendments were justifiable, and should be upheld and enforced by national authority. We should stand at all times for full, free and equal suffrage for colored men, upon the same terms that apply to white men, and should put forth every legal effort in our power to maintain the right of suffrage.

That for the furtherance of our political rights, we urge the organization of colored voters in the North and West by congressional districts for the sole purpose of electing to Congress and to the State Legislatures men who, at all times, will vote for measures promotive of the rights of the Negro race.

In the South, both in those states which have revised their constitutions and in those which have not, we urge each eligible Negro voter to qualify and to vote at every election.

3. That we are opposed to all restrictions of our civil rights in matters of travel and public accommodations, and we urge the institution of suits against common carriers in cases of discrimination and that efforts be made to secure absolutely equal accommodations on all public conveyances. We stand for no compromise, or equivocal statement, respecting our civil rights, but insist on the equality of all men before the law.

4. That the education of the Negro race should consist of:

(1) Thorough training of leaders and teachers in the higher institutions of learning;

(2) Thorough elementary training for every Negro child;

(3) Industrial training of the masses in trades and handicrafts.

5. That we vigorously denounce lynching and all modes of punishment without due process of law; and, while we condemn rape and every other crime, we are certain that skillfully exaggerated reports of rapeful assaults by Negroes have been and are being used

to discredit the race and blacken its reputation. Means should be devised of carefully investigating and publishing the truth of all such accusations.

6.   That Negroes should cooperate with the fair-minded and progressive element of the Southern white people, in so far as they can do so without compromise of manhood.

7.   That the Northern white man, the Southern white man and the Negro are the three constituent factors of the race problem, and that there should be a conference of representatives of these three elements to consider methods of solution.

8.   That effort should be made to disseminate a knowledge of the truth in regard to all matters affecting our race, so that the North, the South and the Negro himself may be adequately informed as to race data and conditions.

RESOLUTION 1.   It is the sense of this conference that there should be appointed by this body

a Committee of Safety

1.   That this committee should be composed of twelve (12) men;

2.   That the duties of this committee be as follows:

  (a)   To be a bureau of information on all subjects relating to the race;

  (b)   To seek to unify and bring into cooperation the action of the various organizations;

  (c)   To be a central bureau of communication between all parts and sections of the country.

3.   That this committee meet several times a year, at the discretion of the chairman.

This resolution was signed by:

Booker T. Washington, W. E. B. Du Bois, A. Grant, Charles W. Anderson, Archibald H. Grimke, Robert Russa Moton, H. T. Kealing, T. Thomas Fortune, S. Laing Williams, Fredrick L. McGhee, E. H. Morris, Samuel E. Courtney, J. C. Napier, G. L. Knox, I. B. Scott, Clement G. Morgan, E. C. Morris,[1] A. Walters, R. L. Smith, P. B. S. Pinchback, John S. Trower,[2] William H. Steward, James H. Hayes, Judson W. Lyons, Kelly Miller, C. T. Walker,[3] Whitefield McKinlay, Emmett J. Scott, Hugh M. Browne, and was formally passed unanimously by the conference.[4]

Booker T. Washington, W. E. B. Du Bois and Hugh M. Browne

386

were made members of the Committee of Safety and authorized to select the other 9 members.

RESOLUTION 2. That the conference request of the publishers of McClure's Magazine the privilege of reprinting the article by Hon. Carl Schurz in the January issue.

RESOLUTION 3. That we extend to Hon. C. W. Anderson, of New York, our sincere appreciation of his generous services in furnishing the conference with the conveniences and comforts that have made the proceedings pleasant and agreeable.

RESOLUTION 4. That, in consideration of the thoughtful initiative of Dr. Booker T. Washington in calling the conference, we express our gratitude to him for taking the lead in this movement, and also we extend to him our thanks for his helpful address delivered before the closing session of the conference.

KELLY MILLER, *Secretary.*

TMSr   Con. 25   BTW Papers   DLC.

[1] Elias Camp Morris (1855–1922) was pastor of Centennial Baptist Church in Helena, Ark., from 1879 to 1922. He was president of the National Baptist Convention beginning in 1894, and was an organizer of the Baptist Home Mission Board in 1899. Morris was a delegate to several Republican national conventions, and was active in the NNBL in Arkansas.

[2] John S. Trower was a successful caterer and confectioner in Philadelphia.

[3] Charles Thomas Walker (1858–1921) was pastor of the Tabernacle Baptist Church in Augusta, Ga., during most of his career, except for five years from about 1899 to 1904, when he was pastor of the Mount Olivet Baptist Church in New York City. He was a founder of the black branch of the YMCA while in New York.

[4] Two conferees, William H. Lewis, who left early, and Henry H. Proctor, did not sign the report.

From William Henry Baldwin, Jr.

[New York City] January 7th., 1904

Dear Mr. Washington: I was sorry not to have been able to see you yesterday or to-day. I knew you were busy, and I never was put to it so hard. Both last night and to-night I am working.

I have received an invitation to come before your conference to-morrow, and have telegraphed you that I will be there at three thirty if that is convenient, and I hope it will be. If you have any special points that you want me to refer to, send them to me.

I had a conference with Mr. Carl Schurz, and also have a note about a small matter from Mr. Carnegie, about which I want to see you.

I have talked with Mr. Jesup, and with Mr. Harrison[1] of the Southern Railway, about the Pullman Car matter, and I want to discuss it with you and some of your friends.

I expect Mr. Adler[2] is going to take up the Negro question at his Carnegie meeting on Sunday. Perhaps all your members will want to hear him.

The letter from Cassius Carter[3] is the most striking thing I have ever seen, except another letter I have from Mr. Bassett.[4] I want you to let me show that Carter letter to Mr. Schurz. Yours very truly,

W. H. Baldwin, Jr.

TLpSr Copy   Con. 18   BTW Papers   DLC.

[1] Fairfax Harrison (1869–1938) was president of the Southern Railway for many years beginning in 1913. Earlier he was solicitor (1896–1903), assistant to the president (1903–6), and vice-president (1906–10).

[2] Felix Adler (1851–1933), born in Alzey, Germany, came to the United States as a child and graduated from Columbia University. In 1876 he founded the New York Society for Ethical Culture. After 1902 he was professor of political and social ethics at Columbia.

[3] Possibly the letter of Jan. 6, 1903, above.

[4] John Spencer Bassett wrote to Baldwin, Dec. 16, 1903, that when the editor of the Raleigh *News and Observer* condemned a Baptist minister for proposing to restrict the license of the press and demanded his ouster, his Baptist brethren stood by the minister. This seemed to him evidence of more independence of spirit among southerners. (Con. 792, BTW Papers, DLC.)

From John Henry Washington

Tuskegee, Ala., Jan. 9, 1904

Dear Brother: For the last two days there have been numerous rumors on the school grounds, in town, and inquiries have come from Montgomery and other places in the State. These rumors are as follows:

(1)   That Mr. E. J. Scott was shot in Washington.

(2) That Mr. E. J. Scott was confined to his room in Washington City very sick.

(3) That you got shot near Washington City.

I have remained quiet about the matter for two days, hoping to hear something definite, this was the cause of my sending the telegram to you today. I have been watching the papers very carefully to see if there was anything in them concerning the matter, and while I do not believe there is any truth in it, yet some of the inquiries come so direct from graduates and ex-students that I will not feel content concerning the matter until I hear from you. Yours truly,

J. H. Washington

TLS Con. 553 BTW Papers DLC.

To Samuel Edward Courtney

Stevens House Hotel, New York City. January 10th, 1904

PERSONAL AND CONFIDENTIAL.

Dear Dr. Courtney: It is persistently reported that Trotter has a plan for giving out later on, either in his own paper, or in some white paper, the entire proceedings, real or imaginary, of our conference.

I hope that you will see that Mr. Grimke keeps his hand on Trotter to restrain him from doing this. Do not use my name.

Mr. Grimke has promised to do this. Very truly yours,

[Booker T. Washington]

TLc Con. 2 BTW Papers DLC.

From Edward Elder Cooper

Washington, D.C., Jan. 12, 1904

Dear Mr. Washington: I have your letter of the 11th inst., and note what you say concerning the matter of Mr. Hayes. I quite agree with you in the opinion that the Suffrage League, Afro-American Council and other political leagues should combine and unite for a common cause, and a common purpose. Nor do I think it advisable to make any mention whatever of Mr. Hayes' Suffrage League until he has pooled issues with the other leagues and councils. I shall make no further reference to him in any way until the unification of the various organizations have been effected. How do you like the way I treated Lawyer Smith's handling of the case before the U.S. Supreme Court? He made a good impression down this way, and the concensus of opinion is, that he has won his case. But of that we shall know later.

I did not hear of your New York Conference until yesterday.[1] The brethren down this way managed to keep me in the dark as far as possible. I presume you have heard of the death of Col. Pledger. Too bad. Poor fellow. Lawyer Edward H. Morris of Chicago was banqueted here last Saturday night and a most representative gathering was in attendance. He speaks tonight before the Bethel Literary, taking for his subject "Shams." I will let you know about it, as I expect to attend the lecture. With very best wishes, I am, Yours very truly,

E E Cooper

TLS   Con. 2   BTW Papers   DLC.

[1] Cooper wrote to BTW: "Messrs. Dancy, Terrell and some of your other friends are sore because they did not know of it and was not invited to the New York Conference." (Jan. 15, 1904, Con. 20, BTW Papers, DLC.)

To Phil Waters

[Tuskegee, Ala.] Jan. 15, 1904

My dear Mr. Waters: I understand that our mutual friend, Mr. Fortune, is to visit Charleston within the next few days, and I am very anxious that all of our friends in West Virginia and the Kanawha Valley unite to give him a royal welcome. I hope that in every way possible everything will be done to show real appreciation of the services which he has rendered the race. One thing, however, bear in mind, and that is do not make the mistake of doing anything in the direction which I have so often cautioned you. Yours truly,

[Booker T. Washington]

TLc   Con. 296   BTW Papers   DLC.

From Louis G. Gregory[1]

Washington, D.C. January 15 1904

Personal

My dear Sir, It is seldom a difficult matter to answer the arguments of those who oppose you and your work, as they generally display the weakness of vituperation. And still it would be manifestly improper and unfair to say that all of those who oppose you do so out of ignorance or malice. The question around which opposition centers is whether your policy in spirit and results, accepts a lower plane of manhood and recognition for your own people than that accorded other Americans.

Mr. Edward H. Morris of Chicago, on Tuesday evening last before a crowded house at the Bethel Literary and Historical Society, maintained the affirmative view with great force.[2] His speech was, all in all, about the cleverest piece of sophistry I've ever heard. He made skillful use of extracts from your books and speeches, which, taken out of their original settings, were twisted and construed to make you a sham and a traitor to the best interests of the Negro. Your friends were present to take issue. But Mr. Morris brought to bear all the skill and address of a trained lawyer and without doubt captivated the audience.

I am fully convinced from listening to your speeches and a careful reading of your books and magazine articles, that your aims are as high for your people as those of any others of the world's leaders. You would make the race strong in a strength from within and adopt measures and methods which are most effective through their stability and permanence. It is the principal lesson for a struggling people to learn, that we reach the acme not by a single bound, but slowly, painfully, step by step. It is not only idle but insane to arouse the prejudices of powerful foes when no principle is sacrificed and nothing is gained.

But I write to make this suggestion: It is best for your influence and prestige with your people to maintain a dignified silence with respect to any wrong attitude of the South, rather than use words which may be construed as an approval. For while men of breadth will see in your statements about jim crow cars and lost political rights only encouragment to those who labor under adverse conditions, your enemies may argue them, cleverly, plausibly, if not convincingly, to mean a sordid approval of race prejudice and inferiority of the Negro.

You have long since learned, that however elevated your motives may be, the good you can do your people is largely proportional to their faith in your wisdom and integrity. If any number of them regard you merely as a "white folks' nigger," you can still be kind to the unthankful; but they serve to defeat in a measure your good offices by standing in their own light. Of course these things do not discourage you, for no leader has ever escaped opposition from within the ranks, which is far more annoying than that which comes from without.

Hoping in any event, that your wise and aggressive leadership may be long spared us, I have the honor to be, Very truly yours,

Louis G. Gregory

ALS Con. 288 BTW Papers DLC.

1 Louis G. Gregory, a graduate of Fisk University (1896) and Howard University Law School (1902), was a government clerk and an attorney in Washington, D.C.

2 Edward Morris attacked BTW for inconsistencies in *The Story of My Life and Work* and *Up from Slavery*. "Washington said in his first book that his father was a white man," the Washington *Bee* reported, "but in his second book he omits his father. He was improving." The Washington *Bee*, almost gleeful over the meeting and the speech, praised Morris for his manly utterances and condemned the few defenders of BTW such as Robert H. Terrell and P. B. S. Pinchback who rose to object to Morris's words. About 1,500 persons were present and the *Bee* reported that four-fifths of those in attendance heartily approved of the speech. (Washington *Bee*, Jan. 16, 1904, 1.)

To Walter L. Cohen

[Tuskegee, Ala.] Jan. 16, 1904

Personal

My dear Mr. Cohen: I think I telegraphed you a few days ago from New York to the effect that I talked with the President about the case of yourself and Col. Lewis. The President had been of the impression that both of you had been reappointed sometime ago, but after I showed him that this was not true he promised to reappoint both of you just as soon as a vote has been taken on the Panama question. He fears just a little to do anything that might arouse any of the Southern senators just now and thus run the risk of losing their vote and influence in favor of the Panama treaty. I think I ought to say to you that I found that somebody had been talking to the President against you and made him a little prejudiced, but I had no difficulty in assuring him that you were entirely worthy and he promised to reappoint both of you just as soon as I reminded him of it after the ratification of the Panama treaty. As I have so many things to attend to, it would not be out of place for you or Col. Lewis to drop me a card of reminder after the Panama vote has been taken. Yours truly,

[Booker T. Washington]

TLc Con. 19 BTW Papers DLC.

To Cyrus Field Adams

[Tuskegee, Ala.] Jan. 16, 1904

Dear Mr. Adams: Will you be kind enough to send me a short outline of Morris's address? I mean the points that he made against me. I want to meet them as far as I can without calling his name or making direct reference to him when I speak in Washington. Yours truly,

[Booker T. Washington]

TLc Con. 283 BTW Papers DLC.

To James Sullivan Clarkson

[Tuskegee, Ala.] Jan. 18, 1904

Personal

My dear General Clarkson: I want to speak to you about a matter in which I hope you will not mention my name to either of the Referees[1] as I do not want them to feel that I am meddling with their business. I am wondering whether or not it will not be a good plan for you to suggest that in the filling of important positions, especially Presidential offices, that all three of them get together and agree unanimously as to the man to be recommended. I find just now that there is a little disposition for one or two of them to recommend an individual without the consent of all. Of course in filling minor positions it would not be expected that unanimous consent could be secured, as I understand the three men have the state divided up into divisions over which each one exercises control in minor appointments.

Secondly, extreme caution will have to be exercised to prevent a rebellion among the colored people on account of too much favor being shown to the Lily Whites. The enclosed letter will illustrate a case for which Mr. Aldrich is responsible.[2] I agree thoroughly with the policy which gradually brings the Lily Whites back into the party in proportion as they confess their error and treat the colored people with some consideration, but in the case of Mr. F. F. Conway, about whom Dr. Nelson writes, who has been among the most abusive enemies of President Roosevelt and myself in this state through his daily paper, up to the time of his appointment had shown no evidence of repentance. As Dr. Nelson expresses it, to appoint such a man to any office without his making any apology for his insult to the colored people and the Republican party looks like putting a premium upon Lily Whiteism. I repeat, I hope if you write Mr. Aldrich that you will not mention this matter to him because, on the whole the Referees have done might[y] well; I only write to prevent future mistakes being made.

The three Referees have just united and recommend Mr. Armbrecht of Mobile, for the position of District Attorney. He was a former Lily White, but in his case I insisted that he get the endorsement of the leading colored people in his section before he was appointed; that was done, and of course the colored people are satisfied. The same course should have been followed in the case of Mr. Conway. Yours truly,

[Booker T. Washington]

TLc Con. 261 BTW Papers DLC.

1 William Farrington Aldrich, Charles Herrington Scott, and Joseph Oswalt Thompson.

2 W. H. Nelson of Huntsville wrote to BTW on Jan. 14, 1904, complaining that F. F. Conway of that city, who had criticized the President in his newspaper for inviting BTW to dinner, had been given one of the most lucrative federal appointments in the state by one of the referees, W. F. Aldrich, also a lily white. (Con. 19, BTW Papers, DLC.)

To Addison Wimbs

[Tuskegee, Ala.] Jan. 18, 1904

My dear Mr. Wimbs: For sometime Gen. Clarkson, Mr. Thompson and others have been making an effort to get me to stand for an election before the State Convention as one of the delegates at large for the state of Alabama. This I have decided, however, not to do, but in a conversation with Mr. Thompson Saturday when the matter was finally settled, I told him I preferred that you go in my stead, and I hope he and his friends will throw their influence in this direction. Mr. Thompson readily consented to this and said he would have all the Referees throw their influence in the direction of sending you as a delegate at large. If this is satisfactory to you and I can help further in carrying out the plan please let me know. Yours truly,

[Booker T. Washington]

TLc Con. 26 BTW Papers DLC.

To Robert Donaldson Townsend

[Tuskegee, Ala.] Jan. 18, 1904

Dear Mr. Townsend: I am in receipt of your letter and have no objection to your carrying out your plans with reference to the publication of my article on the Negro Potato King,[1] but in leaving out any portion of it I hope you will be very careful to consider that in the case of a Negro many things are not taken for granted that are taken for granted in the case of a white man. For instance, in my article I think I described with some detail the interior of the house, including the bath room for example. I do this because the average white man who knows little about the successful Negro takes for granted that they have nothing in the way of such conveniences as a bath room in their houses. I am very sorry for the same reason that the photographs were not in such condition that you could use them. I was especially anxious to have the people see a picture of the dwelling house, but I shall be very glad to see the article published in one of your un-illustrated numbers. Yours truly,

[Booker T. Washington]

TLc   Con. 23   BTW Papers   DLC.

[1] See An Article in *Outlook*, May 14, 1904, below.

From William Goodell Frost

Dayton, Ohio. Jan. 18. 1904

My Dear Dr. Washington: I write to ask your advice, in confidence, on an important matter.

As you know for near 40 years Berea has admitted colored students on the same basis as whites, and with no unfortunate results.

The wave of anti Negro sentiment has reached Kentucky, and a bill is up prohibiting this. Should this become a law we shall *certainly* not drop our work for the colored people. We might divide funds and have twin schools, we might sacrifice buildings and move to Ohio, we might use a part of our income for publications and extension work, lectures, traveling libraries etc. (a work *much* needed, and which could be made very effective). I have never pushed our principle of "admitting all of good moral character["] offensively. There is no tendency toward "race wars,["] nor inter-marriage in Berea.

Now the question is should Berea resist this proposed law to the utmost (of course in christian spirit) or might we find a way to do as much good as now in a manner less offensive to the South-erners?

My instincts are for "standing pat" on platform vindicated by so many years. But I wish to know what others would say. Do you think Berea's advanced position ought to be fought for? Most cordially yours,

Wm. Goodell Frost

Please address me at Berea, Ky.

ALS   Con. 288   BTW Papers   DLC.

From Cyrus Field Adams

Washington, D.C., January [ca. 18] 1904

Dear Mr. Washington: Replying to your request for the "strong" points made against you by Mr. Morris in recent address at Washington, I beg to say:

Mr. Morris first stated that it made little difference what you really thought, the important point being what the people imagined you thought, their interpretation of your meaning. He cited Justice Taney's famous decision in the Dred Scott case, showing that the general opinion among well-informed people is that Taney said, "The Negro has no rights that the white man is bound to respect." The facts in the case being that Taney did not deliver such opinion. "It is generally believed that Booker Washington believes in the natural inferiority of the Negro, that he should

397

have a special place in American civilization, separate and distinct from other peoples and that he should consider the suffrage as of secondary importance." The quotation is not exact but that is the idea I caught.

He attacked your story of the boy studying the French grammar in the log cabin and brought in to view the fact that Abraham Lincoln studied in a log cabin by the light of a pine knot.

Mr. Morris claimed that the people in the shanty had a perfect right to have a piano if they wished to.

He quoted from a number of anthropologists of eminence to prove that the Negro is the equal of the white man.

He disputed your contention that the Southern Constitutions place a premium on thrift and proved that they were formed for the express purpose of disfranchising the Negro.

He found objection to your funny stories showing up the weaknesses of the race and claimed that no one of the race should bring out the bad features as the enemy would look after that matter.

The Negro has the right to work or not just as he chooses; he should not be forced to work any more than the white man.

He claimed that lawyers, doctors and teachers are needed now.

He claimed that the spirit of submission and compromise would never solve the race problem, that had been tried for many years but the prejudice against the race was increasing. There must be a manly contention for all of the manhood rights. The Negro should have all of the rights given to other American citizens.

Mr. Morris mentioned the toothbrush story, saying that it gave the whites a wrong idea of the race. It may be true that the Colored people of the South have no knowledge of the toothbrush, but the members of the race in the North use it as often as their white brethren.

I have thrown this together hurriedly as I am about to leave the city, but I trust it will give you some idea of Mr. Morris' paper on "Shams." I am, Yours faithfully,

C. F. Adams

TLS Con. 4 BTW Papers DLC.

To Fredrick L. McGhee

[Tuskegee, Ala.] January 19, 1904

Dear Mr. McGhee: I have read your letter of January 12th with very great interest, and note what you say respecting your visits to Senator Nelson, Platt,[1] and others; also, what you say respecting the Catholic Eclesiastic[2] whom you visited at Baltimore.

I think it will be worth a very great deal if we can bring some pressure to bear in opposition to the proposed disfranchisement in Maryland, and I hope that your church can see its way clear to lend a hand in this direction.

Thanking you again for the kindly words of your letter, as well as for the services which you have rendered in this matter, service for the race itself, I am, Very truly yours,

[Booker T. Washington]

TLc   Con. 4   BTW Papers   DLC.

[1] Actually Moses Edwin Clapp, U.S. senator from Minnesota (1901–17), who arranged for McGhee to see the President.

[2] James Gibbons (1834–1921), born in Baltimore, was ordained a priest in 1861. He became bishop of Baltimore in 1877 and cardinal in 1887.

McGhee urged Cardinal Gibbons to use his influence with the Catholic members of the state legislature of Maryland to defeat any legislation designed to disfranchise blacks, but he could not get a definite promise from him. (McGhee to BTW, Jan. 12, 1904, Con. 4, BTW Papers, DLC.)

To Walter Hines Page

[Tuskegee, Ala.] Jan. 19, 1904

My dear Mr. Page: A few days ago while I was going North on a Southern train, I noticed a large group of young men in the front end of the dining car while I was taking my dinner, and I became a little suspicious on account of the size of the crowd and their constant gazing at me, and did not know what was likely to take place and so kept my eye on them. The dining car conductor had to request them to stay out of the car several times. Finally, however, one of the men broke through the other crowd and came to my table and stated that there were 12 or 15 students aboard returning from their recess to Trinity College and Chapel Hill, and that they requested him to ask me that I consent to have all of them introduced to me. You can imagine my surprise and pleasure at this very pleasant occurrence. Yours very truly,

[Booker T. Washington]

TLc   Con. 565   BTW Papers   DLC.

To William Henry Baldwin, Jr.

[Tuskegee, Ala.] Jan. 19, 1904

Dear Mr. Baldwin: At our recent conference held in New York in the parlors of Carnegie Hall, where practically all the race interests were represented, we came to a pretty general and definite agreement as to our future policy. One of the most important things to do is first to establish a strong national Negro paper which will unify the race and keep it at work along sensible and constructive directions. We could either buy a paper now established and reorganize it, or start a new paper outright; in any case, it would require some capital, and if through you or any of our friends we could secure sufficient money to carry out either of these plans it would help the interests of the race immensely. Of course as we get nearer to either plan we could find out the definite amount needed. Yours truly,

[Booker T. Washington]

TLc   Con. 18   BTW Papers   DLC.

To Timothy Thomas Fortune

Tuskegee, Alabama. Jan. 19, 1904

My dear Mr. Fortune: I have your kind favor of January 13th written from Rochester. I hope you are well and succeeding admirably on your lecture tour.

One thing you should keep constantly in mind, and that is to organize local Afro-American Councils as far as possible. There are very few of these Councils at present.

I have written Mr. Waters to see that you are given a royal time in West Virginia.

I hope you will let up on our friend Hayes for a few weeks at any rate.

Judging from all the reports that I have received from Washington concerning Morris's address before the Bethel Literary, I fear that he is a hard and difficult creature without any sense of honor. If he wanted to attack me he had an opportunity during the three days we were together face to face in a manly, straightforward way, but he was too big a coward for that, but waited until he got an opportunity to do so behind my back. It is very trying to deal with such creatures. Yours very truly,

Booker T. Washington

TLS   Con. 1   BTW Papers   DLC.

To Louis G. Gregory

[Tuskegee, Ala.] January 19, 1904

Personal

My dear Mr. Gregory: I received your very kind note of recent date and thank you for writing me in the frank manner that you have.

It is very difficult for one placed in my position to know the course of action that is best to pursue at all times, but of one thing I am convinced, and my own experience bears me out in it, and that is if one is doing what he honestly feels is right regardless of whether for the time being it meets with cheers or condemnation, I am sure that he will succeed. Of one other thing I am determined, and [that] is I will under no circumstances get down into the mud and wallow with the people who are trying to draw me into a controversy. Oliver Wendell Holmes very wisely said, "Controversy equalizes wise men and fools, and the fools know it." I believe that if one goes on bravely, without flinching, doing the work that he feels the people ought to have done for them in their present generation and in their present condition, he will meet with a praiseworthy reward. Of course it would be a very easy thing for me to flatter the people and receive their cheers on all occasions. For example, to tell them that they are wealthy when I know they are poor, to tell them that they are influential when they have little influence, to tell them that they are the equals of the whites when in reality they have not developed to that point, in a word, to urge them to disregard all of the intermediate steps in reaching the very highest point of development and jump at once to the top of the ladder without going through the preparation that other races have gone; all this would meet with great success and make me immensely popular with the unthinking, but I shall yield to no such temptation.

Referring to the gentleman who spoke at the Bethel Literary a few days ago I would say that, I have always up to the present time regarded him as being a brave and frank man. He had an opportunity during three days of last week to make the same statements in my presence and to my face which he made before that organization, but in the three addresses which he delivered in my presence he refrained practically from criticism because he knew that he could not palm off the same kind of sophistry in my presence that he did in my absence. The plain, common, hard-working people, however, I am sure, understand every move that I make and no man was ever more loyally and faithfully backed up by these classes than I am. I shall strive, however, more in the future than I have in the past, to have all classes understand my motives. There is not a single accomplishment or privilege in possession of any other race which I do not demand and strive for for my race, but I do not at all times agree with others as to the methods of reaching these ends. Of course any man can take advantage of another in his absence and use extracts from his speeches or writings to his disadvantage. One difficulty in dealing with such people is that you cannot reply in kind, because, as a rule, you can find no writings that they have left in permanent form.

I wish to assure you again, Mr. Gregory, that I appreciate most heartily and deeply the friendship of yourself and Mr. Cobb, and I shall always esteem it a privilege to merit your confidence and good will.

Sometime in the near future I am to speak in the Metropolitan Church, and I shall hope to have the opportunity of meeting both of you.

I wonder if you have ever seen a copy of my book, "Up from Slavery." I take the liberty of sending you one by this mail, also some copies of addresses delivered by me recently; one, an address before the Brooklyn Institute of Arts and Sciences, and the other delivered before the Afro-American Council in Louisville, Ky., last summer. Yours very truly,

[Booker T. Washington]

TLc   Con. 21   BTW Papers   DLC.

To Leigh S. J. Hunt[1]

[Tuskegee, Ala.] January 19, 1904

My dear Mr. Hunt: I have yours of December 6th,[2] written off Dueim,[3] with enclosure of copy of letter to Lord Cromer.[4]

The letter which you mention as having [been] sent to me at the embassy of London did not reach me. As a matter of fact, I did not go on to London from Paris.

I have very great faith in the plans which you outline, and, as I said to you before, you have my full sympathy in the matter. If there is any way that I can be of assistance, I am only too anxious to render that assistance.

As I think I have said to you, I am not in favor of wholesale colonization of the Negro people in Africa, or anywhere else, but the opportunities which you suggest that Sudan offers are opportunities which, it seems to me, large numbers of our Negro people should take advantage of.

With sincere good wishes for the new year, I am, Very truly yours,

[Booker T. Washington]

TLc   Con. 29   BTW Papers   DLC.

[1] Leigh S. J. Hunt (1855–1933) was a former midwestern educator and superintendent of schools in Des Moines, Iowa. Hunt moved to Seattle in 1886 and became

owner and editor of the *Post-Intelligencer*, Seattle's first daily newspaper. He became a successful entrepreneur in public utilities, banks, and real estate but lost heavily during the Panic of 1893. He traveled to Korea, where he established the Oriental Consolidated Mines Co. Hunt regained his fortune, and in 1903 he moved on to new enterprises in the Anglo-Egyptian Sudan, where he introduced cotton-growing as a feasible industry. Hunt turned to Tuskegee for three assistants to help on the plantation. In 1910 Hunt returned to the United States, and in 1924, after several years in Maryland and the Pacific Northwest, he settled in Las Vegas, where he engaged in the real estate business, buying large tracts of desert property in anticipation of the completion of Boulder Dam.

2 Hunt's letter of Dec. 6, 1903 (Con. 29, BTW Papers, DLC), sketched in glowing words his plan to colonize American blacks on cotton plantations in the Sudan.

3 Ed Dueim, Sudan.

4 Evelyn Baring, first Earl of Cromer (1841–1917), was British agent and consul-general in Egypt from 1883 to 1907, with broad diplomatic powers that allowed him to contribute to the economic and political modernization of Egypt. The Cromer letter mentioned is not attached to Hunt's letter.

Emmett Jay Scott to Charles Alexander

[Tuskegee, Ala.] Jan. 19, 1904

Dear Mr. Alexander: Mr. Washington has received your telegram and notes carefully all the suggestions which you make. Enclosed you will find check for $400 as requested. He prefers that you get this check cashed in Xenia so that there may be no discussion about it at Wilberforce. Mr. Smith has already been notified about your coming and will be ready to turn the paper over to you. Mr. Washington is particularly anxious to have you understand that he will help you to the extent that he has mentioned, but wants the paper to get upon its feet after that so it will pay its own way. Of course this arrangement is strictly between you and Mr. Washington and he expects that his name will not be used by you even in private conversation with any one. Yours truly,

[Emmett J. Scott]

TLc   Con. 19   BTW Papers   DLC.

To Samuel Abbott Green[1]

[Tuskegee, Ala.] January 21, 1904

My dear Dr. Green: I see by the papers that the Trustees of the Peabody Fund are to meet in Washington on January 26th for the purpose of electing Dr. Curry's successor and of devising some plan for the use of the Fund itself or the interest on the Fund.

In any decision that the Board may make, I am very anxious to impress the fact that the colored people's interests should not be overlooked. I notice that it is suggested in some quarters that the bulk of the money should be spent in establishing a large central normal school somewhere in the South. If this course, for example, is followed, it would mean that the colored people would be deprived of any interest in the Fund because they would not be permitted to attend such a school. My point is to impress upon you and others, as far as I may, that I hope the Board will pursue the plan which it has heretofore stood by, that of seeing that the colored people have an equitable share of the Fund, no matter how it is used in the future. The amount of money given to the colored schools in many of the rural districts of the South is very, very small, and if any proportion of the Fund is used to stimulate education in the rural districts, I hope that emphasis will be laid upon the need of helping not only the white schools, but the colored. I think you know that I stand firmly upon the principle that we should not only look after the education of the colored children in the South, but that of the white children as well, but I mention the interest of the colored race because in many cases I find that people are likely to overlook their welfare in a board where the race is not directly represented. Yours very truly,

[Booker T. Washington]

TLc   Con. 288   BTW Papers   DLC.

[1] Samuel Abbott Green (1830–1918), physician, author, and former mayor of Boston, was a trustee and secretary of the Peabody Education Fund beginning in 1883.

From Addison Wimbs

Greensboro, Alabama, Jany 21st 1904

Dear Mr Washington: I own your letter and appreciate its contents very much. It would please me to be of service to the President and to the Referees in the next National Convention. This much is to be considered, and that is, the Lily Whites would rather see any one, other than you or the writer go to the National Convention. Of course if the Referees have the convention well in hand and are not afraid of "wetting their feet" they can elect any one they please. In all my experience in "nigger publican politics" I have never run up against any three white republicans who stood more faithful to the cause they held out as representing.

If the Referees could win so signal a victory against the Lily Whites as sending me as a delegate it would be a death blow to the Lily Whites and even the slumbering ashes would be smothered completely.

If I can get myself in shape for sending my boy over there next session I expect to do so. He is just about old enough now. I would have sent him last Fall but he was hardly old enough and then too I was running about so much and spending so much that I could not do so.

Well they seem to want to discuss "Washington" up north. Pearson[1] is now putting a first class tin roof on our New Baptist Church building, Will Thomas is shoeing horses and Cleveland is making harness. They are all well dressed every Sunday and I am quite sure are better off than the fellow with an A. M. Diploma on the walls and no occupation. Your Friend

Ad Wimbs

TLS   Con. 26   BTW Papers   DLC.

[1] William Pearson, a tinsmith, was an 1896 graduate of Tuskegee.

To Robert Russa Moton

[Tuskegee, Ala.] Jan. 22, 1904

Personal

My dear Major Moton: Perhaps I had better write you what I had in mind about not inviting Dr. Du Bois to Hampton. Some months ago Mr. Baldwin invited him to his house for a frank conference, and I learn from two or three sources that Dr. Du Bois afterwards said that it was the purpose of Mr. Baldwin to try to bribe him or change his opinion regarding Hampton and Tuskegee and myself.[1] I was wondering if he was invited to Hampton at this time if he would not place some such interpretation upon the invitation? You remember in his opening address that he said to the effect that persons had attempted to bribe him in order to pull him off from his course. Of course later on, after we get our committee of twelve selected we can perhaps thrash out all these matters and come to a full understanding. Yours truly,

[Booker T. Washington]

TLc Con. 873 BTW Papers DLC.

[1] In 1940 Du Bois still recalled the conversation at Baldwin's home, and believed that Baldwin brought undue pressure on him to work at Tuskegee and to conform to the Washington racial program. (Du Bois, *Dusk of Dawn*, 78.)

To William Henry Lewis

[Tuskegee, Ala.] January 22, 1904

Dear Mr. Lewis: I thank you for your very kind letter and for your word of congratulation as to the success of the New York conference. I am very sorry that you could not remain through to the finish.

Trotter made an effort to get a pretended account of the meeting into the New York Sun and nearly succeeded in doing so. Mr. Chas. W. Anderson and Mr. Scott repaired to the Sun office however, and going directly to the managing editor succeeded in holding it out. They were not able, however, to get the manuscript. It was an article which any one could have written who wanted to do so and was not based on information directly given respecting the conference. Among other things he said that he himself was a member of the conference and took a strong stand against me in the meeting, and similar misstatements of this kind.

I shall hope to speak to you at some time respecting other matters which you bring to my attention. Yours truly,

[Booker T. Washington]

TLc   Con. 3   BTW Papers   DLC.

To William Goodell Frost

Tuskegee, Alabama. January 22, 1904

Personal

My dear Dr. Frost: Your kind letter has been received, and I have kept it in my hands for a few hours trying to decide what advice I ought to give, but I find myself unable as yet to reach any satisfactory conclusion. One thing, however, I am sure of, and that I advise as strongly as I can, and that is every effort should be made to convince the members of the legislature that your present organization of the college ought not to be disturbed, and that no harm has taken place by reason of your present policy. If I can reach any further conclusion, that is in case the legislature takes such action that it becomes necessary for your Trustees to act, I shall be glad to write you further.

I hope that you or some member of your faculty will be present at our Conference, February 17th and 18th. Yours truly,

Booker T. Washington

TLS   KyBB.   A carbon copy is in Con. 288, BTW Papers, DLC.

To Timothy Thomas Fortune

[Tuskegee, Ala.] Jan. 22, 1904

My dear Mr. Fortune: I hope by the time I see you that you will go over the whole matter of the committee of twelve and as far as possible have some good strong names selected.

The more I think of it, the more I feel convinced that in the end your interests will be conserved by selling the Age. You would get the cash in hand which you could use in buying outright a home and discharge your present obligations, and could be connected with the Age in a permanent capacity in a way that would enable you to earn as much or more than you are now earning. I would think about the matter from this point of view.

I hope that you have had a magnificent time in West Virginia and the other places where you have visited. Yours very truly,

[Booker T. Washington]

TLc   Con. 3   BTW Papers   DLC.

To William Henry Baldwin, Jr.

[Tuskegee, Ala.] January 22, 1904

My dear Mr. Baldwin: I have your good letter of January 18th for which I thank you. Except what you tell me from time to time I find that I have little knowledge of what is being done by the two boards and friends of Southern education. The fact is, that either consciously or unconsciously, I very much fear it is the policy of those in charge to drift out of touch with the colored people engaged in education in the South. I can remember six or seven years ago when almost every important step bearing upon education in the South some colored man was consulted. Now such consultation is becoming more and more rare, and if matters go on as they now are, within a few years no attention will be paid to the colored people at all, I mean so far as conferences are concerned. I meet Southern people here in the South constantly in business conferences, and as you know, such men as Mr. Hare, Mr. Campbell and Mr. Simpson meet with our colored trustees both here in the South and in New York and think nothing of it. There is no earthly reason why a Southern man whose opinion and influence are worth a pinch of salt should refuse to sit in a business conference in New York City with one or two colored people present. The social feature, the dinners, etc., is entirely another matter, and no colored man with any self-respect would seek to obtrude himself in a dinner party where he is not wanted. There is one difficulty in my speaking so plainly to others as I am to you, and that is the minute I should make these suggestions one would get the idea that I was urging myself for recognition. That is far from being true. I have all the responsibilities at present that I care for, but when these meetings take place from time to time, as they do in New York and in the Southern States, as for example at Richmond last year, without even the presence, to say nothing of the voice, of a single invited colored man however important his work in education in the South, and the colored people learn gradually, I fear, to distrust the whole effort and become critical and cold when they should be warm and sympathetic. This attitude is taken largely because of ignorance and neglect and oversight on the part of those in control. Now I understand perfectly well that it is easier to make such criticisms and to find fault than it is to find a way out of the difficulty. I realize some of the difficulties, but at the same time I think that some way can be found gradually to improve present conditions. In one way or another, and perhaps more than you or any member of the board can realize, the colored people blame me for their not getting such representation as I have suggested.

What you say about the dinner to Mr. Carl Schurz is very interesting, and I am most grateful for the information you have given me about the various conferences.[1]

Now in regard to our conference I . . .[2] say that after threshing out matters pretty fully for three days and we reached this decision, that a central committee of twelve should be appointed who should as far as possible, take charge of the race's interest during the year, and this committee was to meet at the call of myself. The members of this committee have not been appointed as yet, but are to be appointed by Prof. Hugh M. Browne, Dr. Du Bois and myself at a meeting which we shall perhaps hold in New York sometime in

February or March. I am quite sure that several of the members, perhaps the majority of them who have been in opposition, are either silenced or won over to see the error of their way. There were others of whom this cannot be said, but will have to be watched in the future in order to determine how they should be classed. All of them, however, I am sure, were overwhelmed by the general sentiment of the conference and by the high character of the men present. I feel that it was a very helpful meeting from every point of view and among the most important efforts that I have ever had part in.

I am very anxious for a long conference with you.

Please remember me kindly to Mrs. Baldwin. Yours very truly,

[Booker T. Washington]

TLc   Con. 18   BTW Papers   DLC.

1 Baldwin wrote, "Dr. Dabney and Alderman did not seem to take any objection to Mr. Schurz's article. McIver had not read it, but Murphy was very bitter, and did not want to see Mr. Schurz. I urged him to and finally he agreed to. The lunch was a great success. They found that Mr. Schurz meant all right. It was another illustration of Murphy's sensitiveness and Southern blood. He said that that article would make the Alabama people 'hate the negroes,' where they had not before. I wanted to say to him it ought to make the Alabama people hate themselves, but there is no use in stirring up bad blood." (Jan. 18, 1904, Con. 18, BTW Papers, DLC.)

2 Obliterated word.

To Theodore Roosevelt

[Tuskegee, Ala.] January 23, 1904

My dear Mr. President: I have just had your letter dealing with the color question while you were a Civil Service Commissioner, which Mr. Jacob Riis uses in the last number of The Outlook,[1] recopied and sent out to a large number of colored papers. This is admirable in showing your position on that question even before you came into the Presidency. I am trying to arrange also to have several of the white papers in the North use it. Yours very truly,

[Booker T. Washington]

TLc   BTW Papers   ATT.

411

1 Jacob Riis's account of Roosevelt's career as civil service commissioner appeared in *Outlook,* 76 (Jan. 2, 1904), 25–33. Roosevelt said that if blacks passed the civil service examinations, they should be hired without regard to race.

From William Edward Burghardt Du Bois

Philadelphia, 24 Jan., 1904

Dear Sir: I might possibly get to the Conference if I could be of any particular use. Had you anything especial in mind? I am here at present lecturing for the University Extension and shall return just about the time of your conference.

As to the sleeping-car matter I did nothing more. Martin's[1] fee seemed to me too high. I have additional complaint now. I wanted to come north on the regular express & was refused even a ticket on the ground that the train was all Pullman's now & they could not accommodate me on account of the law. This is a clear case. I cannot afford to spend as much as Martin wanted, but I am willing to push the matter if the cost is lowered. Yours sincerely,

W. E. B. Du Bois

ALS   Con. 272   BTW Papers   DLC.

1 William C. Martin.

To George F. Richings

[Tuskegee, Ala.] Jan. 25, 1905 [1904][1]

My dear Mr. Richings: I thank you very much for what you have written me regarding the "Successful Training of the Negro" and the other pamphlet. Now there is one phase of your suggestion which I fear you have not thought over when you mention your distributing these circulars at the places where you lecture. We could easily furnish any number of these pamphlets but for you to distribute them or sell them, would it not give the impression that you were a mere agent of this institution and that the illustration of the work of other schools was merely incidental? Of course the minute people get the idea that you are an agent of Tuskegee, that minute in a very large degree your influence would be modified. Please think of this and let me hear further.

I wonder what kind of pictures you are selling of me? I have two kinds made from a large plate in Chicago some years ago and have not disposed of very many of them. I am wondering if I could not help you in the way of getting these photographs at a cheaper rate than you are now getting them. In order to make the matter a little more definite, I send you by this mail samples of three kinds. Yours truly,

[Booker T. Washington]

TLc   Con. 23   BTW Papers   DLC.

1 This letter is a reply to an autograph letter from Richings dated Jan. 23, 1904, and is filed in a 1904 container.

From Charles William Anderson

New York   January 26th, 1904

My dear Dr. Washington: I beg leave to hand you herewith a clipping from the Boston Guardian relative to Industrialism. As you will notice from this editorial, and especially from the paragraph which I have marked, some one has been guilty of a ruthless violation of the pledges of the Conference. The reference to the willingness of Mr. Baldwin to help finance through the Pullman Company matter must have been the result of information given by some one who was a member of the Carnegie Hall Conference. If so, it is a sad commentary on the alleged culture of the gentlemen from the City of "Beans and Brains." I think you will ultimately conclude to come around to my proposition of "smoking out" these fellows. I may be wrong, but I am strongly of the opinion that there are but two ways of meeting opposition; one is by submission, and the other is by resistance. Now, resistance does not necessarily mean violence or force. *It far more frequently means the display of that spirit which satisfies your opponent that opposi-*

tion is not safe. My experience in politics is, that, he is whipped oftenest who is whipped easiest, and I long ago made up my mind to give my opponent the very best I have in my shop, when he sets himself the task of fighting me. The opposition to you and your work, is confined to a little coterie of men who have graduated from some of the best Universities of the country, — *and have done nothing else.* A good thrashing would convince these young upstarts, with their painful assumption of superior intellectuality, that they had better spend their time in some less dangerous occupation. This is merely my opinion, and I pass it on for what it is worth.

I want to thank you again for that nice box of cheese, and assure you that I shall enjoy it with much gratitude to you. Perhaps after all, you had better burn this letter, that you may the more surely remember its tenor. By and by, you may think it more sensible than it now appears to be. Let me hear from you, when you have time, and advise me definitely when you conclude to make another visit to the North. Yours faithfully,

Charles W. Anderson

P.S. Congratulations on the recent decision of the Supreme Court in the Alabama case. I have been confounding Wibecan and others, who tried to sneeze me out of court, when I told them that in my opinion, Wilford Smith would win his case or cases, if any were won. When I came upon the newspaper report of the Supreme Court decision, I shouted "glory, Hallelujah!!" It was the first time I had used this old Hebrew expression of joy since the opening of this suffrage fight. It is the preliminary skirmish; and we have won.

C. W. A.

TLS Con. 550 BTW Papers DLC. Postscript in Anderson's hand.

To William Edward Burghardt Du Bois

[Tuskegee, Ala.] January 27, 1904

Dear Dr. Du Bois: Even before our committee is formed, I think there are one or two matters that we might attend to effectively.

First. I presume you have seen something of the recent decision handed down by the U.S. Supreme Court bearing upon the question of colored men serving upon juries. So far as I can get hold of the facts, this is a clear, clean cut decision in our favor, and I think it will be a good idea for you, Mr. Browne and myself to arrange to have Mr. Wilford H. Smith, the lawyer who had charge of the case, make up a letter of instruction that might serve as a guide to colored people throughout the South and have this circular printed as far as possible in the colored papers and distributed also separately as far as possible. If the facts and proper instruction as to methods of procedure are put before the colored people and they do not secure representation upon the juries they will have no one to blame but themselves. Please let me have your idea as soon as possible upon the advisability of taking this course.

Second. Either before or soon after the committee of twelve has been formed, I think it well to get Mr. Smith, or some competent authority, to make a digest of the various requirements for voting in the various Southern States and put it in pamphlet form for large circulation among the colored people throughout the South. I find that in many cases the people do not vote simply because they are careless or ignorant of the law. For example, as the law now stands in Alabama, a very large number of colored people could vote if they were aware of the fact that they must pay their poll tax between now and February 1st. Unless some individual however, takes it upon himself to keep the poll tax matter constantly before them between now and February, comparatively few of them will pay this tax. It seems to me that our committee might have for one of its objects the keeping of such matters constantly before the people.

I do not mind saying for your private information that I think I could get Mr. Smith to compile the circular bearing on the jury system without charge since I employed him to take the case through the Supreme Court. Yours very truly,

[Booker T. Washington]

TLc   Con. 20   BTW Papers   DLC.

To Timothy Thomas Fortune

Tuskegee, Alabama. January 27, 1904

My dear Mr. Fortune: I have been thinking a good deal about the reorganization of the Age within the last few days. And there are one or two points which I want you to think about and act upon as soon as possible. First. I think it is very clear that in the near future somebody is going to see the opening that now exists and start a large national weekly paper that will control in a very large degree the whole Negro situation, and I am anxious for the Age to see the opening and occupy it. Second. I believe that the money can be gotten to reorganize and put upon its feet such a paper, but the people furnishing the money will look upon it from a bold, business standpoint and will want control. Third. I believe that if you and Peterson could see your way clear to sell at a reasonable price — $10,000 I fear is more than the parties will give — the money could be secured to buy your interests and at the same time enough secured to expend in further developing and pushing the paper. Fourth. In the meantime I believe that such an arrangement could be made by which you and Peterson would be put upon a salary that would leave you in control of the paper very much as you now have control, of course bearing in mind the idea that the paper would have to have some new men on it and the policy would have to be changed somewhat from a local one to a national one. There is an immense call for such a paper, and I am very anxious to see the Age occupy the field, and I believe it can be done with financial advantage to yourself and tremendous advantage in other directions to all concerned. Yours very truly,

Booker T. Washington

TLS Con. 1 BTW Papers DLC.

To Allerton D. Hitch[1]

[Tuskegee, Ala.] January 28, 1904

My dear Sir: I am very glad to receive your kind letter of January 25th and to be reminded that we met at the home of your grandfather some years ago.² I remember Captain Delano very well and my visit to his home. I hope that I may have the privilege at some time of seeing you in New York.

I would state in a word, that I think the main difference between Dr. Du Bois' position and that of my own is, that he believes that what the race is entitled to can be secured mainly through making "demands" and asserting "grievances." My belief is that we will secure more quickly and have in our possession more permanently the rights which we should possess through the more slow but sure channel of development along all commercial and industrial lines in connection with education, morality and religion. I believe that one successful Negro operating a bank is more potent in securing respect and justice for the race than a hundred men making mere abstract speeches or abstract demands for justice; but to make a long story short, I send you by this mail a copy of my book, "Up from Slavery," which will show you clearly my position. If I can send you further information please be kind enough to let me know. Yours truly,

[Booker T. Washington]

TLc   Con. 289   BTW Papers   DLC.

¹ Allerton D. Hitch, an international coal contractor with offices in New York City and Washington, D.C.

² Hitch wrote BTW that he had read Du Bois's *The Souls of Black Folk* and was surprised at the attack on BTW. He asked BTW to give his side of the story, since "Mrs. Hitch and I are both thoroughly in sympathy with your work. . . ." (Jan. 25, 1904, Con. 289, BTW Papers, DLC.)

From Theodore W. Jones

Chicago Ill. Jan. 28, 1904

Dear Sir: It has been my intention for sometime, to write you a letter relative to your standing in Chicago among colored people: but a heavy press of business has prevented my doing so. Recently word reached me through Dr. A. J. Carey, that you will be here next month, that decided me. A longer delay is not consistent with my endorsement of, and my proclaimed friendship for you.

I wish to set before you certain facts concerning our people in

Chicago, which I think you do not know, that you may determine how best to handle the situation upon your next appearance here. Chicago is slipping from you and I feel that you cannot afford to let her go.

The situation, Mr. Washington, is this: in Chicago your followers may be equal in number to those arrayed against you, but they are far out classed by brain, tact, and influence: the opposing faction has the ear of the public and the courtesy of the press; while we have neither.

Not long since "The Equal Opportunity Association" had an over-flow meeting at which you were severely criticised, abused and condemned. Every paper in this city had a reporter present, and the next morning every speech made was read by the public. Hoping to off set this The Business League had a meeting at Quinn Chapel. Mr. Baldwin of the Associated Press, promised to have a reporter present and assured us that if the speeches were not too long and too bitter, they should be published in their entirety. The meeting was well advertised. The speeches on that occasion were short, strong and to the point. No reporter appeared and the next day the daily papers did not even mention that the meeting had been held. The attendance was very small. A street car strike was in progress at the time and it was claimed that was responsible for the slim attendance. But all lines of transportation were not affected by the strike, yet the fact remains the people were not at that meeting.

The one colored paper supporting you and some of your endorsers claim that the opposing faction is composed of "bums, ward-heelers, cheap politicians, grafters, and envious men." This is not true. They are some of our brainiest lawyers, best physicians, dentists, druggists, clerks, teachers and good moral citizens: men and women whose influence is felt, who sway and largely control public opinion. This, Mr. Washington, does not reflect upon those who endorse you. Your followers are good, honest men and women in various walks of life, some are brainy and have influence where they are known. Unfortunately we have not the public ear and the press.

Now a word regarding The Business League of this city. The President, Secretary and Treasurer, with several floor members joined the opposing faction. To prevent complete surrender or dissolution we were forced to reorganize, and with all my business cares and responsibilities I was obliged to accept the presidency. Much of the dissatisfaction lies in the fact that our men are accustomed to *secret orders*, in which the Grand-head never appears in the city without first notifying the order. They complain here, that the National President of The Business League never communicates with the League save at the call for the annual session. There is dissatisfaction even since the reorganization. The only information the League has of your intended visit is through Rev. A. J. Carey. Our Secretary, S. Laing Williams, informed us that you "wish the League to join or seem to join with Dr. Carey in arranging for a demonstration in February." Now, being the President, I appointed a committee to wait upon Dr. Carey and ascertain if he will permit the League to join with him in arranging for your reception, but the men are chagrined to that extent that the committee has not even convened. If any thing is done along that line it will be through the effort of Mr. Williams or myself. The claim of your opponents that "Mr. Washington is not in touch with the colored people and gives no recognition to his colored friends," is readily believed and under such circumstances hard to disprove; it in no measure aids us in obtaining public or press recognition when we announce a Washington meeting.

This is the situation and I feel that you should know it and thereby be enabled to meet the issue and win over the opposers. Knowing the personnel of the other faction you may better judge wherein they find grounds for their opposition. Hence, if you see fit, when you come to Chicago in February you will be able to overcome much of their opposition. I firmly believe that this constantly criticising so severely, a man who has risen from our own ranks to your point of prominence, must redound to the race's detriment. I would be glad to see harmony, as near absolute harmony as can exist, between all lovers of the race.

Trusting that I have made myself perfectly clear to you and that your next visit to this city will be a great success, I am, Yours Resp'tfully,

Theodore W. Jones

TLS Con. 22 BTW Papers DLC.

From Robert Heberton Terrell

Washington, D.C. January 31, 1904

My dear Dr. Washington, Mrs. Terrell and I are delighted to have you consent to be our guest on the occasion of your visit to Washington in the near future. We shall look forward to your coming with a great deal of pleasure.

I have your letter with reference to myself and the conference in New York. I have noted carefully what you have to say about the composition of the meeting. While I do not believe that it is possible to harmonize the forces represented in New York, yet I can see clearly the force of the position taken by you relative to your own friends and supporters. While I should like to have been present at the conference — not for what I could have contributed to it but for what it would have done for me — yet our question is so large and so important I am always willing to make a personal sacrifice if by so doing it can be helped along any line making for its solution.

The men who are prominent in opposition to you and your work are moved by envy and jealousy. There may be a few exceptions. I hope there are. It is impossible to reconcile these men to anything you may do or say. If you had assumed their attitude and had advocated their doctrines in their words and had thereby gained prominence they would have adopted your present methods and would have still made you the target of their spite. This is an awful charge to make, but I am afraid that it is true. We are the only people on earth whose leaders cannot enjoy and appreciate success in each other. It has always been so. It must be due to the fact that so few of our people get that prominence that an inordinate ambition craves. They will not wait their turn. I have thought deeply about Morris and his speech here. The more I think of it the more contemptible the man and his utterances appear. If Morris had not been a part of the Conference he, perhaps, would not have merited the contempt of thoughtful people however much we might have disagreed with him. It is hard to reconcile his conduct under the circumstances with all that is best in man. His attack is not one to be ignored by your friends. It was specious, it was unfair, but it was calculated to catch a crowd willing to be swayed by him. It was a cleverly arranged assault. At some time it must be answered by one who knows you and who has read your books and followed your work. I don't believe that you can afford to answer it. Any reply of yours will simply give additional prominence to Morris and dignity to his utterances. Your books explain fully all the excerpts that he touched upon, but he would not do you the justice of reading further than suited his purposes.

I think that we sometimes make a mistake in not laying stress on your work in a more emphatic way on all occasions. It can be done in so many ways, and so effectively, without inviting a discussion of the "Man behind the guns." We who know and appreciate what you are doing for our race must hold up your hands and let the opposition call us all manner of names and charge us with all kinds of crimes and misdemeanors. The crisis is here and we must meet it. The great common enemy, prejudice, must engage our whole attention, if we would save our wives and our sisters and daughters from a degradation little less than that which slavery brought to their mothers.

Mrs. Terrell joins me in expression of pleasure at your contemplated visit to us. With kindest regards for Mrs. Washington, Faithfully yours,

Robert H Terrell

I am looking into Mr. Rose's case.

ALS   Con. 295   BTW Papers   DLC.

To Joel Chandler Harris

Tuskegee, Alabama. February 1, 1904

My dear Sir: Will you allow me to thank you most sincerely and earnestly for your very liberal and helpful article published in last week's Saturday Evening Post.[1] It has been a long time since I have read anything from the pen of any man which has given me such encouragement as your article has. It has been read already by a large number of colored people, and it would surprise and delight you to hear the many pleasant things which they are saying about it. In a speech on Lincoln's Birthday which I am to deliver in New York, I am going to take the liberty to quote liberally from what you have said. Yours very truly,

Booker T. Washington

TLS   Joel Chandler Harris Papers   GEU.

¹ Joel Chandler Harris, "The Negro of To-day: His Prospects and His Discouragements," *Saturday Evening Post*, 176 (Jan. 30, 1904), 2–5. Harris concluded that the Negro race was improving and that the great majority of blacks in the South led "sober and industrious lives." Harris wrote of BTW: "He is an orator of great power, a writer of unusual ability, and an extraordinary administrator of large and complicated interests."

To James H. Hayes

[Tuskegee, Ala.] Feb. 2, 1904

Personal

My dear Mr. Hayes: Both of your kind letters have been received. I am very sorry that Mr. Fortune continues to hammer on the suffrage convention. I made an earnest effort with him to get him to stop and supposed I had succeeded, although I could not get a promise that he would stop. He was considerably agitated when I spoke to him about it, but I have the feeling that the best thing is to let him alone and he will forget all about it in a few weeks and will find some other fellow or some other institution to hammer on and will forget you and your organization at least for a while. You will note that the other papers I think without exception, that I promised to help with have ceased to trouble you.

When I see you, I am particularly anxious to talk over the questions raised in Mr. Asbury's letter. More and more I feel inclined that Mr. Asbury is one of the most level headed and square men in the race and I think a great deal of his suggestions on any point.

Mr. Humphreys¹ was the man that I wanted you to see with me sometime when in New York. I am to be in New York on the 12th of February but my stay there will be so very short that I very much fear I cannot find time to see you at any length. I shall be there, however, next month when I shall have more time to see you and talk over important matters. Yours very truly,

[Booker T. Washington]

TLc   Con. 3   BTW Papers   DLC.

1 Andrew B. Humphrey, a white man, was secretary of the Constitutional League of the United States, with headquarters in New York City.

To Wilford H. Smith

[Tuskegee, Ala.] February 2, 1904

My dear Mr. Smith: Enclosed I send you copy of letter which I sent to Professor Hugh M. Browne some days ago, together with his reply.

What I want you to do is to undertake the preparation of the jury decision circular at once, and follow it later on by instructions for voting, etc. Of course we want to pay you for your work.

I am surprised that I have heard nothing regarding that Boston matter. What is the trouble there?

I want to congratulate you most heartily upon the moral effect of the recent decision. I have not heard from you as to whether or not in any degree it reached the vital purpose which we had in mind, but I do know that the whole thing has paid so far as the jury part of it is concerned because it has given the colored people a hopefulness that means a great deal, and I have spared no pains to let everybody know that you are entitled to great credit for the victory. I am sure in the end it is going to help you in your business. Very truly yours,

[Booker T. Washington]

TLc   Con. 25   BTW Papers   DLC.

To Timothy Thomas Fortune

[Tuskegee, Ala.] February 3, 1904

Personal and confidential.

Dear Mr. Fortune: The enclosed editorial I hope you will use. In case you do, please send me to this address three dozen copies of the paper as early as possible.

In this connection, it is interesting to note that the proposed separation in the street cars is violently protested against by the proprietors of the street cars in the principal cities of Mississippi. These street car magnates have already learned what has been the result in other cities where separate street car laws have been passed. Very truly yours,

[Booker T. Washington]

TLc   Con. 3   BTW Papers   DLC.

From William H. Steward

Louisville, Ky., Feb 3 1904

My Dear Mr Washington: I am glad to be able to inform you that my prediction made in New York has been verified. The proposition to disfranchise the Negroes in this state was indefinitely postponed in the lower house of our Legislature in Frankfort yesterday by a vote of 47 to 42. This means the death of the measure, as the motion was made by a Democrat and 29 votes of the 47 were cast by Democrats. Our Committee has been working quietly at the matter for some weeks and we are happy. The bill to prevent the co-education of the races, aimed at Berea College, will I think pass. It has been reported favorably, but so was the disfranchising law. The sentiment however is more in favor of the co-education bill. Yours &c.

Wm H. Steward

ALS   Con. 296   BTW Papers   DLC.

From Leigh S. J. Hunt

Zeidab [Sudan] Feb. 3rd [1904]

My Dear Dr Washington   Your boys arrived in good health and good cheer and have taken hold in a manner which augurs well for their future. If their beginning is a true index of their character and worth then I congratulate you upon the kind of men Tuskegee sends out into the world. To tell you the truth I am delighted with these boys and therefore very hopeful that my experiment in blazing the way to this land of promise is going to prove beneficial to at least some of your race. I hope to live to see those who come to me make fortunes at any rate. The boys here have recommended L. N. Spurlock[1] of Tuskegee and Ocie R Burns[2] of St Joseph Missouri whom I should like to have come to us if they will accept the same terms as you gave for me to Triplett,[3] Smith[4] & Powell[5] providing you are willing to let them come. If they decide to come send them along without delay. Gen. Clarkson will furnish them tickets. The boys here will write their views of the Sudan which I shall in no way attempt to influence. They know better than I what is likely to satisfy your boys. With great regards   I am yours &c

Leigh Hunt

ALS   Con. 29   BTW Papers   DLC.

[1] Lewis Nathaniel Spurlock of St. Albans, W.Va., was a postgraduate student at Tuskegee in 1903–4.

[2] Ocie Romeo Burns was a senior at Tuskegee in 1903–4.

[3] Cain Washington Triplett, of Mashulaville, Miss., was a senior at Tuskegee in 1903–4.

[4] Poindexter Smith, of Winona, W.Va., was a postgraduate student at Tuskegee from 1902 to 1904.

[5] John Perry Powell of Blakely, Ga., was a senior at Tuskegee in 1902–3.

To William Henry Baldwin, Jr.

[Tuskegee, Ala.] February 4, 1904

Dear Mr. Baldwin: So much is being said about Governor Vardaman's charges that it injures the Negro to educate him that I have determined to devote the major portion of my address on Friday evening, the 12th, to a refutation of that charge. I think this subject is so much in the public mind that something ought to be said on the other side. I shall discuss other important matters bearing upon our progress later. Yours very truly,

[Booker T. Washington]

TLc   Con. 18   BTW Papers   DLC.

To Theodore W. Jones

[Tuskegee, Ala.] February 6, 1904

My dear Mr. Jones: I am sure you will forgive me for my rather tardy reply to your kind letter which came to me a few days ago. This has been an exceedingly busy week with me and hence the delay.

I thank you for your frankness in expressing yourself as to the situation in Chicago. I confess that the thing that gives me the most concern is whether or not my course is the right one, and with that thoroughly settled in my own mind I care very little for personal criticisms or even direct opposition or hostility. In making this statement I do not do so with any degree of stubborness or foolhardiness. I realize that any man who is before the public ought to seize every opportunity to let his friends and the public know his position and to educate them as far as possible into seeing things as he does, and this is the policy I have always tried to pursue, and mean to in the future as far as possible. I have pass[ed] through, however, so many scenes of opposition that I do not perhaps look upon hostile criticism with the same degree of seriousness that some of my friends do. For example, I can remember the time in Montgomery, Birmingham, and elsewhere when persons would hardly speak to me upon the street and when I would not be permitted to speak in a church or in any public gathering, and students who came here to school were laughed at and held up to public scorn. Though my life has not been a long one, I have lived to see the time when some of the very individuals who have opposed me most bitterly at the beginning of this work, have had their children graduate here, and from having to beg students to come we are now to the point where we have over 1500 and have refused admission to about 1200 others for whom we have not room. I do not say this in a spirit of boastfulness, but to show that if a person is pursuing the proper course and keeps at it the world will come around to his position in the long run.

Now as to the suggestion that some people criticise me because I do not go among the colored people. I grant that there is something in that view of the case. I have regretted more than once that I could not attend more of the colored people's meetings in their churches, etc., that is[,] could not mingle with them more freely, but during the last ten or twelve years this has been almost a matter of impossibility. I had to choose between getting this institution financially upon its feet and spending my time with the colored people. I was compelled to go among the people who had the money. Now that we have succeeded in getting the school pretty well upon its feet financially and otherwise, I can see my way clear in the future I think, to spend more time among the people of my race and let them know more fully my own views.

Now as to my Chicago trip. You can easily understand that, consulting my own feelings, it would have been much more agreeable to me to have gone there wholly under the auspices of the Business League, but at the same time I could not wholly overlook the invitation that came to me though the pastor of Quinn Chapel backed up by Bishop Grant; this invitation came to me before any suggestion came from the Business League. I shall remember, however, what you say in my future visits to Chicago and elsewhere and will give the Business League the first opportunity wherever it is possible. I want to get my program for Chicago settled just as soon as possible, and I therefore ask that you and Mr. Williams get together and advise me what, in your opinion, ought to be done under the circumstances. You can easily understand that I owe something to Quinn Chapel because the invitation came from there first. It seems to me that it must either be arranged for me to speak jointly before the Business League and the church, or give the Business League if possible, a separate evening; I should not like to do the latter, however, unless it is absolutely necessary as my time is very valuable at this season of the year.

Do not become too much alarmed over newspaper reports of meetings and addresses. The public in the long run is able to separate the wheat from the chaff. I have learned long since that if 999 people in an audience cheer a speaker and his position and one individual hisses the newspaper will give more attention to the one man who hisses than to the 999 who cheer. The papers are always looking for the unexpected and the unnatural, and nobody knows better than you how often they can find it among our people.

Lastly, while I regret exceedingly that there are so many professional men and others in Chicago who seem to be against me, I feel just as absolutely sure in the end they will see that my course is the proper one and that in many matters they have misunderstood me. What we want is progressive, constructive work, not mere whining, complaining and criticism at the present period.

May I thank you again for your very kind and frank letter. You know how much faith I have in you and how much I admire you. Yours very truly,

Booker T. Washington

TLpS   Con. 22   BTW Papers   DLC.

An Item from the Chicago *Broad Ax*

Chicago, February 6, 1904

Prof. Booker T. Washington, his little lackey Emmett J. Scott, Dr. S. E. Courtney of Boston, Mass., who is unable to lead himself, "Race horse," Charles W. Anderson of New York, Old Drunken T. Thomas Fortune, who has rode every political horse in this country, Col. Jim Crow George L. Knox, Frederick L. McGhee, Saint Paul, Minn., who beat the writer out of three dollars as subscription to The Broad Ax, Col. Edward H. Morris, who was never known to give up one dollar of his great wealth for the benefit of the Negro race, unless he had a string to it, Judge S. Laing Williams, who resembles a woman more than a man, and many other self-constituted leaders of the Afro-American race, met in New York City recently in a secret conference under the guise of formulating plans for the improvement of the Negro. It is said, that those who attended the conference took an oath not to acquaint the public nor the rank and file of the colored race with its aim and object, which is conclusive proof that the conference was simply held in the interest of the cold-blooded and selfish would-be leaders of the race whose names have already been mentioned.

Chicago *Broad Ax*, Feb. 6, 1904, 1.

From John Davison Rockefeller, Jr.

New York   Feb 8 [1904]

Mrs. Rockefeller and I delighted to have you dine with us quarter of seven Friday evening of this week before your address in Carnegie Hall[1] please answer DH.[2]

John D. Rockefeller, Jr.

TWSr Con. 294 BTW Papers DLC.

[1] BTW accepted the invitation by telegram on the same date. (Con. 294, BTW Papers, DLC.)
[2] Deadhead, presumably meaning collect.

A Lincoln's Birthday Address in New York City

Concert Hall, Madison Square Garden, New York, February 12, 1904

NEGRO EDUCATION NOT A FAILURE

The anniversary of the birth of Abraham Lincoln and the presentation of the claims of the Hampton Institute furnish a fitting occasion to discuss the condition of my race.

Several persons holding high official position have recently said that it does not pay, from any point of view, to educate the Negro; and that all attempts at his education have so far failed to accomplish any good results. Except that these utterances come from official sources, they would have little claim to a place in a meeting of this character. But the Southern States, which out of their poverty are contributing rather liberally for the education of all the people, as well as individual and organized philanthropy throughout the country, have a right to know whether the Negro is responding to the efforts they have made to place him upon a higher plane of civilization.

It is not possible to improve the condition of any race until its mind is awakened and strengthened. Does the American Negro desire to improve his mind, and what has been the result of his efforts? Will it pay to invest further money in this direction? In partially answering this question, it is hardly fair to compare the progress of the American Negro with that of the American white man, who, in some unexplained way, got thousands of years ahead of the Negro in the arts and sciences of civilization. But to get at the real facts and the real capability of the black man, let us compare for a moment the American Negro with the Negro in Africa, or the black man with the black man. As was recently suggested by Mr. Carnegie, in South Africa alone there are five million black people who have never been brought, through school or other agencies, into contact with a higher civilization, in a way to have their minds or their ambitions strengthened or awakened. As a result, the industries of South Africa languish and refuse to prosper for lack of labor. The native black man refuses to labor because he has been neglected. He has few wants and little ambition, and his crude and few wants may be satisfied by laboring one or two days out of the seven. In the Southern part of the United States there are more than eight millions of my race who, both by contact with the whites and by education in the home, in school, in church, have their minds awakened and strengthened — have thus had their wants increased and multiplied many times. Hence, instead of a people in idleness, we have in the South a people who are anxious to work because they want education for their children; they want land, and houses, and churches, books and papers. In a word, they want the highest and best in our civilization. Looked at, then, from the most material and selfish point of view, it has paid to awaken the Negro's mind, and there should be no limit placed upon the development of that mind.

Does the American Negro take advantage of opportunities to secure education? Practically no schoolhouse has been opened for the Negro since the war that has not been filled. Often hungry and in rags, making sacrifices of which you little dream, the Negro youth has been determined to annihilate his mental darkness. With all his disadvantages the Negro, according to official records, has blotted out 55.5 per cent of his illiteracy since he became a free man, while practically 95 per cent of the native Africans are illiterate. After years of civilization and opportunity, in Spain, 68 per cent of the population are illiterate; in Italy 38 per cent. In the average South American country about 80 per cent are illiterate, while after forty years the American Negro has only 44.5 per cent of illiteracy to his debt. I have thus compared the progress of my race not with the highest civilized nations, for reason that in passing judgment upon us, the world too often forgets that either consciously or otherwise, because of geographical or physical proximity to the American white man, we are being compared with the very highest civilization that exists. But when compared with the most advanced and enlightened white people in the South we find 12 per cent of illiteracy for them and only 44 per cent for our race.

Having seen that the American Negro takes advantage of every opportunity to secure an education, I think it will surprise some to learn to what an extent the race contributes towards its own education and works in sympathetic touch with the whites at the South. In emphasizing this fact I use the testimony of the best Southern white men. Says the State Superintendent of Education of Florida in one of his recent official reports: "The following figures are given to show that the education of the Negroes of Middle Florida (the Black Belt of Florida) does not cost the white people of that section one cent." In those eight Black Belt counties the total cost of the Negro schools is $19,457. The total contributed by the Negro in direct and indirect taxes amounted to $23,984, thus leaving a difference of $4,527, which according to the Superintendent went into white schools. In Mississippi for the year ending in 1899, according to [an eminent][1] authority, the Negroes had expended on their schools about 20 per cent of the total school fund, or a total of about $250,000. During the same year they paid toward their own education in poll taxes, state, county, and city taxes, and indirect taxes, about $280,000, or a surplus of $30,000. So that, looked at from any point of view, it would seem that the Negroes in that state are in a large measure paying for their own education.

But all this has little to do with my main purpose, and that is to emphasize the fact that with all the Negro is doing for himself, with all the white people in the South are doing for themselves, and despite all that one race is doing to help the other, the present opportunities for education are woefully inadequate for both races. In the year 1877–78 the total expenditure for education in the ex-slave states was a beggarly $2.61 per capita for whites and only $1.09 for blacks; on the same basis the United States Commissioner of Education reasons that for the year 1900–01, $35,400,000 was spent for the education of both races in the South, of which $6,000,000 went to Negroes, or $4.92 per capita for whites and $2.21 for blacks; on the same basis, each child in Massachusetts has spent upon his education $22.35 and each one in New York $20.53 yearly.

From both a moral and a religious point of view, what measure of education the Negro has received, has paid, and there has been no backward step in any state. Not a single graduate of the Hampton Institute or of the Tuskegee Institute can be found today in any jail or state penitentiary. After making careful inquiry I cannot find a half-dozen cases of a man or woman who has completed a full course of education in any of our reputable institutions like Hampton, Tuskegee, Fisk, or Atlanta, who are in prisons. The records of the South show that 90 per cent of the colored people in prisons are without knowledge of trades, and 61 per cent are illiterate. Mr. Clarence H. Poe, Editor of the Raleigh *Progressive Farmer*, says: "In the two years during which the North Carolina Prison at Raleigh has kept a record, the proportion of Negro prisoners from the illiterate class has been 40 per cent larger than from the class which has had school training." These statements disprove the assertion that the Negro grows in crime as education increases. If the Negro at the North is more criminal than his brother at the South, it is because the North withholds from him the opportunity for employment which the South gives. It is not the educated Negro who has been guilty of or even charged with crime in the South; it is, as a rule, the one who has a mere smattering of education or is in total ignorance. While the Negro may succeed in getting into the state prison faster, the white in some inexplicable manner has a way of getting out faster than the Negro. To illustrate: the official records of Virginia for a year show that one out of every three and one-half white men were freed from prison by executive clemency, and that only one out of every fourteen Negroes received such clemency. In Louisiana it is one to every four and one-half white men and one to every forty-nine Negroes. So that when this feature is considered, matters are pretty well evened up between the races.

As bearing further upon the tendency of education to improve the morals of the Negro and therefore to prolong his life, no one will accuse the average New York insurance company of being guided by mere sentiment towards the Negro in placing its risks; with the insurance company it is a question of cold business. A few months ago the chief medical examiner for the largest industrial insurance company in America stated that after twenty years' experience and observation, his company had found that the Negro who was intelligent, who worked regularly at a trade or some industry and owned his home was as safe an insurance risk as a white man in the same station of life.

Not long ago a Southern white man residing in the town of Tuskegee, who represents one of the largest and most wealthy accident and casualty companies in New York, wrote to his company to the effect that while he knew his company refused to insure the ordinary, ignorant colored man, at the Tuskegee Institute there were some 150 officers and instructors who were persons of education and skill, with property and character, and that he, a Southern white man, advised that they be insured on the same terms as other races, and within a week the answer came back: "Insure without hesitation every Negro on the Tuskegee Institute grounds of the type you name." The fact is that almost every insurance company is now seeking the business of the educated Negro. If education increased the risk, they would seek the ignorant Negro rather than the educated one. As bearing further upon the effect of education upon the morals of the Negro during the last forty years, let us go into the heart of the Black Belt of Mississippi and inquire of Alfred Holt Stone, a large and intelligent cotton planter, as to the progress of the race. Mr. Stone says: "The last census shows that the Negro constitutes 87.6 per cent of the population of the Yazoo-Mississippi delta. Yet we hear of no black incubus; we have had few midnight assassinations and few lynchings. The violation by a Negro of the person of a white woman is with us an unknown crime; nowhere else is the line marking the social separation of the two races more rigidly drawn; nowhere are the relations between the two more kindly. With us race riots are unknown, and we have but one Negro problem — though that constantly confronts us — how to secure more Negroes."

There are few higher authorities on the progress of the Negro than Joel Chandler Harris, of the Atlanta Constitution, of "Uncle Remus" fame. Mr. Harris had opportunity to know the Negro before the war, and he has followed his progress closely in freedom. In a printed statement two weeks ago, Mr. Harris says:

"In spite of all, however, the condition of the Negro has been growing better. . . .

"We cannot fairly judge a race, or a country, or a religious institution, or a social organization, or society itself, nay, not the republic in which we take pride, unless we measure it by the standard set up by the men who are its best representatives. . . .

"We are in such a furious hurry. We are placed in a position of expecting a race but a few years from inevitable ignorance imposed on it by the conditions of slavery to make the most remarkable progress that the world has ever heard of, and when we discover that in the nature of things this is impossible, we shake our heads sadly and are ready to lose heart and hope.

"The point I desire to make is that the overwhelming majority of the Negroes in all parts of the South, especially in the agricultural regions, are leading sober and industrious lives. A temperate race is bound to be industrious, and the Negroes are temperate when compared with the whites. Even in the towns the majority of them are sober and industrious. The idle and criminal classes among them make a great show in the police court records, but right here in Atlanta the respectable and decent Negroes far outnumber those who are on the lists of the police as old or new offenders. I am bound to conclude from what I see all about me, and what I know of the race elsewhere, that the Negro, notwithstanding the late start he has made in civilization and enlightenment, is capable of making himself a useful member in the communities in which he lives and moves, and that he is becoming more and more desirous of conforming to all the laws that have been enacted for the protection of society."

In connection with this testimony from Joel Chandler Harris, may I add, no one has a right to pass final judgment upon the moral status of a race unless he has visited the homes, the intellectual gatherings, the schools and churches, where he can observe something of the higher life of that people. Our moral progress must not be judged by the man on the street. You may not know it, but the moral lines are beginning to be as strictly drawn in my race as in yours, and it must not be forgotten that we are as proud of our race as you are of yours, and that the more progress we make in education, the more satisfaction do we find in our own homes and social circles.

We are to live in the South, and sympathy between the races is vital. We must convince the Southern white people of the value of educating the Negro, and this we are doing according to the testimony of Southern people themselves.

Sometime ago I sent out letters to representative Southern men, covering each ex-slave state, asking them, judging by their observation in their own communities, what effect education had upon the Negro. To these questions I received 136 replies as follows:

1. *Has education made the Negro a more useful citizen?*

Answers: Yes, 121; No, 4; Unanswered, 11.

2. *Has it made him more economical and more inclined to acquire wealth?*

Answers: Yes, 98; No, 14; Unanswered, 24.

3. *Does it make him a more valuable workman, especially where skill and thought are required?*

Answers: Yes, 132; No, 2; Unanswered, 2.

4. *Do well trained, skilled Negro workmen find any difficulty in securing work in your community?*

Answers: No, 117; Yes, 4; Unanswered, 15.

5. *Are colored men in business patronized by the whites in your community?*

Answers: Yes, 92; No, 9; Unanswered, 35. (The large number of cases in which this question was not answered is due to scarcity of business men.)

6. *Is there any opposition to the colored people's buying land in your community?*

Answers: No, 128; Yes, 3; Unanswered, 5.

7. *Has education improved the morals of the black race?*

Answers: Yes, 97; No, 20; Unanswered, 19.

8. *Has it made his religion less emotional and more practical?*

Answers: Yes, 101; No, 16; Unanswered, 19.

435

9. *Is it, as a rule, the ignorant or the educated who commit crime?*
Answers: Ignorant, 115; Educated, 3; Unanswered, 18.

10. *Does crime grow less as education increases among the colored people?*
Answers: Yes, 102; No, 19; Unanswered, 15.

11. *Is the moral growth of the Negro equal to his mental growth?*
Answers: Yes, 55; No, 46; Unanswered, 35.

But it has been said that the Negro proves economically valueless in proportion as he is educated. Let us see: All will agree that the Negro in Virginia, for example, began life forty years ago in complete poverty, scarcely owning clothing or a day's food. Right here I lay emphasis upon conditions in Virginia for the reason that the Hampton Institute, whose claims we are considering, is located in that state, and is the oldest and most widely known of all our schools. From an economic point of view, what has been accomplished for Virginia alone largely through the example and work of the graduates of Hampton and other large schools in that state? The reports of the State Auditor show that the Negro today owns at least one twenty-sixth of the total real estate in that commonwealth exclusive of his holdings in towns and cities, and that in the counties east of the Blue Ridge Mountains he owns one-sixteenth. In Middlesex County he owns one-sixth; in Hanover one-fourth. In Georgia the official records show that, largely through influence of educated men and women from the Atlanta schools and others, the Negroes added last year $1,526,000 to their taxable property, making the total amount upon which they pay taxes in that State alone, $16,700,000. From nothing to $16,000,000 in one state in forty years does not seem to prove that education is hurting the race very much. Relative progress has taken place in Alabama and other Southern states. Every man or woman who graduates from Hampton or Tuskegee Institutes who has become intelligent and skilled in any of the industries of the South, is not only in demand at increased salary, on the part of my race, but there is equal demand from the white race. One of the largest manufacturing concerns in Birmingham, Alabama, keeps a standing order at the Tuskegee Institute to the effect that it will employ every man who graduates from our foundry department.

When the South had a wholly ignorant and wholly slave Negro population, she produced about 4,000,000 bales of cotton; now she has a wholly free and partly educated Negro population, and the South produces nearly 10,000,000 bales of cotton, besides more food products than were ever grown in its history. In the making of these statements, it should not be overlooked that it is not the Negro alone who produces cotton, but it is his labor that produces most of it. And while he may pay a small direct tax, his labor makes it mighty convenient for others to pay direct taxes.

Judged purely from an economic or industrial standpoint, the education of the Negro is paying and will pay more largely in the future in proportion as educational opportunities are increased. A careful examination shows that of the men and women trained at the Hampton and Tuskegee schools, not 10 per cent can be found in idleness at any season of the year. They have learned the beauty of work, the disgrace of idleness. But my real object, I beg to repeat, is not to enter into a controversy on this or that point of the progress of the race, but to emphasize the fact that with all the Negro is doing to help himself, with all that the Southern white people are doing, the opportunities for education for my race are inadequate almost beyond description, and the same may be said of the poor white people in certain sections of the South.

Years ago some one asked an eminent clergyman in Boston if Christianity is a failure. The reverend doctor replied that it had never been tried. When people are bold enough to suggest that the education of the Negro is a failure, I reply that it has never been tried. The fact is that 44.5 per cent of the colored people in this country today are illiterate. A large proportion of those classed as educated have the merest smattering of knowledge, which means practically no education. Can the Negro child get an education in school four months and out of school eight months? Can the white child of the South who received $4.92 per capita for education or the black child who receives $2.21 be said to be given an equal chance in the battle of life, or has education been tried on them? The official records in Louisiana, for instance, show that less than one-fourth of the Negro children of school age attend any school during the year. This one-fourth was in school for a period of less than five months, and each Negro child of school age in the state had spent on him for education last year but $1.89, while each child of school age in the state of New York had spent on him $20.53. In the former slave states ninety per cent of the Negro children of

437

school age did not attend school for six months during the year 1900.

I would seek to convince you that wherever the race is given an opportunity for education it takes advantage of that opportunity and that the change can be seen in the improved material, educational, moral, and religious condition of the masses. Contrast two townships, one in Louisiana where the race has had little chance, with one in Farmville, Virginia, says the United States Bulletin of the Department of Labor. In the Louisiana township only 10 per cent attend school, and they attend for but four months in a year, and 71 per cent of the people are illiterate. And as a result of this ignorance and neglect we find only 50 per cent of the people living together as man and wife are legally married. Largely through the leadership of Hampton graduates, 56 per cent of the black children in Farmville, Virginia, attend either public or private school from six to eight months. There is only 39 per cent of illiteracy. Practically all the people living together as man and wife are legally married, and in the whole community only 15 per cent of the births are illegitimate.

But the vital point which I want to emphasize is the disposition [of the Negro to exercise self-help in the building up of his own schools]² in connection with the state public school system. Wherever we send out from Hampton, Tuskegee, or any of our Southern colleges a Negro leader of proper character, he shows the people in most cases how to extend the school term beyond the few months provided by the state. Out of their poverty the Southern states are making a tremendous effort to extend and improve the school term each year, but while this improvement is taking place, the Negro leaders of the character to which I have referred must be depended upon largely to keep alive the spark of education. But when all this has been said, the question as to the elevation of the black man goes deeper than the interests of the Hampton Institute, deeper than the interests of a single race, deeper than the interests of the South. In the last analysis it means that we shall have in this country either a democratic form of government or a mere sham and semblance of the same.

It now seems settled that the great body of our people are to reside for all time in the Southern portion of the United States. Since this is true, there is no more helpful and patriotic service than to help cement a friendship between the two races that shall be manly, honorable, and permanent. In this work of molding and guiding a public sentiment that shall forever maintain peace and good will between the races on terms commendable to each, it is on the Negro who comes out of our universities, colleges and industrial schools that we must largely depend. Few people realize how, under the most difficult and trying circumstances, during the last forty years, it has been the educated Negro who counseled patience, self-control, and thus averted a war of races. Every Negro going out from our institutions properly educated becomes a link in the chain that shall forever bind the two races together in all the essentials of life.

Finally, reduced to its last analysis, there are but two questions that constitute the problem of this country so far as the black and white races are concerned. The answer to one rests with my people, the other, with the white race. For my race one of its dangers is that it may grow impatient and feel that it can get upon its feet by artificial and superficial efforts rather than by the slower but surer progress which means one step at a time through all the constructive grades of industrial, mental, moral and social development which all races have had to follow which have become independent and strong. I would counsel: We must be sure that we shall make our greatest progress by keeping our feet on the earth, and by remembering that an inch of progress is worth a yard of complaint. For the white race the danger is that in its prosperity and power it may forget the claims of a weaker people; may forget that a strong race, like an individual, should put its hand upon its heart and ask if it were placed in similar circumstances how would it like the world to treat it; that the stronger race may forget that in proportion as it lifts up the poorest and weakest even by a hair's breadth, it strengthens and ennobles itself.

All the Negro asks is that the door which rewards industry, thrift, intelligence, and character be left as wide open for him as for the foreigner who constantly comes to our country. More than this, he has no right to request. Less than this, a republic has no right to vouchsafe.

Neither must the nation grow impatient and faithless. It must remember that during the last forty years the South has been passing through a tremendous industrial and social crisis. This is true of the white race, equally true of the black race. The change from slavery to freedom could not be accomplished without mistakes on both sides, without each race going to extremes. Time, the great leveler, will exercise a modifying, a sobering influence upon all concerned, and in all proper directions.

With all his faults the Negro rarely betrays a trust or manifests a spirit of ingratitude. Whenever he has been called upon to render service in behalf of his state or nation, such service has been ungrudgingly given. Further, whether in ignorance or in intelligence, whether in slavery or in freedom, the Negro has always been true to the Stars and Stripes and the best interests of the nation; and no black-skinned citizen has ever lifted his hand to strike down the Chief Magistrate of the nation, or raised the red flag of anarchy. Every dollar that is put into our education by the North or South through such agencies as the Hampton Institute, the race will more than repay by a life of industry, intelligence, high Christian character, and in helpful friendship between the races; and because of our elevation, it shall be said of the South: "The wilderness and the solitary place shall be glad, and the desert shall rejoice and blossom as the rose."

Ernest Davidson Washington, ed., *Selected Speeches of Booker T. Washington* (Garden City, N.Y.: Doubleday, Doran and Co., 1932), 118–34.

1 Thus in typescript version, ATT.
2 Thus in typescript version, ATT.

Timothy Thomas Fortune to Emmett Jay Scott

Red Bank, N.J., Feb. 15, 1904

My dear Scott: Have to-day sent the Wizard additional names for consideration in the committee of 12.

Sorry I did not have a fuller talk with the Wizard this time. You may want to know why I have consented to sell my interest in The Age. I have got to the end of my rope as an editor, with no more reputation in that line, unless I take up the cudgels against the damned Republican policy of hands off, and the President's policy of much talk and no do, and in doing that I should have to collide with Mr. Washington's idea of running politics in the South, with a lot of rank Democrats here and there on top, which I can't stomach. And then I am making no living out of the Age and have to spend more than I make all the time, with irritation of feeling to make life happy. I would have asked under the new arrangement that I go to Tuskegee and have the departments of history and political economy, but the Wizard has not seem[ed] to care to have me at Tuskegee of late years, and I am no butter in; and hence have in mind to go to Jacksonville and with my brother in law engage in private banking and real estate on what I realize on sale of Age, and follow my literary bent. I have no faith in the President and the Wizard is afraid I will kick the traces all the time; so I want to get out and let the Negro business go except as a matter of business and make some money, which I can do all right, if I dump the Negro load I have on my back.

We all send love to you and yours, Yours as ever,

T. Thos. Fortune

TLS   Con. 284   BTW Papers   DLC.

From Charles William Anderson

New York. February 17th, 1904

Confidential

My dear Dr. Washington: I am telling you, in strictest confidence, of the result of my visit to the "General"[1] on yesterday.

Relative to my Club House matter, the General informed me that he was in receipt of a letter from Mr. Loeb, stating that the matter had been turned over to Governor Crane,[2] and that the Governor felt that nothing ought to be done along this line at this time. Thus you will see, that the whole thing has come to "pot," as I predicted. At our interview of last week, the General promised me that he would write directly to the President, but it seems now that he must have written to Mr. Loeb instead. Probably it is all for the best as, it will save me from contributing $200 as I promised.

On leaving the General I found Bruce-Grit cooling his heels in the outside office. He at once approached me and begged me to put in a good word for Chisum, whereupon I replied, "I thought you and Chisum were not friendly. Some one told me that you had parted company with him over the policy of the 'Impending Conflict.'" Bruce then told me that Chisum had asked him to write a letter stating that the paper had gone down because he (Bruce) refused to allow the publication to be turned over to the support of Booker T. Washington. He informed Bruce that such a letter would be of service to him, as he could do "some business" with it, and secure Mr. Washington's support to land a place for himself. Bruce told me that the letter was written to help Chisum in this way, and that Chisum had been showing it with his knowledge and approval.

Thus you will see, the whole scheme was put up by these two men, who are still *warm friends*. I told Bruce that he was making a great mistake, in his attitude toward you, and had not talked five minutes with him before I discovered that General Clarkson had also been talking to him. Doubtless this will account for the article in the Progressive American of this week, which I am enclosing to you. This is all fine business, and leaves a bad taste in my mouth. I told Moore the whole story, and asked him to see Bruce and get the facts for himself. Bruce thinks well of Moore, and I am sure will tell him candidly of the entire transaction. This I am sure will give you a glance at the real character of this man Chisum.

Hoping you are very well, I remain   Yours truly,

Charles W. Anderson

TLS   Con. 551   BTW Papers   DLC.

1 James Sullivan Clarkson.
2 Winthrop Murray Crane (1853–1920), governor of Massachusetts (1900–1902) and U.S. senator (1904–13).

To Robert Curtis Ogden

[Tuskegee, Ala.] February 19, 1904

My dear Mr. Ogden: I wish to speak to you about a matter which is important to be kept private as far as possible.

I find that Mr. Tanner is in rather a tight place financially, owing to the large expense in connection with the sickness of his wife, and together with the fact that he finds it is not so easy to sell pictures in America as it was in Paris. I have been trying to think of some way by which we might be of some service to him. He tells me that he is to exhibit some of his pictures in one of the galleries in April. I wonder if it would be out of order to send a note to some of our friends calling attention to his pictures? I have almost no knowledge of the proper method to proceed, neither do I know what to suggest, but I am anxious to be of service to him. Yours very truly,

[Booker T. Washington]

TLc   Con. 255   BTW Papers   DLC.

To Columbus Augustus Barrows[1]

[Tuskegee, Ala.] February 19, 1904

Mr. Barrows: I fear that you do not understand the policy of the school regarding the girls who work in your division. It is our aim to give the girls the very best training in poultry raising, and to this end I wish you to see that they are encouraged to remain in the department and are treated with every proper consideration. I am more anxious to have the girls learn poultry raising than the boys, and wherever girls can do any work as well as boys I wish the girls given the preference; in a word, I wish you to have just as few boys in your division as possible and as many girls. This policy I hope you will not deviate from. In order to get the girls to remain in your division and be satisfied, you must treat them with consideration, and not only be sure they are taught to do the work but learn something from day to day.

Booker T. Washington

TLpS   Con. 551   BTW Papers   DLC.

[1] Columbus Augustus Barrows, an 1894 graduate of Tuskegee, managed the Marshall Farm and taught in the night school there from 1898 to 1902; from 1902 to 1904 he taught poultry-raising and beekeeping.

To William Demosthenes Crum

[Tuskegee, Ala.] Feb. 19, 1904

Private and Confidential.

Dear Dr. Crum: Together with Mr. McKinlay, Mr. Cyrus Field Adams and others of your friends, I have been putting forth quite an effort during the last few months to try to secure your confirmation. It has been necessary to spend considerable money in sending telegrams direct to the senators in various parts of the United States. I do not mind telling you that most of the money I have had to take out of my own pocket, although I feel it was a good cause in which to spend money. It is almost impossible to get these senators to act properly unless influence is brought to bear on them direct from their own homes. I hope you will do everything possible in Charleston to keep down active opposition. If you can keep the people in Charleston away from Washington awhile, I think your confirmation will be secured.

Please remember me kindly to Mrs. Crum. Yours very truly,

Booker T. Washington

TLpS Con. 20 BTW Papers DLC.

From William Henry Baldwin, Jr.

N.Y. [City] February 19, 1904

PRIVATE AND CONFIDENTIAL.

Dear Mr. Washington: I have a report that it is proposed to take concerted action through the Brotherhood of Locomotive Engineers "to abolish negro firemen on the ground that he is a menace to their Order, and that the day is not far distant when he will be running an engine, unless he is abolished; also on the plea that he is not a success as he can not be depended upon to look out for signals and that wrecks occur thereby." Very truly yours,

W H Baldwin Jr

TLS Con. 18 BTW Papers DLC.

To John C. Asbury

[Tuskegee, Ala.] February 22, 1904

Personal and Confidential

My dear Mr. Asbury: I have read with interest your editorial in the last issue of your paper bearing upon the attitude of the Conservator. What the Conservator has said about you in this regard will give you some idea of the manner that that paper and two others of the same caliber have been treating me for over a year. I do not know what has put it into their heads to make this charge of subsidizing which they now seem to be industriously engaged in advocating. I have never paid out a single dollar, nor has this institution done so, for the purpose of influencing any editorial opinion and do not intend to do so. You and I both know that even if I wished to accomplish such a result, that an editor who could be bought one month would have to be bought the next month, and so on throughout the year. The Negro press has been most generous to this institution as well as to myself, and it is very largely owing to the generosity of the Negro press that this school has been built up to the point where it is, and I naturally feel very kindly towards the papers. I believe thoroughly in the wisdom of keeping an institution before the public in every legitimate way, but I repeat that I would not pay out a single dollar for the purpose of influencing editorial opinion. Time and time again propositions have been made to me of the most flattering character to get me to invest money in the whole or part ownership of Negro papers; this I have also refused. The Odd Fellows Journal is just as much subsidized by me as any other paper in the United States.

May I repeat again that I have always appreciated in the highest degree your unselfish generosity to this institution.

I wonder if you have had time to look over my New York address? I tried to refute some of the statements that Vardaman made without calling his name. Yours very truly,

Booker T. Washington

TLpS Con. 283 BTW Papers DLC.

445

To Francis Jackson Garrison

[Tuskegee, Ala.] February 22, 1904

My dear Mr. Garrison: I am very glad to receive your kind letter, together with your check and the photographs of your father. We appreciate your thoughtfulness in sending these photographs and wish to assure you that our students and teachers will be constantly helped by the sight of the face of your father. One of them I have caused to be placed in our library, the other I have given to Miss Clark to place in our main girls' building, and the third I am going to take the liberty of using as you suggest in my home.

Enclosed I send you a copy of an address delivered in New York City a few days ago in which, without calling his name, I attempted to refute the recent statements of Vardaman and others regarding Negro education.

In regard to the sleeping car matter, I think that Robert T. Lincoln, son of Abraham Lincoln, is largely to blame. If Mr. Lincoln would stand up straight there would be little trouble regarding Negroes and the sleeping cars. George M. Pullman let the world understand that no discrimination was to be tolerated, consequently there was practically no trouble while he lived. I think the present policy of the Pullman Car Company is to discourage colored people riding, and for the agents and conductors to tell them some falsehood as far as possible, but I find that wherever a colored man knows his rights and has the courage to assert them that they accommodate him in the Pullman cars. Personally I have never been given any trouble. I find that several of my colored friends have recently, in fact within the last two days, ridden in Pullman cars without difficulty, one came from Chicago this week and another from Washington.

I presume you have noticed the decision of the Supreme Court which compels the courts in the South to make no discrimination between the races as to the juries. This is the most encouraging thing that has occurred for some time.

Mrs. Ruffin is spending the winter with Mrs. Washington and me, and desires to be remembered to you. Miss Clark also asks to be remembered. Yours very truly,

Booker T. Washington

TLpS Con. 288 BTW Papers DLC.

A Protest against Lynching

Tuskegee, Ala., February 22, 1904

Within the last fortnight three members of my race have been burned at the stake; of these one was a woman. Not one of the three was charged with any crime even remotely connected with the abuse of a white woman. In every case murder was the sole accusation. All of these burnings took place in broad daylight and two of them occurred on Sunday afternoon in sight of a Christian church.

In the midst of the nation's busy and prosperous life few, I fear, take time to consider where these brutal and inhuman crimes are leading us. The custom of burning human beings has become so common as scarcely to excite interest or attract unusual attention.

I have always been among those who condemned in the strongest terms crimes of whatever character committed by members of my race, and I condemn them now with equal severity; but I maintain that the only protection of our civilization is a fair and calm trial of all people charged with crime and in their legal punishment if proved guilty.

There is no shadow of excuse for departure from legal methods in the cases of individuals accused of murder. The laws are as a rule made by the white people and their execution is in the hands of the white people; so that there is little probability of any guilty colored man escaping.

These burnings without a trial are in the deepest sense unjust to my race; but it is not this injustice alone which stirs my heart. These barbarous scenes followed, as they are, by publication of the shocking details are more disgraceful and degrading to the people who inflict the punishment than those who receive it.

If the law is disregarded when a Negro is concerned, it will soon be disregarded when a white man is concerned; and, besides, the rule of the mob destroys the friendly relations which should exist between the races and injures and interferes with the material prosperity of the communities concerned.

Worst of all these outrages take place in communities where there are Christian churches; in the midst of people who have their Sunday schools, their Christian Endeavor Societies and Young Men's Christian Associations, where collections are taken up for sending missionaries to Africa and China and the rest of the so-called heathen world.

Is it not possible for pulpit and press to speak out against these burnings in a manner that shall arouse a public sentiment that will compel the mob to cease insulting our courts, our Governors and legal authority; cease bringing shame and ridicule upon our Christian civilization?

Booker T. Washington

PDSr Con. 1107 BTW Papers DLC. The statement originally appeared as a letter to the editor in the Birmingham *Age-Herald*, Feb. 29, 1904, 2, and the Associated Press sent it to many other newspapers. The New York *Times*, Feb. 29, 1904, 5, printed part of the letter.

To Walter L. Cohen

[Tuskegee, Ala.] February 23, 1904

Private and Confidential

My dear Mr. Cohen: Your kind letter has been received, and the same mail brought one from Dr. I. B. Scott on the same subject as yours. Just as soon as the Panama treaty has been reported as passed I shall telegraph the President urging him to reappoint you and Col. Lewis.

I confess that I am thoroughly disgusted with conditions in Louisiana so far as the treatment of Negroes is concerned by the Republican party. Practically everything has been straightened out in all of the Southern states except in Louisiana, and I cannot understand why this disgraceful condition should be permitted to obtain in that state. Especially in Alabama has it been agreed upon, and the plan is now being carried out, that two colored men and two white men shall go as delegates at large to the National Convention, and there shall be one colored man and one white man from all the congressional districts. The Lily White movement has been completely killed in this state. I have hesitated to bother the President directly with Louisiana matters owing to the fact that I have had to take up so many matters with him recently and then in a few days shall have to put your case and that of Col. Lewis

448

before him, hence I thought it a good policy to go directly to him with just as few matters as possible. I am writing, however, today a letter to Postmaster General Payne, of which I send you a copy. This is rather a thrust in the dark as I do not know just how much authority Postmaster General Payne has, but I have heard from one or two sources that he has charge of Louisiana matters. In case I fail to get anything of a satisfactory nature from him I shall write directly to the President or see him. Yours very truly,

Booker T. Washington

TLpS Con. 19 BTW Papers DLC.

To William Edward Burghardt Du Bois

[Tuskegee, Ala.] February 23, 1904

Dear Dr. Du Bois: Enclosed I send you manuscript for a circular on the question of the Negro and the Jury. This was compiled by Lawyer Wilford H. Smith, the gentleman who secured the favorable decision from the Supreme Court, and he says that it answers all purposes. I would suggest that some explanatory acts be added.

What do you think of the wisdom of having this put in pamphlet form and getting the colored newspapers to republish it and get it before the masses of the colored people in every possible way? This might be done at once. Yours truly,

Booker T. Washington

TLpS Con. 20 BTW Papers DLC. BTW sent the same letter to Hugh M. Browne on the same date, Con. 19, BTW Papers, DLC.

From Robert Curtis Ogden

New York. February 23, 1904

My Dear Mr. Washington: Concerning Mr. Tanner: In the same confidence with which you write me I desire to tell you that last

449

week I gave him my check for $500. He desires to give me a picture in return which I will very gladly accept if it will be a comfort to him, but my contribution to his needs is not made with any hope or expectation of compensation.

It would, of course, be perfectly proper for us to call the attention of friends to his pictures when exhibited, and I will do so with the utmost cheerfulness. I am anxious to help him. I fear that, in the development of his art, difficulties have arisen that will operate against the sale of his recent work. I have seen a half dozen of his pictures which are very mysterious in spirit, very abstruse in art, full of delicate sensitivity, and altogether too transcendental for popular appreciation.

Please consider these hints as only for yourself. We must all help him to the extent of our ability. He is altogether too fine to be allowed to suffer, but I am anxious about his ability to succeed on his own artistic lines. It is not impossible that real genius may go to such abstract extremes as to place its product outside of and above the range of human sympathy and thereby useful influence and material return both be sacrificed. But we must help him, and I can be counted on for anything within my power. Yours very truly,

Robert C Ogden

TLS   Con. 255   BTW Papers   DLC.

To Henry Clay Payne

[Tuskegee, Ala.] February 24, 1904

Personal

My dear Sir: I hesitate to trouble you about a matter which I consider of great importance to the President and to the Republican Party, but I do not wish to trouble the President directly with the matter if I can avoid it.

I do not know whether you are keeping up with conditions in Louisiana or not, but I think in case you are not informed that you ought to know that the Negro Republicans are being completely barred out of all Republican councils in that state. This refers to both national and state politics. The Lily White party has gone so far as to put a white supremacy plank in their platform.

In the first place, I think you will agree with me that such conduct is unjust to the Negro race.

In the second place, nothing will be gained in the way of representation in Congress or electoral votes for the Republican Party or the President.

In the third place, and this is the most important so far as the interests of the President are concerned, you will find that if this movement goes on unchecked, the Democrats during the national campaign will use it among the colored voters in the doubtful states with telling effect. It may not be known to you and other Republicans of prominence, but it is a fact in New York City that a large majority of the colored voters cast their ballots during the last state election for Tammany Hall, and it is going to require a strong effort to prevent a large proportion from voting the Democratic ticket during the national election, not because they have anything against the President because on the other hand they love him, but once in the habit of voting the Democratic ticket it will be hard to win them away.

Fourthly, the colored Republicans in Louisiana are using the greatest amount of patience and self-control and are bearing all their ill-treatment with remarkable resignation, hoping that something will be done soon that will check the present foolish and unreasonable movement. They are especially anxious that no contesting delegation go to the Convention from Louisiana, and if they are recognized in a reasonable manner no contest will take place.

I hope this letter will reach the eye of no one except yourself, and perhaps the President. Yours truly,

Booker T. Washington

TLpS   Con. 4   BTW Papers   DLC.

To William Edward Burghardt Du Bois

Tuskegee, Alabama. February 25, 1904

Dear Dr. Du Bois: I have not answered your letter in which you enclose suggestions as to "The Committee of Safety,"[1] for the reason that I want to have some days in which to think the matter over.

The more I think of it, the more I am inclined to believe that while the plan outlined by you in many respects would prove helpful and wise, I am inclined to the feeling rather strongly that for a year at least, the Committee would better consist of twelve only. If we can make that a success, it may prove the basis for a larger and more thorough organization. Very truly yours,

Booker T. Washington

TLS W. E. B. Du Bois Papers MU. A press copy is in Con. 20, BTW Papers, DLC.

1 A copy of Du Bois's four-page outline, dated Feb. 20, 1904, is in Con. 164, BTW Papers, DLC.

From Wilford H. Smith

New York City, Feb. 26th, 1904

Dear Mr. Washington: I have your favor of the 24th instant, which had the effect of making me more cheerful over the result of our recent decision at Washington. I felt that I would sacrifice almost everything to have a chance to continue the fight and bring the court to a fair decision, and I am glad you think the same way as to the necessity of continuing the fight.

A case based upon the refusal to allow an unregistered negro to vote for a member of Congress and the presidential electors is the last and only other course open to us. It is the course along which the court has already made two decisions which they will be compelled to follow. In the condition of our cases heretofore, it was not practicable to make our cases along this line because the permanent plan of registration was not fully in operation. We can now make a sweeping attack on both plans of registration by this course through the U.S. Circuit Court, and the Supreme Court will have to invent some new excuse to escape us. I think that we should begin preparations by selecting a person who is unable to read or write, and who does not own any personal or real property, and have him pay all of his poll taxes from 1901 to the present time and have him apply for registration and be refused, and then offer to vote at the election, and I cannot see how this case can fail.

The law requires however, that all poll taxes shall be paid by the first day of February, or his vote may be challenged, still I think if all the taxes are paid now, no one will challenge a vote on that ground, especially when the party offering to vote is not registered.

I had just written you about the circular regarding registration. As soon as it is completed I will send it to you.

Regarding the Boston matter, I shall go up there next week and find out conditions and make a full report. Mr. Lewis has said nothing in reply to my letter. Very truly yours,

Wilford H. Smith

TLS Con. 25 BTW Papers DLC. E. J. Scott wrote in the margin of the third paragraph: "May work against it!"

To William Edward Burghardt Du Bois

[Tuskegee, Ala.] February 27, 1904

Dear Dr. Du Bois: In regard to the decision of the conference to institute a suit against the Pullman Car Co., I would state that I have done everything I could to get such a suit started, but the people in Nashville for some reason have not thought it wise to begin the suit. In the first place, Mr. Baldwin wanted us to wait until he could have opportunity to have a conference with Robert T. Lincoln himself, but as this conference was delayed I wrote urging Mr. Napier to start the suit in accordance with our agreement at New York, but there is failure to act so far. I rather think that this delay or failure comes about by reason of the fact that our people in Nashville find themselves not so much inconvenienced by the recent action of the State Railroad Commission as they thought they were going to be, still the fact is that no action has been taken. Yours truly,

Booker T. Washington

TLpS Con. 20 BTW Papers DLC.

To Edward Augustine Benner

[Tuskegee, Ala.] February 29, 1904

Dear Mr. Benner: I have just written Booker regarding his studies. I am sorry to see by the last report that he does not stand as high as in former reports except in his behavior and in his sloyd. I rather fear that on the whole his coming home for a vacation was not the best thing for him as far as his studies are concerned. I note, judging by his letters since he has been back in school, his mind is considerably on matters at Tuskegee. He found so much here to interest him that I fear he is thinking as much about matters here as about his books. I had a letter from him a few days ago telling me in detail all the repairs that ought to be made at our house; he made a careful note of them while he was here. Yours truly,

Booker T. Washington

TLpS   Con. 2   BTW Papers   DLC.

To William Reuben Pettiford

[Tuskegee, Ala.] February 29, 1904

Dear Dr. Pettiford: As a matter of fact, I do not know what day I was born upon. My family, however, follows the suggestion made sometime ago by a Sunday School at Rochester, N.Y., which, after reading my "Up from Slavery," decided to recommend January 1st as the proper date for celebration, and this has been done ever since.

I am greatly obliged to you and the Negro Business League of Birmingham for its kindly interest in this matter. Yours truly,

Booker T. Washington

TLpS   Con. 293   BTW Papers   DLC.

To Theodore Roosevelt

[Tuskegee, Ala.] March 1, 1904

Am sure real conditions in Louisiana being kept from you. Matters there in very bad shape. Every principle of justice for which you stand being overturned and disregarded. If not checked dissatisfaction will fast spread among colored people in other states. I am taking measures to put the real facts before you after careful investigation as to conditions in the state and as to Cohen.

B. T. W.

TWcIr   BTW Papers   ATT.

To Timothy Thomas Fortune

Tuskegee, Alabama. March 1, 1904

My dear Mr. Fortune: I presume you have read my letter on lynching which was recently sent out through the Associated Press. You will be surprised to know that I have just received the following telegram from Wilkins: "Just read your splendid protest against burning. Like it. Send your latest cut at once. D. R. Wilkins."

In this connection I wish to call your attention to what I have said in "Up from Slavery" on the subject of lynching; you will find what I have said on Monday is no stronger than what I said three years ago. I mention this because Wilkins and his crowd are going to attempt to say that they have driven me to this utterance. Yours truly,

Booker T. Washington

TLS   Con. 301   BTW Papers   DLC.

To Wilford H. Smith

[Tuskegee, Ala.] March 3, 1904

Dear Mr. Smith: I rather suspect that the law which requires that all poll taxes shall be paid by February 1st might work against any contention you should make of the kind mentioned in yours of some days ago.

I would suggest securing some such man as C. O. Harris[1] of Montgomery, who, I understand, has been refused registration and who has been practically conducting the Montgomery Post Office for many years.

A case based upon the refusal to allow an unregistered Negro to vote for a Member of Congress, or for Presidential electors seems to me to offer another opportunity and one which I think it well for us to follow up. Very truly yours,

Booker T. Washington

TLpS   Con. 25   BTW Papers   DLC.

1 Charles O. Harris, born in Alabama in 1852, was a clerk in the Montgomery Post Office, according to the 1900 census.

From William Lloyd Garrison, Jr.

Lexington, [Mass.] March 3, 1904

My dear Mr. Washington: I am indebted to you for many favors which deserved acknowledgment but they have not been unappreciated because I have been remiss. I read with avidity everything from and about you, watching with anxious solicitude the increasingly bitter struggle and wishing for channels of expression. I have long feared the acute stage of the Negro's steady upward progress, seeing no other possibility than increased friction when intelligence and character gathered force among the downtrodden race. You cannot educate men, even in manual skill, and fit them to occupy the menial position that a caste community (like the South) decrees. Revolt is inevitable and the caste system has to be shattered in the nature of things. So instead of a betterment of conditions in the near future I do not see anything but increased strain, precedent to the final grapple. It is not the brutality of the southern whites that discourages, but the letting down of northern protest and the bending of weak-kneed friends of the negro who are intimidated by the revival of southern autocracy. There were never more trimmers and doughfaces in the North before the war than now, their cowardly notes finding expression even on platforms where they lend their presence in your behalf. Eliot, Cleveland, Shepard, Lyman Abbott especially, betray by their apologetic and circumspect utterance

> "the little rift within the lute
> That by and by will make the music mute,
> And ever widening slowly silence all."

In the Montgomery Advertiser, sent by you and marked with red ink, is your speech at the Tuskegee Conference. You call my attention especially to your emphasis on the importance of the colored people owning the land they work. It cannot be too much impressed upon them. As Louis Post well said, "If the colored people of the South owned all the land there would only be a *white* problem to consider." I know of no oppression in the world where land control is not at the bottom of it.

In a little pamphlet which I mail herewith is an illustration of the fact borrowed from South Africa, where the natives employed in the Rand mining companies successfully resisted a cut down of wages because they all had patches of land from which they could support themselves. By refusing to work at the cut price and simply getting their living from their mealie patches, after 18 months' struggle they beat the billionaire mine owners and got their old wages. It is an object lesson and explains why Chinese cooley labor is now to be substituted. And one of the imperative conditions is that no Chinese shall be allowed to buy or lease land. Everywhere he who owns the land owns the labor upon it.

So what you urge with such good sense may and will benefit the colored people who profit by your advice, but it does not touch the all important necessity of putting land outside of private monopoly. Always free land should be the refuge of every man who prefers to employ himself rather than work for an employer. Very soon colored speculators will become landowners and in turn oppress those who must work upon the land or starve. The trouble is with the whole land system, as important to the whites as to the blacks. The basis of all liberty is equal opportunity, which simply means accessible land and unhindered exchange of products. I am sure you have an apprehension of the philosophy and understand that your mission is a special and practical one, and it is not for you to champion the abstract principle; but I trouble you with this dissertation hoping it may lead you more and more to feel that no men can be free while there are fellow men to make them pay for the privilege of living and working on God's earth. While less than ten per cent. of the inhabitants of the planet own it absolutely it is small wonder that 90% are discontented and that social problems tax the wit of reformers and philanthropists. The only problem in all the strifes of men is equal justice and opportunity. With kind regards,

Wm. Lloyd Garrison

TLS   Con. 288   BTW Papers   DLC.

From Henry Ossawa Tanner

Mount Kisco N.Y. March 3rd 1904

My dear Mr Washington. I am having a small exhibition of 5 or 6 of my pictures at the National Arts Club. This is however not the exhibition that I spoke to you of about the later part of March. But if any possible purchaser could be sent around I should appreciate it. As I am not a member of this Club I shall send tickets out as they were sent to me.

I am sending a large picture "Daniel in the Lions Den" to the Exhibition spoken to you of. I am asking $3000. for it & Mr Ogden would be willing to give $500. of this sum if the picture could be placed in the Metropolitan Museum of Art. This I should like if we could get others who would subscribe the balance. Of course I should first have to approach the authorities of [the] Museum to see if the picture would be agreeable to them.

Do you think there is any practi[ca]bility in such a move?

Desiring to be kindly remembered to Mrs Washington   I am Yrs Sincerely

H. O. Tanner

ALS   Con. 296   BTW Papers   DLC.

To Hugh Mason Browne

[Tuskegee, Ala.] March 4, 1904

My dear Mr. Browne: I am glad to have your letter of March 1st. I note what you say about the composition of the committee of twelve.[1] In my opinion, I do not think the fact that a man is an office-holder should weigh very much against him, or very much in his favor. My general feeling is that each man ought to be taken at his real worth. However, I do not attempt to say that your general idea in this regard is not correct.

I shall not do anything further regarding the Schurz article until I have heard from you again.

I presume you have already received copies of the jury article. I did not put anything on it to indicate from whom it was because I thought it better that our committee should make a decision on that point before any definite label was put upon our publications. Of course, the general preface should also be in a large measure uniform, and I did not know what was the wish of the committee in that regard either.

I think the plan of Dr. Du Bois[2] has some good points in it toward which we should work, but I have the feeling that it is rather large and complicated for our present purposes. I do not know how much experience you have had in dealing with large numbers of colored people, but my own experience leads me strongly to the feeling that the smaller the number, the more effectively one can work. I have written Dr. Du Bois that my thought is that if we can make a success of a committee of twelve for a year or two, we will then be in a position to take on a larger number. Then, too, since a good portion of our work will be confidential, I think we should go slowly in revealing ourselves to men unless we are very sure that they can be thoroughly trusted.

I have been having some correspondence lately with Dr. Frissell regarding the meeting with Dr. Buttrick, yourself and himself but I have not quite gotten the Dr. around to the point where he agrees to attend the meeting, but I think I will before the 21st.

By this mail I send you a dozen copies of a circular which I have just printed on lynching. Very truly yours,

Booker T. Washington

TLpS   Con. 19   BTW Papers   DLC.

1 Browne had expressed the opinion that no person who held an appointive government position should be allowed to serve on the Committee of Twelve. (Browne to BTW, Mar. 1, 1904, Con. 19, BTW Papers, DLC.)

2 Du Bois had proposed, in addition to the Committee of Twelve, a much larger general committee which would be divided into six subcommittees for political action, legal redress, social reform, defense and information, economic cooperation, and organization and finance. A copy of his proposed plan is in Con. 164, BTW Papers, DLC.

From Charles Waddell Chesnutt

Cleveland, O., March 5, 1904

Dear Dr. Washington: Some one has sent me from Tuskegee a copy of part of the Montgomery Advertiser containing your letter to the Age-Herald concerning the shocking outrages against negroes in the South. It is a timely word and I hope may make some impression. I fear however that the race has not yet touched the depths to which the present movement seems tending. The refusal of the Kentucky Legislature to adopt the disfranchising amendment scarcely offsets the destruction of Berea College. The bill to disfranchise the negroes in Maryland went through with no more commotion, no more show of interest, than would have gone a bill to repair a bridge across a creek.[1]

I have always admired your cheerful optimism, and I sincerely hope it may stand the strain upon it. But the present state of public opinion upon the race question is profoundly discouraging. I had imagined that we had reached the depths of contemptuous disregard in the case of Senator Tillman, but Governor Vardaman has gone far beyond him, and Bishop Brown[2] of Arkansas — a product of this city, by the way or at least a former resident, and a bishop of my own church here — had out-herod's Herod. Even these things could be endured, but when Pres't Eliot of Harvard comes out with his curious speech in New York, justifying by inference the rigid caste system of the South which is the real thing that is holding the colored people down, I feel the foundations falling. I am profoundly convinced that a race without political power or influence is and will continue to become even more so a race without rights. From its present attitude there seems no immediate remedy through the Supreme Court of the United States.

I hope that you do not underestimate the power of education, but these ferocious outbreaks such as that which disgraced the State of Mississippi and called forth your letter, make me wonder if we do not underestimate the power of race prejudice to obscure the finer feelings of humanity. With best wishes for your continued success, I remain, Cordially yours,

Chas. W. Chesnutt

TLS Con. 1 BTW Papers DLC.

1 BTW replied that Chesnutt was "mistaken about the disfranchising bill having passed the Maryland Legislature. It may go through, but so far it has only passed one house." (Mar. 10, 1904, Con. 1, BTW Papers, DLC.)

2 William Montgomery Brown (1855–1937), born near Orrville, Ohio, was the Episcopal bishop of Arkansas from 1900 until his resignation in 1912. He was deposed as a bishop in 1925 for heresy, and he later became bishop of the Old Catholic Church in America. He was the author of a seven-volume work, *The Bankruptcy of Christian Supernaturalism* (1928–34).

From Wilford H. Smith

New York City, March 7th, 1904

Dear Mr. Washington: Replying to yours of the 3rd instant, I have to say, that the suggestion as regards C. O. Harris meets my approval. I was under the impression that registration would not be refused a man like Harris under the permanent plan when the registrars open up in July. I did not like the idea of losing a qualified elector on an experiment when we could get along without it. Why not keep Giles, as he is so well known, and the fact that he comes before the Supreme Court so often will give the race a reputation for determination that it has not heretofore had. Then too, Giles would be perfectly willing to lose his vote for the prestige of having his name before the country. Owing to certain insinuations made in the equity case, and in view of the disposition of the court to invent technicalities, I would suggest that we bring two cases, one for a qualified person like Harris or Giles, and one for a person unable to read or write and owning no property whatever. We will get around the poll tax requirement by selecting a person who was over the age of forty-five when the new Constitution went into effect, and thereby exempt from poll taxes, and if such a person cannot be found, then to take the position that the poll tax requirement was made only to apply to negroes and not to white people. The danger in taking the last position would be that if they denied the fact, instead of demurring to the complaint we would be compelled to find proof that white men were allowed to vote who had not paid their poll taxes. I am quite sure however, that we ought to be able to find somewhere in the State unlettered negroes of good character and without any property who were over forty-five years of age in 1901 when the new Constitution went into effect. It will cost no more, or very little more to bring two cases instead of one, and as this is our last chance we ought to provide against every possible technical objection.

If you have not put out the circular to voters, you might amend by stating that persons over forty-five years of age are not required to pay poll taxes.

I did not go to Boston as I wrote you I would, because I received the enclosed letter from Dr. Courtney and I had reason to expect further information about the matter. I have also been quite busy in the courts. Very truly yours,

Wilford H. Smith

TLS Con. 25 BTW Papers DLC.

From Harry Scythe Cummings[1]

Baltimore, Md., March 8th 1904

My Dear Sir: Your confidential communication to hand. I have begun the work referred to therein and shall do all within my power to contribute to the successful outcome of the case. I shall guard with the greatest precaution your suggestion that no reference be

made to you in the communications. Wishing you great success   I
am   Very Truly

Harry S Cummings

ALS   Con. 2   BTW Papers   DLC.

1 Harry Scythe Cummings (1866–1917), a Baltimore black lawyer and politician,
was a graduate of Lincoln University and of the University of Maryland Law School.
He was the first black to be elected to the Baltimore City Council—in 1890, from the
predominantly black eleventh ward. He was a leader in the successful effort of
Maryland blacks to defeat the Poe disfranchisement amendment in 1905, with aid
from BTW and the Committee of Twelve. Active in the Republican party, he
seconded Theodore Roosevelt's nomination for President in 1904.

To James Sullivan Clarkson

[Tuskegee, Ala.] March 9th, 1904

Personal.

Dear General Clarkson: We have just held in this, the Fifth Congressional District, what I consider a model Republican Convention. All counties of the District were represented. About one third
of the delegates were colored, and the remainder were white, far
above the average type of white people who attend Republican
Conventions in the South. Two delegates and two alternates were
elected to attend the Chicago Convention; two being colored and
two white. Both Mr. Thompson and Mr. Aldrich were present. A
strong, aggressive, and well-to-do white man was nominated for
Congress. There was not a hitch in the whole day's proceedings. In
two counties the whites had seen fit to exclude colored delegates,
and the contests were settled by dividing the delegation between
the whites and blacks; which seemed to give entire satisfaction.

What was done here, can be done in practically every Southern
state, if the proper management is brought about. Very truly yours,

Booker T. Washington

TLpS   Con. 19   BTW Papers   DLC.

To Booker Taliaferro Washington, Jr.

[Tuskegee, Ala.] March 10, 1904

Dear Booker: I will write you a long letter soon. I am writing to-day to Mr. Benner something about your Easter vacation.

I am very sorry that you are charged with breaking some of the things in your room. Please talk with Mr. Benner about it, and I hope you will feel that you can say to him that no more property will be injured by you. Such things trouble me. Your father,

B. T. W.

TLpI Con. 17 BTW Papers DLC.

From Portia Marshall Washington

Bradford, Mass. Mar. 10–04

My dear Papa: I was so nervous and tired when I wrote my last letter that I suppose I said some things I should not have said. Please forgive me — if I did.

Our vacation begins a week from next Friday and I find that none of the girls are going to stay here. Miss Knott finds boarding places for them, else where. Do you suppose that I could board with Mrs. Brehaut in Wellesley — if she can take me? The woman I stayed with before? If you are willing I can write and find out. It is quite near Booker's school. Her address is Mrs. B. H. Brehaut, Wellesley Mass — and I do not think she would charge me very much. I shall have to know quite soon.

I hope you are better, mamma said you were not well in her last letter and I was worried about you.

I am still getting along nicely although I am quite tired.

Tell Mamma I had a nice letter from Miss Downing. Please also say to her that I am getting quite shabby. I need shoes, gloves, etc.

With lots of love for you all. Your loving daughter

Portia

ALS Con. 17 BTW Papers DLC.

From Charles William Anderson

New York, March 11th, 1904

My dear Dr. Washington: Replying to your good favor of the 8th, I beg to say that I did not receive a telegram from you on last Sunday. It must have miscarried in some way. However, I did not reply to the Bishop's letter, for I rather suspected that he was forming some sort of a Committee in which your friends would be in the minority. You will notice in his letter, which I sent you on last Sunday, that he says that my name was suggested to him by Secretary Loeb. Like yourself, I do not know what he is aiming at, and therefore thought it best to allow his letter to go unanswered for a time.

I am in receipt of about a dozen copies of your "Lynching letter," and I want to congratulate you most heartily, upon its tenor. I have sent them out to men around here who are supposed not to be altogether satisfied with your utterances, and much to my surprise and delight I have since met three of these men, and all of them commended this letter with all the strength of language at their command. Thus, you see, it is a good document for missionary work among the kickers and crocheteers. I have not sent it to any of the faithful, but to those who are considered a little weak. Happily there are not many such hereabouts. I forgot to say that your letter on lynching was most timely. The recent events in Ohio will give the letter a national significance, and no one can accuse you of addressing it exclusively to the South. It is a letter to the American people without regard to section.

Concerning the Club matter, it is looking a great deal better. I concluded that I would have this house or break a shoestring, and to that end secured promises of support from many of our leading citizens here. When I advised the General of this move, he soon cleared all obstacles away and started in to help me. I expect, therefore, to be able to have things started in a very short time. I of course need a little more assistance, but I think we can arrange that when you reach here and get a chance to see Governor Crane. The Club has now over 500 members, and bids fair to reach the thousand mark before next election day. To show you how thoroughly I have canvassed this City, I will relate a circumstance to you. In some of the lower East side districts, where colored people do not reside ordinarily, I requested the "Republican leader" there to send me the names of any colored persons living in his district, that I might have representation in the Club from each of the 35 assembly districts in this City. The leaders of one or two of these districts, notably the 1st Assembly District which includes Wall St. and Broad St., and the downtown business section, answered that there were no colored people in their districts. Thereupon I made a house to house canvass, and located from 12 to 20 colored persons in each of these districts. I found several families living on the top floors of banking houses in Wall Street where they were employed as janitors, etc. I repeated this in two or three other districts, and when I showed the result to the Chairman of the Republican County Committee, he was greatly amazed to find that I had unearthed 12 or 15 colored voters in one district who were unknown to the district leader. This of itself shows the need of such a Club as I have under consideration.

Begging your pardon for this long letter and expecting definitely to see you in Washington on the 17th, I remain   Yours truly,

Charles W. Anderson

TLS   Con. 550   BTW Papers   DLC.

To Portia Marshall Washington

[Tuskegee, Ala.] March 12, 1904

My dear Portia: In regard to your Easter vacation. How would you like to go to Brooklyn, N.Y., and spend the time in the family of Mr. Fred R. Moore? He is a very nice man and has several very nice daughters. Perhaps you have met them. If you go to New York at all I prefer you to be in the home of some family with whom I am acquainted rather than at a boarding house. You would have plenty of opportunity of consulting with Jessie. Please write me what you think of this, sending your letter to Hotel Manhattan, New York. Your papa,

B. T. W.

TLpI   Con. 17   BTW Papers   DLC.

To William Henry Baldwin, Jr.

[Tuskegee, Ala.] March 12, 1904

Personal

Dear Mr. Baldwin: I send you a clipping from a Birmingham paper which contains a portion of an interview from Mr. Murphy. This interview illustrates how almost impossible it seems to be for even the most advanced Southern people to be frank and honest. You will note that he names practically all the places that the Ogden party plans to visit except the colored schools. I do not believe that anything is to be gained by this kind of evasion. It is much better to be perfectly frank and straightforward with the Southern people; they will see in the end that other places have been visited, and what is more, the Southern people expect Northern people to take interest in the colored schools, and they will have no respect for or confidence in a Northern man who at this late date pretends to be interested in the white schools and not interested in Negro schools. Yours truly,

Booker T. Washington

TLpS   Con. 288   BTW Papers   DLC.

To William Henry Baldwin, Jr.

[Tuskegee, Ala.] March 15, 1904

My dear Mr. Baldwin: There are one or two vital points upon which I want you to be informed.

First, I have spent more time upon the school grounds this year than I have for a good many years; largely in consequence of this we are more behind at this time than we have been financially for a good while. I am sure in the long run the wisdom of my staying here is going to be apparent. I have given my attention mainly in two directions: (a) In bringing about a proper relation between academic and industrial education. I believe we have worked out and put in operation here the best system of education in the South and perhaps in the country; this was the verdict of nearly all the superintendents who visited here a few days ago. When you come I want you to go into the details of it. (b) My time has been given again largely in enlarging and planning for the future of the farm. It has been very costly indeed, but in the long run I am sure we are going to be justified in what we have been doing. Yours truly,

Booker T. Washington

TLpS   Con. 284   BTW Papers   DLC.

A Fragment of an Address
at the Metropolitan A.M.E. Church

Washington, D.C., March 18, 1904

Mr. Commissioner,[1] I thank you most heartily for your words of welcome to this city. I am most grateful to Mr. Lassiter,[2] to Dr. Scott,[3] and to the Trustee Board of this church for permitting me to have some part in connection with the success of their effort to build and sustain a church work which shall be a credit to the people of this city and to our whole country; and I wish also to express my thanks to the cadet corps of the Armstrong Manual Training School of the District of Columbia for the kindly and generous services which they have rendered me since I have been in this city.

Sometime ago, in a little town in the South, a boy rode into the village one morning with a large load of hay upon his wagon, and while upon his wagon and when he got to about the center of the village, the hay fell off of the wagon and the little fellow, in distress, went in search of a friend to help him reload the hay. By some fortune he came upon a friend of his by the name of Jones and earnestly besought him to go to the place of disaster and help him reload the hay. But Jones said "It is now nearly 12 o'clock; let's go home and have some dinner together; afterwards I will go back to the wagon and help you reload the hay." The little fellow replied "I would like to accept your invitation to dinner but I am sure papa would not like it." However, the little fellow was over-persuaded and he went on and had dinner with Jones, but as soon as that was over the little fellow again took up the refrain: "I am sure papa won't like it. I am sure papa won't like it." Finally Jones said: "Well, where is your papa anyway?" to which the little fellow rejoined: "Papa is down there under the hay." (laughter.)

Well, now, my friends, whether we like it or not, in a measure, for a number of years at least, we, as a race, have been somewhat "under the hay" in this country, and I am glad of this slight opportunity to have the privilege to help, in some ways perhaps, to lift the race an inch or two out of the hay.

Every individual race and nation has its peculiar trials and difficulties. One generation is not permitted to perform all of the service. Each individual, each race and each nation is likely to think that the difficulties confronting it are more serious, more embarrassing than the difficulties that confronted the preceding generations. But if one nation, one generation were permitted to clear away all of the difficulties, to solve all of the perplexing problems, nothing would remain for the succeeding generations to accomplish; and out of these trials — out of the very obstacles which are seemingly placed in our way, each race — each nation gets a strength — gets an experience and confidence which it could receive in no other manner. And so, my friends, I hope that as a people we will not suffer ourselves to become discouraged, nor suffer ourselves to enter into the Valley of Despair, but feel that there is a future for our race — a proud and a great future. (applause.) Every individual, every race and nation should have its goal, toward which it is continually making progress and in each case that goal should be the very highest and best things which the nation has to furnish. There is a certain work for each individual to perform and he should be fortified by the most complete education of the hand, of the head and of the heart for the performance of that work. He should go forward unspoiled by praise, unruffled by adverse criticism; he should not, however, mistake stubbornness for wisdom; he should attempt to live in a high atmosphere and should welcome, I repeat, criticism in the same spirit that he welcomes commendation. It is impossible for all the individuals of any race to agree upon the details concerning their advancement, but there are certain great fundamental principles upon which all of us are agreed, and I believe that among these elements is the one of frankness. We cannot advance very far unless we are absolutely frank and straightforward with each other.

(applause.) We must face the fact that in a large degree ours, as yet, is but a child race[4] — very largely an undeveloped race, and when I say that I do not indicate an INFERIOR race; a child race — an undeveloped race is a far-different thing from an inferior race. (applause.) The child in his place — the youth in his place, deserves as much respect as the full grown man. Two thousand years ago the proud representatives of the Anglo-Saxon race who sit upon this platform, were in heathenism, were in a more complete barbarism than is true of any black man in America. They had their period of undevelopment; we have had ours, and perhaps are having it at the present time. The main question, however, is not as to whether we are a child race or an undeveloped race, but it is — are we growing? Are we going upward as a people? And as has already been intimated a study of our history during the last 40 years will prove to any man that no race of people in history under similar circumstances have begun to make the progress that is true of our people in every part of this country. (applause.)

My friends I was never prouder of the race than I am to-day. (applause.) I am proud that I am a black man. (applause.) There are few kinds of individuals for whom I have supreme contempt, and one is the man who is ashamed of the race to which he belongs. (applause.) I was never prouder of the achievements and the progress of the black man of this country than I am tonight. We must however be sure that our house is being builded upon the rock and not upon the sand. (loud applause.) Very often the medicine that will tomorrow purify the body and make it strong and healthy, is to-day the medicine which the patient most dislikes to take; but the wise physician, the brave physician will administer the medicine whether it pleases the patient or not. (applause.) Whether it brings to him praise or curses, the wise physician knows that if he is cursed to-day he will be praised tomorrow. We cannot, however, reach our end — we cannot accomplish what we have in view by merely "willing" to do something — by merely "demanding" something, and in our willing and in our asking, and in our demanding I would SET NO LIMIT IN ANY SPHERE OF LIFE in which the Negro is expected to accomplish. (applause.)

Freedom, in its largest and broadest and highest sense can never be a BE-QUEST, it must be a CON-QUEST. (applause.) And the Negro can be no exception to that rule which has obtained with reference to all nations who have gotten upon their feet and who exert an influence among the civilized nations of the world to-day. Among the fundamental principles upon which all of us will agree is that every race of people must have enlightenment, must have education, a thorough education — and when I say "education" I mean that education which is most modern — that education which is best adapted to the needs of the country in which those people live. In a very large degree we represent a new race of people in this country. We are about 40 years of age and in a new country, among a new people. It naturally and logically follows that the first concerns of those people are very largely those that relate to their material condition. The people want at first, food — they want houses, they want clothing, they want a bank account, they want manufactories, they want all of those material possessions upon which every race of people rests whose civilization is secure and permanent. (applause.)

Two young men enter college, remain there during a period of four years; they sit at the feet of the same professors; they study from the same text books. At the end of the four years they receive the same diploma. One is black — the other white. In nine cases out of ten the white boy receiving that diploma goes to his father's home in New England or in New York City to become a partner, to become an overseer, to become a bank clerk or a cashier in the counting room or elsewhere of a business that was founded years, and, in some cases, centuries ago by his grandfather or his great-grandfather. (applause.) Nine cases out of ten the black boy receiving that same diploma, upon going to his home, finds no such business opening for him. (applause.) Therefore, in our present primary condition, it is important while we are educating our people, that a number of our brightest and best young men and women — not all, but a very large proportion, receive that education which will help them most to go home and CREATE A BUSINESS out of the raw material before them. (long applause.) It is not, my friends, so much a question of getting an education in our heads. The doors of the District of Columbia, so far as the schools are concerned, fly open willingly to every black boy and every black girl who would receive an education in this District. The doors of the school room and of the high school, of the colleges and of the universities in Boston and in New York fly willingly open to every black boy and black girl who would enter, but, my friends, the great problem that is beginning to confront us more and more as a race, is not that of getting an education in the head, but ask those gray-headed fathers and mothers if the problem that is pressing more and more upon them is the finding of employment for their sons and daughters after they have received that education. (long and continued applause.)

It was proper that in the earlier days of our freedom the main emphasis should have been placed upon turning out ministers and teachers and all those persons who wanted to do the various lines of missionary work. That was proper. We need ministers, we need doctors, we need lawyers of the very highest efficiency; no race that is so largely segregated, as is true of ours, can get along without its professional class of men and women. But at the same time we need back of this professional class, and beneath this professional class, a number of intelligent artisans and producers out of the soil. (applause.) In proportion as we have this intelligent producing class —the lawyer, the doctor and the minister will be sustained and supported. (applause.) Now I claim that we have reached that stage in our development where a large number of our educated men and women — I don't care where you graduate, get the best mental equipment possible, in high school, in university, in college or in industrial or manual training school — I don't care where you get it, you GET THE BEST MENTAL EQUIPMENT — but I claim that the time has come when a large proportion of our men and women, after graduating from college and university, should go out and start some kind of industry upon which, and from which a large number of our people can draw an independent and decent support. (applause.) In too large a measure we have looked to the ignorant class of people to sustain these industries; they need to have come to their relief this educated class, the men and women to whom I have referred. I was in a city of the North not very long ago and I met a friend of mine. He came up to me and said: "Mr. Washington, I like you as an individual very much, but I don't like the emphasis which you place upon manual and industrial education for the Negro." "Well," I said, "we won't fall out about that; we will simply agree, perhaps, to disagree." And I said to him: "What are you engaged in in this city?" He said: "I am pastoring a church." I said:

"I shall be very much pleased to see your church." He told me that he would be only too glad to show me his church, he said it was a brand new church, just built at a cost of $25,000. I went with him and soon saw a very fine, attractive, well built church house, and I said to him "$25,000 is a good deal of money"; I said, "Where did you get this money?" He said that three-fourths of it came from the nickels and dimes and quarters that the women and their daughters earn over the washtub, the iron board and the cook stove; (Dr. Washington pointing to the Ministers on the platform said: "all of you ministers know that") (laughter.) I then said to him: "Your church certainly is beautiful, it is perfect in design, and will you tell me who drew the plans for your building?" "Well," he said, "Jones-Smith-and-Company up here on Broadway." I asked him to tell me who was Jones-Smith-and-Company. "Well," he said, "they are a very prominent firm of white architects in this city." "Well," I said, "those are very fine brick you have laid into your building; will you tell me where you bought those bricks; who manufactured them?" He said: "Why, a German firm out here about two miles from the city manufactured those bricks, and they are a very fine quality of brick, I tell you." (laughter.) "Well," I said, "that is a beautiful job of brick masonry; who laid those bricks into the walls?" He told me that "up there in the center of the town, near the post-office, there is an Irish firm, the senior partner of which came over to this country from Ireland about 20 years ago and began making a living by digging ditches and he soon grew into a big contractor and now he is putting up all the finest buildings in this city and," said he, "I thought it would be a fine thing to have that prominent firm to lay the bricks in this house." (laughter.) I went inside of the church with him and he showed me the excellent job of plastering; I said, "Who did that?" He said some rich firm did the plastering. (continued laughter.) Then I noticed the job of painting and decorating and I said, "Who did that?" He said: "There is an Italian firm here (laughter.) that does very fine painting and decorating — you know they are good at that — these Italians are noted for their skill in colors, and I thought it would be just the thing to get those Italians from Sunny Italy to do the decorating and painting in this house." I said: "I see you have got the church lighted by electricity; will you tell me who did that?"

"Well," he said, "a firm of Americans, just simply Americans, did that." And I said seriously: "My friend, do you mean to stand here as a Christian minister, an intelligent man, a leader of your people in this community — do you mean to tell me that you have taken out of the pockets of these washerwomen and from the pockets of these men who earn their living by working on the street and as hod-carriers, barbers, draymen and the like — you mean to tell me that you have taken $25,000 of their hard-earned money and paid it all out to these white firms and have not given a single black boy or a black man a chance to lay a brick or drive a carpenter's plane on that building?" (continued applause, mingled with laughter.) "Well," I said, "with this building standing here as an object lesson, do you mean to tell me that I must not advise our people to educate the hand so that they may make bricks, paint and decorate and build, and light buildings by electricity as the white man is doing? (long and continued applause.) NOW WE NEED MINISTERS TO PREACH THE GOSPEL IN THESE FINE CHURCHES AND YOU GET THE PEOPLE TO HEAVEN WHILE WE, at Tuskegee and other places where they have manual and industrial training, WILL BUILD THE CHURCHES IN WHICH THEY CAN PREPARE THEMSELVES FOR G-L-O-R-Y! (laughter and applause.)

Now those of you, my friends, who have studied education (and there are a number of people in this room who have studied more about education than I ever had the privilege of doing) know that the trend of education during the last 50 years, not only in America but in every civilized country of the world, including Europe, has steadily tended in one direction — the cementing of mind to matter — of bringing about, as the Hon. Mr. Watson said "of the partnership of head and hand"; it is tending in the direction of specialization. When we studied chemistry in the olden days, it was by the book method; we committed to memory certain formulas; when we study chemistry to-day, in a degree we throw aside the book and go into the laboratory where we come in direct contact with the particles of matter. When we studied botany in the old days, it was by the book method; to-day, in a very large measure, we go into the field with the boys and girls and get into direct contact with the plants they are studying. Where was once the old classical course, we now have in every university not only a classical course but a scientific course as well, and in addition to that you have an agricultural school, a manual training school and a dressmaking school in every civilized country of the world.

Now some have gotten the idea that industrial education is something that has been especially prepared and created during the last 40 years for the special benefit of the black people of this country. (laughter and applause.) Now let us see, my friends, to what extent that is true. Do you know that in Saxony, Germany, there is one industrial school for every 14,000 individuals in that province or a total of 287 industrial schools in only one part of Germany? In the South we have only one to every 500,000 Negroes. Do you know how industrial education has spread, and is spreading over every section of the North? Why, in the University of Minnesota, which I visited a few months ago, I found 50 bright, intelligent, cultured white women in the agricultural department of that university studying agriculture. I saw in England a few years ago — when I went to what is known as the Girls' Agricultural College at Swanley — there I found young women, graduates of high schools and of universities and colleges, from the best sections of England, studying agriculture, horticulture, bee-raising — studying everything that relates to agricultural development in that section. My friends, if it is necessary for a people, who are in the advanced condition as are the masses of the people in England, to secure an industrial education, how many times more necessary is it for our people in this country? (applause.) You will find an agricultural college in every state of the Union, and, my friends, let me tell you this — do you know that there is more money to-day being spent in the South for the industrial and technical education of white boys and white girls than there is for the same kind of education for our own people? I do not want to make a general statement, I want to give you definite facts. Let us take the state of Georgia for instance. In the city of Atlanta the sum of $40,000 annually is spent in the industrial education of the white boys of that city. At Milledgeville the sum of $22,000 is spent for the industrial education of white girls annually. At the State agricultural college $10,000 annually is spent for the agricultural education of white boys. They spend in the whole state of Georgia the pitiful sum of $10,000 for the industrial education of the black boys and girls, while they spend $72,000 for the same kind of education for the white children of that state. The State legislature of Mississippi, a few days ago, passed a bill appropriating $175,000 for the education of white girls along in the Industrial. . . .

TDf   Con. 802   BTW Papers   DLC.

¹ Henry B. F. Macfarland, president of the Commissioners of the District of Columbia, gave BTW an address of welcome.

² Henry Lassiter, a Washington black man.

³ Oscar Jefferson Waldo Scott.

⁴ BTW's black critics made much of his acceptance of the popular Social Darwinism that white supremacists employed to justify racial discrimination. Though BTW denied in his speech that he intended to imply innate inferiority, he was in fact approving a social hierarchy in which blacks were assigned the place of children. Despite the criticisms, BTW continued to use the phrase, which reveals his ambivalence on the question of the appropriate "place" of blacks in the social order. A defense of BTW by a New York black leader is Samuel R. Scottron to the editor, New York *Age*, May 19, 1904, Clipping, Con. 871, BTW Papers, DLC.

To Walter L. Cohen

Washington, D.C. March 20th, 1904

PERSONAL.

Dear Mr. Cohen: Please do not let this letter pass out of your hands.

I have had two long and interesting interviews with our friend here about your case. There is no question about it that those fellows have been getting in some pretty hard work against you. One of the charges made was that you at present own an interest in a bar-room, or a house of ill-fame of some sort. I need not tell you how earnestly Dr. I. B. Scott, Mr. E. J. Scott, and myself have sought to overthrow this impression, and I think we have done so.

He remarked before we left that he would not remove you; and that, of course, secures you in your position. But we want more. We wish your reappointment. The fact is, I fear, that he dislikes to offend the referees there, who have control of affairs; but he admires the manly stand you have taken in behalf of your race, and was especially pleased with your manly letter to Payne.

To sum up, the whole matter has been taken out of the hands of Payne, and placed in the hands of Elmer Dover,¹ whom you know, and who is one of your best friends. I do not think it safe for you at present, (without notifying me) to communicate with Dover, or let him know that you have information from me, but wait until he communicates with you, and at the proper time it might be well for you to come to Washington and see Dover. You will remember that he was Secretary Hanna's private secretary.

I have no fear of the final result; the matter only needs nursing. Very truly,

[Booker T. Washington]

TLc   Con. 19   BTW Papers   DLC.

1 Elmer Dover (1873–1940) was secretary to Mark Hanna from 1897 to 1904, secretary of the Republican National Committee from 1904 to 1908, and Assistant Secretary of the Treasury from 1921 to 1922.

Emmett Jay Scott
to Roscoe Conkling Simmons

[Tuskegee, Ala.] March 23, 1904

Dear Mr. Simmons: Herewith I am sending you all of the Washington papers with reports of the Doctor's address. I am sure you can use it to good advantage. I ordered the papers sent to you from Washington, but it has occurred to me that perhaps they were not received, and so I am sending you these additional copies.

Of course it will occur to you that the reception at the banquet and at the church, as well as the splendid meeting, at Congressman Porter's,[1] prove exclusively that the Doctor has the enemy on the run. Important also, it seems to me, was the splendid ovation given Mr. Washington when he came from Lassiter's house to go to the church when fifteen hundred or more people made the streets impassable and gave him such an ovation as resounded for blocks and blocks. When he proceeded to the church he had to pass through lines of people and a way was made by the police with much difficulty. It was a splendid triumph in every way, and the fact that he invaded the enemies' territory in Boston and gave the lie to the enemy there as well as in Washington, is the strongest evidence of his courage in carrying the message directly to the people and telling his own story. It was a great week and I found real pleasure in being with the Doctor and in helping somewhat. Very truly yours,

Emmett J. Scott

TLpS   Con. 25   BTW Papers   DLC.

¹ Henry Kirke Porter (1840–1921) of Pennsylvania, who served in the U.S. House of Representatives from 1903 to 1905.

To Emmett J. Scott

Hotel Manhattan, New York City. March 27th, 1904

Dear Mr. Scott: Perhaps you can take up and arrange in a private manner with Mr. Langston¹ of St. Louis the program for Negro Day. I prefer to let Du Bois draw his own crowd, and I will draw mine. I understand that there will be two or three sessions. Very truly,

B. T. W.

TLI   Con. 550   BTW Papers   DLC.

¹ Arthur D. Langston, born in Ohio in 1865, was principal of the Dumas School in St. Louis. He was also president of the Egyptian Club, organized to entertain black visitors to the St. Louis Exposition.

To Henry Ossawa Tanner

Hotel Manhattan, New York City. March 28th, 1904

Dear Mr. Tanner: I have already spoken to one or two people about your pictures. One of them is Mr. Wm. Jay Schieffelin, whom I am writing today and asking to call to see them. I saw the exhibition yesterday morning, and was very glad to see your pictures, as well as the others.

Enclosed I send you the address of Mr. Volk,¹ one of the judges who passed upon your pictures. He is anxious to see you, and seems a generous and whole-souled man. He might be of assistance to you. Very truly yours,

[Booker T. Washington]

TLc Con. 295 BTW Papers DLC.

1 Stephen Arnold Douglas Volk, later Douglas Volk (1856–1935).

To Theodore Roosevelt

Hotel Manhattan, New York City. March 29th, 1904

Personal and Confidential.

My dear Mr. President: I do hope that you will stand by what you told me to say to Mr. Thompson regarding the Chairmanship, when I saw you a week ago at the White House. I telegraphed Mr. Thompson what you said, namely, that you had no objection to his being chairman if it came about in a natural way, that is, provided that he would have been the choice of the people if he had not held a federal office. The candidacy has been urged upon Mr. Thompson, and while I take no sides in the matter, I hope that you will let the voters settle the question as they think wise. You know that Mr. Aldrich is a very busy man, engaged in large business enterprises; and that Mr. Scott is much out of the state. Mr. Thompson is really the man who has taken off his coat, gone down among the masses and done the work; and has thus brought the two wings of the party together. Because of his hard and unselfish work for you and the party, the people like him, and feel that he is very close to them; he is very strong with the masses. I am not urging that he or anyone else be elected but that the matter be left to its natural course if you see your way clear to do so.

Any change from what you said at the White House will place both Mr. Thompson and myself in an awkward position.

Any answer sent to me here will reach me. Very truly yours,

[Booker T. Washington]

TLc BTW Papers ATT.

From Wilford H. Smith

New York City, March 31st, 1904

Dear Mr. Washington: I have gone over, several times, the matter of the probable course proceedings will take in a suit against the election officers, and I feel quite confident that I can so frame the case as to compel a demurrer and bring the cases up to the Supreme Court on questions of law rather than facts, and thus avoid a voluminous and expensive record. I still think that two cases should be made in order to reach both plans of registration.

If you are willing to risk so much, I can cover the expenses and pay myself out of $1500. This is as close as I can possibly cut the figures, and I fully appreciate the sacrifices you have already made in this matter, and the unsatisfactory result so far, as well as the advantage it will be to me to finally triumph in the fight.

My letters to Dr. Courtney and Mr. Lewis at Boston written the day I saw you are still unanswered. Just as soon as I hear from them [I] will communicate with you.

As to the Palisade Park lots, the party who was speaking of buying them is expected from Cuba any day. As soon as she comes I will try to close out to her. If I cannot I would feel very much relieved if some arrangement could be made so as to make the payments in the future without using my friend from Texas. Very truly yours,

Wilford H. Smith

TLS   Con. 25   BTW Papers   DLC.

To Walter L. Cohen

Hotel Manhattan, New York City. April 1st, 1904

Personal.

Dear Mr. Cohen: I do not intend to answer your letter fully at present, but to acquaint you with the following facts.

The President himself wrote a card to Secretary Hitchcock, appointing Col. Lewis at once. The card was given to Mr. Scott, my secretary, who fortunately delayed delivering it until I had arrived. When I saw the card, I took the liberty of holding it up until I saw the President, when I frankly told him what I had done. He smiled. I think you will agree that if Col. Lewis had been reappointed, but you had not, the Lily-whites would have concentrated the fight on you, and would have claimed a victory. Col. Lewis knows what has been done, and takes it in good part. I think you should let him know that you are grateful to him for his generosity. There is no fight on him, and he cannot possibly fail of reappointment.

Enclosed I return the letters from Mr. Dover which you sent me.

If this letter does not reach you too late, I should like to see you here when you come to Washington to see Mr. Dover. I shall probably be here, excepting from the 2d to the 6th, until the 18th of April. Please keep me informed as to how the fight goes. Very truly yours,

[Booker T. Washington]

TLc Con. 19 BTW Papers DLC.

To Margaret James Murray Washington

[Hotel Manhattan, New York City] April 11th, 1904

Shall call tonight before eight o'clock to take you to recital.

B. T. W.

TWlr Con. 553 BTW Papers DLC. Addressed to 235 West Thirteenth Street, New York City.

From Ellen A. Craft Crum[1]

Charleston S.C. April 15. [1904]

Dear Mr. Washington: Dr Crum has requested me to write you and to return Mr. Morton's letter and to thank you for sending it, and also to say that he will write you shortly.

We both feel deeply grateful to you for all your kindnesses and know you have done all in your power.

Dr. is broken in health and spirit, he has been quite sick this week having to go to bed. I am afraid it is the beginning of the end with him should this senate neglect to confirm him as the papers here seem to be sure it will. He says the President could not be expected to rename him and that the night work he is compelled to do to keep up his practice, to keep the home going is very taxing. His lungs are weak. Two brothers have died in the past 6 months of consumption.

We still have a flickering hope from the letter you sent of Senator Gallinger.[2]

Better be dead than an Afro-*American.* Still we trust in God. Kind regards to Mrs. Washington. Very Sincerely

Ellen A. Crum

ALS Con. 20 BTW Papers DLC.

[1] Ellen A. Craft Crum, born in England in 1866, married William D. Crum in 1883. Her parents were runaway slaves who were befriended by Theodore Parker and Samuel May, who helped arrange their passage to England in 1850. They returned to the United States in 1871 and purchased an 1,800-acre plantation in Savannah, Ga., which became the site of their industrial school, Woodville Co-operative Farm School.

[2] Jacob Harold Gallinger (1837–1918), a Republican, was U.S. senator from New Hampshire (1891–1918).

To Bettie G. Cox Francis[1]

[Tuskegee, Ala.] April 21, 1904

Personal

Dear Mrs. Francis: Yesterday I sent you a telegram reading as follows:

"Have you done so or are you intending to employ a Miss Murrell recently connected with this institution? If she has not begun work, I think it well that you should hear from me before she does. Answer my expense."

Miss Murrell was employed to teach in this institution during the present school session. While I was North she received an offer of a position in Washington, as I understand it, on Friday and left here on Saturday. The manner of her leaving was to me a great disappointment and mortification.[2] I must say that during the two years in which she was a teacher here, she conducted herself in a lady-like manner, giving satisfaction in her deportment and in her teaching, but the thing that surprised and mortified me was that she was unable to see that she had a moral responsibility in connection with the manner of her leaving this institution. She did not give me time to make any provision for anyone to take her place. She did not receive the permission of the acting principal, nor did she notify Mr. Bruce, the head of the Academic Department that she was going away. The notification which she left for me I received only yesterday. To me it is perfectly inconceivable how an educated person can act in such a manner. I telegraphed you with this in mind, and now write with the same point in view. I have the feeling more and more that those who are in authority in educational matters ought to teach our young people that mere book education or industrial education amount to little except as they are re-enforced by high moral standards of life. I would say further that I would not think of receiving into this institution any person as a teacher who would leave another institution in the same manner that Miss Murrell left the Tuskegee Institute. I do not believe that a person with such loose ideas of moral obligation can be a teacher in the broadest and strongest sense. What Miss Murrell ought to do would be to leave this institution in a correct and business-like manner. Further, I believe that by making an example of such persons that the lesson would be impressed upon them that the securing of money is not all, that in the long run the individual receives the highest salary and is placed in the most responsible positions who can be depended upon to act from a high sense of right, whether for the time being it means a large or small salary. I place these considerations before you for your own decision. Yours very truly,

Booker T. Washington

TLpS   Con. 868   BTW Papers   DLC.

[1] Bettie G. Cox Francis (1861–1925), originally of Galveston, Tex., was the first woman to serve on the D.C. Board of Education (1899–1906), and was president and co-founder of the black branch of the YWCA in Washington, D.C. She and her

husband, John R. Francis, a physician, were social leaders in the black community of the nation's capital.

2 BTW later wrote to John R. Francis: "Perhaps I feel more keenly and deeply about such conduct than the average person." (Apr. 25, 1904, Con. 868, BTW Papers, DLC.) He wrote Margaret P. Murrell ten days after her sudden resignation that her actions "gave me such a shock and a disappointment that I have not been able to bring myself to the point where I could write you before this date." (Apr. 25, 1904, Con. 869, BTW Papers, DLC.) The Washington, D.C., school board advised her that she would not be hired until she had satisfied BTW and Tuskegee Institute. She wrote BTW expressing her "extreme mortification" upon learning that BTW had written the school board placing her in a "bad light." She explained to BTW that she had been seeking a new position for some time because of her difficulty in becoming acclimated to Alabama and problems with her eyesight stemming from too much night work. (Apr. 27, 1904, Con. 869, BTW Papers, DLC.) BTW replied that "to my view you have not brought out a single fact which justifies your actions." He told her that he wrote the Washington school board not "to humiliate and punish you, but I did seek to teach a lesson for the future which would be of profit to yourself and to others." (May 3, 1904, Con. 869, BTW Papers, DLC.) BTW had copies of all the correspondence typed and read before the Tuskegee Executive Council and then considered the matter closed. (BTW to Scott, May 3, 1904, Con. 869, BTW Papers, DLC.)

To William H. Steward

[Tuskegee, Ala.] April 21, 1904

Dear Mr. Steward: Some days ago you wrote me about the wisdom of accepting Mr. Fortune's resignation. Since that time I notice that the letter has been in the public prints, and on the whole, I believe it is just as well to let the resignation stand and for you to take charge of the Council as President. If you desire it, I feel quite sure that you will be elected permanent President at the St. Louis meeting. Of course Mr. Fortune is poor, and the constant attendance on these meetings is not only injurious to his health but also brings about an expense which he is unable to bear. The position of President, of course, calls for expenditures that it is hard for a layman to understand. I think that what I have said would meet with Mr. Fortune's wishes. Yours very truly,

Booker T. Washington

TLpS   Con. 5   BTW Papers   DLC.

To Nathalie Lord

[Tuskegee, Ala.] April 21, 1904

My dear Miss Lord: I thank you very much for your kind and thoughtful letter. I have just returned from the North where I have been for nearly a month and find many matters to occupy my time and strength, but I must write you.

In regard to my birthday.[1] I am not at all sure of the day, but I think it was in April 1856. What you say about the little book is very interesting.

Your letter gives me the excuse for writing you about another matter which has been on my mind for several weeks. You will perhaps remember that several years ago you gave me a Bible in which you wrote your name. I have kept the Bible and read it almost daily from the time you gave it to me until about three months ago, when I seem to have left it in the Chapel and it disappeared and I have not been able to get hold of it since, though I have made diligent inquiry and it has been well advertised among the students and teachers, so I think I may just as well give it up as lost. I am very anxious to have another Bible from you with my name written in it as before, but I do not want you to pay for it. If you will let me have another and will also send me the bill I shall be very glad to see that the account is settled. I hope at some time that you can come by Tuskegee either going to or returning from the North.

I am planning to be in Bar Harbor sometime during the month of August, and shall hope to see you and your sister. Yours very truly,

Booker T. Washington

TLpS Con. 869 BTW Papers DLC.

[1] In a list of birth dates of her friends she had written BTW's birthday as Apr. 18, 1855, and wrote to ask if that was correct. (Apr. 18, 1904, Con. 869, BTW Papers, DLC.)

To Charles William Anderson

[Tuskegee, Ala.] April 22, 1904

Personal

My dear Mr. Anderson: Perhaps you have already noted that a bill has been introduced into Congress for the purpose of sending a Commercial Agent or a Consul to represent this country in Abyssinia. I have talked with the President several times with a view of getting him to send a colored man to represent this country since Abyssinia is practically a Negro nation, and I believe, if you and I can unite in recommending a man that the President will appoint him. Even if the bill does not pass which calls for an appropriation of $3500 annually, I think the Secretary of State can provide for the salary out of his contingent fund. I am free to act in the matter in any manner that may seem wise.

I will write you later about the San Domingan matter, which I hope I can get in a more satisfactory shape than it now seems to be in.

Mr. and Mrs. Fassett[1] have been spending the day here, and he made an excellent speech to the students. Both seemed quite pleased, and Mr. Fassett spoke of you with the greatest appreciation.

The enclosed clipping may interest you. Yours very truly,

Booker T. Washington

TLpS Con. 5 BTW Papers DLC.

[1] Jacob Sloat Fassett (1853–1924), a banker and lumber dealer in Elmira, N.Y., was a Republican congressman from 1905 to 1911 and a donor to Tuskegee. The theme of his talk to the Tuskegee students was that they should not ask, "Is this world my oyster and how can I open the shell?" but rather, "What can I do for the world? How can I so strengthen my body; how can I so fortify my mind; how can I so prepare my soul as to best be of service to this world." (*Tuskegee Student*, 16 [Apr. 30, 1904], 1.)

To Emmett Jay Scott

Tuskegee, Alabama. April 23, 1904

Dear Mr. Scott: I note from your letter the impression that Mr. Barber got concerning my interview with Mr. Hertel. I would say that

I am quite sure that neither Dr. Bowen nor any one else connected with the magazine will in the end misunderstand me. I understood that Mr. Hertel was one of the proprietors of the magazine, and he asked me when in Chicago a few days ago, what I thought about it. I told him that I thought it was a valuable and timely publication, that it had strong points and at the same time it had, in my opinion, some weak points that would be overcome by time and experience. Among the features that I thought might be improved was the one of making a summary each month that would indicate in a very thorough and broad manner everything that has taken place relating especially to the Negro race and emphasizing matters in the direction of constructive progressive effort. I told him that I did not think much of some of the paragraphs in the magazine that dealt with matters in general; as a rule, such matters are covered by either the daily press or weekly press which our people read. The way to make the magazine strong in my opinion is to have it understood that one can find in it that which he cannot find elsewhere. Any colored man who will read a magazine will read either a daily or weekly paper and will keep himself abreast of the general news of the world through these mediums, but this is not always so in relation to matters bearing upon the interests of the race. There are some matters which I did not call to Mr. Hertel's attention that I think should be looked after pretty closely by some one. For example, I notice that a great deal is made of titles such as A.B., A.M., D.D., LL.D. The fact is that you will find in the very best literature of the country that such titles are made very little of at the present time. I happen to have a degree from Harvard and another from Dartmouth College; I have never used either of these degrees in any publication and do not suppose I ever will, and I do not think that I have lost anything by not emphasizing this feature. The world in the long run cares very little about titles or degrees, what it wants is results.

Some one connected with the magazine should read it so closely as to not make the mistake of saying, for example, that Mr. Grimke was once Minister to San Domingo, this is not true; neither should it be said that Henry W. Blair is dead, this is not true.

Now while I have spoken of some of the weak points, I want it understood thoroughly that the magazine is growing in strength and in influence and has many strong and commendable features.

The last number contains several editorials and articles that are in the highest degree commendable, and I think all connected with the publication have reason to feel proud.

I always speak frankly because in the end I consider frankness the greatest kindness. I have gotten more from people who have criticised in a very frank way the work of the Tuskegee Institute than I have from those who have spoken words of mere fulsome praise, and I think you will find it so in the publication of a magazine.

Booker T. Washington

TLS   Con. 261   BTW Papers   DLC.

To William Henry Baldwin, Jr.

[Tuskegee, Ala.] April 27, 1904

Dear Mr. Baldwin: Among other things, when Mr. Gates examined Rockefeller Hall and found out the cost, which was about $200 per student, he said it was very remarkable that we could put up a building in which to house students at $200 when at other institutions it cost from $600 to $1000 per student. Yours truly,

Booker T. Washington

TLpS   Con. 284   BTW Papers   DLC.

To Edward Elder Cooper

[Tuskegee, Ala.] April 28, 1904

My dear Mr. Cooper: I am in receipt of your kind letter, and I will say in reply that I shall be passing through Washington on Saturday night and shall be very glad to see you at the train.

In a general way, however, I must say that I shall be very glad in the future, as I have tried to do in the past, to encourage your paper in every legitimate way that I can. I have always made it a practice to aid and encourage Negro newspapers because I have realized their tremendous value in the uplifting of our race. I am very sorry indeed that your own paper is not as prosperous as you desire it.

In regard, however, to the direct subject discussed in your letter I would state that, I have never paid out a single cent for the purpose of getting a newspaper to change its policy toward me nor have I ever paid out a cent for the purpose of keeping a paper from expressing the views which its owners desired it to express, and this policy I shall pursue in the future. You of course know that there is a publication in Washington that has been abusing and misrepresenting me for years, and if I had desired to I could have changed its policy or brought about silence at any time by the payment of a very few dollars, but I have realized, as any public man must, that bought friendship does not amount to very much and that if one has to pay for silence or a change of policy at one time it will only be a matter of a few weeks or months when he will have to pay for it again, so that looked at from any point of view all public men realize that the payment of money for a change of policy or for silence never pays. Looked at, however, as I have stated in the beginning of this letter, in a broader view, I have always tried to encourage the Negro papers that were working along the same lines which I am trying to pursue, but if for any reason they choose to take a different course I have always let them go their way without hindrance. For the same reason that I have mentioned, I have always refused to own a newspaper [or] to have a single dollar's worth of stock in one.

I thank you very much for writing me so frankly. As I have stated, I shall see you when I pass through Washington.

Would it not be a good plan for you to call a small meeting of your friends there to discuss some method of putting the Colored American upon its feet? Yours truly,

Booker T. Washington

TLpS   Con. 20   BTW Papers   DLC.

To John Stephens Durham

[Tuskegee, Ala.] April 28, 1904

Personal

My dear Mr. Durham: Mr. Scott has just returned from Washington where he had a long conference with the President at my request. The status of the San Domingan matter is this: The Dominicans have diplomatically made the President understand that they do not wish a Negro sent as Minister and the President, of course, says that he will be under the necessity for the reason mentioned, to send a white man to occupy the place temporarily at least.

I think I am not violating any confidence when I say to you that in the course of the conversation, even before your name was brought up by Mr. Scott, the President remarked that if he were to send a colored man you would be his choice. Yours very truly,

Booker T. Washington

TLpS   Con. 20   BTW Papers   DLC.

To the Editor of the Birmingham *News*

[Tuskegee, Ala.] 28 April 1904

Private and Confidential

Dear Sir: I have just had the opportunity of reading the enclosed editorial taken from the issue of your paper dated March 26. For your private information, because you have been so kind to me and our Institution that I do not like to see you imposed upon, I wish to say that, in the first place, I did not on the occasion referred to discuss the subject of lynching with the President, nor have I ever done so; and in the second place, that the President asked me to come to the White House to discuss with him the advisability of employing colored men to do various kinds of work in connection with the construction of the Panama Canal.

The subject of lynching was not even mentioned. Very truly yours,

Booker T. Washington

TLpS   Con. 867   BTW Papers   DLC.

To Cora Lina Cherry White[1]

[Tuskegee, Ala.] April 29, 1904

My dear Mrs. White: Replying further to your kind letter, which has been recently received, I will state that I send you by this mail a catalog of the Bradford Academy, Bradford, Mass. This is the institution where my daughter Portia attends, and before making any attempt to get your daughter[2] into that institution, I want to find out if the conditions laid down in the catalog are satisfactory to you. Of course I am not sure what the decision of the authorities will be, but there is no reason why an attempt may not be made. If she were accepted there, I am sure she would be treated in a very satisfactory manner. It is one of the oldest institutions in the country. Of course there are some of these schools that are willing to admit one or two colored persons but object when more apply; it is not at all agreeable to have to deal with such conditions, but we must face the facts. My daughter Portia is very anxious to have your daughter enter while she is there. Portia graduates next year, and she feels that it will be best for both your daughter and yourself if arrangements could be made so that your daughter could enter next fall. Yours very truly,

Booker T. Washington

TLpS   Con. 872   BTW Papers   DLC.

[1] Cora Lina Cherry White (1864–1905), a public-school teacher from North Carolina, married the black congressman George H. White in 1886.

[2] Mary A. White.

Wilford H. Smith to Emmett Jay Scott

New York City, May 2nd, 1904

Dear Friend: I have your favor of the 28th ultimo, and hope that I shall have the opportunity of conferring with our friend over the matter therein referred to.

I have had a bad case of the blues ever since the Supreme Court sat down on me, and I have not been disposed to have much to say. I have been doing a great deal of thinking against the Supreme Court, which I am unable to express. If, however, I could have the opportunity of forcing them to a decision, I would greatly relieve myself as much as the people of Alabama. But I am sure that I should not neglect to write my friends because I have been disappointed, so in the future I shall aim to have more to say, so as not to seem selfish.

I wish you would have the "Voice of the Negro" sent to me, and I will pay the subscription. We hope to interest you in our Afro-American Realty Company, which is doing far better than Mr. Payton[1] and I dreamed of when we first projected it. We have in mind to publish pictures of our ten flats which we have under five years leases, with a group of the ten partners, in the Colored American of Boston, and we hope to follow it up by a repetition in your "Voice of the Negro."

Mr. Payton and I are figuring out a good place in the concern for you when we incorporate.

I wish to be kindly remembered to Mrs. Scott and the children. Very truly yours,

Wilford H. Smith

TLS Con. 25 BTW Papers DLC.

[1] Philip A. Payton, Jr., was born in Westfield, Mass., in 1876, and was educated at Livingstone College, Salisbury, N.C. He moved to New York City in 1899, where he began speculating in real estate. He was successful in opening Harlem to blacks desiring better living conditions and became known as "the father of Colored Harlem." In 1904 Payton organized a ten-man partnership, the Afro-American Realty Co., which specialized in leasing white-owned buildings and renting to blacks. The business had the support of many black small entrepreneurs and professionals. The first president was James C. Thomas, a black undertaker, who became known as the wealthiest black man in New York. Other officials included Charles W. Anderson, Fred R. Moore, Wilford H. Smith, and Emmett J. Scott. The company did well for a while, and became a symbol of black business success.

The company, however, was not as sound as its inflated claims indicated. Payton was a spendthrift as well as a shrewd investor, and many buildings that he claimed the company owned were actually heavily mortgaged. In 1906 Wilford H. Smith, representing a group of stockholders, sued Payton for fraud. Payton was acquitted since he was legally only one of the partners despite his virtual control of the company. The Afro-American Realty Co., however, was found guilty of misrepresentation. The company floundered in 1907–8 as a recession caused a declining housing market. Payton continued to overspend and make inflated claims about the company's financial condition. Payton urged BTW to write him a letter of introduction to Andrew Carnegie, but BTW refused on the ground that it was not a philanthropic matter. In 1908 the company collapsed. Payton continued on in Harlem as a private real estate dealer, and never issued a statement concerning the company's downfall despite protestations from Emmett J. Scott and others.

To James Nathan Calloway

[Hotel Manhattan, New York City] 3 May, 1904

Dear Mr. Calloway: I think it would be a good plan for you to use one half of each day circulating in a quiet way among the white people of Macon County. I fear that in the past we have neglected too much the education of the white people, and that we should begin to let them know what we are doing. It would be a good plan to take them one by one in your buggy over the farm and through the shops. I hope that you will keep me informed from time to time of your accomplishments and plans. Very truly yours,

[Booker T. Washington]

TLc   Con. 548   BTW Papers   DLC.

From Andrew B. Humphrey

New York. May 4, 1904

Personal

Dear Mr. Washington: I take pleasure in sending you the *second* dictated letter, issued from the *first Official Headquarters* of this League. The *first* letter was sent to *The President*.

From our frequent conversations, I think you understand our proposed work fairly well. In brief, it is to maintain and enforce the

493

Constitution: to establish the rights of all citizens by carrying test cases to the Supreme Court: to conduct a propaganda of education; to discountenance lynching, peonage, and mobs, and to advance legislation that seems to be necessary to make the Constitutional Amendments effective.

At present, we are conducting our work without notoriety, as you know, and all our correspondence is confidential. At a later period, the present Provisional Committee will give way to a National Organization.

I understand perfectly well that, for many reasons, you cannot co-operate with us in certain portions of our work. You are making great strides in the direction of industrial education for your race, and other organizations are doing all they can along strictly moral lines. Our work must, from its nature, be more or less legal and political, hence we shall be always on the "firing line," between the oppressors and the oppressed, and always facing the *judicial* branch of the United States Government, as well as the *legislative*.

The colored man, as you know, so far as his Constitutional rights are concerned, has been buffeted back and forth between the Supreme Court and the Congress. We propose to carry the rights of citizens to both of these dignified bodies with all the legal and political power we can command. You will understand that this is no easy task and may not be accomplished in your lifetime and mine but the work is in the right direction and the "right *will* prevail" in due time. It took a century of struggle, billions of treasure, and the best blood of the Nation, North and South, to write a single sentence into the *Thirteenth* Amendment of the Federal Constitution, and it may take another century to demonstrate that the Fourteenth and Fifteenth Amendments are an essential part of the "Supreme Law of the Land."

We appreciate *your* position and we are sure *you* appreciate *ours*. Let us co-operate in every possible way to advance the cause in general. I am sure you can be of great assistance to us in furnishing *information* which we cannot readily secure. We shall appreciate this *information* and any, and all, *literature* that you can send us concerning the negro problem. I shall be pleased to confer with you when in New York. Sincerely yours,

Andrew B. Humphrey

We have a "Law Com." to investigate cases *before* they are brought.

TLS   Con. 3   BTW Papers   DLC.

To Edward Augustine Benner

Hotel Manhattan, New York City. 5 May, 1904

Dear Mr. Benner: Please tell Booker that I am to be here for a week, and that I should like to hear from him.

He has a tendency, I have noticed, to stoop over when he sits, and to stand not at all erect when he walks. I hope you will do all that you can to correct this habit. Very truly yours,

[Booker T. Washington]

TLc   Con. 2   BTW Papers   DLC.

From D. Robert Wilkins

Chicago, May 5, 1904

My Dear Sir and Friend: Your favor of the 22nd inst. was duly received and highly appreciated. Kindly pardon the delay as I am rushed to death with work and am therefore neglecting and missing many of my best friends. I am certainly proud to learn that you appreciate anything the Conservator says in commendation of your great work, and incline to the idea that we wish to treat you fairly though we may differ as to the propriety of some things, etc.

Referring to your speech at Quinn Chapel this city, I am pleased to say and have often said before, that I never listened to a speech, which I enjoyed and approved more thoroughly. It was in every way grand and nobody in Chicago, so far as I am aware, found any ground to complain of it.

The Chicago Conservator is no enemy of yours, Mr. Washington, and never has been and has never sought to do other than place your work at Tuskegee before the people as the greatest of the kind in the country. Notwithstanding the past criticism of the Conservator of many of your utterances, touching our race, your Chicago speeches convinced me that it would be an easy matter for you and the Conservator to labor together for the betterment of the condition of our people which I should deem both a privilege and a duty to do, should we find it possible to agree on the modus operandi of the uplift.

Thanking you for your kind words and wishing you success in your great work, I am, Respectfully,

D R Wilkins

TLS   Con. 867   BTW Papers   DLC.

To Charles Alexander

Hotel Manhattan, New York City. 7 May, 1904

Personal.

Dear Mr. Alexander: I think it wise for you to be very careful to see that no one sees your private correspondence which reaches you from time to time.

I have sent you today the remainder of what I told you I would send,[1] and, as I have told you before, this is all that I shall be able to do.

I should like to see you try this experiment. Hire a good man or woman, and have him or her devote the time for a month to making a house to house canvass among the colored people of Boston for the purpose of securing subscriptions. These might be taken for three months, six months, or a year. If a small per cent. is given to the canvasser in addition to a weekly salary, it ought to stimulate him or her to good work. You ought to get such a person for $10 a week or less. That salary, with a small per cent. on each subscription ought to produce good results. If [you] think this plan wise, and will put it into execution at once, I know a friend who will bear the expenses for a month. Very truly yours,

[Booker T. Washington]

TLc   Con. 19   BTW Papers   DLC.

1 Attached are receipts for postal money orders totaling $500.

From Henry Ossawa Tanner

Paris 7th May 1904

My dear Mr Washington — I had intended dropping you a line before I left New York but at last moment was so hurried that I have delayed.

As you know by this time Miss Olivia E. P. Stokes bought a picture of mine & has temporarily sent it [to] Phelp[s] Hall. I hope it arrived in good condition. I was unable to see it off as the frame maker was unable at the last moment to finish it at time promised. However he is a very responsible man & I imagine all has been well. Although I have had no definite word.

Do you know what I thought it *might be* possible for you to do for me. To bring my work &c. &c. to the attention of some persons or person like Mr Carnegie, who might be willing to give me for a period of 3 or 4 years $2000. — (Two thousand) dollars for the picture of the year the best I could do, & thus for this period the question [of] money would be settled & I would have a "square" chance to see what I really could do. It might be said in my favor that I am not completely unknown & while it would be a great help for me to know that the money would come I could make a picture which would I believe be well worth the money. I believe if such a scheme could be properly presented it might succeed, and I am sure that if the occasion offered itself you would use your influence in my favor. Would you not?

Thanking you for your past interest   I am   Vy Truly —

H. O. Tanner

ALS   Con. 872   BTW Papers   DLC.

From Theodore Roosevelt

White House, Washington. May 9, 1904

My dear Mr. Washington: My attention has already been attracted to the situation set forth by you in your memorandum to Mr.

Leupp. In view of the contest between the two delegations I do not think it would be well for me to reappoint Mr. Cohen and Mr. Lewis now — at least not until after the convention meets. You will notice that all of the federal office-holders voted against the so-called "Lily White" movement. I trust that they were not properly reported in the reasons they gave. Mr. Williams[1] has sent me up violent complaints of the fealty of Cohen and his adherents, who he insists have helped the Democrats in the last election. Sincerely yours,

Theodore Roosevelt

TLS Con. 16 BTW Papers DLC.

[1] Frank B. Williams was the leader of the lily whites in Louisiana. He and the rest of his delegation were ultimately seated in the Republican convention with a half-vote each, while the black-and-tan faction was also recognized and received the other half-votes.

Emmett Jay Scott to John Mitchell, Jr.

[Tuskegee, Ala.] May 10, 1904

Dear Mr. Mitchell: While publishing the Texas Freeman at Houston, Texas, you will remember that it was the writer's privilege always to refer to you as "brave John Mitchell." There is no especial reason why I should change this appellation except that on second thought I do not believe that you will be willing to stand by the attached which I clipped from your last issue. Differences which you may have with Dr. Washington as such I am sure have not inclined you to do him an injustice. I am not writing for publication now, and so the information I send is sent simply for the reason that I would have you properly informed. I would ask to start with, if you can substantiate your charge that Dr. Washington "has gone away back and sat down" since the hullabaloo about Dr. Crum's appointment. I would ask you if you yourself or any of your special friends have contributed toward the confirmation of Dr. Crum in direct ways, that is, either in money or personal pressure, and would say that for Dr. Washington it can be stated that he has spent not less than $450 as Dr. Crum well knows, on this case, besides a prodigious amount of time and energy, and did spend a day before the last congress adjourned in seeing the leaders of the Senate in person with reference to Dr. Crum's confirmation. The President knows fully everything that Dr. Washington has done and is fully pleased as he said to the writer himself, with the tremendous amount of work which Dr. Washington has done to bring about Dr. Crum's confirmation.[1] Yours truly,

[Emmett J. Scott]

TLc Con. 877 BTW Papers DLC.

[1] Mitchell replied: "We should accept the leadership of somebody and we were content to give him the right of way. I am free to say to you that the one blunder he made was his accepting the position of referee in political matters." The Crum case, Mitchell said, showed BTW's weakness as a political broker: "It has required more effort to secure his confirmation than it took to secure any five of the colored appointees since the Civil War and he is as yet unconfirmed." He promised to continue to treat BTW with fairness. (May 25, 1904, Con. 869, BTW Papers, DLC.)

Scott replied that BTW was merely responding to President Roosevelt's requests for advice, though as BTW's secretary he knew that BTW was more aggressively involved in politics than that implied. (May 30, 1904, Con. 869, BTW Papers, DLC.)

An Article in *Outlook*

[May 14, 1904]

A NEGRO POTATO KING

Junius G. Groves, of Edwardsville, Kansas, is often referred to as "The Negro Potato King." He is practically a full-blooded negro, and was born a slave in Green County, Kentucky, in 1859. He and his parents were made free a few years later by the proclamation of Abraham Lincoln. As soon as he was old enough, he began attending the public schools in his neighborhood, but as he could be in school during only two or three months in the year, he did not secure a great deal of book knowledge. What he learned was enough, however, to give him a desire for education, for we find him, after leaving school, continuing to study as best he could. By the time he reached manhood he was able to read and write and had some knowledge of figures.

In 1879 occurred what was known as the "Kansas Exodus," and

Mr. Groves, with a large number of other colored people from the South, caught the emigration fever. When he reached Kansas he had just ninety cents in his pocket. The sudden influx of so many colored people into the State caused it to be rather overrun with cheap labor, and employment was hard to find. After an earnest search of some days, however, Mr. Groves succeeded in finding employment on a farm at forty cents a day. He told me that he agreed to begin work for this wage because he knew that within a few days he could convince his employer that he was worth more. So faithfully did he work that by the end of three months his wages had been increased to seventy-five cents a day. This was the pay which the very best farm hands were receiving in that neighborhood. Out of this small sum he had to pay for his board and laundering.

By the end of the year he had saved enough to go in search of what he hoped would be a better job. His travels through different parts of the State availed him nothing, and he finally decided to return to the place where he had first found employment. He had made such a favorable impression upon his old employer that the latter offered to let Groves have a portion of his farm to cultivate on "shares." The conditions of the contract were that the farmer should furnish nine acres of land, a team, seed, and tools, and Groves should plant, cultivate, and harvest the crop for one-third of what was made. This offer was gladly accepted, and Mr. Groves planted three acres in white potatoes, three in sweet potatoes, and three in watermelons.

Soon after getting the crop planted Mr. Groves decided to get married. When he reached this decision, he had but seventy-five cents in cash, and had to borrow enough more to satisfy the demands of the law. But he knew well the worth and common sense of the woman he was to marry. She was as poor in worldly goods as he, but their poverty did not discourage their plans to marry. Both Mr. and Mrs. Groves told me with a good deal of satisfaction how they managed, with much difficulty, the day after their marriage, to get a few yards of calico to make a changing suit for Mrs. Groves, so that she might begin work at once in the field by his side, where she has ever since been his steady companion. During the whole season they both worked with never-tiring energy, early and late; with the result that when the crop had been harvested and all debts paid they had cleared $125. Notwithstanding their lack of many necessities of life, to say nothing of comforts, they decided to invest $50 of their savings in a lot in Kansas City, Kansas. They paid $25 for a milk cow, and kept the remaining $50 to be used in the making of another crop.

The successes of the first year's work had convinced the landlord that he would be taking no risk in renting Groves and his wife a larger acreage; so their holding for the second year was increased to twenty acres. From this year's earnings they purchased a team. They now began to feel that they could take even more independent steps. I say *they* advisedly, because through all these laborious years Mrs. Groves worked on the farm constantly at the side of her husband, and even now, when occasion demands it, she does active work in the field. They had farmed with success the first year on a small acreage; they had been even more successful the second year on a larger acreage; and the third year they rented sixty-six acres of good farm land near the town of Edwardsville, Kansas, at an annual rental of $336. Of this amount they were able to pay one-third cash in advance. As this was more land then they could personally cultivate, a small portion was sub-rented. Seldom have two people worked harder, or sacrificed more, than did Mr. and Mrs. Groves that year. They not only farmed the land, but raised pigs and fowls, and sold milk and butter. In the winter, when the other farmers were idle, they cut wood, and sold it in town. They were determined to succeed.

Omitting many interesting details, I shall merely state that at the end of the year, in 1884, after they had paid all debts, and their bank-book was balanced, they found that they had to their credit in the local bank, as a result of their labor for the last three years, $2,200. During the greater portion of the time they were earning this money, this young man and his wife were living in an old shanty, with one broken-down room. They decided now that they would buy a farm for themselves, and agreed to pay $3,600 for eighty acres of land near Edwardsville, in the Great Kaw Valley — a section comprising about 3,940 acres of the most fertile land in the State. Mr. and Mrs. Groves paid on the land the $2,200 which they had saved, and closed a contract to pay the remaining $1,400 at the end of the year. Letting the hired man live in the house on the place, they built a shanty for themselves until the crop was grown. After

Mr. Groves had taken possession of his farm, nearly all of the neighbors began to tell him that he had made a bad bargain, and to prophesy that he would not only be unable to pay the $1,400 at the end of the year, but would besides lose his $2,200. Mr. Groves told me that this was the first and only occasion in his life when he became discouraged; and that he could not take heart again until he began to inquire who they were who were seeking to discourage him, and found that they were poor shiftless people, who owned no land themselves. After discovering who his "Job's comforters" were, Mr. Groves determined to succeed, not only for his own sake, but to disappoint those who had predicted his failure. He and his wife exerted themselves unusually this year, and their efforts were not without reward. Enough was realized from the one year's crop to pay for the whole farm, with a neat little surplus, which they used in improving their house and stocking their farm.

Mr. and Mrs. Groves continued to work hard and prosperously on this farm, until they were able in 1887 to pay cash for two small adjoining farms. In 1889 they bought a fourth farm, and in 1896 the fifth one. They now own 500 acres of the finest land in the Kaw Valley — land that is easily worth from $125 to $250 an acre. They no longer occupy the original little one-room shanty, but have progressed into a large, beautiful, well-appointed dwelling, built at a cost of $5,000. It has fourteen rooms and modern improvements, including a private gas-plant which furnishes twenty-seven lights, a private water system, and a local telephone. The house is supplied with bath-rooms, and everything necessary to make it comfortable and convenient.

There are eleven children in the family — three girls and eight boys. The children are all being educated with care. Three of them — two boys and one girl — are already in the Kansas State Agricultural College, and their oldest boy will complete the course in June. All the children take as much interest in the success of the farm as do the parents.

In addition to the dwelling-house, one finds upon the farm a modern two story, well-painted barn that cost $1,500, a smoke-house, granary, tool-house, hen-house, and a warehouse, in which are kept six thousand bushels of seed potatoes during the winter. Mr. Groves's business has grown to the extent that he has a private railroad track which leads from his shipping station to the main line of the Union Pacific Railroad, which runs through Edwardsville. Mr. and Mrs. Groves also own and operate a general merchandise store in which they carry a large stock of goods. They have several fine orchards upon their farm. In the apple orchard there are seven thousand trees six years old, from which last year four car-loads of apples were gathered. The peach orchard contains eighteen hundred trees, the pear orchard seven hundred trees, and the cherry orchard two hundred and fifty trees. They also grow extensively apricots and grapes.

But why is Mr. Groves called "The Negro Potato King"? Let me answer. Last year he produced upon his farm 72,150 bushels of white potatoes, averaging 245 bushels to the acre. So far as reports show, this was 12,150 bushels more than any other individual grower in the world produced. And besides the potatoes raised on his own farm, Mr. Groves buys and ships potatoes on a large scale. To illustrate, last year he bought from white growers in the Kaw Valley and shipped away twenty-two cars of white potatoes. He also bought fourteen cars of fancy seed potatoes in North and South Dakota, which he sold to growers in the Kaw Valley, and in Oklahoma and Indian Territory. Mr. Groves says that he ships potatoes and other farm products to nearly every portion of the United States, and to Mexico and Canada. He says that he has never found his color to be a hindrance to him in business. During the busy season as many as fifty laborers, white and black, are employed on his farm. It is maintained at its highest productivity by persistent energy and constant effort on the part of Mr. Groves. As I have said, he received but little education as a boy, but he has persevered until he has now reached the point where he can analyze and classify the soils upon his farm, and apply just the proper fertilizer to the various plots. He uses nothing but the latest improved cultivators, potato-planters, potato-weeders, and diggers, and in fact all work that can be done with machinery is done in that way.

And Mr. and Mrs. Groves have other interests than those of farming. They have large holdings in mining stocks in both the Indian Territory and Mexico, as well as banking stock in their own State. They own four-fifths interest in the Kansas City Casket and Embalming Company, of Kansas City, Kansas, and take the deepest interest in the progress of the race both in their own State and throughout the country. Mr. Groves, in speaking of his large interests, always says "we," meaning Mrs. Groves and himself. In the most beautiful manner, and with the greatest tenderness, he never fails to give Mrs. Groves due credit for all that she has helped him to accomplish.

Having prospered in a material way, the Groveses do not overlook the moral and spiritual side of life. They are both members of the church, as are also their older children. In fact, the little church near their home was organized by Mr. Groves and his wife, and they gave $1,500 for the erection of the church house. Mr. Groves drew the plans for the building and directed the work of construction.

Mr. Groves is held in very high esteem by men of wealth and standing in his State. Mr. Porter Sherman, President of the Wyandotte State Bank, Kansas City, Kansas, in speaking of him said: "I regard Mr. Groves as a man of especial ability. We have no better customer in the county than he is. He is a man of peculiar tact and ability. His standing as a citizen and business man is high in the county, and his papers never pass due. He is easily worth between $40,000 and $80,000 after all obligations are met." Mr. Groves does a great deal of business with this bank, the cashier of which also spoke of him in very high terms.

Mr. C. L. Brokaw, cashier of the Commercial and National Bank of Kansas City, Kansas, said of Mr. Groves: "The credit of Mr. Groves is as great with this bank as is that of any man in Wyandotte County, and not only with this bank but in all banking circles. He is known as a man of exceptional ability, of keen insight, courteous manners, and good financial sense. I consider him one of the best business men in this county, and a citizen of unquestionable character. I have the utmost confidence in the man's worth and intelligence."

It was especially gratifying to me to hear Mr. Thomas Jefferson Barker, of Kansas City, Kansas, speak of Mr. Groves. Mr. Barker is an ex-slaveholder, and is, I am told, the richest man in Wyandotte County. He said: "Mr. Groves came to Wyandotte County about twenty-five years ago, and has always conducted himself in the most creditable manner. As a business man he is intelligent and indisputably honest. He is upright in all of his transactions and meets his obligations on the day that they are due. He is a man of influence and ability in all business connections. Groves is one of the best citizens in the county."

Mr. J. D. Waters, cashier of the Farmers' State Bank of Bonner Springs, Kansas, said of Mr. Groves: "I have known Mr. Groves for fifteen years, and during that time I have never heard anything but good about him. He is a first-class business man, and stands high in his community. His character is unquestionable. For several years he was Secretary of the Kaw Valley Potato Association, of which Senator Taylor was President, and while in this position exhibited unusual ability in conducting the affairs of the Association."

Senator Edwin Taylor, of Edwardsville, Kansas, is a near neighbor to Mr. Groves, and, like him, is a potato-grower of note. In speaking of Mr. Groves he said: "I regard Mr. Groves as one of the best men, white or black, in the valley. He is not only one of the most progressive and astute potato men in the valley, but is also a man of acknowledged general intelligence. Some twenty years ago Mr. Groves came to the valley almost penniless, whereas he is now a man of enviable financial standing. He is a man of quick perception, of fertility of resource; a man interested in every movement making for the good of the community — in fact, a good all-round citizen."

In speaking of what they had been able to accomplish, Mr. Groves said in a very modest way (both he and his wife are among the most simple and modest people I have ever met): "I think our success shows that a negro can and will make his way in the world if given a chance. If we could start with but seventy-five cents and succeed as we have, other people of our race can do the same thing."

Outlook, 77 (May 14, 1904), 115–18.

To William Henry Baldwin, Jr.

[Tuskegee, Ala.] May 19, 1904

Personal

Dear Mr. Baldwin: When you get a few spare moments I hope you will read with care the enclosed newspaper articles written by special correspondents who came here with Mr. Ogden's party.

These articles are interesting as much for what they do say as for what they fail to say. It is rather strange that all of them should strike the same chord, and I can't help but feel that the articles were made up very largely as a result of conversations on the train rather than by what they observed here. Of course since all the articles lay emphasis upon making a compromise between Hampton and Tuskegee I think it is but fair for me to say first that Tuskegee is placed at a great disadvantage by reason of the "social scare" it can have no direct representatives on the train with these parties or at other places where they talk things over with leisure, and cannot have opportunity to explain in detail the methods and results of the school as can the Hampton officials.

Secondly. This party spent two days at Hampton and about four hours at Tuskegee. During the four hours we attempted to give them an idea of the farm, workshops and to witness the Industrial Exercise as well as get a general idea of the school. Of course you know that no proper impression could have been gotten in this length of time. I fear that there are those who feel that we should follow the Hampton Institute completely. This I do not think we should attempt to do, we should be ourselves. There are some inexcusable statements. For instance, Mr. Brown had no basis upon which to make the statement that we attempted to sing classical music to the exclusion of plantation singing. During the whole stay of the party here there was sung only one song that might be called classical; all the others, including some twelve or fourteen pieces, were either plantation songs or songs of a Southern flavor such as "Old Kentucky Home" etc. Four-fifths of the singing was purely plantation. It is wholly untrue that our students refuse to sing or dislike to sing the plantation songs; that question is never raised here. They sing the plantation songs just as willingly as they do any other class of songs, and there is absolutely no feeling against singing them. Of course you can easily understand that we had to do everything in a great hurry, and for example, to have the party see the students at work on the farm at ten o'clock and then to have the same students come from the farm and make some change of clothing, get into the line of march and get to the Chapel by a quarter to eleven required pretty quick work, and there must have been a good many weak points.

If one really knew the history, struggles and sacrifices back of the rough looking buildings to which one correspondent refers, I am sure that he would have nothing but a feeling of reverence for these buildings and would see that in real self-help they meant more in the upbuilding of a race than many fine buildings erected by the hands of outside people.

All the correspondents are in error, in my opinion, in attempting to show that our students are not as wide-awake and alert as the Hampton students. As you know, I spend a good part of my time in speaking before audiences, and I have spoken a good many times to the Hampton students and I . . .[1] in saying that in keen appreciation of what is really worth listening to our students are equal to those at Hampton. On the occasion referred to there was only one [real?] speech made and that was by Dr. Mitchell of Virginia, and I am sure that the students showed their appreciation in as hearty a manner as any speaker could have expected. Owing to the lack of time, all the visitors had to confine their speaking to two or three minutes which of course did not furnish a proper occasion for students or anybody else to show their appreciation of any one's efforts.

I will not, however, take up more of your time in details except to say that it is rather strange that all these special correspondents should point in the same direction. Yours truly,

Booker T. Washington

In my opinion there is not a genuine note of sympathy or encouragement for what we are trying to do in the entire correspondence. It is wholly unfair to make a comparison as Mr. Higginson has done between the speaking of our students and that of the Hampton students. I explained to the audience before the exercises began that ours was an industrial exhibit and that the students' speaking would be confined to a description of the object of the exhibition. There was no attempt at oratorical display, while at Hampton they had their regular literary commencement exercises, and ours come next week. But even the speaking of the students on the day the Ogden party was here was from every point of view good, it was clear, clean cut and thoroughly interesting. What these correspondents said seems to me to be at variance with nearly everything that was said to me by the visitors who were present. The whole matter puzzles me I confess.

B. T. W.

TLpS Con. 284 BTW Papers DLC.

¹ Several words obliterated.

To D. Robert Wilkins

[Tuskegee, Ala.] May 19, 1904

Personal

My dear Sir: Replying further to your kind favor of May 5th permit me to say that I am very glad to know that you seem to be understanding me and my position and words better. I feel that both of us have the same end in view, that is the uplift of the race. While we may have differed in the past as to the means and may differ in the future in details, I believe that, as you suggest, there is no reason why we cannot work together harmoniously for the good of all, and I should be only too glad to cooperate in any manner that I can.

I have never at any time on any occasion done or said anything which in my opinion would in the least compromise the highest and best aspirations of the race. Living constantly in the heart of the South, I may from time to time see things in a manner that one who is living in the North cannot be expected to see and appreciate them. I think if you will review the history of the Negro you will find that never since Freedom were the curses of the entire South centered upon one man for weeks as they were upon me for my dining with President Roosevelt, and if any of my actions have been founded upon fear or a mere desire to please the South then certainly would have been a time for me to have spoken out and said something that would have seemed to please the South. In dining with the President I felt I was simply accepting such an invitation as any American citizen had a right to accept and I have never uttered a word of explanation or regret.

However, I hope to be passing through Chicago soon and shall hope to see you with more satisfaction than I have in the past. Yours truly,

Booker T. Washington

TLpS   Con. 867   BTW Papers   DLC.

From Frederick Randolph Moore

New York. 5/20/04

Dear Mr Washington: Wrote you today — I am to have a further talk with Fortune next week — was interrupted, and thought about the magazine also prevented extended or satisfactory results except he said he wasn't going to fight you. His talk was not so sharp as on previous occasions. Did not say anything about work on the book you spoke of — will write you fully after talk. Think you had best hold up until then. I agree with you as to magazine. Shant connect you with it in any way — you can rely on this.[1] I shall work out its policy in my own way with your quiet advice — shall be glad to receive suggestions from Scott. I find Fortune agrees with my plans of making it the exponent of the material progress of the race.

I shall not engage him until I see that I can pay him and [he] is willing to write in accordance with my ideas. There will be no sentiment in the matter. Business will govern all the way through. Jerome is tickled to death — some folks think the magazine will hurt the Age. I have told such that there is no reason why it should as one is weekly and the other monthly and that the hustling fellow will get there. Yours very sincerely

Moore

ALS   Con. 23   BTW Papers   DLC.

[1] BTW wrote Moore on May 18, 1904, expressing pleasure that Moore had acquired the *Colored American Magazine*, but saying that "it will be best, considering all things, for me not to be represented in it as you suggest." (Con. 268, BTW Papers, DLC.)

To Charles Winter Wood

[Tuskegee, Ala.] May 21, 1904

Fear Booker still unwell. Go Wellesley at once and have full consultation with Mr. Benner. If you and he think wise and necessary
have good physician give Booker thorough examination and do
whatever is best for him at any reasonable expense. Have all your
dealings with Mr. Benner and do nothing he does not approve.
Find out how Booker getting on in every way. Telegraph answer
my expense after you have been to Wellesley.[1]

Booker T. Washington

TWSr   Con. 5   BTW Papers   DLC.

[1] Wood telegraphed: "Dr says Booker nervous little run down all right otherwise.
Booker wants to leave Wellesley come to Boston with me. Benner away." (May 27,
1904, Con. 5, BTW Papers, DLC.)

To Thomas Seymour Barbour

[Tuskegee, Ala.] May 21, 1904

My dear Dr. Barbour: Replying to your very kind letter which was
suggested by a communication from Mr. Gates, I wish to say that,
I shall be very glad to serve you in any manner I can in calling the
attention of the country to the awful conditions prevailing on the
Congo, and I shall be disappointed if something cannot be done to
change the present state of affairs.

When Congress meets in December, if you approve of the plan
I shall be very glad to call personally upon as many members of
the Foreign Affairs Committee as possible and urge action. I have
also thought of another plan by which I might assist. If I could have
a short but pointed statement of the case which I might put before
the President and then after my interview with the President I
could give the same statement out to the press, making the point
at the same time that I had placed the matter before Mr. Roosevelt,
that would give the matter a publicity that perhaps it could get in
no other way as the newspapers are always anxious to give the

greatest publicity to whatever is even remotely connected with the White House or the President. This plan, however, may have some objections and I should not act upon it without your full endorsement. Yours truly,

Booker T. Washington

TLpS   Con. 284   BTW Papers   DLC.

To William Henry Baldwin, Jr.

Tuskegee, Alabama. May 24, 1904

Dear Mr. Baldwin: Enclosed I send you another article evidently written by Talcott Williams, striking the same note as the other correspondents who visited us lately. What Mr. Williams means by his constant emphasis upon low standards I cannot understand, and the whole thing is all the more inexplainable to me because of the fact that most of these people were here three of four years ago, and some have been here several times, and in previous visits they spoke most highly of everything. The institution cannot certainly be in worse condition than it was years ago. Why there should be this sudden change of opinion I cannot understand. Besides, in a private letter, copy of which I send you, you will find that Mr. Williams speaks most highly of what he saw here; this letter is in response to one which I wrote him calling his attention to the inexcusable mistake made in saying that every instructor employed here is a college graduate except myself.

None of the correspondents bring out the fact that all of the work of laying out the grounds and making roads, as well as putting up the buildings, is done by student labor. At Hampton they have fine imitation granite walks through the grounds, but the whole thing is done by outside labor. We are "subsoiling" at Tuskegee, and in doing so, while we may not present to the public such a finely finished picture as some other institutions, I do think that we are doing work that is needed to be done in this generation and in this section of our country. Some one has said that one generation clears the forests and the next builds the palaces. We are clearing the forests. The conditions of climate and soil in Alabama make it impossible, even with the expenditure of large sums of money, for our grounds to have the appearance of the grounds at Hampton. Yours very truly,

[Booker T. Washington]

TLc   Con. 18   BTW Papers   DLC.

From Marcus M. Marks[1]

New York. May 24, 1904

My dear Mr. Washington: Allow me to acknowledge your letters of the 18th and 20th insts. Regarding the former, I regret sincerely that on June the 9th my family leave the city for the summer, and that we will have to postpone the pleasant evening with you which I am looking forward to at our home till after October 1st. If it is not taxing you too much, will you *let me know*, some time in the fall, *when* it will be convenient for you to be with us for dinner, so that the matters which we discussed and which I have so much at heart may be further developed. I may say that I intend to do some missionary work during the summer in the direction indicated.

I think your idea of having a Hebrew on your Board of Trustees at Tuskegee is splendid. It is, in my opinion, a step in the right direction. You ask which of the two Warburgs[2] is preferable for the position: I would suggest Felix M. Warburg, for the reason that he is School Commissioner of Greater New York, also a Director in the Educational Alliance, and therefore more in the line of educational work than his brother Paul, who is also a fine man. Felix M. Warburg is not only a gentleman of wealth, but a noble-man by instinct; a big, broad, liberal, refined, warm-hearted man, with whom it is a privilege to be a friend. I most cordially endorse the wisdom of his selection.

Assuring you of my very kindest regards, I remain, Sincerely yours,

Marcus M. Marks

TLS   Con. 18   BTW Papers   DLC.

1 Marcus M. Marks (1858–1934) was a partner with his father in the wholesale clothing business of David Marks and Sons until 1913, when he retired to devote his life to philanthropy. He was elected president of the borough of Manhattan in 1913. He founded the Educational Alliance, to help Americanize immigrants, and was a strong advocate of daylight saving time.

2 Paul Moritz Warburg (1868–1932) and his brother Felix Moritz Warburg (1871–1937) were New York investment bankers of the firm of Kuhn, Loeb and Co. Both were substantial contributors to Tuskegee Institute, and Paul Warburg was a trustee from 1904 to 1909. In 1911 BTW sought unsuccessfully to interest him in the economic development of Liberia.

From Charles William Anderson

New York, May 25th, 1904

Personal

My dear Doctor: I have your favor of the 23rd inst., before me, and thank you for your thoughtfulness in advising me to consult with your friends who are to attend the next Convention. You did not enclose the list of Delegates however, and I assume that they will come in a separate enclosure.

Relative to Mr. Peterson, you have doubtless noticed that the colored newspapers of the Country are saying complimentary things about him. I am making a collection of these comments and will put the President in possession of them.

I saw Fortune to-day and he was not quite as amiable as I should like to have found him. In strictest confidence, I want to inform you, that he has an editiorial prepared for next week's paper on your "Child Race" allusion. He has fished up a similar statement in Hannibal Thomas' Book and has called attention to the similarity between your statement and that of Mr. Thomas. I tried to convince him that this was a very unwise thing to do, and that if he wanted to be in charge of the Western Bureau, during the Campaign, he would have to depend upon you to place him. This is his ambition, and he gave me to understand that you were agreeable to it. I told him that I would concur with you, and would drop you a line to-morrow expressing my approval of the arrangement. After all, this seems to be a good way to take care of Fortune. If he is put out there in Chicago in this Bureau, he will be out of harm's way, and ought to be happy. Therefore, according to promise I shall write you a letter to-morrow, which I promised to show to him (for he seems to be in doubt about my willingness to write such a letter in his favor) and you can therefore expect to receive it shortly after this one comes to hand.

Every body is pleased over the appointment of Peterson excepting Wibecan. He is as mad as he can be, and is denouncing Peterson in public places — although they have been life-long intimate friends, and so have their families. I think you had better train your guns upon Mr. Cortelyou at once. I am sure he will arrange the Bureaus about as you desire, and I am also sure that the old "hack politicians" will have no influence with him. Yours truly,

Charles W. Anderson

P.S. I am writing Fortune not to print that editorial.

C. W. A.

TLS   Con. 550   BTW Papers   DLC.

To Margaret James Murray Washington

Tuskegee, Alabama. May 27, 1904

Mrs. Washington: Please let me know by bearer if you will go driving at five o'clock.

B. T. W.

TLI   Con. 22   BTW Papers   DLC.   The reply appeared on the letter in Margaret Murray Washington's hand: "Yes—Mrs. W."

From Charles William Anderson

New York, May 27, 1904

Confidential   Return enclosure
My dear Doctor Washington: I beg leave to hand you herewith, a letter which I am this day in receipt of from Mr. Fortune. As I

told you in my last letter, I wrote to Fortune telling him that I felt
that he owed it to you and to the cause to drop that objectionable
editorial which made comparisons between your alleged allusion to
"a child race," and a similar allusion used in Hannibal Thomas'
book. I called attention to the fact that you had always been his
good friend, and would remain so, and that he ought not to take a
lead in his paper, which would be followed up by all the small clip-
pers of reputations in the country. This is his reply. It is very
strange, that whenever this man feels a little cross, he immediately
turns to abusing his friends. I think if he can be placed in that
Western Bureau, under the supervision of a chief who is a strict
disciplinarian, such a chief as Mr. Cortelyou will be likely to appoint, he can be kept in line. This seems to me to be a good way
to keep him from doing any damage during the campaign.

You may be interested to know that I am in receipt of a postal
card, which was handed to me by Senator Platt's private secretary,
for investigation. The card was addressed "To the Colored Leaders
of the 10th Congressional District, Nashville, Tenn." and reads
as follows: "Fifth Avenue Hotel, New York, May 21, 1904. Gentlemen & Brothers: I would suggest that the name of the Hon. Booker
T. Washington be endorsed for the position of Vice-President at
your coming convention to fill up the ticket with that greatest of
soldiers, statesmen and Republicans, Theodore Roosevelt — the
friend of your race. Feelingly yours, (Signed) T. C. Platt." Of
course this card was not written by a colored man as some suspect,
nor by Sen. Platt. I think the phraseology itself will prove that. Besides, a colored man would have been familiar with the names of at
least some of the colored leaders in Tennessee. He would not have
addressed his communication to "The Colored Leaders of the 10th
Congressional District." Neither would he have used the term
"Gentlemen & Brothers." In my judgment it is the work of either
some knave or fool. It is not altogether impossible that it was done
to associate your name with the President's, in the hope that the
association might be offensive to weak-kneed Republicans. I have
the card in my possession at this time, and am trying to get some
sort of clue to the writer. I have promised to return it to Senator
Platt's Secretary.

I am still waiting for the list of Colored delegates to the National
Convention from Alabama, which you omitted to enclose in your

last letter. Now, if there is anything you desire me to do in the Fortune matter, please send me the directions. He is quite angry, and is ready to make trouble. I think we can hold this Chicago matter over his head, and in that way bind him over to keep the peace. Don't you think I had better have a "heart-to-heart" talk with him, and assure him that you alone can place him as he desires, and if he does not turn over a new leaf, and lead a clean life, so far as loyalty to his friends is concerned, he will have small chance of landing in that Western Bureau. You know he is an Indian, and Indians have no respect for anything except a club. It is their natural war weapon, and they fear it when it is in the other fellow's hand. Therefore, I think it best to brandish this Western Bureau club over the head of the New Jersey Seminole. Yours truly,

Charles W. Anderson

P.S. The postal card was not sent to Tennessee, but was sent to Sen. Platt by the New York Post Office officials, who knew the Senator's handwriting, and knew the thing was fradulent. Mr. Howe, his secretary, turned the same over to me to see if I could detect the writer by identifying the handwriting.

C. W. A.

TLS Con. 261 BTW Papers DLC. Postscript in Anderson's hand.

To William Loeb, Jr.

[Tuskegee, Ala.] May 30, 1904

Personal

My dear Mr. Loeb: If it is not asking too much, will you be kind enough to let me know whether the President is expecting to appoint two judges for Panama any time soon, and whether or not it is his intention that one of the appointees be a Democrat. My reason for asking this question is to have in this state a gentleman by the name of Judge Osceola Kyle,[1] a man of the very highest type of character and courage, in fact I can describe him in no better way than to say he represents the type of manhood that Judge Jones does, and I should like very much to have an opportunity to speak to the President about him, and he can get the same kind of evidence from many other public men in this state.

Since it is likely that large numbers of colored people will be employed in one capacity or another in digging the canal, it seems to me that the President would like to consider Judge Kyle since he is well acquainted with the character of the colored people.

I hope for an immediate answer, if it is not asking too much of you. Yours very truly,

Booker T. Washington

TLpS Con. 3 BTW Papers DLC.

1 Born in Tuskegee in 1862, Osceola Kyle was a lawyer in Opelika and Decatur, Ala., and served in the legislature from Lee and Morgan counties. He was an Alabama state railroad commissioner and circuit court judge prior to President Roosevelt's appointment of him as a federal judge in the Canal Zone. Kyle did little in this position to justify BTW's endorsement. Perhaps he was well acquainted with blacks, but Secretary of War W. H. Taft forced him to resign after complaints that he did not know the Spanish language or Spanish law and showed no desire to learn. (Taft to Kyle, Jan. 7, and Kyle to Taft, Jan. 17, 1905, Theodore Roosevelt Papers, DLC; Birmingham *Age-Herald*, Mar. 1, 1905, 2.)

To Henry Ossawa Tanner

[Tuskegee, Ala.] 31 May, 1904

Dear Mr. Tanner: I think that our very purpose would be defeated if I should make a special matter of appealing to Mr. Carnegie, as you have suggested. I think it would be better if I brought his attention to you incidentally when we are speaking sometime of other matters. This method would enlist his sympathies more than would the specific asking that he consider what you desire.

If at any time I can serve you, I shall be very glad of the opportunity.

With best wishes, I am, Very truly yours,

Booker T. Washington

TLpS Con. 872 BTW Papers DLC.

From Charles William Anderson

New York, June 2nd, 1904

My dear Doctor: Yours of the 31st ulto. at hand. Relative to Fortune, I beg to say that my only desire in writing the letter to you and the one to Mr. Loeb was to prevent the publication of that objectionable editorial, and I quite agree with you that he could be of more service under the Eastern Bureau than elsewhere. This did not occur to me until it was suggested by Moore on yesterday. In fact Moore seemed to feel that I had made a mistake in writing at all, and I assured him, as I now want to assure you, that I do not care a fig about Fortune's personality. My only aim in writing the afore-mentioned letters was to serve you. The letter to Loeb was the merest suggestion, and was phrased in very *discreet* language. Mr. Loeb's answer to it, is very interesting. I have shown it to no one, and will not until I show it to you. It proves that the whole thing is in your hands, and it proves some other things that "the Sage of Red Bank" might not find exactly to his taste. So I hope you will not mis-appreciate my motive in writing the letters. As I told you in my letter advising you that one was to follow, Fortune would not be convinced that I would write a letter in his favor, however slightly, and therefore requested me to write them and send them to him at Red Bank, from which point he would mail them. This I did, but sent you an anticipatory letter giving my reasons. As for the editorial, he read the offensive allusions to me and told me he was sure it would make you very mad, as it would be more abhorrent to you to have your language compared with that of Hannibal Thomas, than to have it compared with the words of any living man. Thus you see, it was a rather diabolical scheme to be especially offensive to you. This fact made me feel justified in writing the letter. I hope you will believe me when I tell you that I care no more about the man now, than I have cared in the past, and I give you my permission to say this much to him. *I don't want you to think that I am cultivating pleasant relations with a man who is not "playing fair" with you.* I hope you will believe me incapable of such conduct. What I did, was done to serve you, and for no other purpose. Notwithstanding the fact that Fortune pronounced the statement referred to "a very strong statement," he *did* write the editorial above mentioned, and he *did* intend to publish it. His letter to me, which I have already forwarded to you, will prove this fact. You will notice that he says in it, that he had wired Peterson to return the editorial. I am writing somewhat at length on this heading, but I am very anxious that you shall understand that I am not cultivating Fortune in any way, I was merely making an effort to prevent him from doing a dishonorable turn to you.

I shall make my headquarters, while in Chicago, at the Auditorium, in the headquarters of the New York Delegation to the Convention. I shall live at the place Mr. Williams so kindly provided for me, but will of course spend most of my time at the Auditorium. I sent you copy of a letter to Secretary Ball,[1] of the New York Commission to the St. Louis Exposition on yesterday. It ought to put a quietus on that man Trotter. Kindly let me know when you will be this way again. Yours truly,

Charles W. Anderson

P.S. McKinlay & I can work together harmoniously.

TLS   Con. 261   BTW Papers   DLC.

[1] Charles A. Ball (b. 1850) was secretary of the New York State Commission to the Louisiana Purchase Exposition. He was secretary of the New York State Senate for many years and then its executive officer.

To William Henry Baldwin, Jr.

[Tuskegee, Ala.] June 3, 1904

Dear Mr. Baldwin: Sometime during the week I shall perhaps send you some Alabama papers containing an account of a visit which I made with a number of our teachers to Uniontown, Perry Co., yesterday. Uniontown is 128 miles West of Tuskegee and right in the heart of the Black Belt. The occasion of our going was to visit a school built up by James A. Snead,[1] one of our graduates. The school has 300 or more pupils and five teachers, and it is supported by the combined efforts of the white and colored people in that community.

The meeting where I spoke yesterday was held in a large cotton warehouse, and the audience furnished a very interesting study. In the first place, the mayor of the town met me at the depot and was kind in his words of welcome. In the afternoon when I spoke, the audience was composed of colored people, white men and white women, and I think at least a third of the audience was composed of whites. I was introduced to the audience by the mayor, and after I had gotten through speaking Col. Mallory, the Chairman of the State Democratic Committee, and ex-Attorney General Brown[2] spoke most enthusiastically endorsing everything I said. The court adjourned in order that all interested might attend the meeting, and during the speaking all the business houses in the town closed. I have seldom attended any kind of gathering that has given me more hope and encouragement. When I witness such scenes I constantly wonder why in a meeting such as the one held recently at Birmingham, a colored man or men would be wholly unwelcome as participant in the proceedings. Prominent white men sat upon the platform in equal numbers with prominent colored people, and all seemed cordial and happy. Yours very truly,

[Booker T. Washington]

I neglected to say in the body of this letter that I spoke out from the shoulder to the white people about their duty and obligations to the Negro. For example, I told them that they could not expect to lynch the Negro in the winter and expect him to make cotton in the summer, and they cheered the remark heartily.

TLp   Con. 20   BTW Papers   DLC.

1 James Alcorn Snead, principal of the Uniontown District Academy, graduated from Tuskegee Institute in 1891.

2 Charles Gayle Brown (1844–1913), former solicitor for Perry County, Ala., was Alabama attorney general from 1898 to 1902.

To Leigh S. J. Hunt

[Tuskegee, Ala.] June 3, 1904

Dear Mr. Hunt: Our Executive Council has gone over the list of men who are anxious to go to the Soudan, very carefully, also, we have considered the names of the three men, Cain Triplett, Poindexter Smith and John P. Powell, and agree that no better selection than these three could have been made. We give their selection our heartiest endorsement. I have also talked to the men and find them in entire sympathy with your proposition. I believe then that they will meet your desires most satisfactorily.

Of course you will not hesitate to let me know if I can do anything further in this matter.

I shall be very glad to serve you in any possible manner. Very truly,

Booker T. Washington

TLpS   Con. 868   BTW Papers   DLC.

To Andrew B. Humphrey

[Tuskegee, Ala.] June 4, 1904

Personal and Confidential
My dear Mr. Humphrey: Enclosed I am sending you two planks which I want to entrust to you to get placed in the platform of the Republican Party at Chicago. I say to you frankly that there are several influential friends of mine to whom I could send these planks but in each case I very much fear that in their zeal and earnestness they would use my name as being the author, which I do not want done. I am sure I can trust entirely to your discretion to get them in without the use of my name in any way. Of course you know that in order for them to stand any chance whatever of being inserted they ought to get in the hands of Mr. Lodge within the next few hours, [days?] as I understand Mr. Lodge is drawing the platform.[1]

I think I ought to further say I know what the feelings of the colored people are throughout the country on these subjects, and these resolutions are worded in a way to meet the objections that might be raised by a large class of colored people during the campaign. It is going to be no easy matter for the Republicans to carry

New York State, and such resolutions as I enclose will go a long ways toward keeping the colored vote in harness. Yours very truly,

Booker T. Washington

TLpS Con. 3 BTW Papers DLC.

1 Humphrey wrote to Henry Cabot Lodge on June 9, 1904, enclosing two planks that had been "requested by representatives of the Colored Race" and were "the consensus of the carefully collected opinions of many leading representatives of the Colored Race throughout the country." The planks were:

"The Republican Party avows its unalterable opposition to the establishment of the color line in Republican Party councils, state or national; it condemns unreservedly the policy of any state in so far as it discriminates, on grounds of race and color, against its citizens in the matter of the elective franchise. Equal protection to every citizen in his civil and political rights is demanded and should be guaranteed. Color is no condition precedent in the payment of taxes, and should not be made a condition precedent in the holding of public office.

"Murder in the form of lynching or burning should have no place in a civilized country, and to this end we condemn these practices wherever they exist and contend that all men of whatever color should have the full protection of the law." (Con. 3, BTW Papers, DLC.)

To D. Robert Wilkins

[Tuskegee, Ala.] June 6, 1904

Personal and Confidential

Dear Mr. Wilkins: I note in your paper of a few weeks ago what you had to say concerning the meeting of a committee in St. Louis in a few days. Permit me to say in this connection that there is no reason why practically all the work this committee is to do should not be given to the public in the proper time and in the proper manner, but I have had the feeling for sometime that the race was not as strong and influential in many matters as it should be because our enemies seem to know every move that we make. You will find that the Irish and Hebrews have great influence largely because the public is kept in ignorance in a measure of what they mean to do. Of course I do not mean to indicate that in the long run every colored man should not have the same right as any other colored man to know the actions of our public men and have freedom to criticise such actions, but when plans are being matured it is wise, I think you will agree with me, that a certain amount of secrecy obtain. Yours truly,

Booker T. Washington

TLpS   Con. 249   BTW Papers   DLC.

To James Sullivan Clarkson

[Tuskegee, Ala.] June 6, 1904

Personal and Confidential

Dear General Clarkson: I am writing in hasty response to yours of some days ago. The Negro planks which I am enclosing herewith for the platform have been decided upon by a number of influential colored men who have thought that these planks embody in some measure what should be stated in the platform.[1] I very much hope that you can see your way clear to have them considered by Mr. Lodge or whoever is drafting the platform. Yours truly,

Booker T. Washington

Of course I do not desire that my name shall be used in any way in presenting these planks to Mr. Lodge or that my efforts in the matter shall be known at all.

B. T. W.

TLpS   Con. 19   BTW Papers   DLC.

[1] Clarkson wrote BTW that the "liberty and suffrage plank" was a good one and promised to "see that it is sent forward to the high places." He commented: "I am afraid that the importance as well as the justice of this plank being bold and clear is not as fully comprehended in as many influential quarters as should be, either in the line of justice or in the interest of the party." (June 10, 1904, Con. 867, BTW Papers, DLC.)

To Leslie Pinkney Hill

[Tuskegee Ala.] June 7, 1904

My dear Sir: I have made careful note of your communication[1] of some days ago and in reply beg to say, first: that I am not particularly in sympathy with the suggestion looking to the removal of large numbers of colored people to the North for domestic service. Inevitably, they stray into the larger cities and become cause for concern rather than otherwise. I rather feel that we should do everything we can to persuade our people to keep out of the large cities of the North, and in every way, it seems more satisfactory to suggest that the wisest thing would seem to be the training of the colored people who may be in the Oranges, rather than to import large numbers of others.

Second: With reference further to your communication, beg to say that this has been at Tuskegee, an exceedingly hard year financially. It would please us very greatly if we could see our way clear to advance the Three Hundred and Fifty Dollars you suggest, but in justice to ourselves and to many of our teachers who have faithfully served us & who have been anxious to make overdrafts, in the same way, all of whom we have been compelled to refuse, it would seem impossible for us to comply with your request.

With the hope that you will have a pleasant and profitable Commencement season, I am, Very truly,

Booker T. Washington

TLpS Con. 868 BTW Papers DLC.

[1] Hill asked BTW if he could recommend about thirty persons for domestic service in New Jersey. He also sought a loan to help pay his tuition at Harvard. (June 1, 1904, Con. 868, BTW Papers, DLC.)

Emmett Jay Scott to Charles Alexander

[Tuskegee, Ala.] June 8, 1904

Dear Mr. Alexander: Mr. Washington asks me to remind you that he sent you at a good deal of cost of effort and research, quite a number of personal letters of introduction to firms in Boston from whom he thought you might secure advertising, and that he has received no acknowledgment of these letters, nor have you told him whether or not the letters have been presented. Several of the firms were among Mr. Washington's personal friends and he feels quite sure that if the letters were presented good results would have been accomplished.

He is rather surprised too, in the face of the fact that he told you some weeks ago that a friend would be responsible for $10 a week, if so much were required, for the payment of an agent who could devote himself to securing new subscriptions in Boston and vicinity provided a weekly report of results was sent, that nothing has been done so far as he knows, toward carrying out this suggestion which was certainly a most rare and generous one. It is very seldom that any newspaper man in the country has such offers for help, and it is hard to understand why these suggestions seem not to have been taken advantage of. You will find in the long run that people are willing to help those who make a tremendous effort to help themselves. Yours truly,

Emmett J. Scott

Dear Charley: The "boss" suggests the above & I follow.

TLpS   Con. 867   BTW Papers   DLC.

To Booker Taliaferro Washington, Jr.

[Tuskegee, Ala.] June 9, 1904

My dear Booker: I am very sorry that none of us will be North when your school closes June 14th, but I at least shall see you soon.

You must be very careful to follow in every way the instructions which your mamma gives you regarding South Weymouth. Your papa,

B. T. W.

TLpI   Con. 17   BTW Papers   DLC.

To Portia Marshall Washington

[Tuskegee, Ala.] June 9, 1904

My dear Portia: I have received both of your letters and am very glad to hear from you.

I very much prefer that you not make bills before consulting with either me or your mama. It is not a safe plan. I have paid the bill which was sent me from the Boston house.

I am very sorry that neither of us will be there by June 15th or on the closing, but we shall hope to see you soon.

Your mama has doubtless written you about arrangements at South Weymouth. Your papa,

B. T. W.

TLpI Con. 17 BTW Papers DLC.

To Ernest Davidson Washington

[Tuskegee, Ala.] June 9, 1904

My dear Davidson: I have been trying to find time to write you sooner but have been so busy that I have not been able to do so.

We are all very glad to hear that you are so well satisfied and having such an enjoyable time in St. Louis. We hope very much that you will pin down to hard study during a portion of every day, and that we shall see great improvement when we come to St. Louis. I take for granted that you have already seen the Exposition.

Matters are going on about as usual here. Most of the students of course have left for their vacations.

We are having some very fine peaches in the garden, and I wish that you were here to enjoy some of them.

Please remember me to Mr. and Mrs. Langston and the whole family. We talk about you every day. Your papa,

B. T. W.

TLpI Con. 17 BTW Papers DLC.

To Laura Anna Knott

[Tuskegee, Ala.] June 10, 1904

My dear Miss Knott: I am writing you concerning a matter about which I hope you will be very frank with me, that is in giving your personal opinion. I do not care for you to bother at present, even if you think it necessary, with the opinion of the trustees.

There is a colored girl in Washington who graduates this year from the Manual Training High School, and her parents are anxious to have her enter Bradford Academy. Her father is Hon. George H. White, of North Carolina, who until recently was a member of Congress. The family is a very respectable and intelligent one, and the girl I think is about sixteen or seventeen years old, and so far as I have seen her I think she is a girl of good character and with common sense. In case you thought it wise to permit her to enter Bradford Academy, I think Portia would be glad for the girl to share her room next year.

I can easily realize that there might be an embarrassment in having too many colored girls at one institution, and in case you think there would be such embarrassment I wish you would be very frank with me and I shall not misunderstand you.[1] The parents of the girl view the matter in the same manner that I do, and they have suggested that I should write you. Yours truly,

Booker T. Washington

TLpS   Con. 869   BTW Papers   DLC.

[1] Laura Knott replied that the school was already considering another black girl. BTW wrote to Mrs. George H. White that Bradford Academy did not "think it wise to have more than one or two there during the same year." BTW recommended another New England school and offered to take up the matter in person while he was in New England. (July 8, 1904, Con. 872, BTW Papers, DLC.)

To Samuel Coleridge-Taylor

[Tuskegee, Ala.] June 10, 1904

Dear Mr. Taylor: I am in receipt of your kind letter of recent date[1] which I am very glad to reply to as far as I can.

In the first place, permit me to say that I have long desired the privilege of meeting you, but when I was in Europe last fall I did not go to England. I admire very greatly the work which you have done.

Now, in answer to your direct questions, I would say that it is very difficult to give reliable and satisfactory information on the questions raised in your letter. From some points of view the plan of having an agent in this country is unsatisfactory; from other points of view it perhaps would be an advantage. I think, to begin with, you will have to realize that your name is quite familiar among the intelligent colored people of this country, but I very much fear you are not known very much except in exclusive musical circles among the white people, in the latter respect you would have to advertise yourself.

I would say in a general way that the wise plan would be for you to find a perfectly reliable, unselfish businesslike colored man in the large centers of Negro population and depend upon that individual to arrange the details of your appearing in a given city. The cities where I think it would pay you under proper business arrangements to go would be Boston, New York, Brooklyn, perhaps Newport, R.I., Philadelphia, Washington, Chicago and perhaps two or three others that I might mention later. All of these to which I have referred are in the North and you would be bothered very little with what is known as the color line. Should you decide to come South, I would advise that you make the larger institutions, such as Fisk University, Atlanta University, etc., your principal stopping points; this would take you into such centers as Nashville, Atlanta, New Orleans, etc. We should, of course, in any case, desire you to come to Tuskegee, and I wish in advance to invite you to make this school and my home your headquarters while in this section of the South. So far as your visit to Tuskegee is concerned, I can arrange so that you will have no embarrassment or inconvenience so far as the color line goes. I should like to hear from you as soon as possible definitely about the possible visit to Tuskegee so that I may know how to arrange my own plans.

I would state further that I am going to New York in a few days, and I shall put the whole matter before Mr. Harry T. Burleigh, with whom I think you are already acquainted. Mr. Burleigh's judgment is sound and he is a man on whose word you can depend.

If I can serve you further please do not fail to use me. Yours very truly,

Booker T. Washington

TLSr Copy   Con. 872   BTW Papers   DLC.

1 Coleridge-Taylor to BTW, May 21, 1904, Con. 872, BTW Papers, DLC. Coleridge-Taylor introduced himself to BTW and asked the Tuskegean's assistance in publicizing his first visit to the United States. The Afro-British composer sought to avoid the use of agents and preferred to make direct contacts to schedule his musical recitals. He told BTW: "You have a most ardent admirer in me as you may imagine!"

To William Howard Taft[1]

[Tuskegee, Ala.] June 11, 1904

Personal

Dear Sir: At the President's request I am sending you some information concerning the fitness of Judge Osceola Kyle, of Decatur, Alabama, for the position of a Judge in Panama.

While Judge Kyle is classed as a Democrat in politics, he is one of the cleanest, strongest and most just men in the entire South, one in whom both races have the greatest confidence. I can say no stronger word for him than that he is just such a man as Judge Thomas G. Jones is whom the President selected for a Federal Judgeship in Alabama.

If you have not already received them, there will doubtless be put into your hands very soon recommendations from the Congressmen and Senators in Alabama, also from Mr. Joseph O. Thompson, the Chairman of the Republican State Committee in Alabama, Mr. Nathan Alexander and Mr. H. V. Cashin, both colored men holding Presidential appointments in this state, and from many others of the very best class of people in the state.

You cannot realize how very much it helps the cause of decency in the South to recognize once in a while a Southern Democrat who has stood up against great odds in favor of what is right and proper. Yours truly,

[Booker T. Washington]

TLp   Con. 5   BTW Papers   DLC.

1 William Howard Taft (1857–1930) was Secretary of War from 1904 to 1908 and President of the United States from 1909 to 1913. Though he had carried out President Roosevelt's orders in the dismissal of the Brownsville black soldiers, he escaped some of the onus of this action in the 1908 election because to black voters the Democratic candidate, William Jennings Bryan, did not offer an attractive alternative. Taft alienated black Republicans, however, by removal of black officeholders in the South wherever whites objected to them. BTW occasionally counseled Taft on racial policy but was never as close an adviser as he had been with Roosevelt. In 1912 there was a significant black defection to the candidacy of Woodrow Wilson. Taft was Chief Justice of the U.S. Supreme Court from 1921 to 1930.

To George Bruce Cortelyou

[Tuskegee, Ala.] June 11, 1904

Personal

My dear Mr. Cortelyou: Taking for granted that you will be National Chairman, I am writing to you to request, if possible, that nothing be done in the way of organizing a colored bureau or of doing anything in the direction of providing for special work among the colored voters until I can have an opportunity of having an interview with you. I will arrange to see you very soon after the Chicago Convention. Yours truly,

Booker T. Washington

TLpS   Con. 2   BTW Papers   DLC.

To Theodore Roosevelt

[Tuskegee, Ala.] June 11, 1904

Personal

My dear Mr. President: I shall write you about some other matters later. It has usually been the custom of the National Republican

Committee to place some colored man in charge of a bureau for the purpose of creating special interest among the colored voters during the campaign. I believe it would be wise to follow some such custom, perhaps modifying it and improving it, during the next campaign. And before any move is made in that direction I want to place before you and Mr. Cortelyou the advisability of placing Charles W. Anderson of New York in charge of all such work. I have had occasion to study Anderson very closely during the last two years, and I say without hesitation that he is wise, tactful and energetic in a very remarkable degree and I believe is the best colored man in the country for such work. Besides, he has the advantage of living in New York State[,] a very important one, and has the confidence of the colored people throughout the country generally. Yours truly,

Booker T. Washington

TLpS   BTW Papers   ATT.

To James Sullivan Clarkson

[Tuskegee, Ala.] June 14, 1904

Personal

My dear General Clarkson: I did not attempt to send you all of the names of all the colored delegates to the Chicago Convention, I only sent those that I knew could be relied upon in an emergency.

I have been having a tough wrestle with the President over matters in Louisiana. I have about turned my last card and I fear I have not brought him around to our way of thinking.[1] In some way the two referees, Williams and Clark,[2] have him under a spell I fear. I have just sent him a telegram urging him to use his influence to have at least a compromise before the committee at Chicago. It would be very disastrous, in my opinion, to have it go out from Chicago that the Lily Whites had triumphed in Louisiana and had the confidence of the President. Yours truly,

Booker T. Washington

TLpS   Con. 867   BTW Papers   DLC.

1 Roosevelt had written to BTW on June 8, 1904, that he had kept Cohen in office for BTW's sake but refused to "back the same old Republican gang" which had done nothing for blacks. "The safety for the colored man in Louisiana," he wrote, "is to have a white man's party which shall be responsible and honest, in which the colored man shall have representation but in which he shall not be the dominant force. . . ." Roosevelt considered it sufficient that blacks had the same number of federal offices in Louisiana as in McKinley's time. (Morison and Blum, *Letters of Theodore Roosevelt*, 4:825–26.) On Roosevelt and the lily whites, see Sherman, *Republican Party and Black America*, 45–48.

2 Lewis Clarke, a leader of the lily-white delegation in Louisiana.

From William Garrott Brown[1]

Washington, D.C., 15 June, 1904

Dear Sir, On a tour of the entire South which I recently made, I was deeply impressed with the extent to which white labor, both native & foreign, is now in direct competition with negro labor. My feeling is that the future of your race in this country depends in the long run on its ability to meet this competition.

It is my desire to make a study of the extent, the character, & the outcome of this competition, but it is hard to find reliable data with which to confirm or correct the conclusions drawn from observation and talk. The subject must be of deep interest to you, & I write to ask if you know of any material, statistical or other, bearing on the inquiry, which I can hope to examine. To indicate more specifically the character of the inquiry I wish to make, let me mention the apparent failure of negroes in cotton mills, the employment of Italians & Bohemians in the cotton fields in Mississippi & Texas, of Italians in track-work in the Southern Pacific Railway, the increasing number of white barbers, & even white waiters, in distinctly Southern cities, as among the phenomena with which I should like to deal. I shall also doubtless have to discuss the sort of training which will be of most use to negroes in meeting this competition. Very truly yours,

William Garrott Brown

ALS Con. 867 BTW Papers DLC.

1 William Garrott Brown (1868–1913), born in Marion, Ala., lectured in American history at Harvard and wrote several works on the South. From 1908 until his death he was an editorial writer for *Harper's Weekly*.

To Charles William Anderson

[Tuskegee, Ala.] June 16, 1904

Personal and Confidential

My dear Mr. Anderson: I hope you understand the general scheme which I have in mind, which is to get Mr. Cortelyou to put you in charge of the New York end of the Negro Bureau and also give you supervision over the Chicago bureau, thus unifying the whole work. While you are in Chicago I hope you will see exactly what the situation is there. We shall need to select a good careful and reliable man for that work. Of course the people there would resent a man coming from the East for that position. It is important in my opinion, to get a good strong man, at the same time one who will not incite antagonism but will bring the people together. I wonder if S. Laing Williams would not be as good a man as we can get? Barnett and his wife who had it during the last two campaigns will want it again, but we must defeat Barnett if possible; he is a regular sneak. During the first two years of the Presidential campaign he and his wife spent their time and effort in stirring up the colored people and embittering them against the President, and the last few months of the term they spent their time in trying to prove their loyalty to the powers that be. Both Barnett and his wife abused McKinley shamefully during the first part of his administration and they did the same thing in regard to President Roosevelt, and in both cases at the proper time they laid low and proclaimed themselves loyal supporters of the administration. The time has come when such treachery should be punished as it ought to be. I rather think that Denan[1] will have a good deal to say as to who shall be recognized in Chicago. The situation is a little complicated because Barnett is one of the assistants in his office, but I think there are other colored men in Chicago who have more influence than he has. Just as soon as I can get an interview, however, with Cortelyou, I will know something of the lay of the land. I hope you will confer freely with Mr. Scott on the subject of this letter. Yours very truly,

Booker T. Washington

TLpS   Con. 867   BTW Papers   DLC.

1 Charles Samuel Deneen (1863–1940) was state's attorney for Cook County, Ill., from 1896 to 1904, governor of Illinois from 1905 to 1913, and U.S. senator from 1925 to 1931.

To Wilford H. Smith

[Tuskegee, Ala.] June 16, 1904

Personal

My dear Mr. Smith: It will interest you to know that a half dozen of the best type of colored men in Montgomery County have been summoned for jury duty during the coming session of the circuit court. Sheriff Waller[1] took pains to serve the papers on the individuals personally in most cases.

When one colored man asked a white man why it was that they were just now beginning to summon colored men for jury duty, the white man replied that Negroes' names had been put into the box all along together with white men's names but it seems that they were a long time coming out. The colored people feel much elated and very grateful to you. Yours truly,

Booker T. Washington

TLpS Con. 871 BTW Papers DLC.

1 William R. Waller (b. 1852) was sheriff of Montgomery County from 1903 to 1906, and from 1915 to 1917.

To James Sullivan Clarkson

[Tuskegee, Ala.] June 17, 1904

Many thanks for telegram.[1] The decision will do much good and causes great rejoicing. Victory more complete than I had dared anticipate.

Booker T. Washington

TWSr Copy Con. 867 BTW Papers DLC.

1 Clarkson had wired BTW that the Republican National Committee had turned down the lily-white delegation from Louisiana in favor of the Cohen-Lewis faction. (June 17, 1904, Con. 867, BTW Papers, DLC.)

From Theodore Roosevelt

White House, Washington. June 17, 1904

Personal.

My dear Mr. Washington: Since I wrote you the subject of my letter has become out of date, so to speak, for the National Committee has thrown over the Williams-Clarke organization just because it was tainted with the Lily White business. Politically, I think this may be of momentary advantage. I wish I were as sure that it was a good thing, both for white and black men, in Louisiana. Sincerely yours,

Theodore Roosevelt

TLS   Con. 16   BTW Papers   DLC.

To Ernest Hamlin Abbott[1]

[Tuskegee, Ala.] June 18, 1904

My dear Mr. Abbott: I have read with great interest and profit your third article on the South and the Negro. It is very good, and shows that you have thoroughly mastered the subject. There is one point, however, on which I want to raise a question; on page 362 you speak of "distinguishing negroes from Indians." Why do you use a small "n" for Negro and capital "I" for Indian?

One other point. I can find no evidence of the fact that the interest of the colored people as a whole in education is diminishing as compared with what existed immediately after the war. It is true that there are not so many unusual methods of manifesting their interest in education, but the manifestation is just as sure and even more sensible and earnest. Yours very truly,

Booker T. Washington

TLpS   Con. 293   BTW Papers   DLC.

1 Ernest Hamlin Abbott (1870–1931), son of Lyman Abbott, was a Congregational minister from 1896 to 1902, when he joined the staff of his father's journal, *Outlook*. He was secretary and director of The Outlook Co. for many years beginning in 1913, and was editor-in-chief of *Outlook* from 1923 to 1928.

To James Sullivan Clarkson

[Tuskegee, Ala.] June 18, 1904

Personal

My dear General Clarkson: I appreciate most sincerely the action of the National Executive Committee in properly recognizing the only regularly constituted Republican party in Louisiana. It would really have been suicide if the other faction had been recognized. My only hope is that the action now taken will stand and that it will be ratified by the Convention itself. I feel quite sure that the information sent out by the Associated Press today will be appreciated throughout the country as the only proper thing for the Convention to have done. Yours very truly,

Booker T. Washington

TLpS   Con. 867   BTW Papers   DLC.

To Walter L. Cohen

[Tuskegee, Ala.] June 18, 1904

Personal. Advise that you act very cautiously and conservatively in view of triumph. Seriously question wisdom of letting your name be used for national committeeman. Scott there Sunday afternoon.

W.

TWpIr   Con. 867   BTW Papers   DLC.

To William Garrott Brown

[Tuskegee, Ala.] June 20, 1904

My dear Sir: Permit me, in answering your letter of recent date, to send you a marked copy of the Montgomery Times which contains an account of a recent visit I made to Uniontown, not far, I think, from where you were born. You will notice that your brother was present and spoke briefly.

Now in regard to the direct answer to your question, I will say that it is very difficult to find reliable information in the directions [in] which you are seeking it. My own belief is that the seeming loss of the Negro in industrial directions is relative rather than absolute. We must of course, bear in mind the immense increase of industrial activity of every character in the South during the last twenty-five years; this, of course, has naturally called for a large number of workers. The Negro of course has had to depend upon the natural increase of population rather than emigration. Then, too, I think you will find that the Negro has shifted occupations rather than lost them. For example, while it is true in cities like Philadelphia and New York that the Negro has almost completely lost the barber's trade much to my regret, I think you will be surprised to find how many Negro stenographers of both sexes are employed in important offices in both those cities. When I was in Uniontown a few days ago they told me that for the first time a white barber had that week entered town to begin business; he will doubtless deprive some colored barbers of occupation in time, but on the other hand I was surprised to note that there are in Uniontown 13 colored men engaged in business of various characters, and some of these men represent a line of business that requires the handling of many thousands of dollars annually, especially is this true of the men who own and control the large groceries in that town. What is true of Uniontown is true in a larger or less degree, of every section of the South. In this respect you will note that the Negro is entering a comparatively new field while he is losing in an old one. In Montgomery, Alabama, for example, I believe it will be found there are just as many colored carpenters and brick masons as in former days, but the relative number is smaller because of the influx of Northerners and foreigners.

Further, my belief is that the Negro for the next half century will serve his best interest by sticking pretty closely to the ownership and proper cultivation of the soil. This, of course, will naturally carry with it the training of a large number of our people in the mechanic arts. I believe further that the industries of each community should be as far as possible studied and then the kind of industrial training given to the individuals that will best fit them to be of service and hold their own in that community. This is the policy that we are trying to follow here at Tuskegee.

I do not think that it can be said that the Negro is a failure in the cotton mill. A sufficient trial has not been afforded him. The mill in Charleston failed because the machinery was old and because the mill depended upon a miscellaneous city population for labor. A mill owned largely by colored people in Concord, N.C., I understand is largely not a success because of lack of proper capital to operate it. On the other hand, you will find that there is a mill owned and controlled by colored people in Dallas, Texas, which is successful, and that in Fayetteville, N.C., colored operatives have had control of a large and successful silk factory for 12 years or more. The only way, in my opinion, to control colored labor in a cotton factory is to pursue the same policy that is pursued with white laborers, and that is colonize them at some distance from a city in houses owned and controlled by the factory operators.

I very much fear that I have not given you any valuable information. I wish at some time you might see your way clear to come here and make a study of our work, and then you can then determine to what extent you think we are preparing leaders for service in the lines most needed in the South.

By this mail I send you our catalogue which may show some information on this subject. Yours very truly,

Booker T. Washington

TLpS   Con. 867   BTW Papers   DLC.

From Ernest Hamlin Abbott

New York   June 20th, 1904

My dear Mr. Washington: Please let me say how much I value your expression of appreciation concerning my third article in the series on The South and the Negro. Please accept my hearty thanks for your kind words.

With regard to the spelling of the word negro with a small "n," the rule there followed is simply what has been uniformly adopted by The Outlook. Every journal has to have its typographical rules and in this particular The Outlook is following what it believes to be the best established usage. Personally I think there is good reason for it. The word negro, both etymologically and in current speech, is a synonym simply for black man and there is therefore no more reason for spelling it with a capital than there is in spelling black man, or white man, or yellow man, with capitals. On the other hand the word Indian is derived from a country and although the derivation is geographically false it follows the same custom that other words derived from countries, such as American, African, and the like, follow. The Outlook, as it happens, follows the same custom with regard to the word creole, for instance, as it does with regard to the word negro.

I am very glad to have your testimony with regard to the interest on the part of the colored people in education. I am not old enough, myself, to remember the feeling at the close of the Civil War, and of course my statement concerning the attitude on the part of the negroes toward education at that time, had to be taken on the testimony of those whose memories may have been at fault; but in several instances it happened that the colored people whom I met had the same impression, and were rather discouraged at the indifference of the younger colored people — especially the younger married people — with regard to the education of negro children. My impression is that perhaps the difference ought to be drawn rather between the country negroes and the city negroes; that the country negroes still are interested in getting an education for their children while the city negroes are less so. I may be wrong in this but there are several things that make me feel that it is true and that perhaps the general impression that the present generation are not so eager for education is due to the larger proportion of negroes in the cities than existed at the close of the war. I am sure, however, that, whatever is true with regard to numbers, it is very true that both among the white people and the colored people of the South, there is a saner and truer view of education, more and more prevalent among those who are interested in education at all, and I am only saying what many have said to me that this is due in no small respect to your own labors. I am more and more impressed with the value of the education that comes through the hands. I wish I were trained in that respect myself, and I believe that you have been doing much to open the eyes of people North and South to the value of this sort of education. Indeed I myself am interested and connected with an association which has recently been established to promote this very kind of education in the foreign missionary work. I do not believe that you recognize how much you, yourself, are contributing to this educational renaissance. Very sincerely yours,

Ernest Hamlin Abbott

TLS   Con. 550   BTW Papers   DLC.

From Emmett Jay Scott

Chicago, June 21–04

Immense colored mass meeting Quinn chapel last night. Endorses friend[1] unanimously. Anderson made principal address. Pitched high plane. Trotter meeting fizzle in attendance but captured by Friends and friend endorsed. Opposition Cortelyou dead. He to be here tomorrow. Advise receipt this.

E. J. S.

TWIr   Con. 24   BTW Papers   DLC.   Addressed to BTW in care of D. H. C. Scott, Montgomery, Ala.

1 Theodore Roosevelt.

From Emmett Jay Scott

Chicago Ill   June 22 1904

All telegrams recd. Credentials Committee last night seated C[1] & Lily Whites. Negro delegates threatened to carry contest to Convention to avoid this. Lily whites promised divide Natl Committeeman & State Chrman. Lily whites now repudiate this. Really think lilys will win Everything. Hope friends Washn will hold off appointment Natl Committeeman till you can write to be left to Cortelyou.

Emmett J Scott

HWSr Con. 24 BTW Papers DLC. Addressed to BTW in care of C. F. Adams, Washington, D.C.

[1] Walter L. Cohen.

From Emmett Jay Scott

Chicago Ill   June 23–04

Glad you to see friend. Everything satisfactory except C matter because harmony arrangements to divide committeeman and state chairman between factions repudiated by lily whites after adoption of credential report. This arrangement proposed by Harry New,[1] senators Dick[2] and Scott[3] and agreed to by all concerned. Northern colored delegates angry over C's treatment should insist upon carrying out arrangements. Reybourn's election leaves Lyon only committeeman. Walters trying get control negro bureau. Steward of Louisville is head of Council and refuses cooperation with Walters. Anderson should be named immediately along with Dover and Coolidge. Will prevent unseemly scramble.

E J S

TWIr Con. 24 BTW Papers DLC. Addressed to BTW in care of Whitefield McKinlay, Washington, D.C.

[1] Harry Stewart New (1858–1937), of Indianapolis, Ind., was publisher of the Indianapolis *Journal*. An active Republican, he was state senator from 1896 to 1900, a delegate at four Republican national conventions, and chairman of the Republican

National Committee from 1907 to 1908. In 1916 he was elected U.S. senator and was postmaster general from 1923 to 1929.

2 Charles William Frederick Dick (1858–1945) of Ohio was secretary of the Republican National Committee from 1896 to 1900 and later served three terms in Congress. He was appointed to the Senate after the death of Marcus Hanna, and served from 1904 to 1911.

3 Nathan Bay Scott (1842–1924), U.S. senator from West Virginia from 1899 to 1911.

BIBLIOGRAPHY

THIS BIBLIOGRAPHY gives fuller information on works cited in the annotations and endnotes. It is not intended to be comprehensive of works on the subjects dealt with in the volume or of works consulted in the process of annotation.

Aptheker, Herbert, ed. *The Correspondence of W. E. B. Du Bois.* 3 vols. Amherst: University of Massachusetts Press, 1973—.

Baker, Ray Stannard. *American Chronicle, the Autobiography of Ray Stannard Baker.* New York: Charles Scribner's Sons, 1945.

Carnegie, Andrew. *The Autobiography of Andrew Carnegie.* Boston: Houghton Mifflin Co., 1920.

Chesnutt, Helen M. *Charles Waddell Chesnutt: Pioneer of the Color Line.* Chapel Hill: University of North Carolina Press, 1952.

Daniel, Pete. *The Shadow of Slavery: Peonage in the South, 1901–1969.* Urbana: University of Illinois Press, 1972.

Du Bois, W. E. B. *Dusk of Dawn: An Essay toward an Autobiography of a Race Concept.* New York: Harcourt, Brace and Co., 1940.

Fox, Stephen R. *The Guardian of Boston: William Monroe Trotter.* New York: Atheneum Publishers, 1970.

Garrison, Wendell Phillips, and Francis Jackson Garrison. *William Lloyd Garrison, 1805–1879: The Story of His Life as Told by His Children.* 4 vols. New York: The Century Co., 1885–89.

Harlan, Louis R. *Separate and Unequal: Public School Campaigns and Racism in the Southern Seaboard States, 1901–1915.* Chapel Hill: University of North Carolina Press, 1958.

Harris, Joel Chandler. "The Negro of To-day: His Prospects and His Discouragements," *Saturday Evening Post,* 176 (Jan. 30, 1904), 2–5.

Harris, William H. *Keeping the Faith: A. Philip Randolph, Milton P. Webster, and the Brotherhood of Sleeping Car Porters, 1925–37.* Urbana: University of Illinois Press, 1977.

Hawkins, Hugh, ed. *Booker T. Washington and His Critics.* Lexington, Mass.: D. C. Heath and Co., 1962.

Morison, Elting E., and John M. Blum, eds. *The Letters of Theodore Roosevelt.* 8 vols. Cambridge: Harvard University Press, 1951–54.

Osofsky, Gilbert. *Harlem, the Making of a Ghetto: Negro New York, 1890–1910.* New York: Harper and Row, 1966.

Schurz, Carl. "Can the South Solve the Negro Problem?" *McClure's Magazine,* 22 (Jan. 1904), 258–75.

Sherman, Richard B. *The Republican Party and Black America from McKinley to Hoover, 1896–1933.* Charlottesville: University of Virginia Press, 1973.

Thornbrough, Emma Lou. *The Negro in Indiana: A Study of a Minority.* Indiana Historical Collections, Vol. 37. Indianapolis: Indiana Historical Bureau, 1957.

Washington, Ernest Davidson, ed. *Selected Speeches of Booker T. Washington.* Garden City, N.Y.: Doubleday, Doran and Co., 1932.

Washington Conference on the Race Problem. *Proceedings of the Washington Conference on the Race Problem in the United States under the Auspices of the National Sociological Society, Washington, D.C., November 9, 10, 11, and 12, 1903.* Washington, D.C., 1904.

White, Arthur O. "Booker T. Washington's Florida Incident, 1903–1904," *Florida Historical Quarterly,* 51 (Jan. 1973), 227–49.

INDEX

NOTE: The asterisk indicates the location of detailed information. This index, while not cumulative, does include the major identifications of persons annotated in earlier volumes of the series who are mentioned in this volume. References to earlier volumes will appear first and will be preceded by the volume number followed by a colon. Lyman Abbott's annotation, for example, will appear as: *3:43-44. Occasionally a name will have more than one entry with an asterisk when new information or further biographical detail is presented.